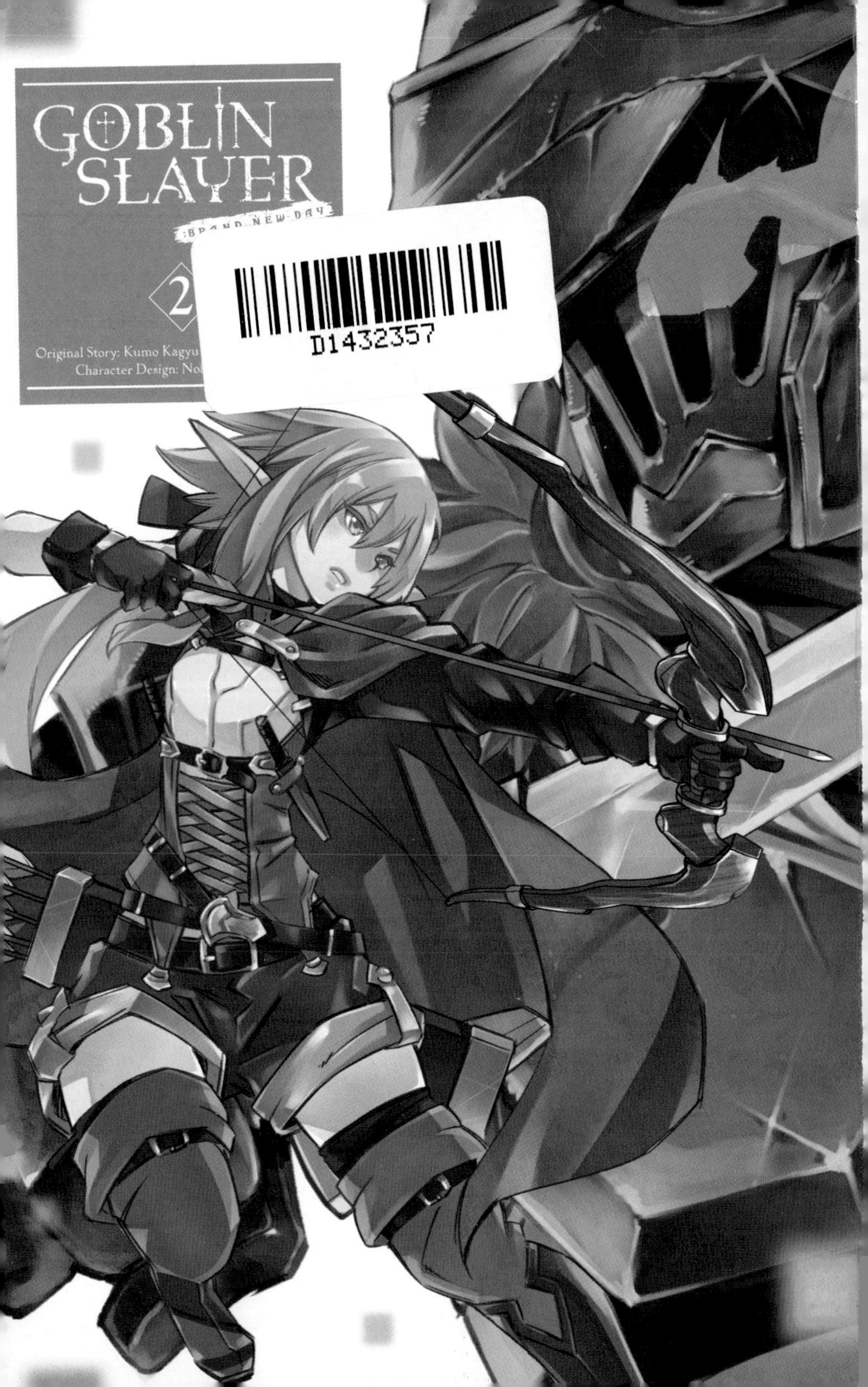
GOBLIN SLAYER
BRAND NEW DAY
2
Original Story: Kumo Kagyu
Character Design:

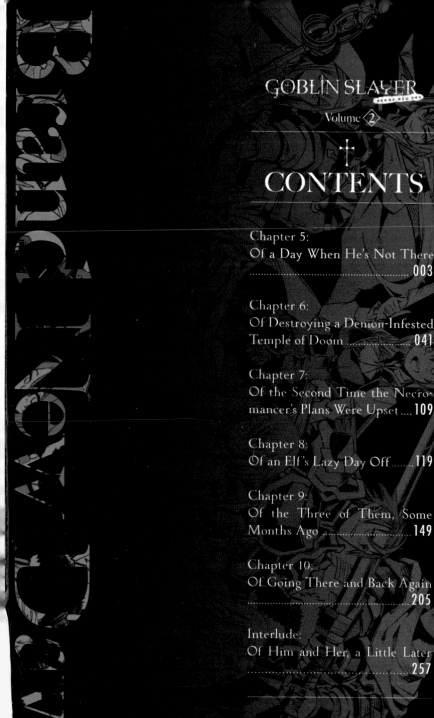

GOBLIN SLAYER
BRAND NEW DAY

Volume 2

†

CONTENTS

Chapter 5:
Of a Day When He's Not There

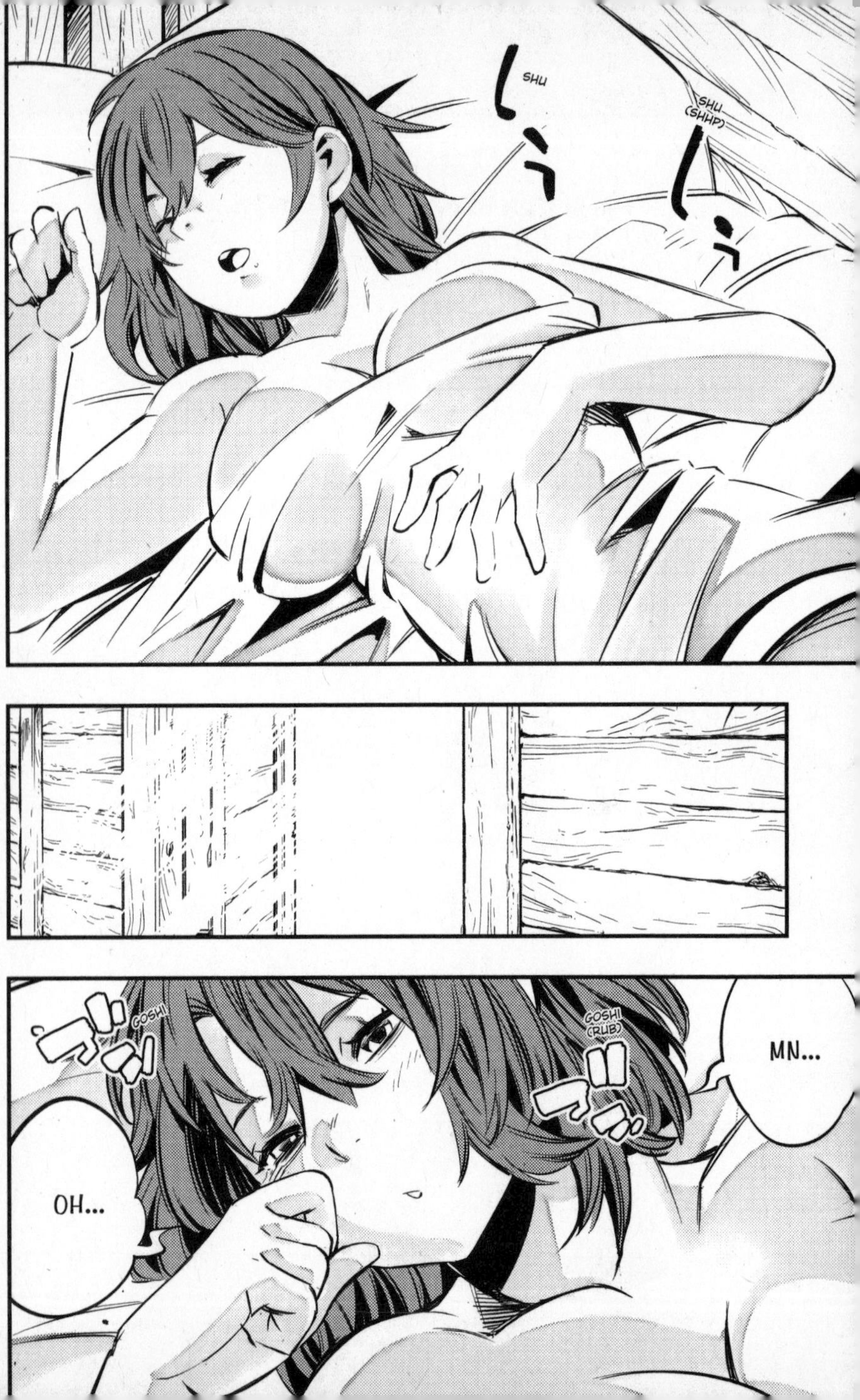
SHU (SHHP)
SHU
MN...
GOSHI (RUB)
GOSHI
OH...

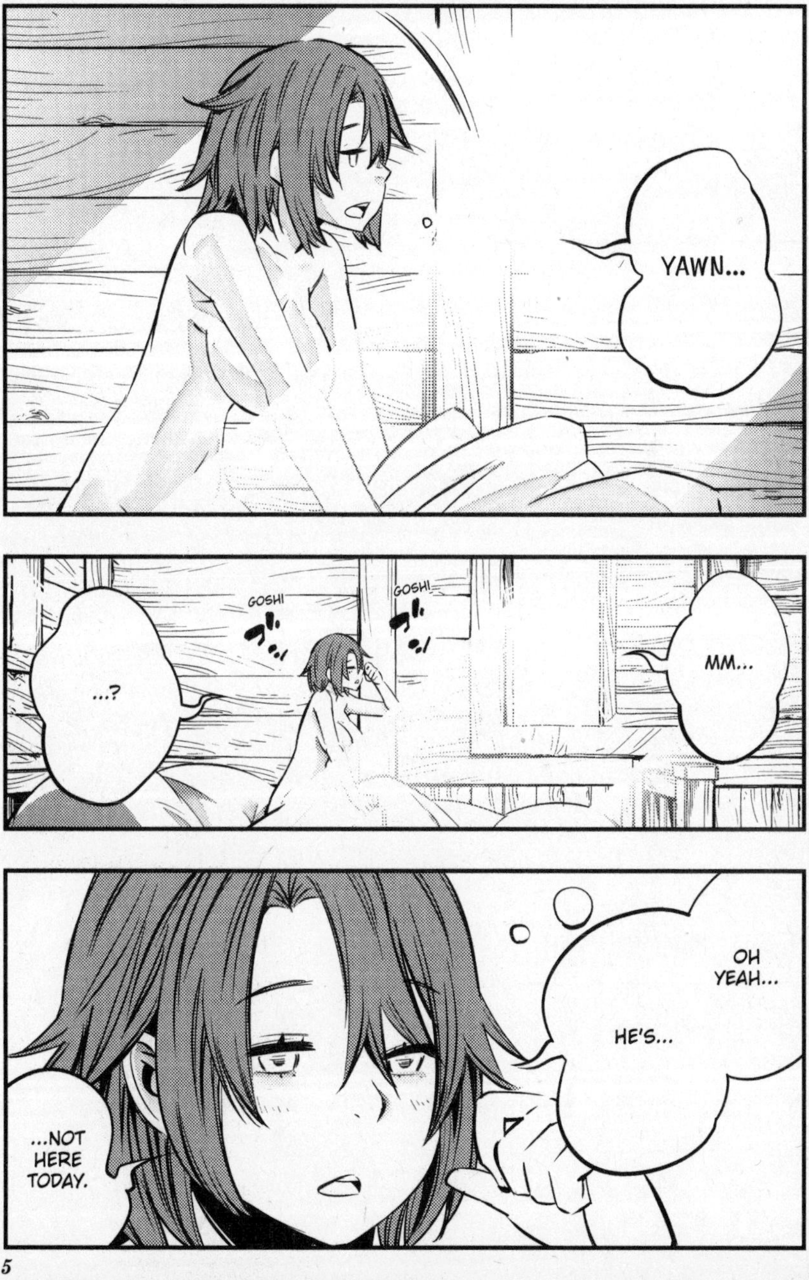
YAWN...
MM...
GOSHI
GOSHI
...?
OH YEAH...
HE'S...
...NOT HERE TODAY.

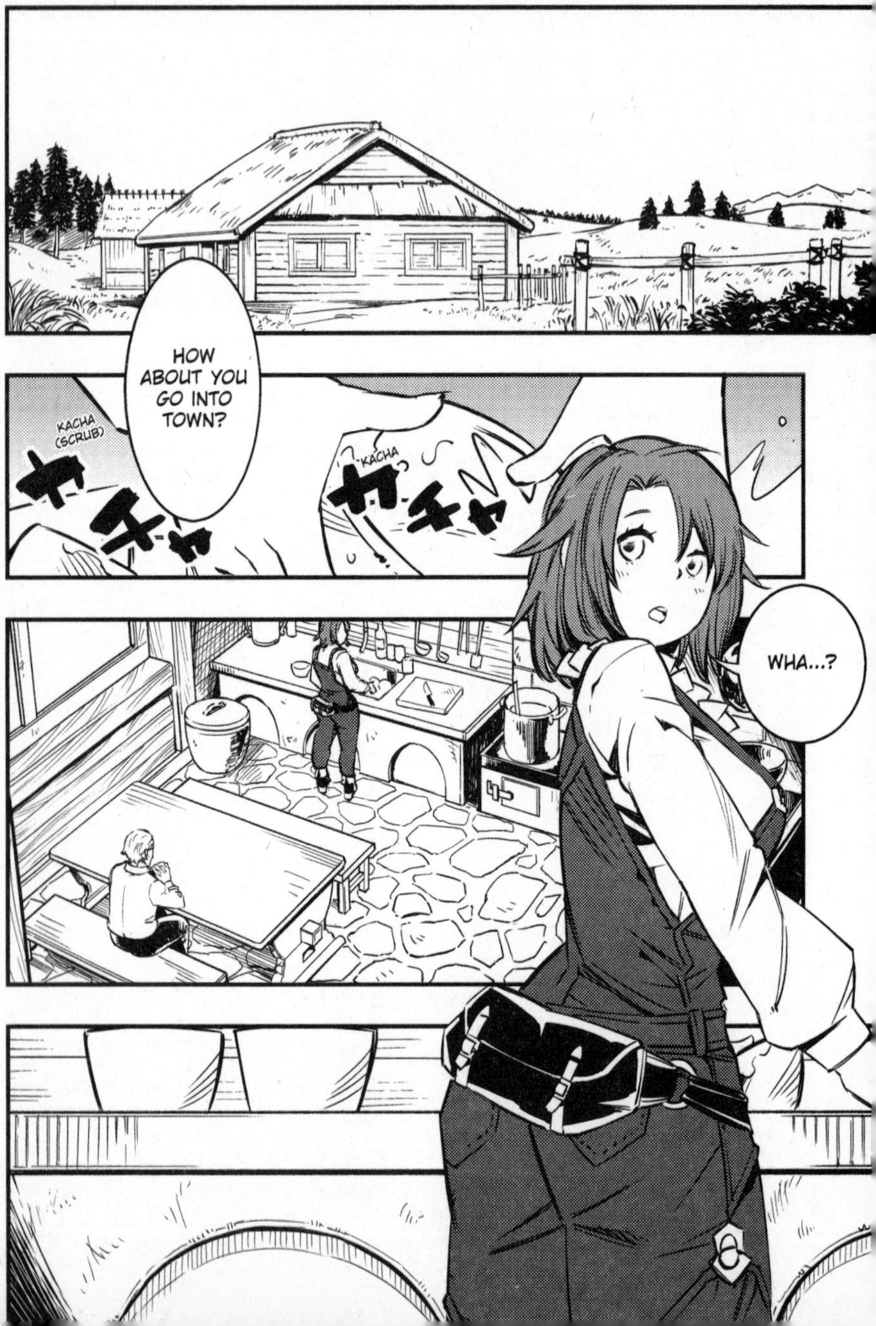
HOW ABOUT YOU GO INTO TOWN?
カチャ
KACHA
カチャ
KACHA (SCRUB)
WHA...?

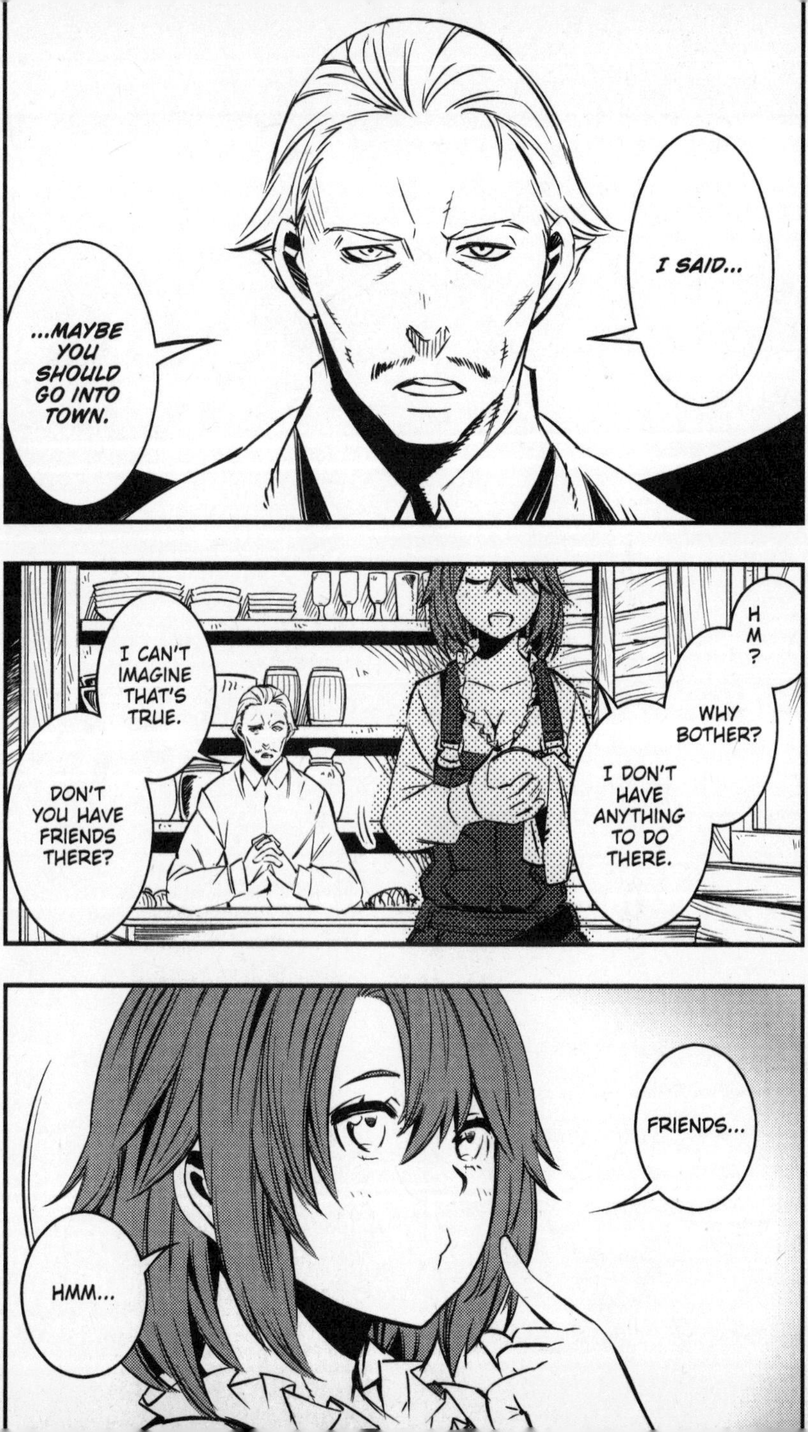
I SAID...
...MAYBE YOU SHOULD GO INTO TOWN.
HM?
WHY BOTHER?
I DON'T HAVE ANYTHING TO DO THERE.
I CAN'T IMAGINE THAT'S TRUE.
DON'T YOU HAVE FRIENDS THERE?
FRIENDS...
HMM...

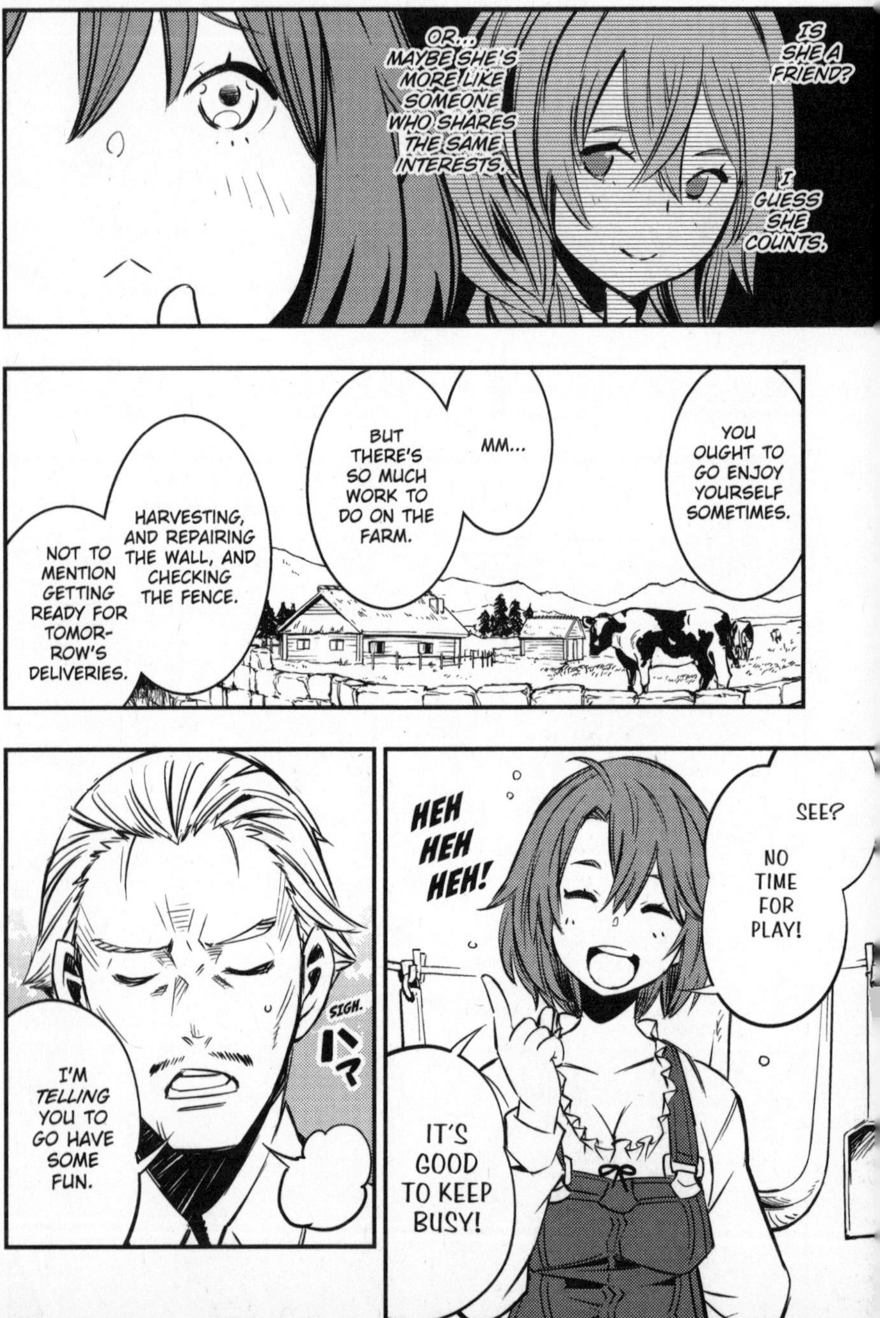
IS SHE A FRIEND?
OR... MAYBE SHE'S MORE LIKE SOMEONE WHO SHARES THE SAME INTERESTS.
I GUESS SHE COUNTS.
YOU OUGHT TO GO ENJOY YOURSELF SOMETIMES.
MM...
BUT THERE'S SO MUCH WORK TO DO ON THE FARM.
HARVESTING, AND REPAIRING THE WALL, AND CHECKING THE FENCE.
NOT TO MENTION GETTING READY FOR TOMOR-ROW'S DELIVERIES.
SEE?
NO TIME FOR PLAY!
HEH HEH HEH!
IT'S GOOD TO KEEP BUSY!
SIGH.
ハァ
I'M *TELLING* YOU TO GO HAVE SOME FUN.

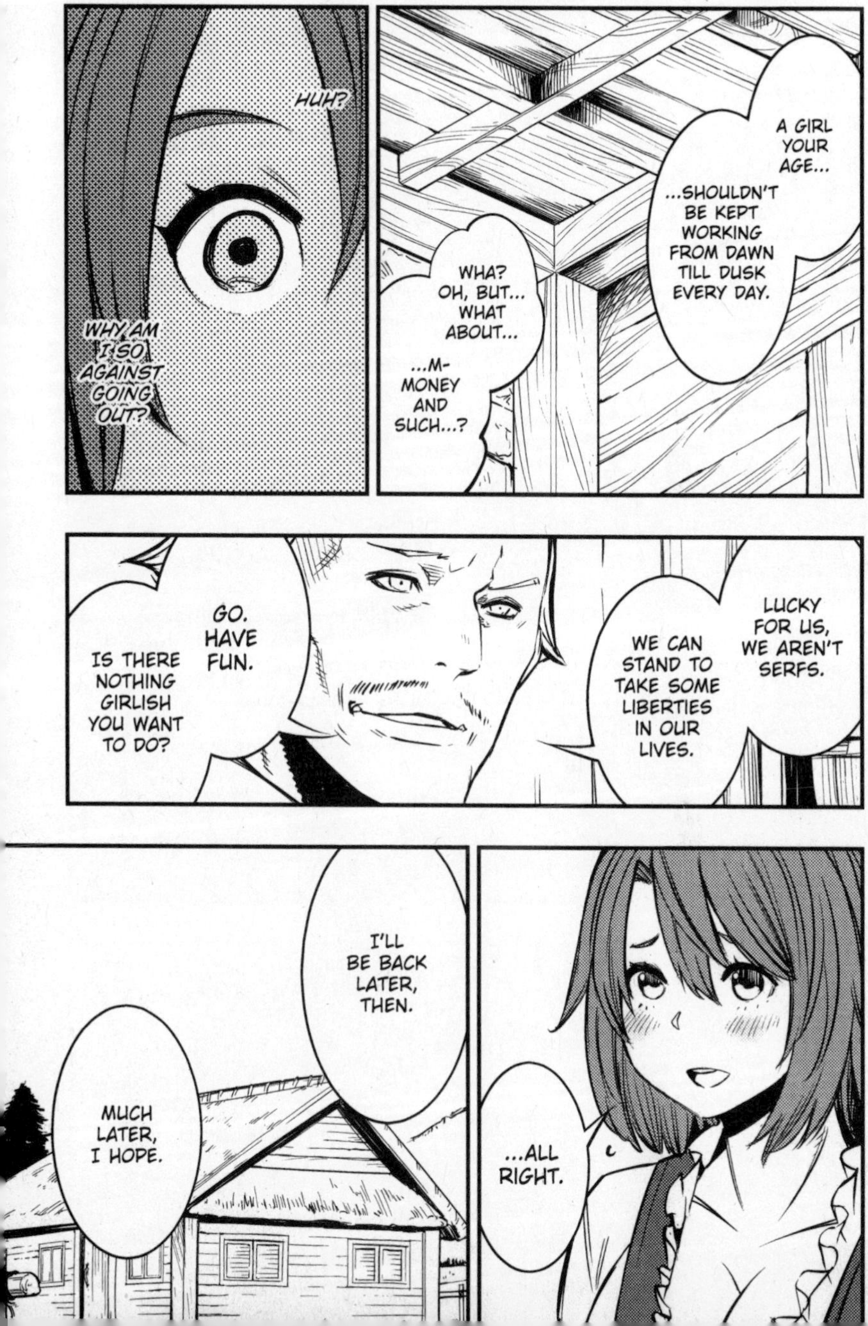
A GIRL YOUR AGE...
...SHOULDN'T BE KEPT WORKING FROM DAWN TILL DUSK EVERY DAY.
WHA? OH, BUT... WHAT ABOUT...
...M-MONEY AND SUCH...?
HUH?
WHY AM I SO AGAINST GOING OUT?
LUCKY FOR US, WE AREN'T SERFS.
WE CAN STAND TO TAKE SOME LIBERTIES IN OUR LIVES.
GO. HAVE FUN.
IS THERE NOTHING GIRLISH YOU WANT TO DO?
...ALL RIGHT.
I'LL BE BACK LATER, THEN.
MUCH LATER, I HOPE.

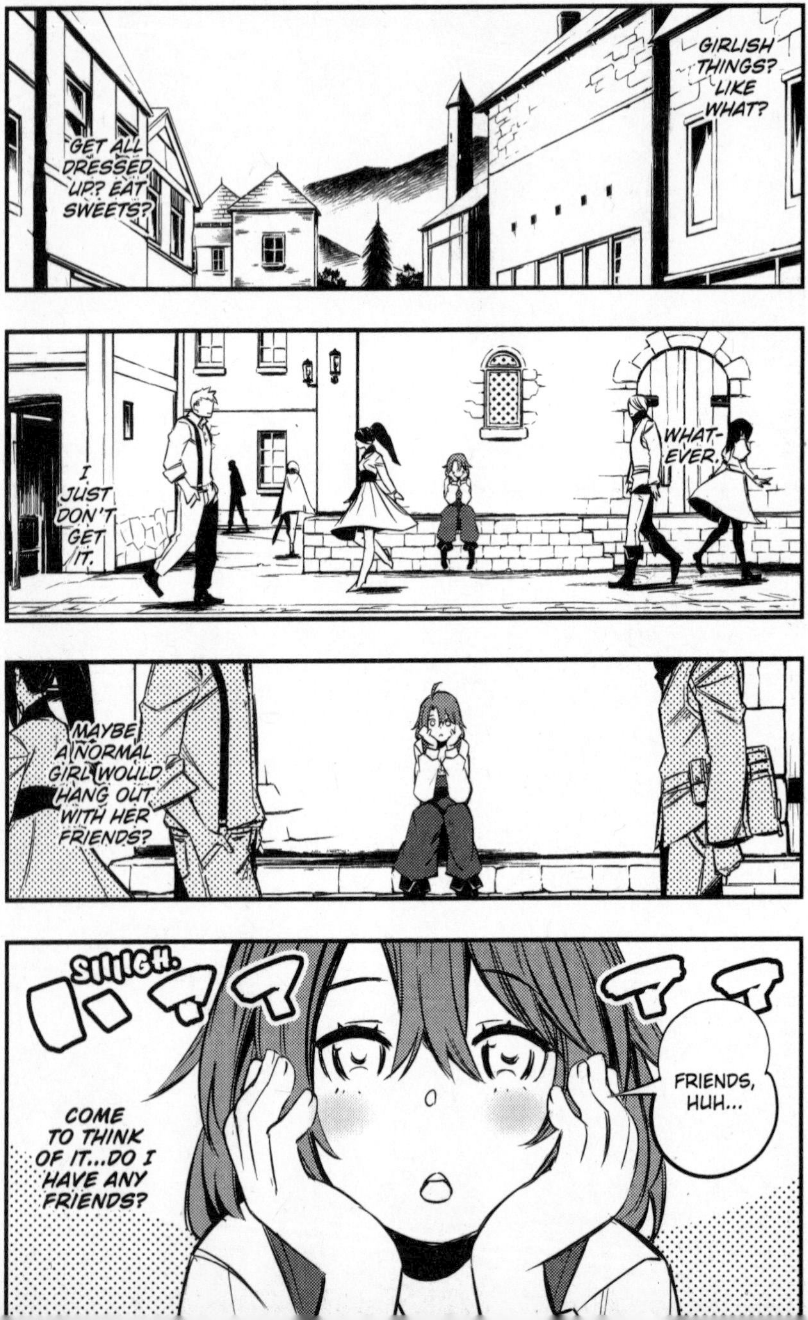
GIRLISH THINGS? LIKE WHAT?
GET ALL DRESSED UP? EAT SWEETS?
WHAT-EVER.
I JUST DON'T GET IT.
MAYBE A NORMAL GIRL WOULD HANG OUT WITH HER FRIENDS?
SIIIGH.
FRIENDS, HUH...
COME TO THINK OF IT...DO I HAVE ANY FRIENDS?

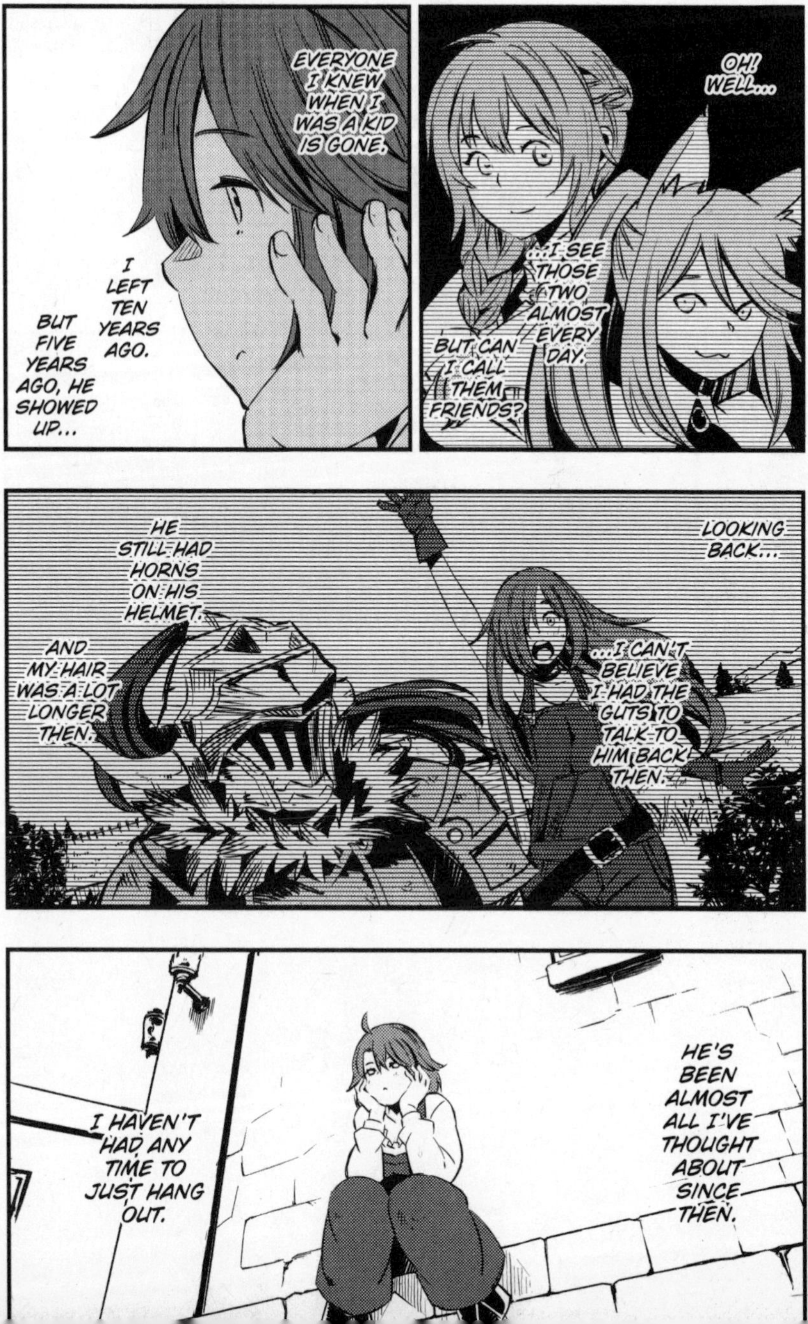
OH! WELL...
...I SEE THOSE TWO ALMOST EVERY DAY.
BUT CAN I CALL THEM FRIENDS?
EVERYONE I KNEW WHEN I WAS A KID IS GONE.
I LEFT TEN YEARS AGO.
BUT FIVE YEARS AGO, HE SHOWED UP...
LOOKING BACK...
...I CAN'T BELIEVE I HAD THE GUTS TO TALK TO HIM BACK THEN.
HE STILL HAD HORNS ON HIS HELMET.
AND MY HAIR WAS A LOT LONGER THEN.
HE'S BEEN ALMOST ALL I'VE THOUGHT ABOUT SINCE THEN.
I HAVEN'T HAD ANY TIME TO JUST HANG OUT.

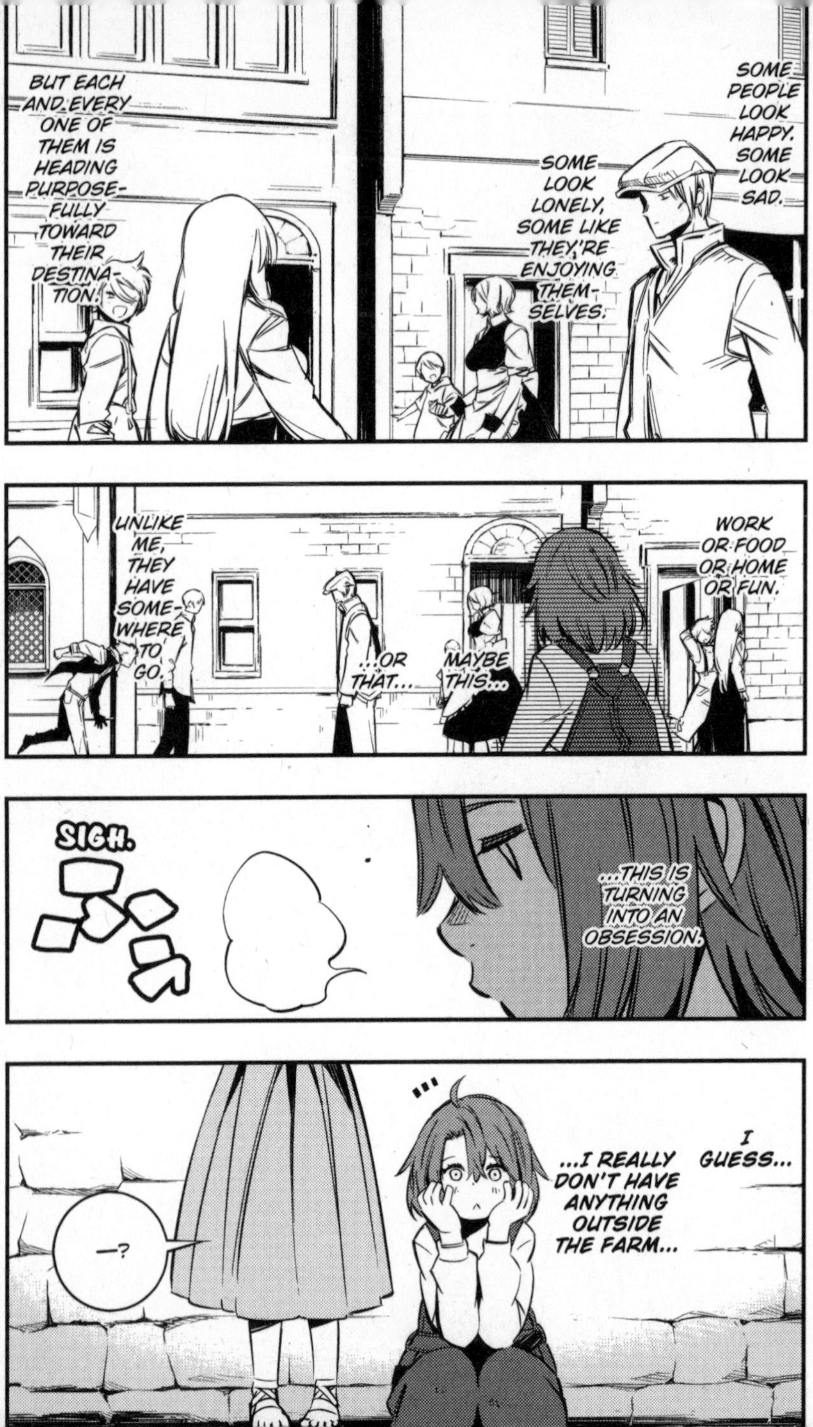
SOME PEOPLE LOOK HAPPY. SOME LOOK SAD.
SOME LOOK LONELY, SOME LIKE THEY'RE ENJOYING THEMSELVES.
BUT EACH AND EVERY ONE OF THEM IS HEADING PURPOSEFULLY TOWARD THEIR DESTINATION.
WORK OR FOOD OR HOME OR FUN.
MAYBE THIS...
...OR THAT...
UNLIKE ME, THEY HAVE SOMEWHERE TO GO.
...THIS IS TURNING INTO AN OBSESSION.
SIGH.
I GUESS...
...I REALLY DON'T HAVE ANYTHING OUTSIDE THE FARM...
...
—?

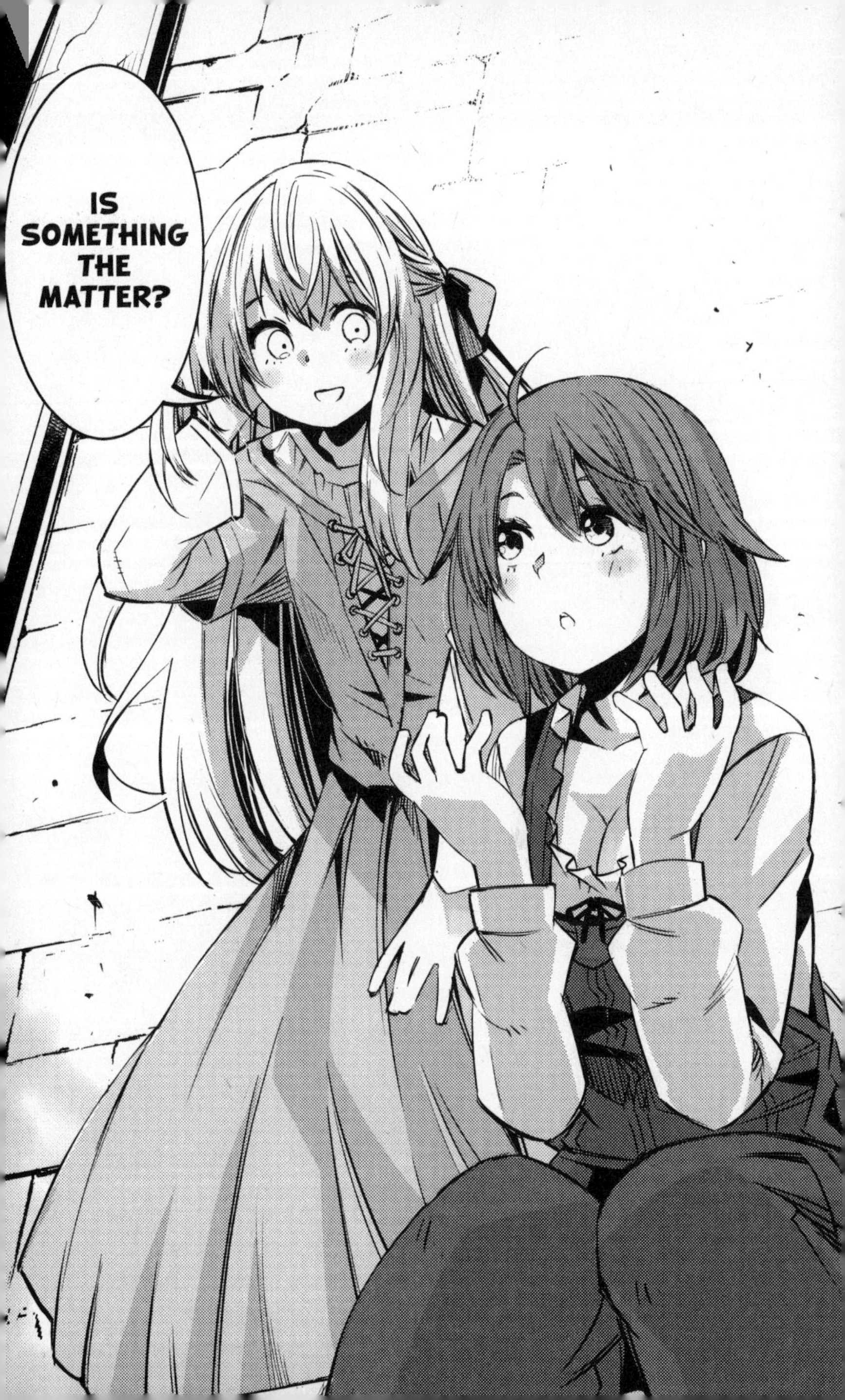
IS SOMETHING THE MATTER?

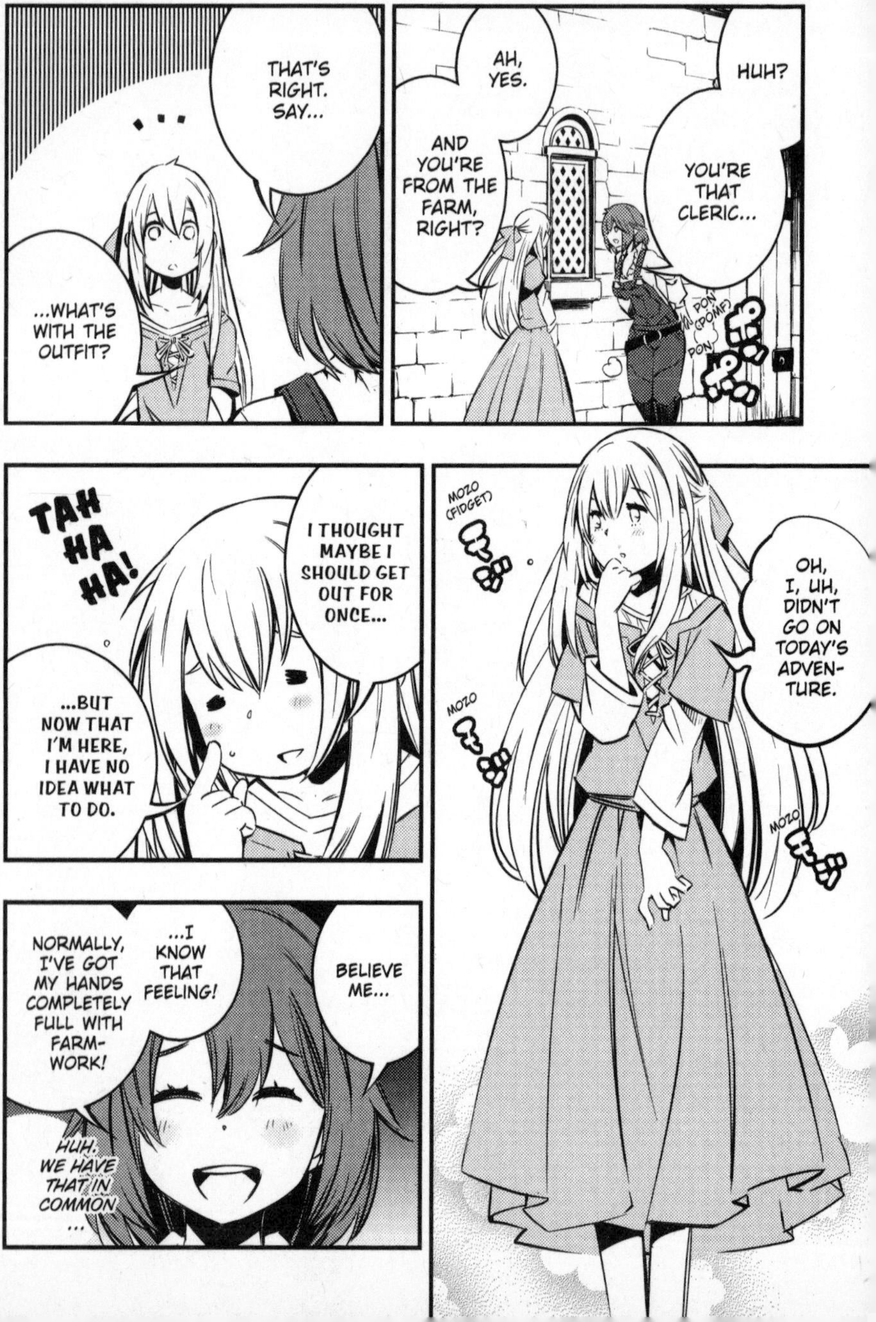
HUH?
YOU'RE THAT CLERIC...
AH, YES.
AND YOU'RE FROM THE FARM, RIGHT?
PON (POMF) PON
THAT'S RIGHT. SAY...
...
...WHAT'S WITH THE OUTFIT?
OH, I, UH, DIDN'T GO ON TODAY'S ADVEN-TURE.
MOZO (FIDGET)
MOZO
MOZO
I THOUGHT MAYBE I SHOULD GET OUT FOR ONCE...
TAH HA HA!
...BUT NOW THAT I'M HERE, I HAVE NO IDEA WHAT TO DO.
BELIEVE ME...
...I KNOW THAT FEELING!
NORMALLY, I'VE GOT MY HANDS COMPLETELY FULL WITH FARM-WORK!
HUH. WE HAVE THAT IN COMMON...

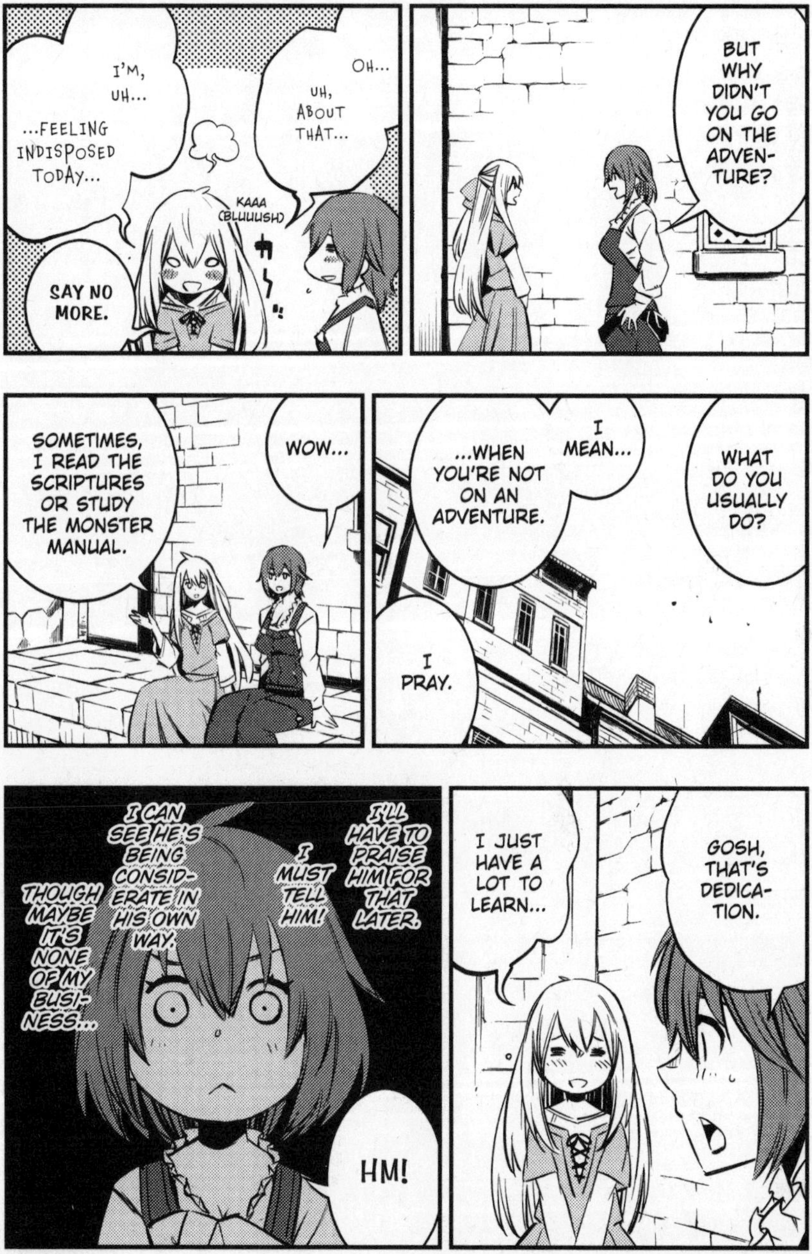
BUT WHY DIDN'T YOU GO ON THE ADVENTURE?
OH... UH, ABOUT THAT...
I'M, UH... ...FEELING INDISPOSED TODAY...
KAAA (BLUUUSH)
SAY NO MORE.
WHAT DO YOU USUALLY DO?
I MEAN...
...WHEN YOU'RE NOT ON AN ADVENTURE.
I PRAY.
WOW...
SOMETIMES, I READ THE SCRIPTURES OR STUDY THE MONSTER MANUAL.
GOSH, THAT'S DEDICATION.
I JUST HAVE A LOT TO LEARN...
I'LL HAVE TO PRAISE HIM FOR THAT LATER.
I MUST TELL HIM!
I CAN SEE HE'S BEING CONSID-ERATE IN HIS OWN WAY.
THOUGH MAYBE IT'S NONE OF MY BUSI-NESS...
HM!

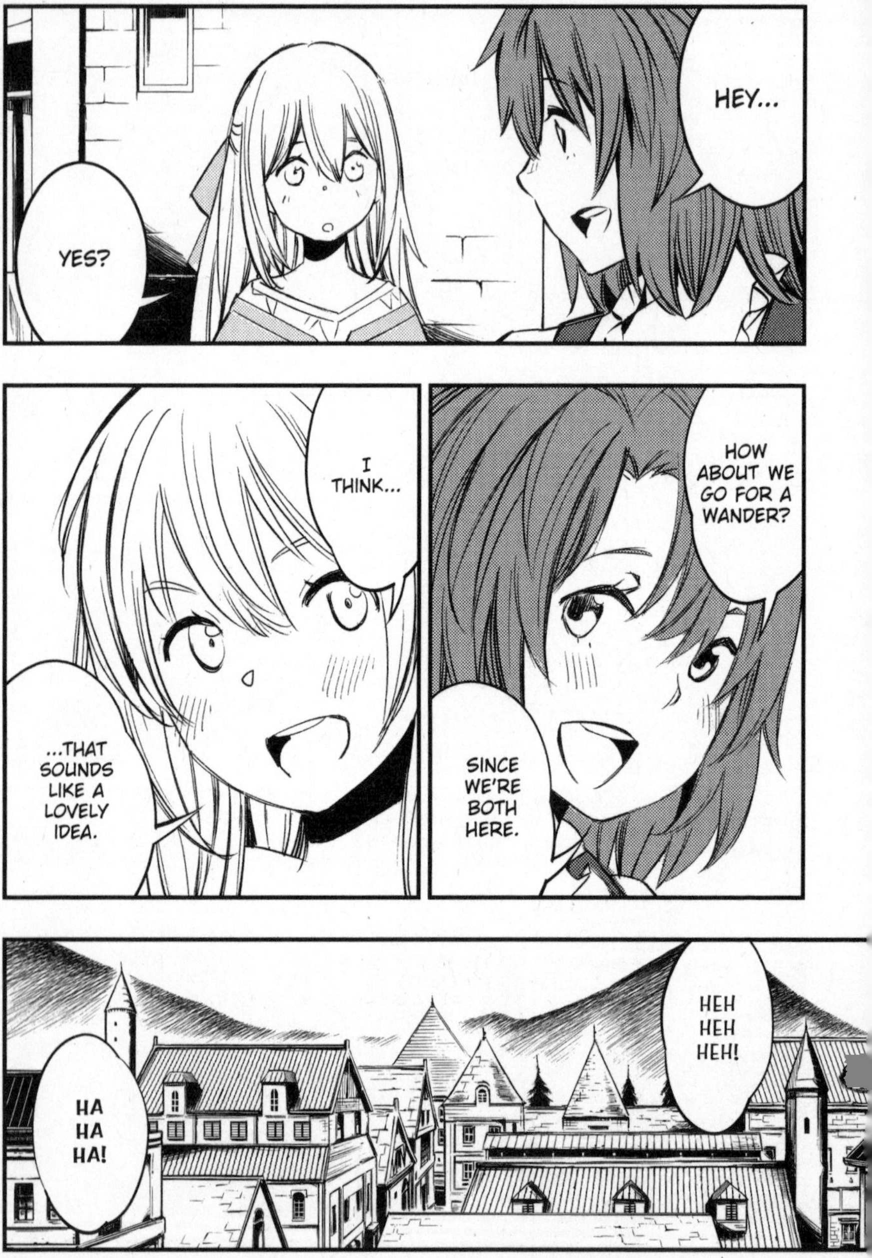
HEY...
YES?
HOW ABOUT WE GO FOR A WANDER?
SINCE WE'RE BOTH HERE.
I THINK...
...THAT SOUNDS LIKE A LOVELY IDEA.
HEH HEH HEH!
HA HA HA!

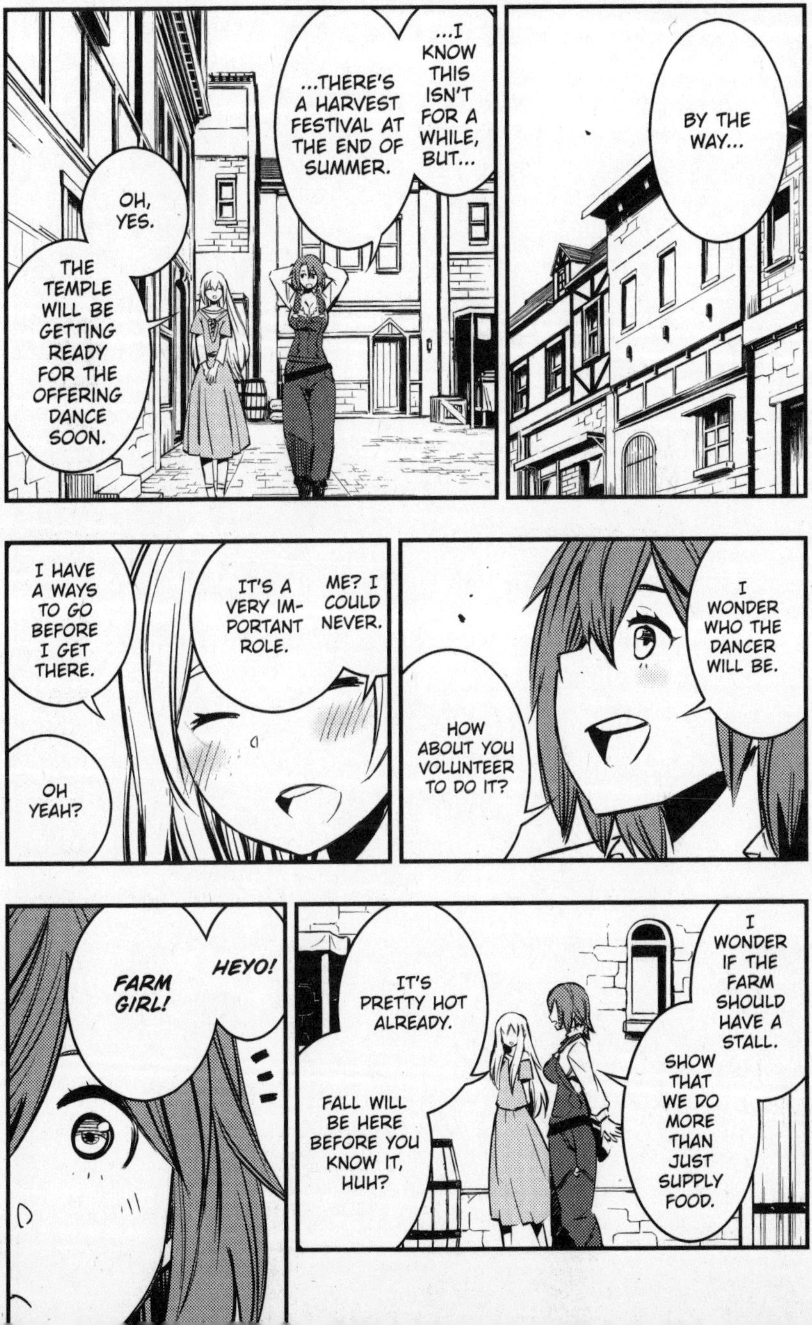
BY THE WAY...
...I KNOW THIS ISN'T FOR A WHILE, BUT...
...THERE'S A HARVEST FESTIVAL AT THE END OF SUMMER.
OH, YES.
THE TEMPLE WILL BE GETTING READY FOR THE OFFERING DANCE SOON.
I WONDER WHO THE DANCER WILL BE.
HOW ABOUT YOU VOLUNTEER TO DO IT?
ME? I COULD NEVER.
IT'S A VERY IM-PORTANT ROLE.
I HAVE A WAYS TO GO BEFORE I GET THERE.
OH YEAH?
I WONDER IF THE FARM SHOULD HAVE A STALL.
SHOW THAT WE DO MORE THAN JUST SUPPLY FOOD.
IT'S PRETTY HOT ALREADY.
FALL WILL BE HERE BEFORE YOU KNOW IT, HUH?
HEYO!
FARM GIRL!

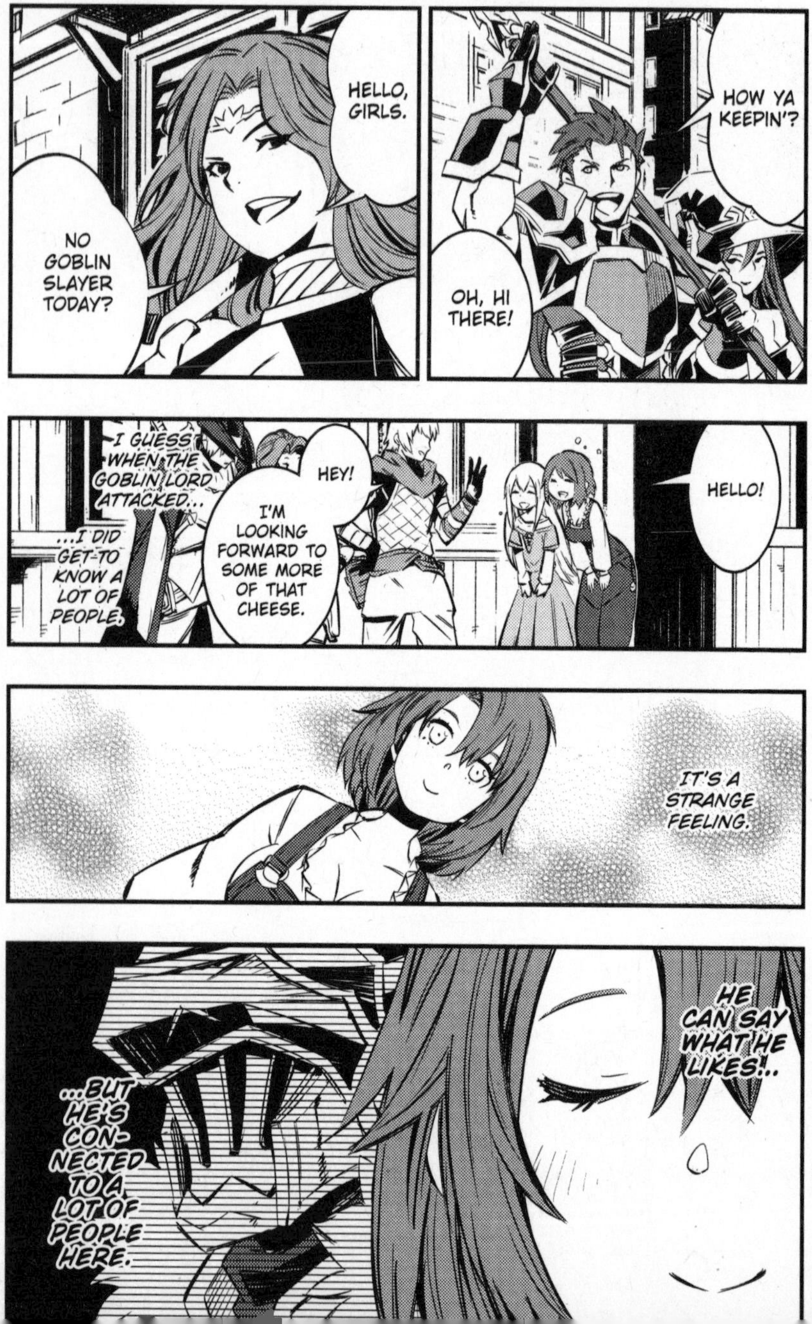
HOW YA KEEPIN'?
OH, HI THERE!
HELLO, GIRLS.
NO GOBLIN SLAYER TODAY?
HELLO!
HEY!
I'M LOOKING FORWARD TO SOME MORE OF THAT CHEESE.
I GUESS WHEN THE GOBLIN LORD ATTACKED...
...I DID GET TO KNOW A LOT OF PEOPLE.
IT'S A STRANGE FEELING.
HE CAN SAY WHAT HE LIKES!...
...BUT HE'S CONNECTED TO A LOT OF PEOPLE HERE.

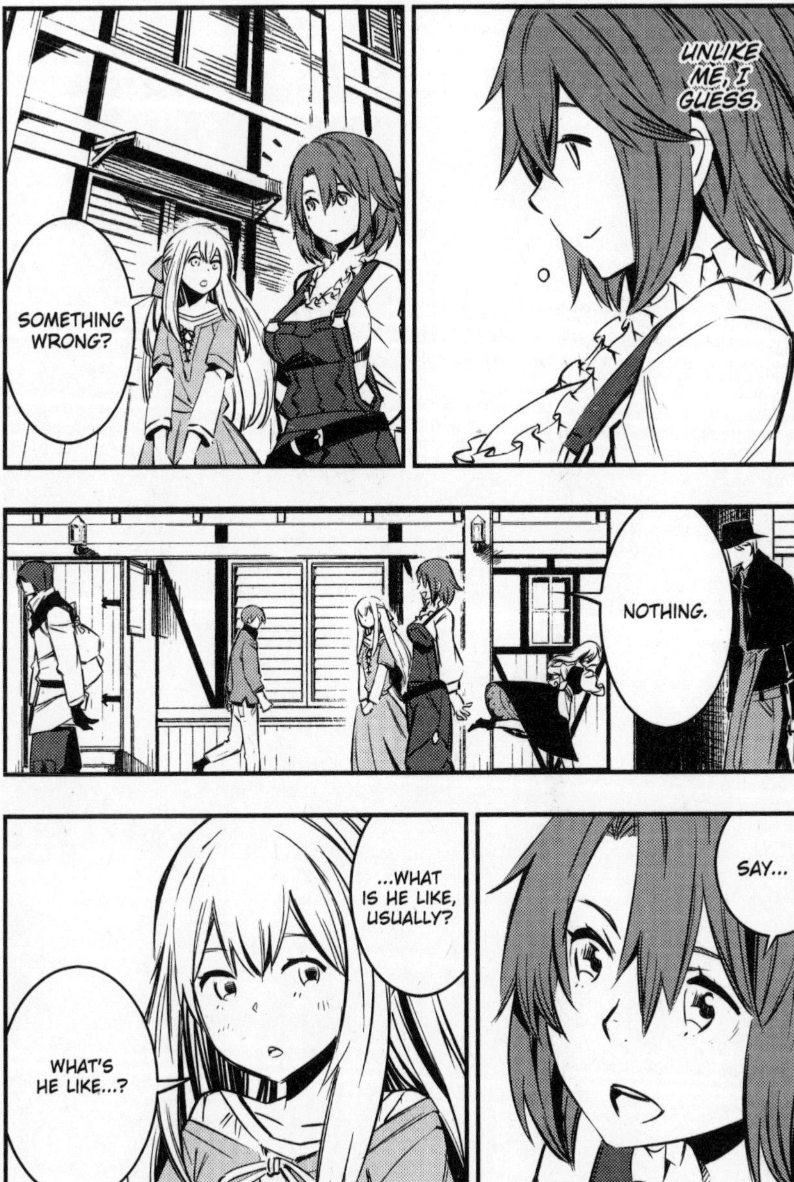
UNLIKE ME, I GUESS.
SOMETHING WRONG?
NOTHING.
SAY...
...WHAT IS HE LIKE, USUALLY?
WHAT'S HE LIKE...?

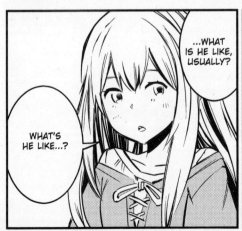

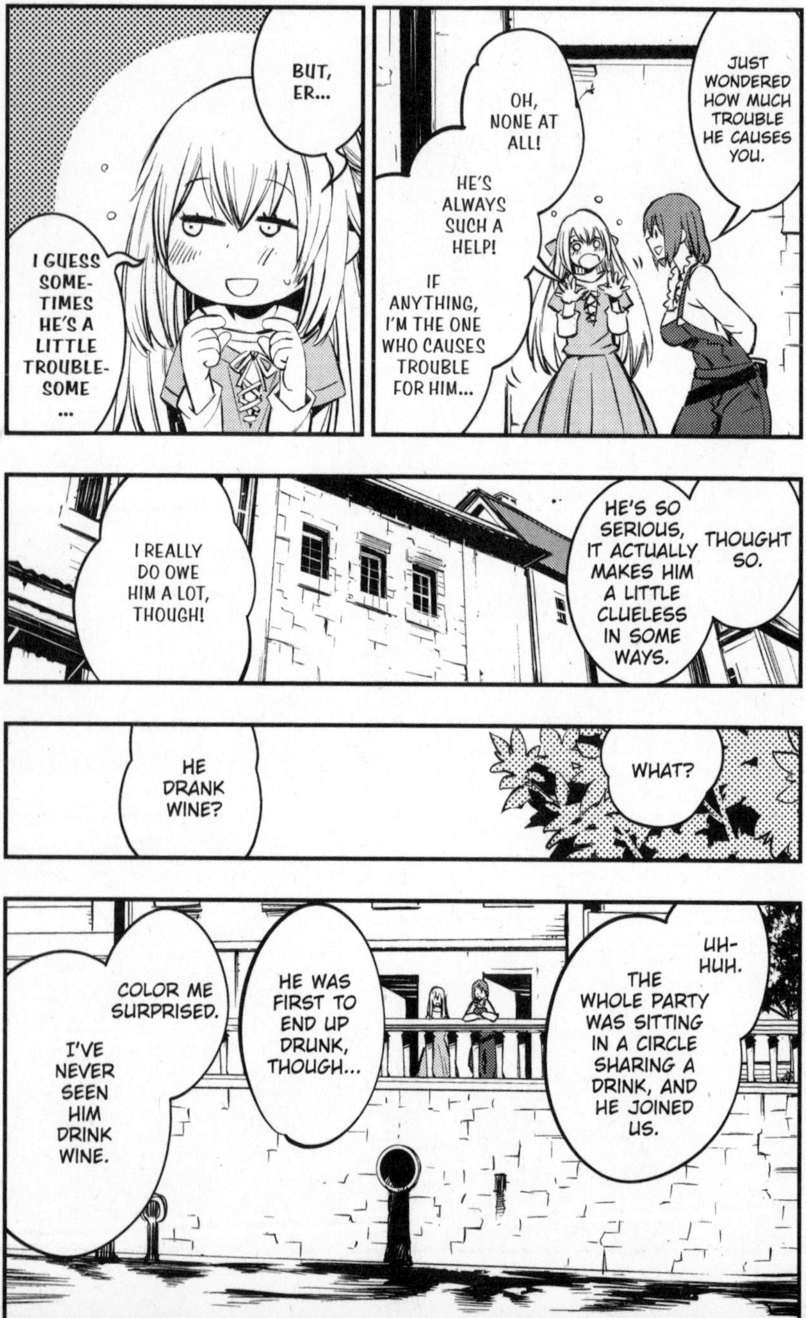
JUST WONDERED HOW MUCH TROUBLE HE CAUSES YOU.
OH, NONE AT ALL!
HE'S ALWAYS SUCH A HELP!
IF ANYTHING, I'M THE ONE WHO CAUSES TROUBLE FOR HIM...
BUT, ER...
I GUESS SOME-TIMES HE'S A LITTLE TROUBLE-SOME...
THOUGHT SO.
HE'S SO SERIOUS, IT ACTUALLY MAKES HIM A LITTLE CLUELESS IN SOME WAYS.
I REALLY DO OWE HIM A LOT, THOUGH!
WHAT?
HE DRANK WINE?
UH-HUH.
THE WHOLE PARTY WAS SITTING IN A CIRCLE SHARING A DRINK, AND HE JOINED US.
HE WAS FIRST TO END UP DRUNK, THOUGH...
COLOR ME SURPRISED.
I'VE NEVER SEEN HIM DRINK WINE.

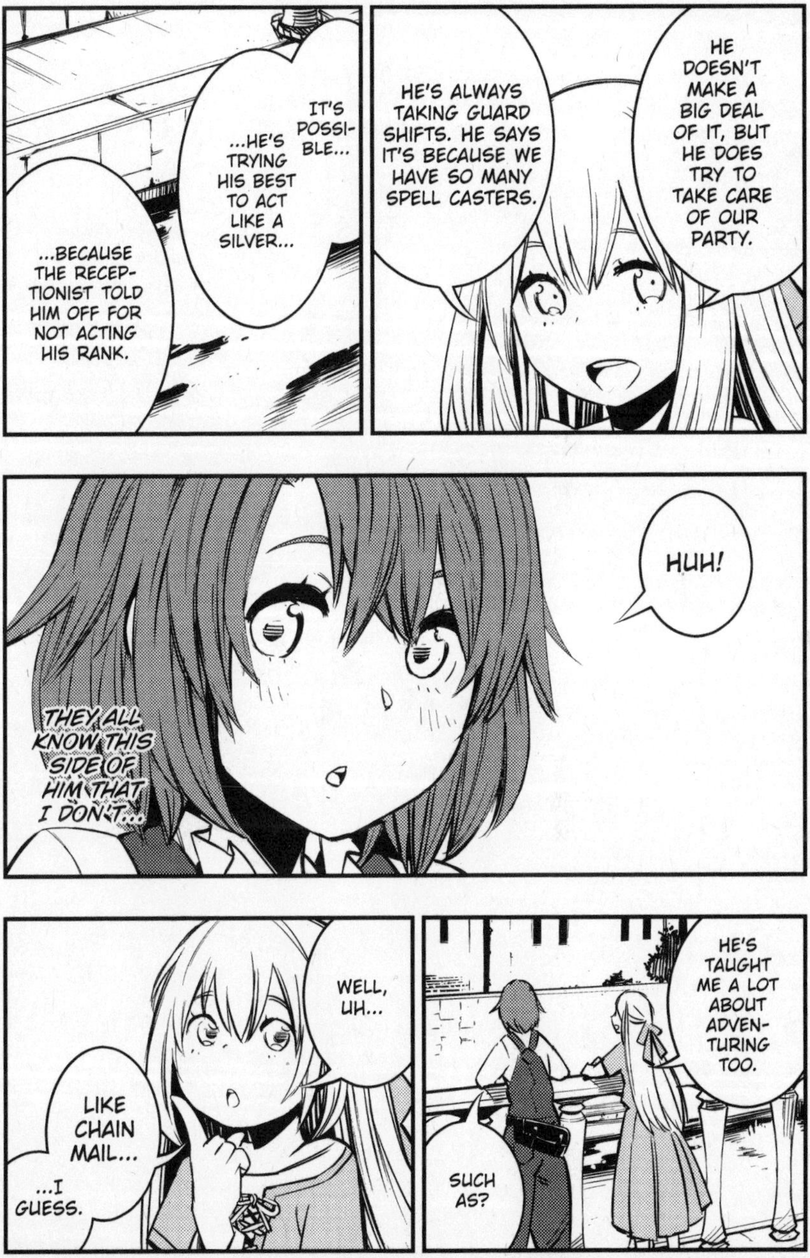
HE DOESN'T MAKE A BIG DEAL OF IT, BUT HE DOES TRY TO TAKE CARE OF OUR PARTY.
HE'S ALWAYS TAKING GUARD SHIFTS. HE SAYS IT'S BECAUSE WE HAVE SO MANY SPELL CASTERS.
IT'S POSSIBLE...
...HE'S TRYING HIS BEST TO ACT LIKE A SILVER...
...BECAUSE THE RECEPTIONIST TOLD HIM OFF FOR NOT ACTING HIS RANK.
HUH!
THEY ALL KNOW THIS SIDE OF HIM THAT I DON'T...
HE'S TAUGHT ME A LOT ABOUT ADVENTURING TOO.
SUCH AS?
WELL, UH...
LIKE CHAIN MAIL...
...I GUESS.

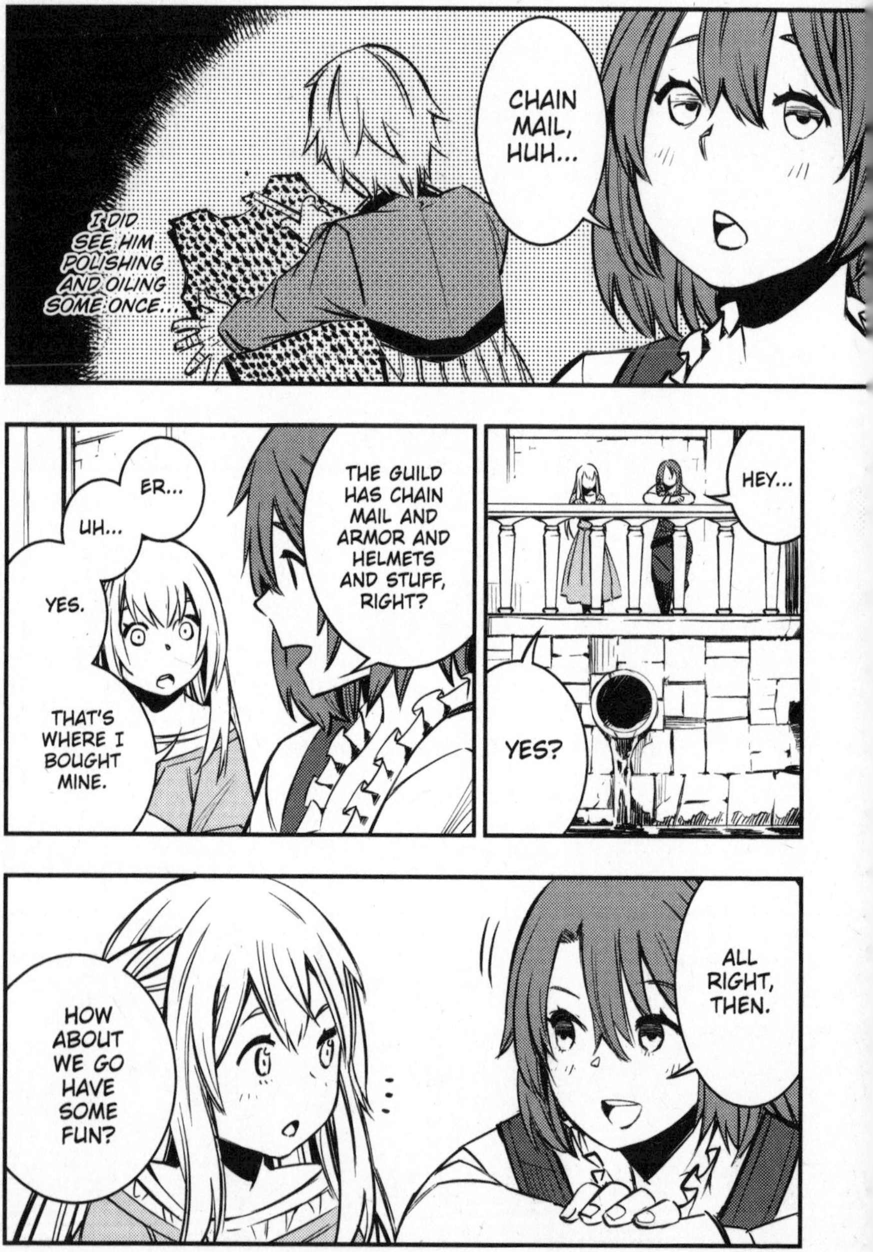
CHAIN MAIL, HUH...
I DID SEE HIM POLISHING AND OILING SOME ONCE...
HEY...
YES?
THE GUILD HAS CHAIN MAIL AND ARMOR AND HELMETS AND STUFF, RIGHT?
ER...
UH...
YES.
THAT'S WHERE I BOUGHT MINE.
ALL RIGHT, THEN.
HOW ABOUT WE GO HAVE SOME FUN?

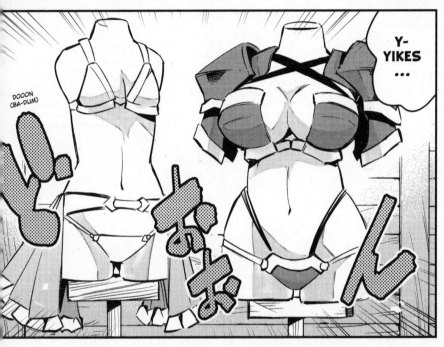

Y-YIKES...

DOOON
(BA-DUM)

NO IDEA...

DOKI!
(BA-DUM)

HUH?

DO YOU... WEAR ANYTHING UNDER THAT...?

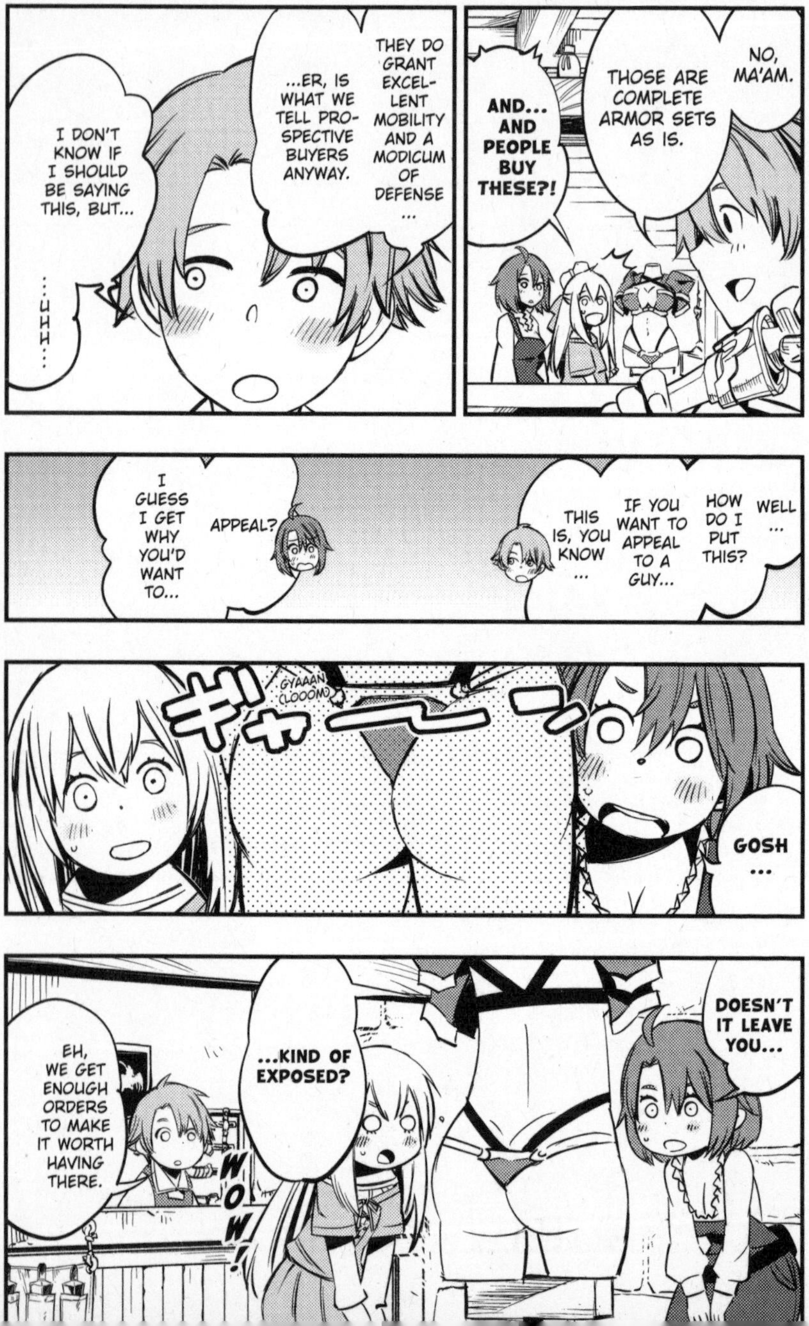
NO, MA'AM.
THOSE ARE COMPLETE ARMOR SETS AS IS.
AND... AND PEOPLE BUY THESE?!
THEY DO GRANT EXCEL-LENT MOBILITY AND A MODICUM OF DEFENSE ...
...ER, IS WHAT WE TELL PRO-SPECTIVE BUYERS ANYWAY.
I DON'T KNOW IF I SHOULD BE SAYING THIS, BUT...
...UHH...
WELL ...
HOW DO I PUT THIS?
IF YOU WANT TO APPEAL TO A GUY...
THIS IS, YOU KNOW ...
APPEAL?
I GUESS I GET WHY YOU'D WANT TO...
GYAAAN (LOOOM)
GOSH ...
DOESN'T IT LEAVE YOU...
...KIND OF EXPOSED?
WOW!
EH, WE GET ENOUGH ORDERS TO MAKE IT WORTH HAVING THERE.

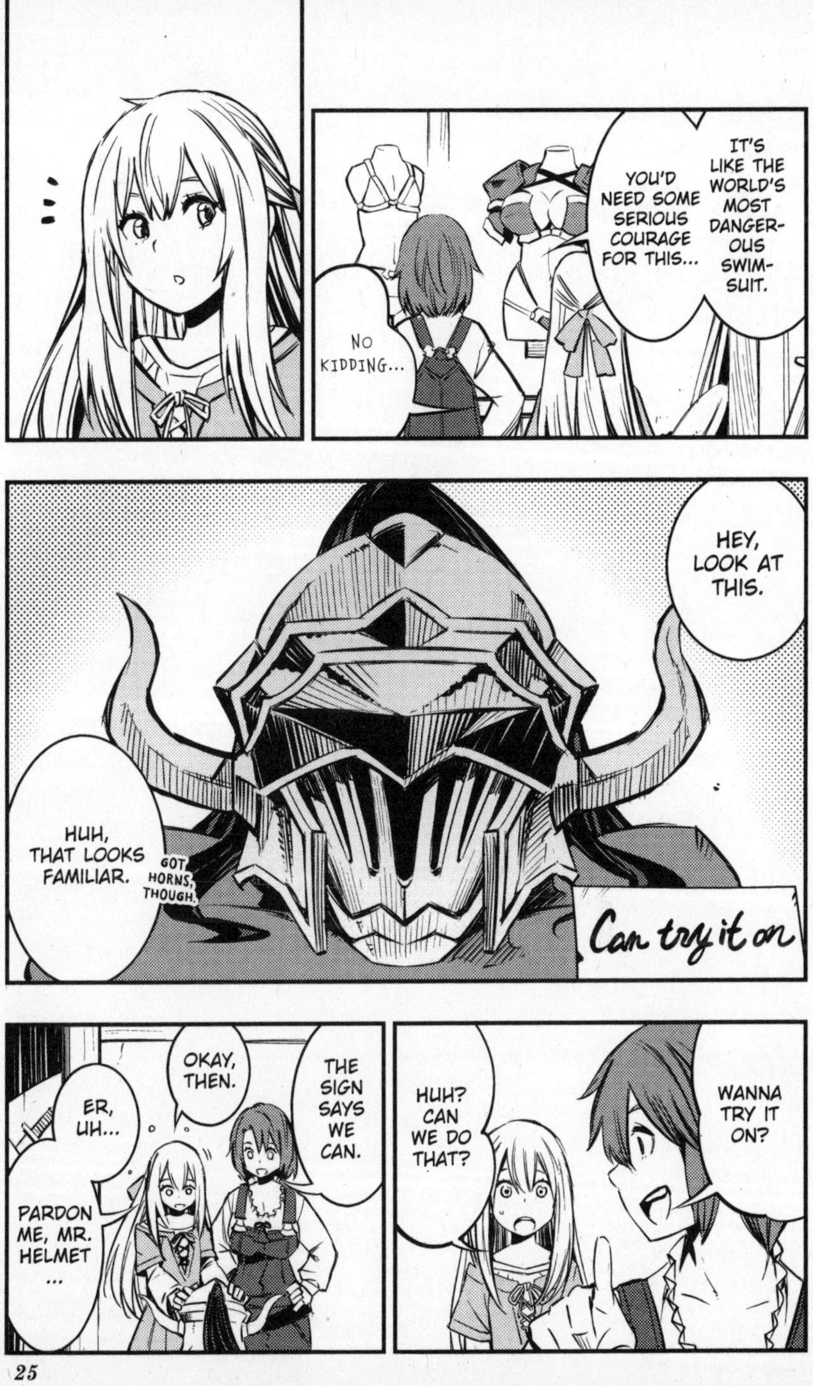
IT'S LIKE THE WORLD'S MOST DANGER-OUS SWIM-SUIT.
YOU'D NEED SOME SERIOUS COURAGE FOR THIS...
NO KIDDING...
HEY, LOOK AT THIS.
Can try it on
HUH, THAT LOOKS FAMILIAR.
GOT HORNS, THOUGH.
WANNA TRY IT ON?
HUH? CAN WE DO THAT?
THE SIGN SAYS WE CAN.
OKAY, THEN.
ER, UH...
PARDON ME, MR. HELMET ...

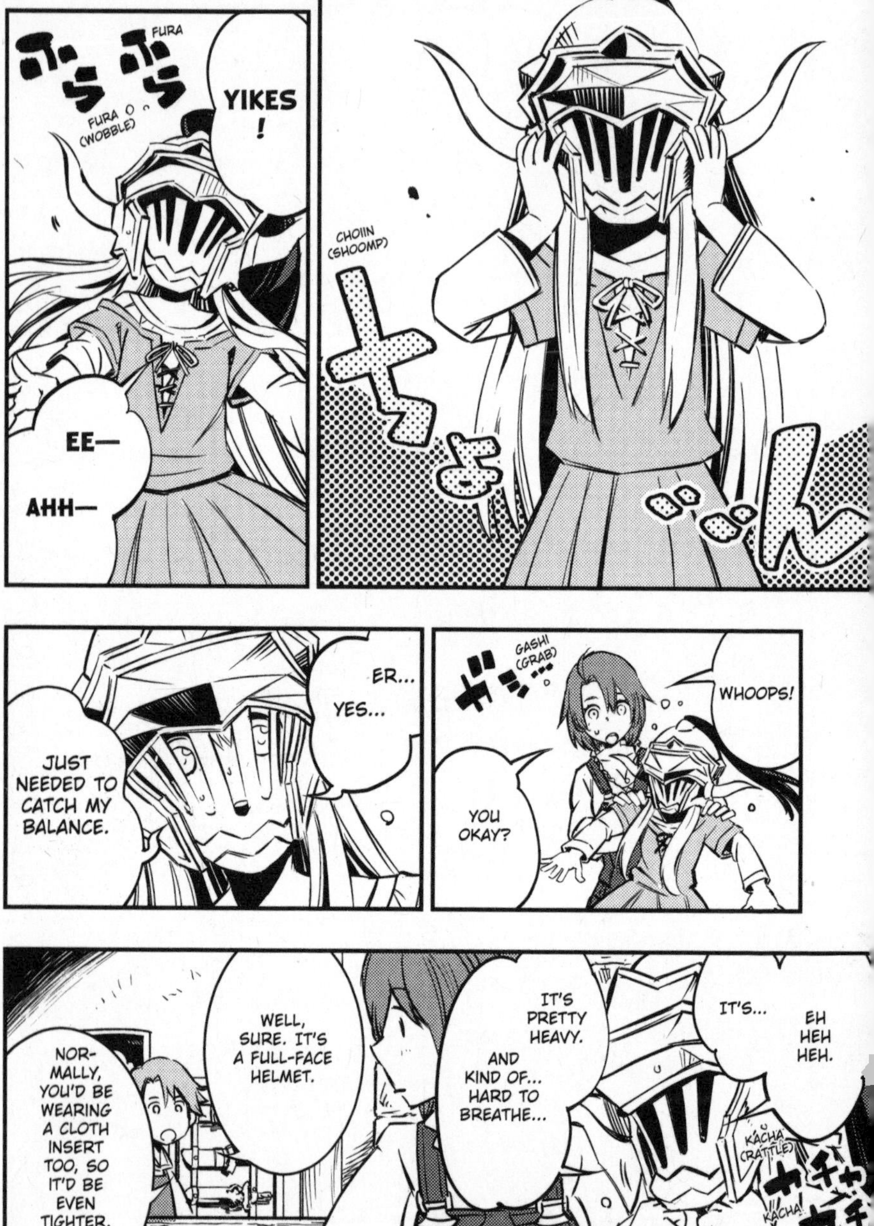
CHOIIN
(SHOOMP)
FURA
FURA
(WOBBLE)
YIKES!
EE—
AHH—
GASHI
(GRAB)
WHOOPS!
YOU OKAY?
ER...
YES...
JUST NEEDED TO CATCH MY BALANCE.
IT'S...
EH HEH HEH.
KACHA
(RATTLE)
KACHA!
IT'S PRETTY HEAVY.
AND KIND OF... HARD TO BREATHE...
WELL, SURE. IT'S A FULL-FACE HELMET.
NOR-MALLY, YOU'D BE WEARING A CLOTH INSERT TOO, SO IT'D BE EVEN TIGHTER.

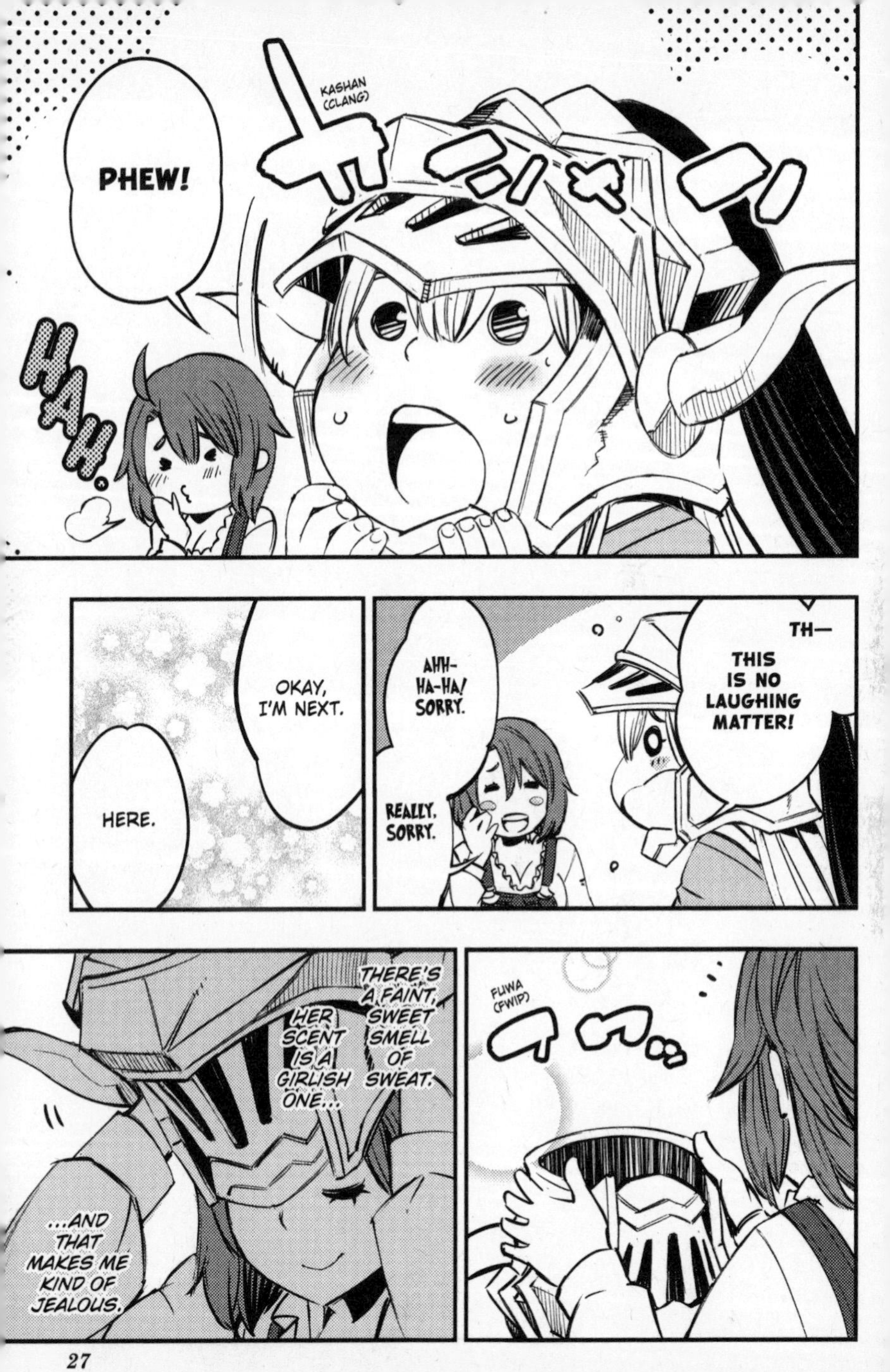
KASHAN (CLANG)
PHEW!
HAH.
TH—
THIS IS NO LAUGHING MATTER!
AHH-HA-HA! SORRY.
REALLY, SORRY.
OKAY, I'M NEXT.
HERE.
FUWA (FWIP)
THERE'S A FAINT, SWEET SMELL OF SWEAT.
HER SCENT IS A GIRLISH ONE...
...AND THAT MAKES ME KIND OF JEALOUS.

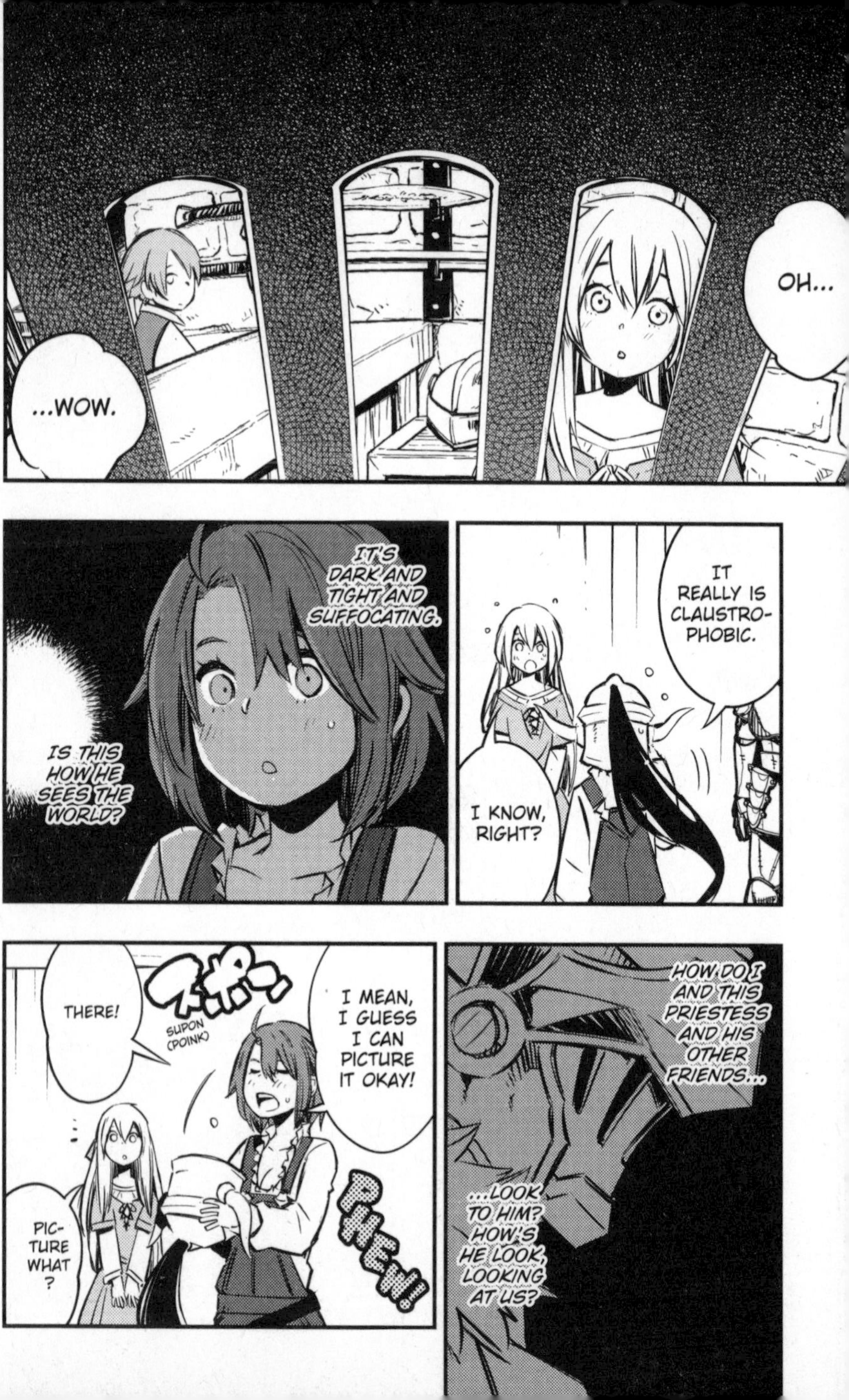

OH...
...WOW.
IT REALLY IS CLAUSTRO-PHOBIC.
I KNOW, RIGHT?
IT'S DARK AND TIGHT AND SUFFOCATING.
IS THIS HOW HE SEES THE WORLD?
HOW DO I AND THIS PRIESTESS AND HIS OTHER FRIENDS...
...LOOK TO HIM? HOW'S HE LOOK, LOOKING AT US?
I MEAN, I GUESS I CAN PICTURE IT OKAY!
THERE!
SUPON (POINK)
PHEW!
PIC-TURE WHAT?

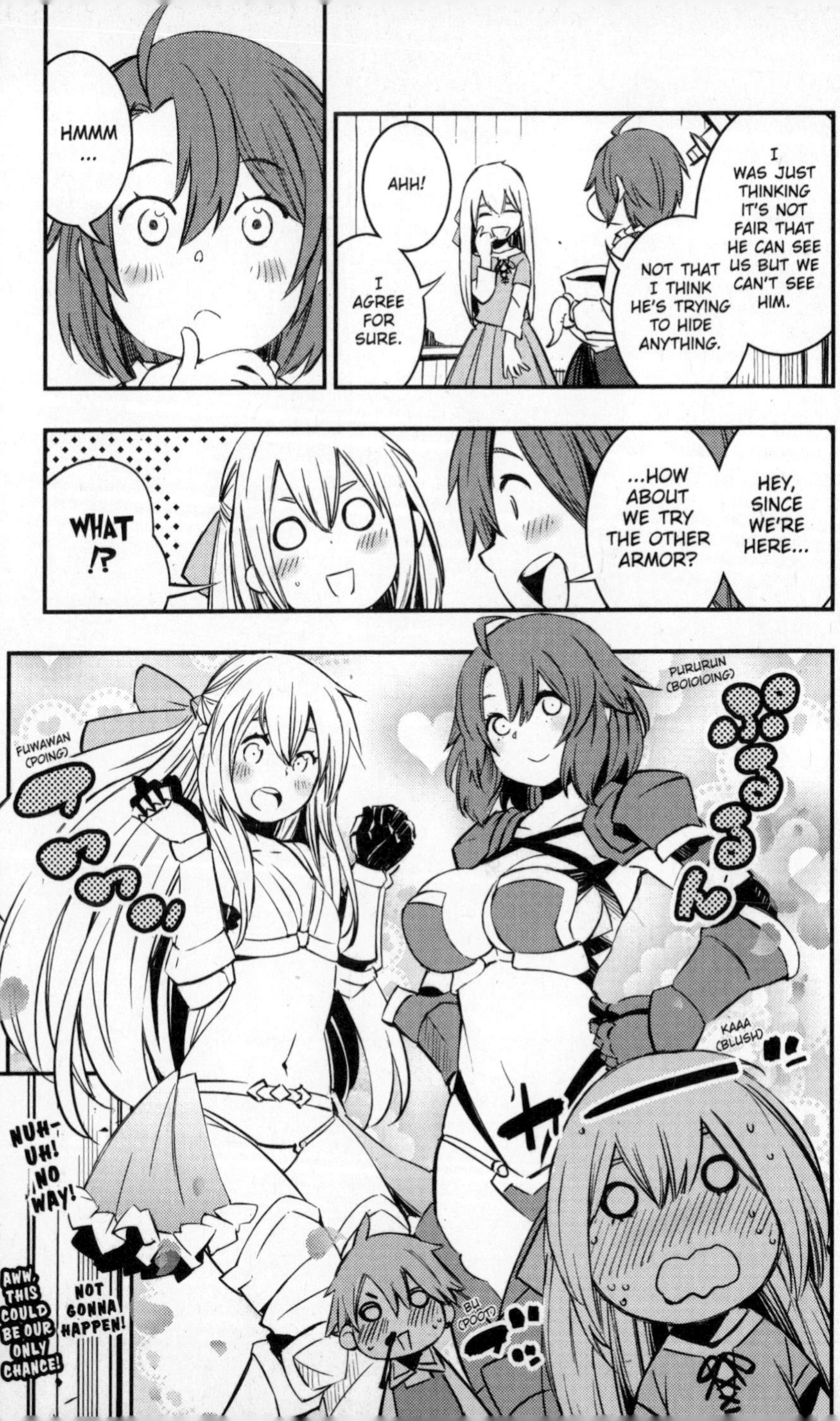
I WAS JUST THINKING IT'S NOT FAIR THAT HE CAN SEE US BUT WE CAN'T SEE HIM.
NOT THAT I THINK HE'S TRYING TO HIDE ANYTHING.
AHH!
I AGREE FOR SURE.
HMMM ...
HEY, SINCE WE'RE HERE...
...HOW ABOUT WE TRY THE OTHER ARMOR?
WHAT !?
PURURUN (BOIOIOING)
FUWAWAN (POING)
KAAA (BLUSH)
NUH-UH! NO WAY!
BU (POOT)
NOT GONNA HAPPEN!
AWW, THIS COULD BE OUR ONLY CHANCE!

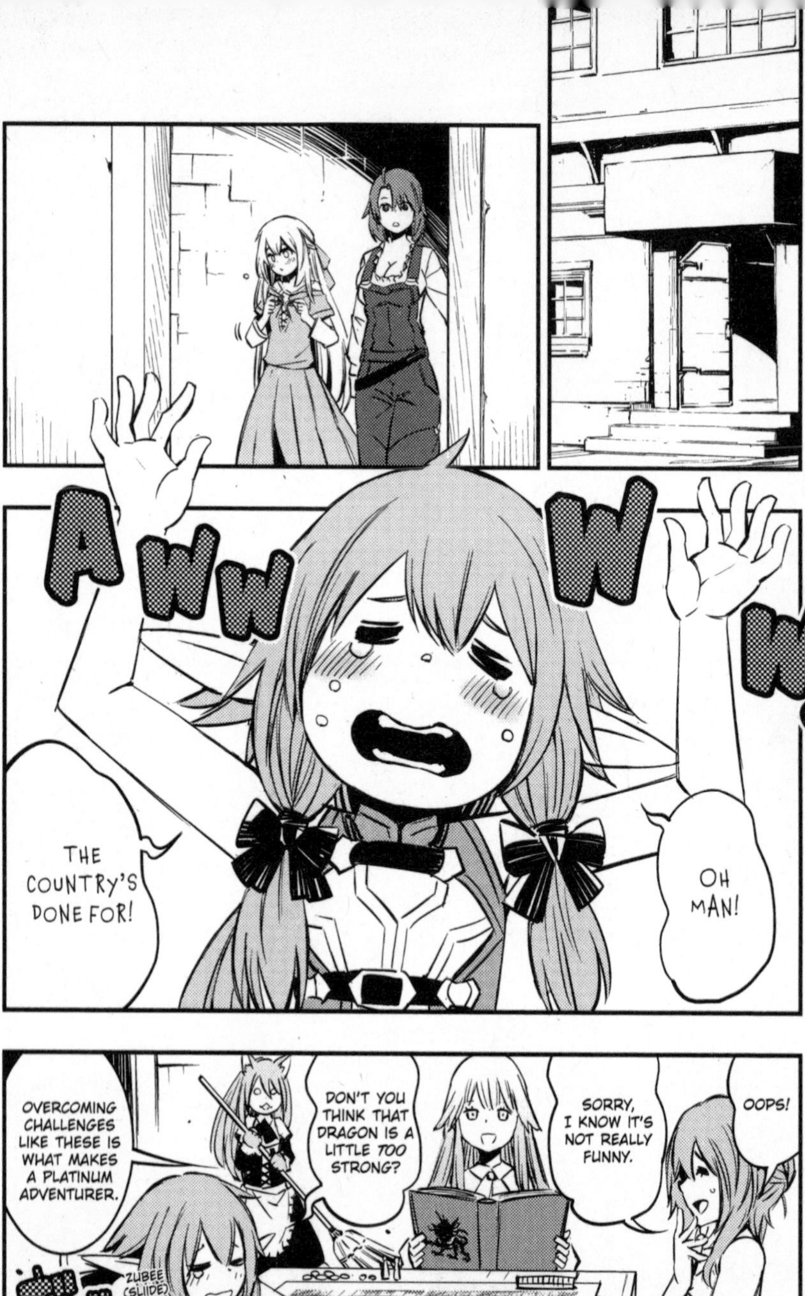
AWWWWW!
OH MAN!
THE COUNTRY'S DONE FOR!
OOPS!
SORRY, I KNOW IT'S NOT REALLY FUNNY.
DON'T YOU THINK THAT DRAGON IS A LITTLE *TOO* STRONG?
OVERCOMING CHALLENGES LIKE THESE IS WHAT MAKES A PLATINUM ADVENTURER.
ZUBEE (SLIIDE)

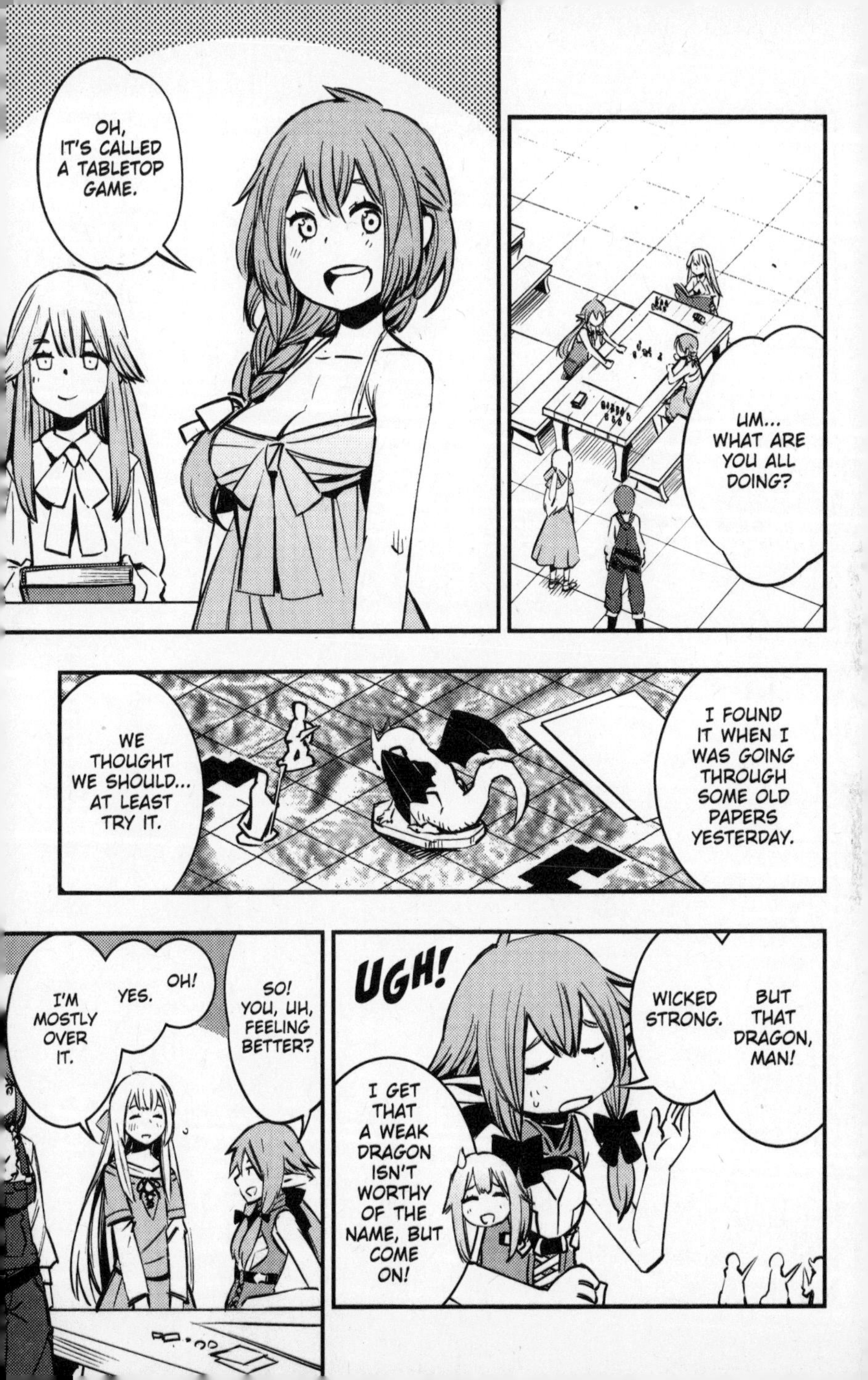
UM... WHAT ARE YOU ALL DOING?
OH, IT'S CALLED A TABLETOP GAME.
I FOUND IT WHEN I WAS GOING THROUGH SOME OLD PAPERS YESTERDAY.
WE THOUGHT WE SHOULD... AT LEAST TRY IT.
BUT THAT DRAGON, MAN!
WICKED STRONG.
UGH!
I GET THAT A WEAK DRAGON ISN'T WORTHY OF THE NAME, BUT COME ON!
SO! YOU, UH, FEELING BETTER?
OH!
YES.
I'M MOSTLY OVER IT.

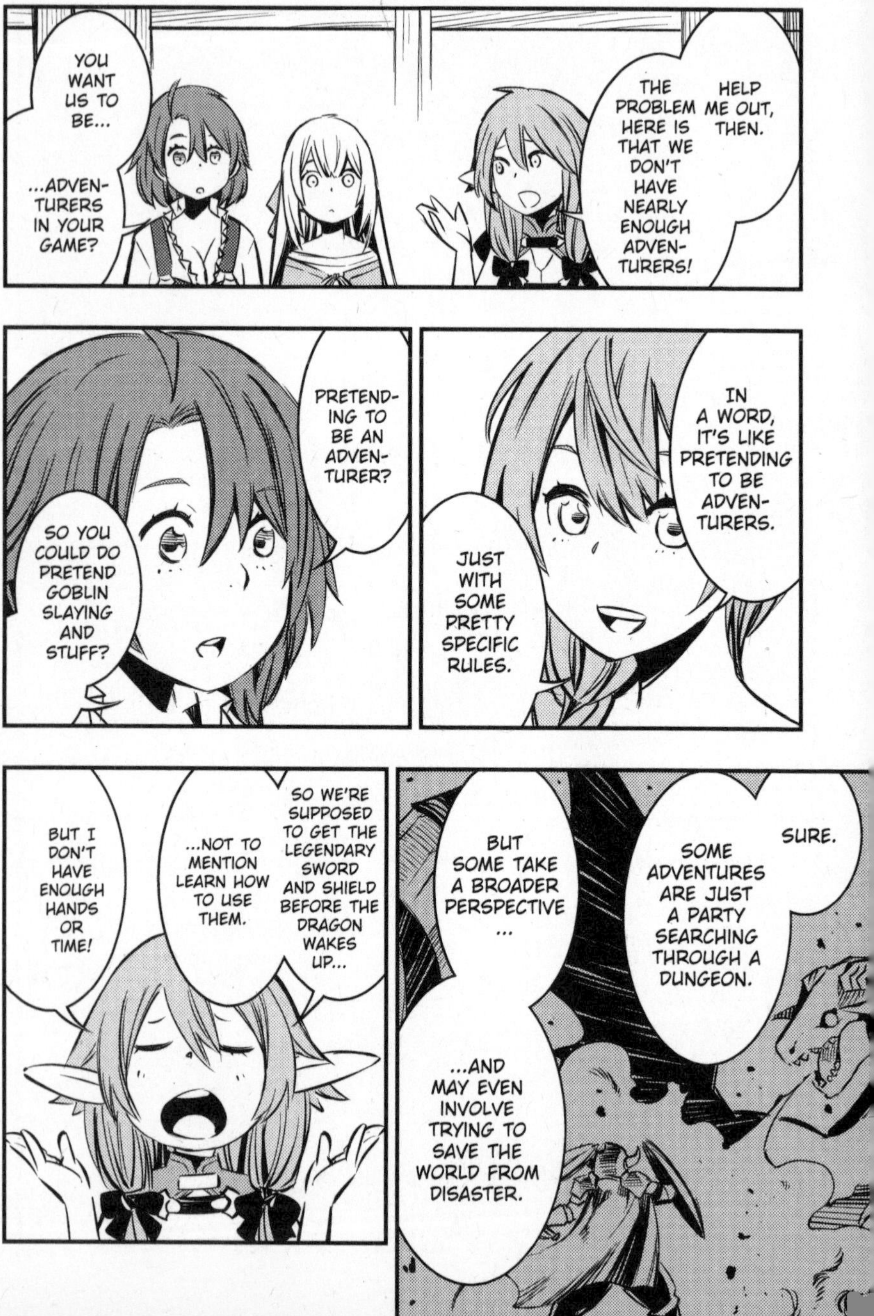
HELP ME OUT, THEN.
THE PROBLEM HERE IS THAT WE DON'T HAVE NEARLY ENOUGH ADVEN-TURERS!
YOU WANT US TO BE...
...ADVEN-TURERS IN YOUR GAME?
IN A WORD, IT'S LIKE PRETENDING TO BE ADVEN-TURERS.
JUST WITH SOME PRETTY SPECIFIC RULES.
PRETEND-ING TO BE AN ADVEN-TURER?
SO YOU COULD DO PRETEND GOBLIN SLAYING AND STUFF?
SURE.
SOME ADVENTURES ARE JUST A PARTY SEARCHING THROUGH A DUNGEON.
BUT SOME TAKE A BROADER PERSPECTIVE...
...AND MAY EVEN INVOLVE TRYING TO SAVE THE WORLD FROM DISASTER.
SO WE'RE SUPPOSED TO GET THE LEGENDARY SWORD AND SHIELD BEFORE THE DRAGON WAKES UP...
...NOT TO MENTION LEARN HOW TO USE THEM.
BUT I DON'T HAVE ENOUGH HANDS OR TIME!

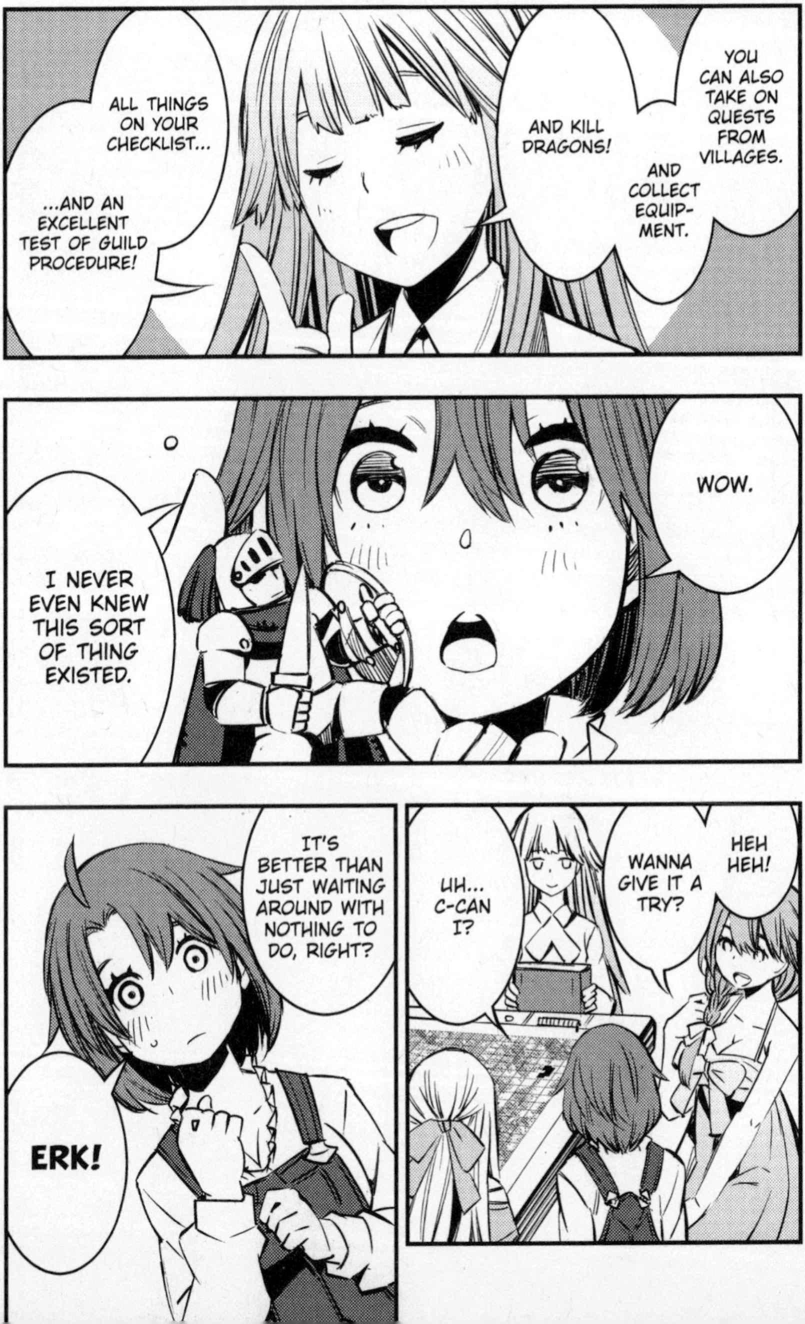
YOU CAN ALSO TAKE ON QUESTS FROM VILLAGES.
AND COLLECT EQUIP-MENT.
AND KILL DRAGONS!
ALL THINGS ON YOUR CHECKLIST...
...AND AN EXCELLENT TEST OF GUILD PROCEDURE!
WOW.
I NEVER EVEN KNEW THIS SORT OF THING EXISTED.
HEH HEH!
WANNA GIVE IT A TRY?
UH... C-CAN I?
IT'S BETTER THAN JUST WAITING AROUND WITH NOTHING TO DO, RIGHT?
ERK!

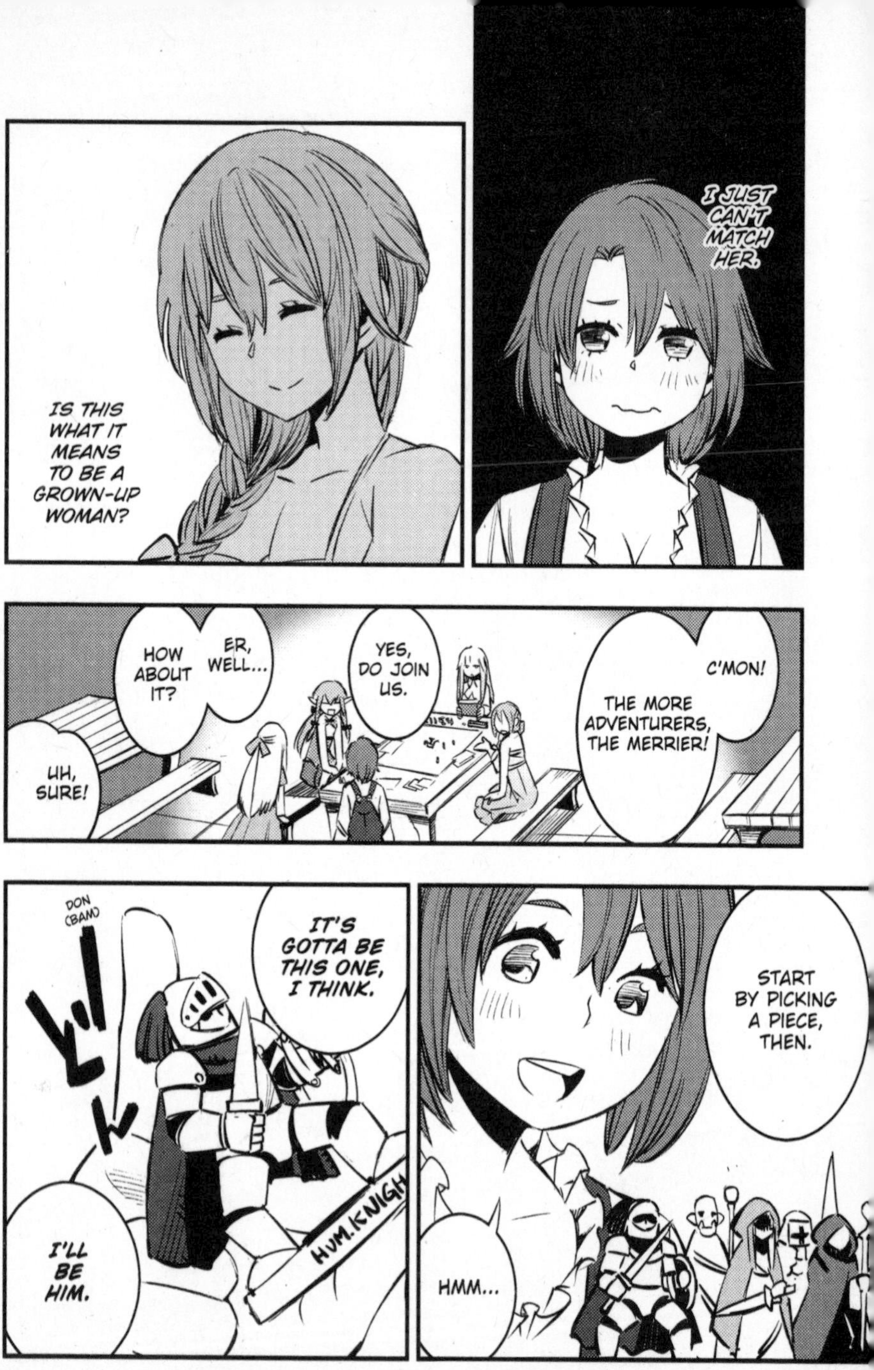
I JUST CAN'T MATCH HER.
IS THIS WHAT IT MEANS TO BE A GROWN-UP WOMAN?
C'MON!
THE MORE ADVENTURERS, THE MERRIER!
YES, DO JOIN US.
ER, WELL...
HOW ABOUT IT?
UH, SURE!
START BY PICKING A PIECE, THEN.
HMM...
IT'S GOTTA BE THIS ONE, I THINK.
DON (BAM)
HUM.KNIGH
I'LL BE HIM.

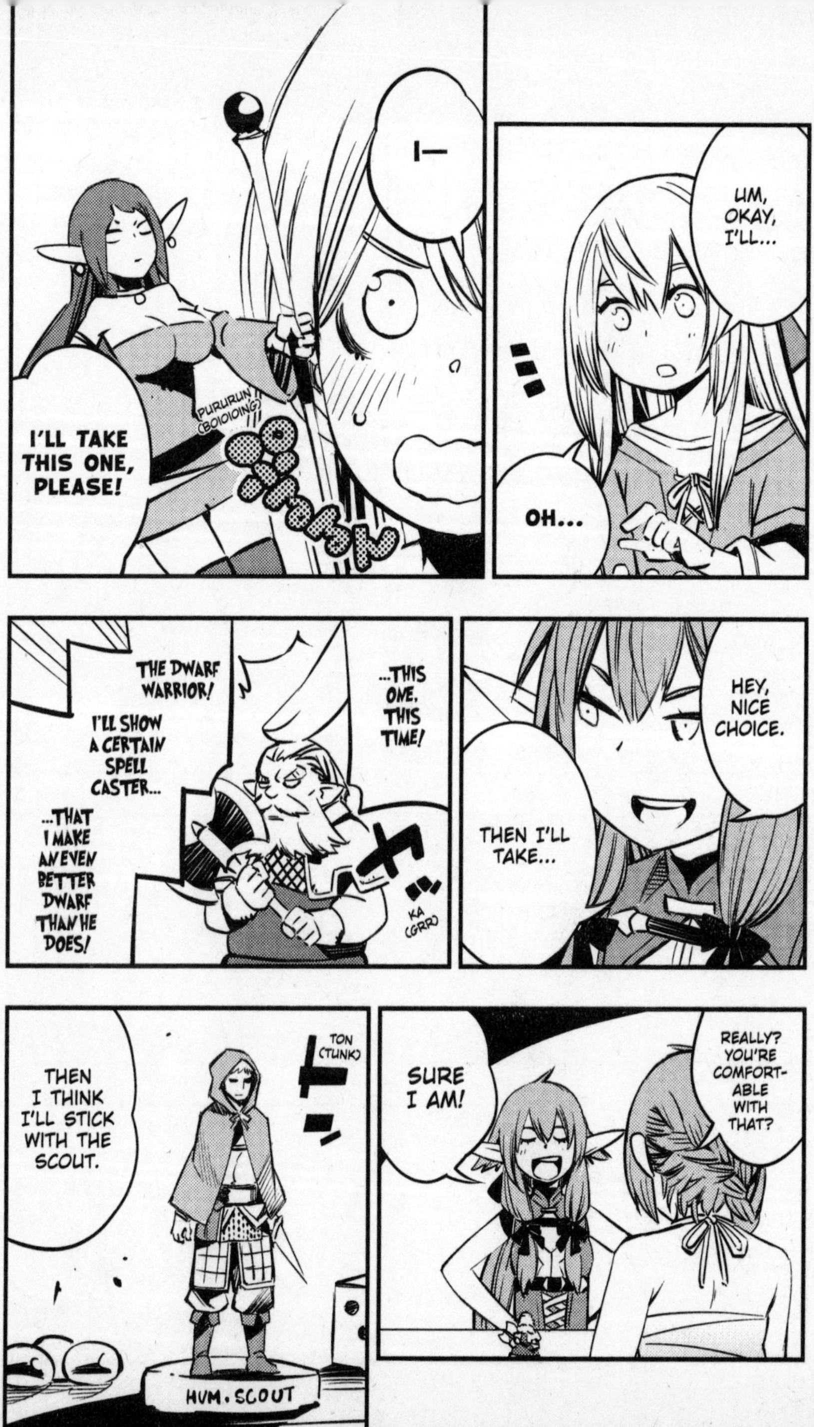
UM, OKAY, I'LL...
OH...
I—
I'LL TAKE THIS ONE, PLEASE!
PURURUN (BOIOIOING)
HEY, NICE CHOICE.
THEN I'LL TAKE...
...THIS ONE, THIS TIME!
THE DWARF WARRIOR!
I'LL SHOW A CERTAIN SPELL CASTER...
...THAT I MAKE AN EVEN BETTER DWARF THAN HE DOES!
KA (GRR)
REALLY? YOU'RE COMFORT-ABLE WITH THAT?
SURE I AM!
TON (TUNK)
THEN I THINK I'LL STICK WITH THE SCOUT.
HUM. SCOUT

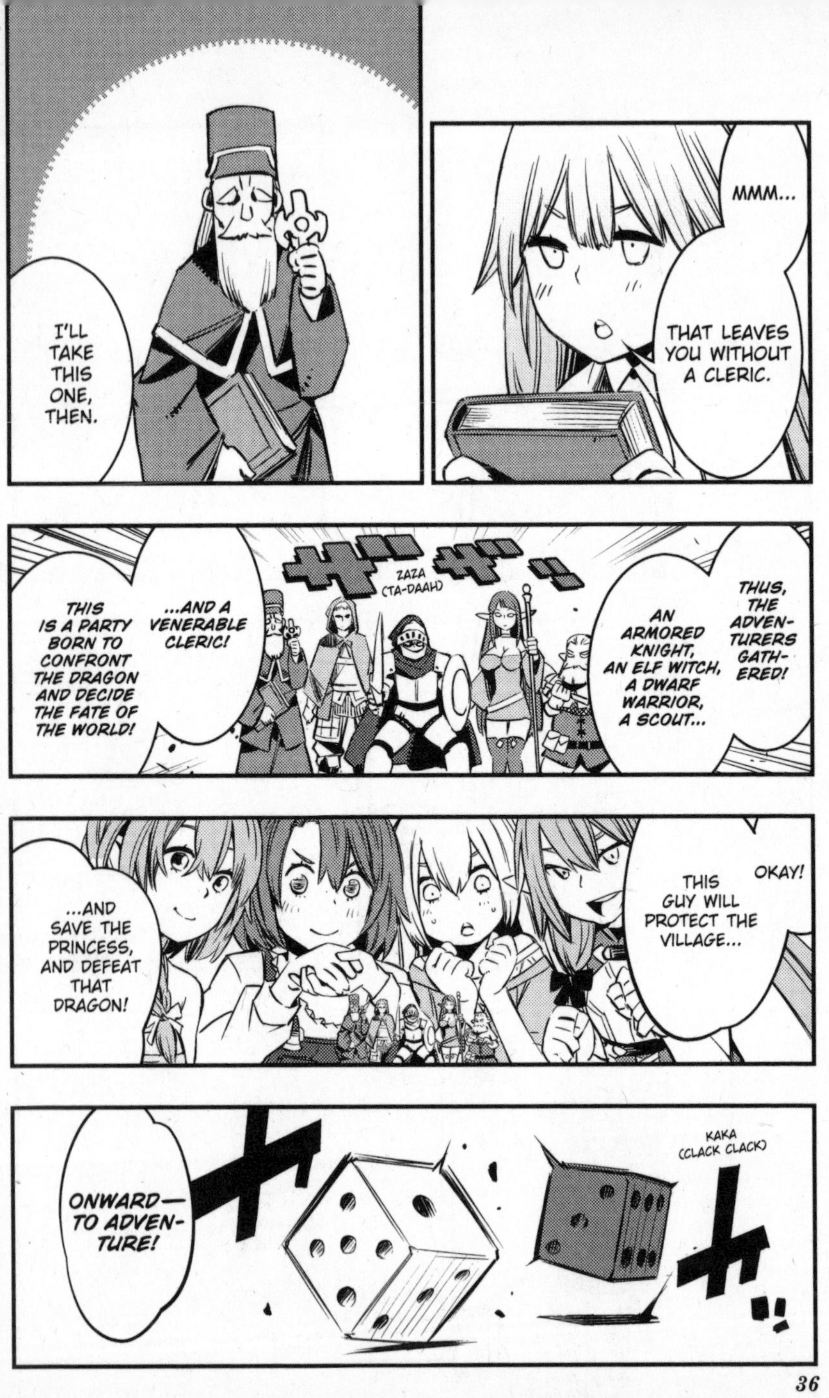
MMM...
THAT LEAVES YOU WITHOUT A CLERIC.
I'LL TAKE THIS ONE, THEN.
THUS, THE ADVEN-TURERS GATH-ERED!
AN ARMORED KNIGHT, AN ELF WITCH, A DWARF WARRIOR, A SCOUT...
ZAZA (TA-DAAH)
...AND A VENERABLE CLERIC!
THIS IS A PARTY BORN TO CONFRONT THE DRAGON AND DECIDE THE FATE OF THE WORLD!
OKAY!
THIS GUY WILL PROTECT THE VILLAGE...
...AND SAVE THE PRINCESS, AND DEFEAT THAT DRAGON!
KAKA (CLACK CLACK)
ONWARD—TO ADVEN-TURE!

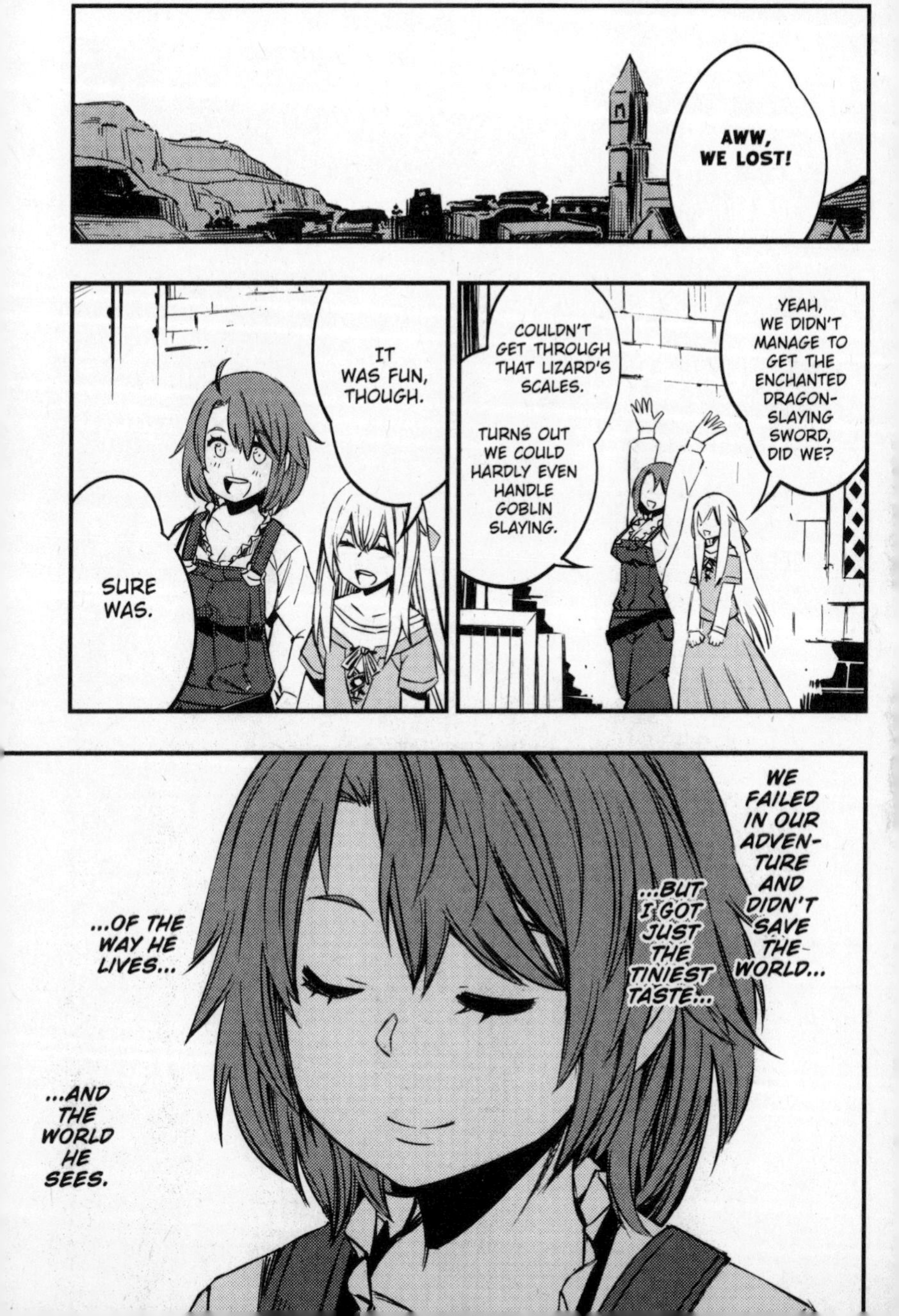
AWW, WE LOST!
YEAH, WE DIDN'T MANAGE TO GET THE ENCHANTED DRAGON-SLAYING SWORD, DID WE?
COULDN'T GET THROUGH THAT LIZARD'S SCALES.
TURNS OUT WE COULD HARDLY EVEN HANDLE GOBLIN SLAYING.
IT WAS FUN, THOUGH.
SURE WAS.
WE FAILED IN OUR ADVENTURE AND DIDN'T SAVE THE WORLD...
...BUT I GOT JUST THE TINIEST TASTE...
...OF THE WAY HE LIVES...
...AND THE WORLD HE SEES.

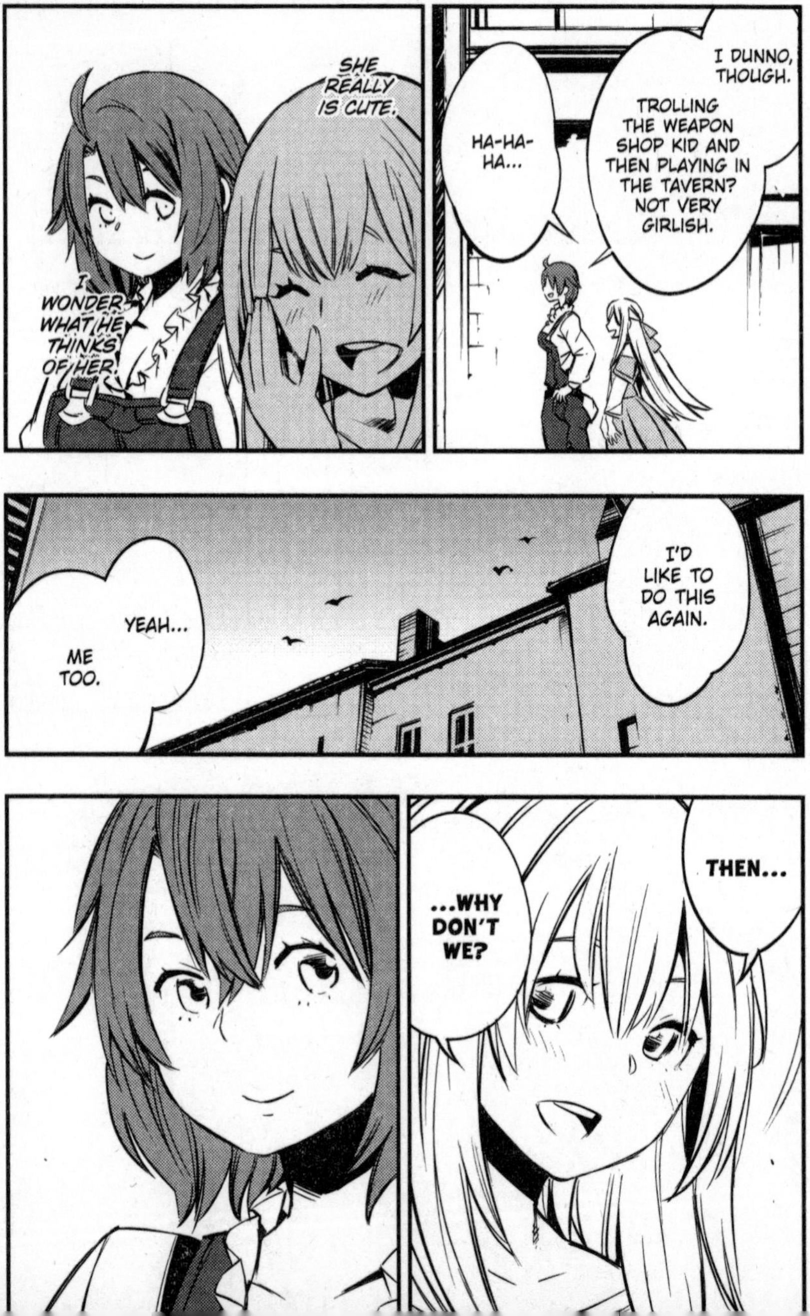
I DUNNO, THOUGH.
TROLLING THE WEAPON SHOP KID AND THEN PLAYING IN THE TAVERN? NOT VERY GIRLISH.
HA-HA-HA...
SHE REALLY IS CUTE.
I WONDER WHAT HE THINKS OF HER.
I'D LIKE TO DO THIS AGAIN.
YEAH...
ME TOO.
THEN...
...WHY DON'T WE?

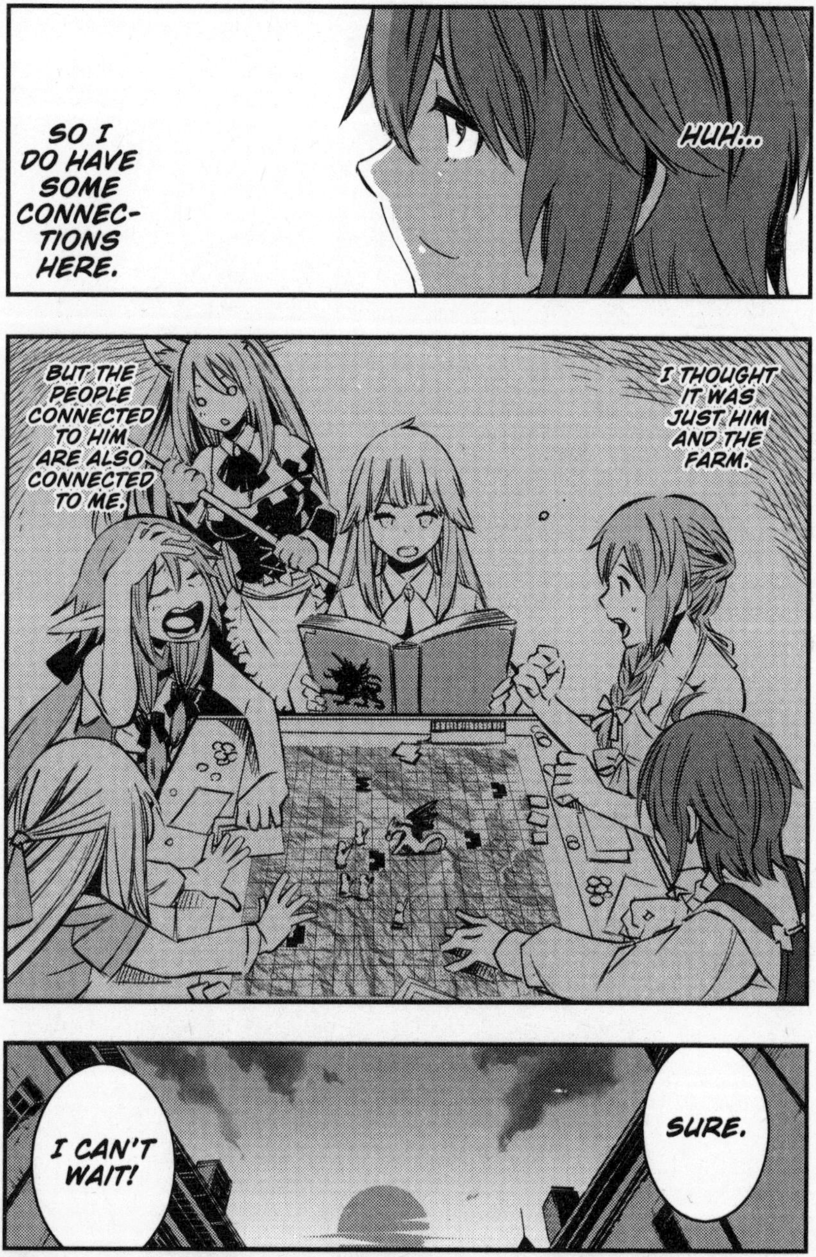
HUH...
SO I DO HAVE SOME CONNECTIONS HERE.
I THOUGHT IT WAS JUST HIM AND THE FARM.
BUT THE PEOPLE CONNECTED TO HIM ARE ALSO CONNECTED TO ME.
SURE.
I CAN'T WAIT!

GOBLIN SLAYER

BRAND NEW DAY

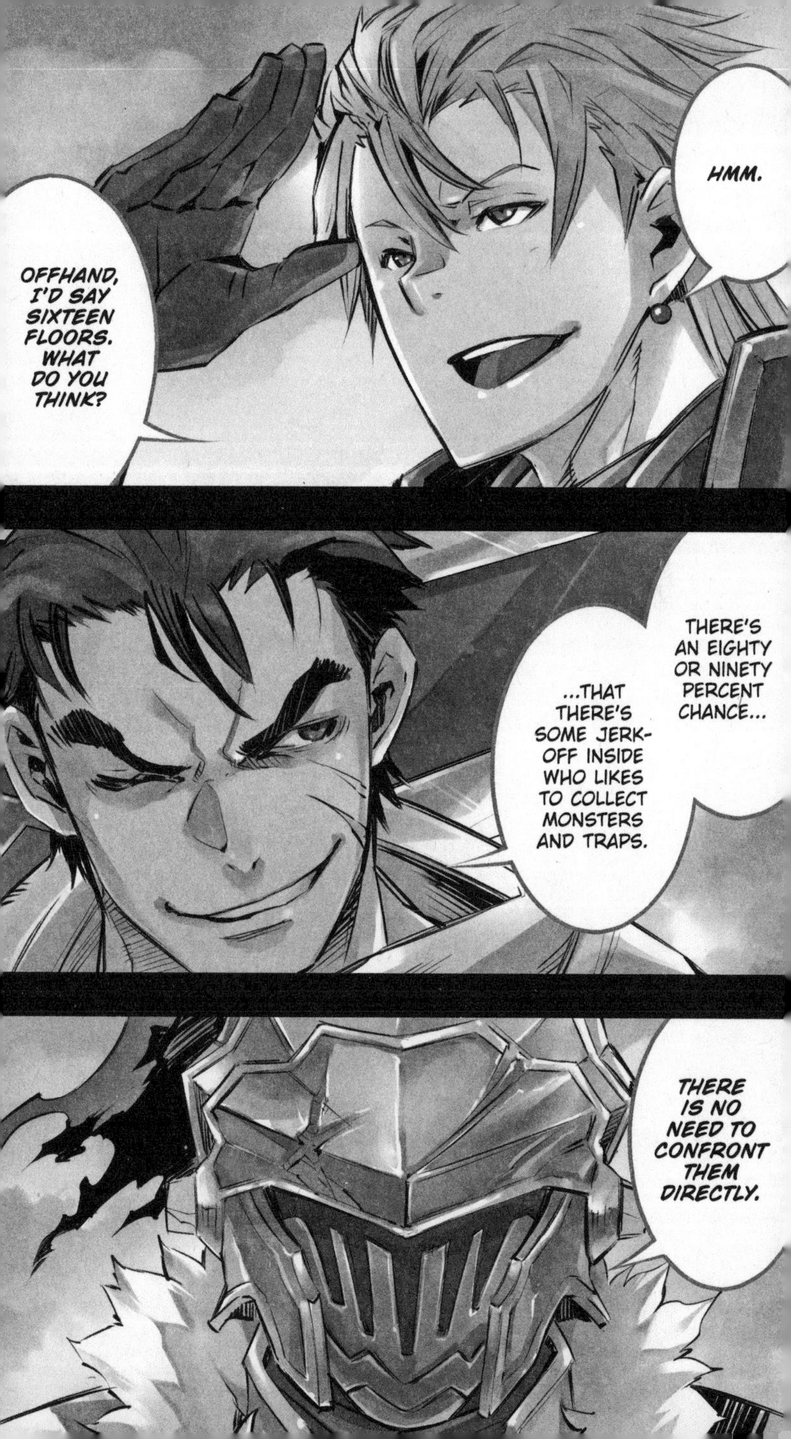
HMM.
OFFHAND, I'D SAY SIXTEEN FLOORS. WHAT DO YOU THINK?
THERE'S AN EIGHTY OR NINETY PERCENT CHANCE...
...THAT THERE'S SOME JERK-OFF INSIDE WHO LIKES TO COLLECT MONSTERS AND TRAPS.
THERE IS NO NEED TO CONFRONT THEM DIRECTLY.

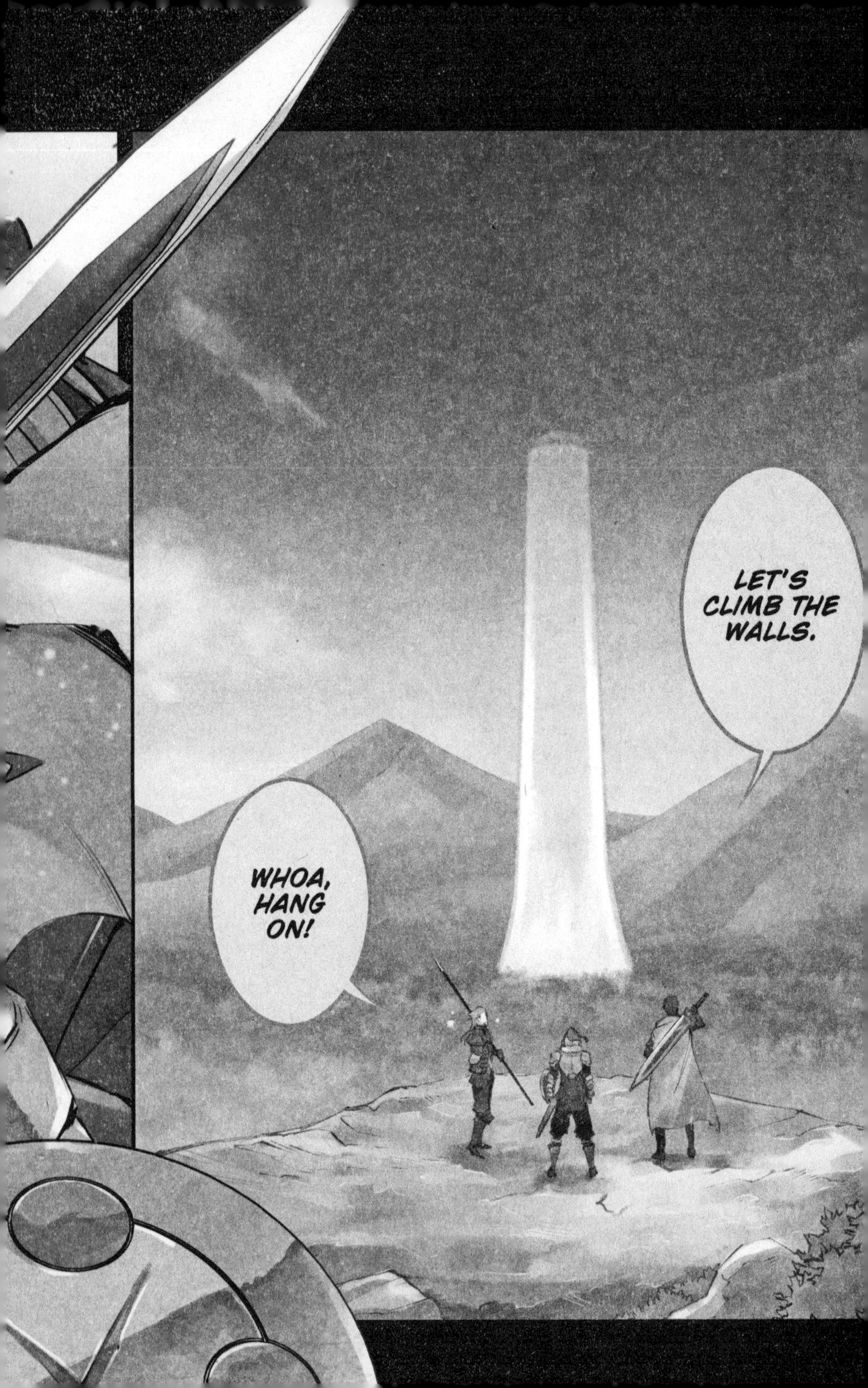
LET'S CLIMB THE WALLS.
WHOA, HANG ON!

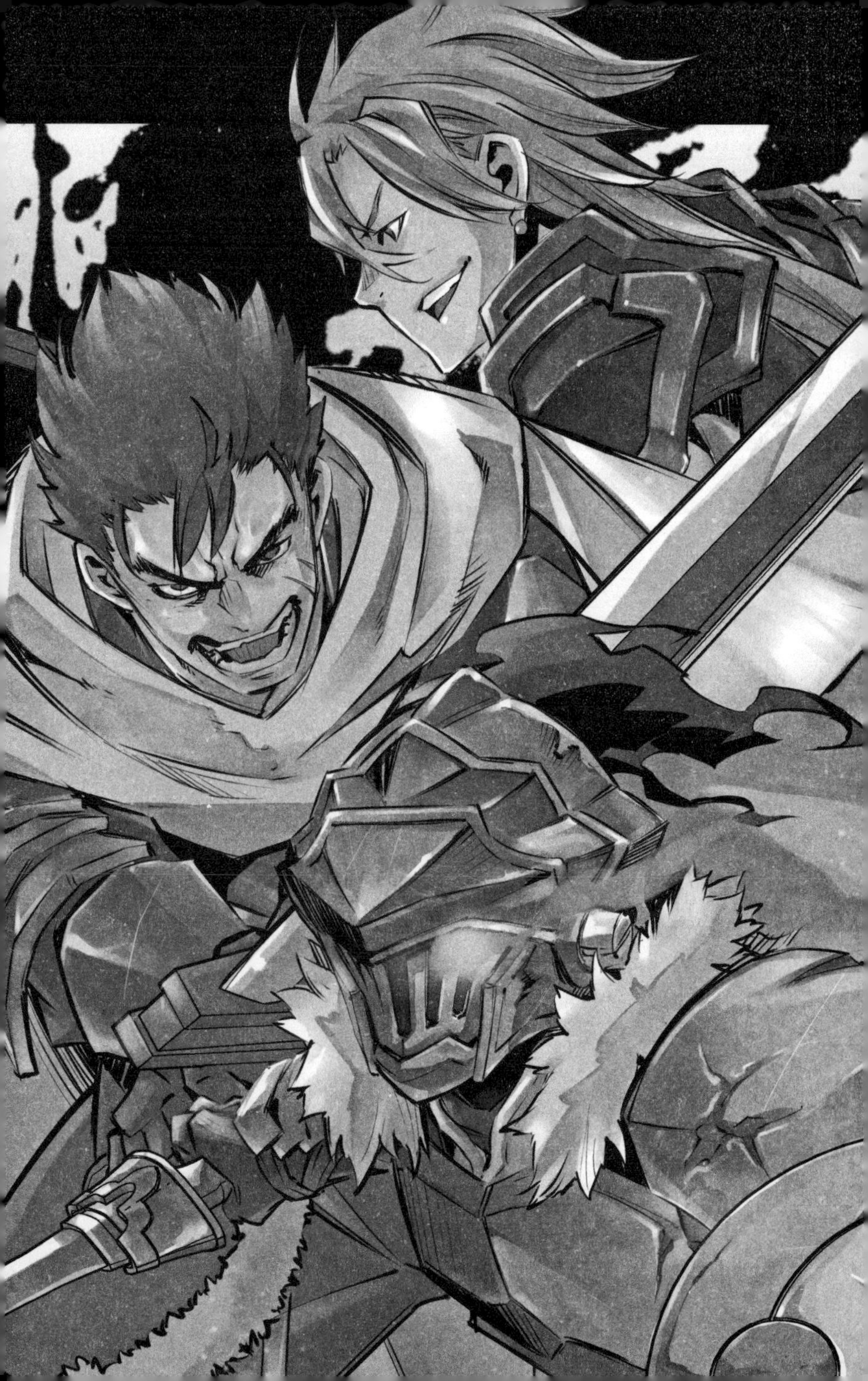

Chapter 6:
Of Destroying a Demon-Infested Temple of Doom

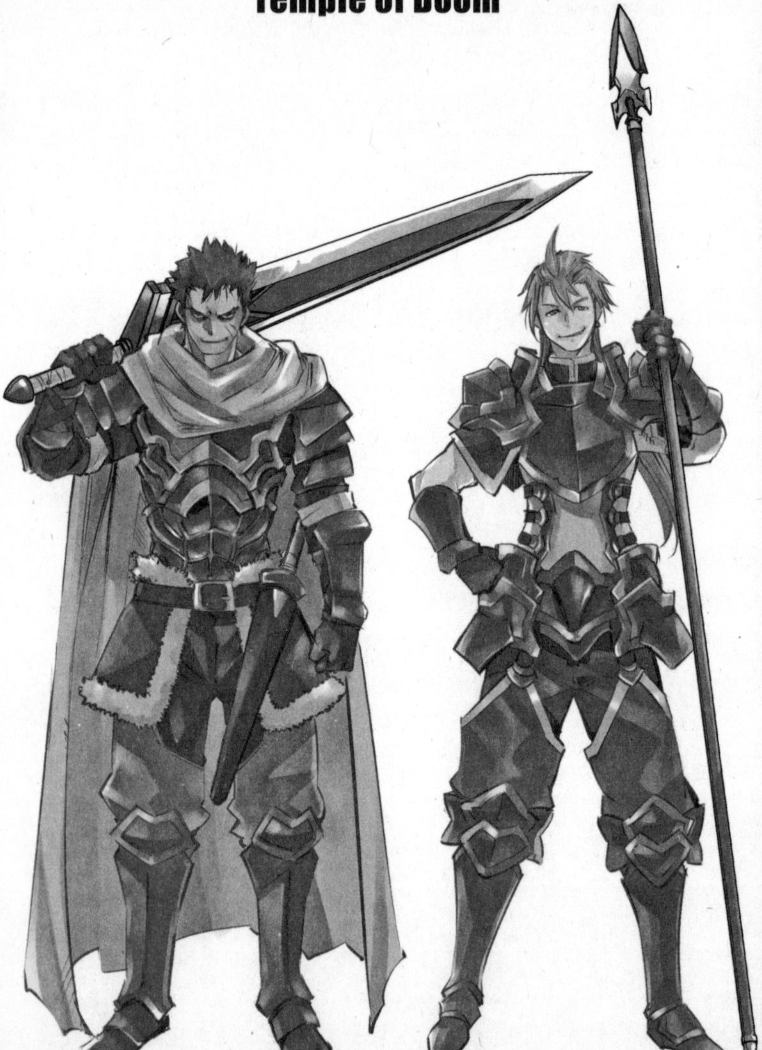

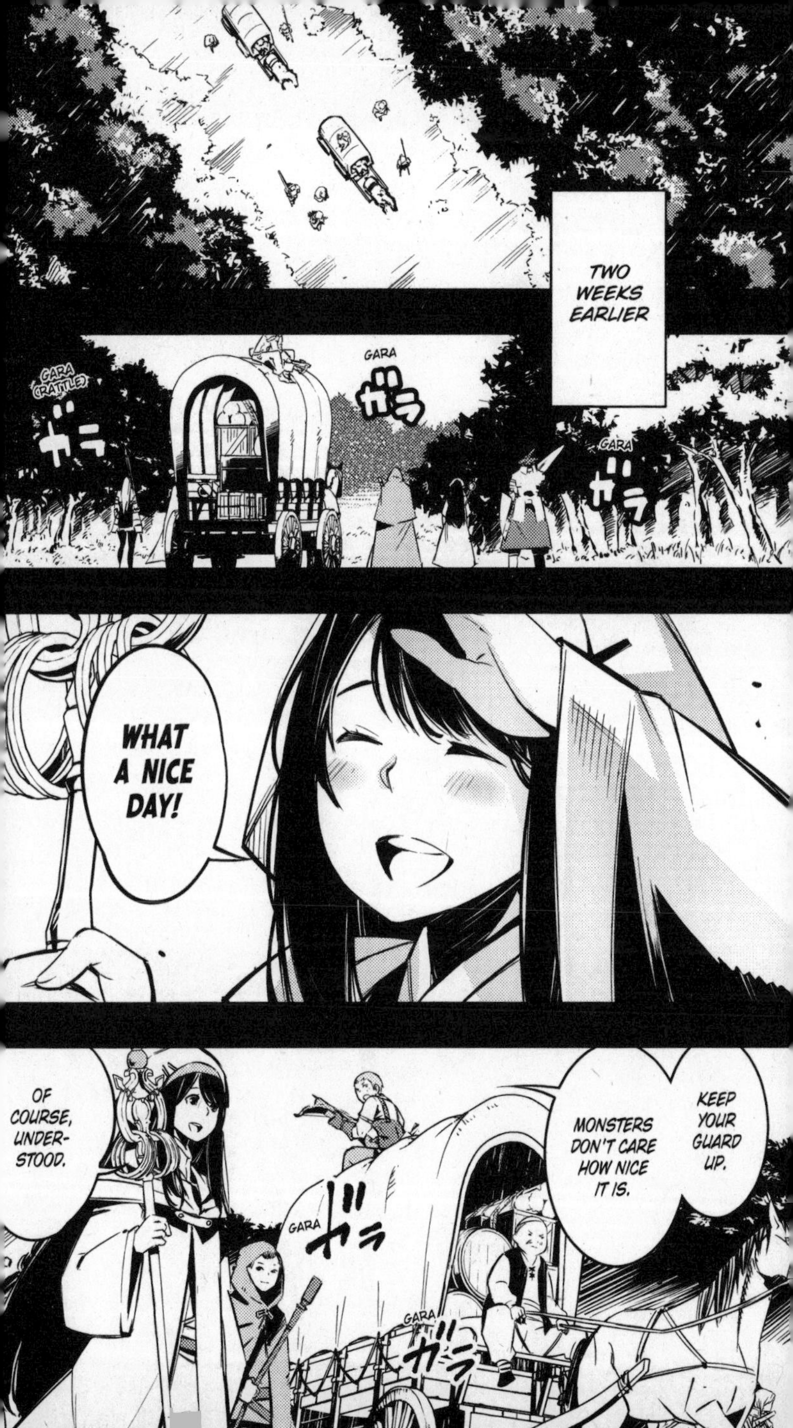
TWO WEEKS EARLIER
GARA
ガラ
GARA
ガラ
GARA (RATTLE)
ガラ
WHAT A NICE DAY!
KEEP YOUR GUARD UP.
MONSTERS DON'T CARE HOW NICE IT IS.
GARA
ガラ
GARA
ガラ
OF COURSE, UNDERSTOOD.

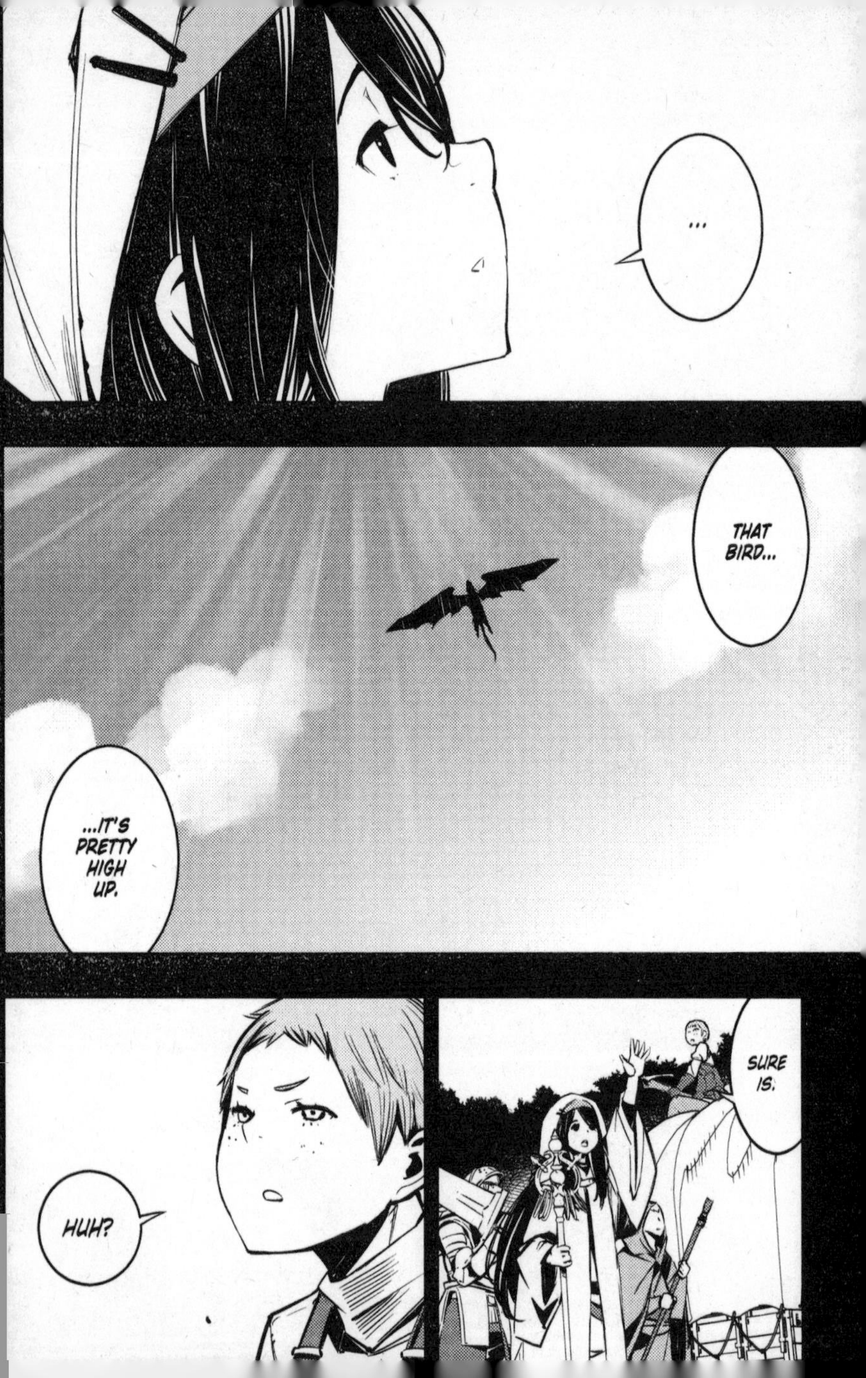
...
THAT BIRD...
...IT'S PRETTY HIGH UP.
SURE IS.
HUH?

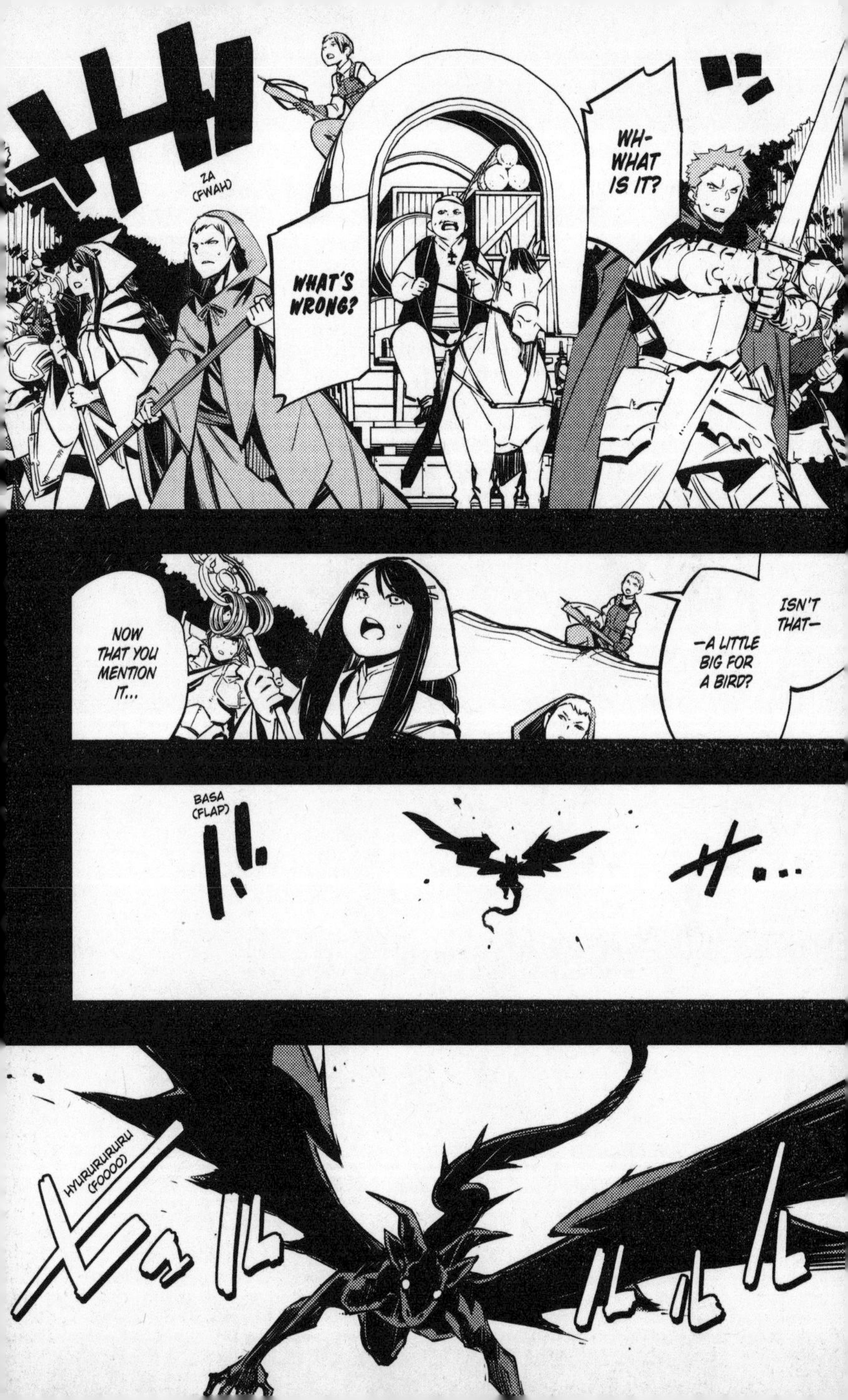
WH- WHAT IS IT?
WHAT'S WRONG?
ZA (FWAH)
ISN'T THAT—
—A LITTLE BIG FOR A BIRD?
NOW THAT YOU MENTION IT...
BASA (FLAP)
HYURURURURU (FOOOO)

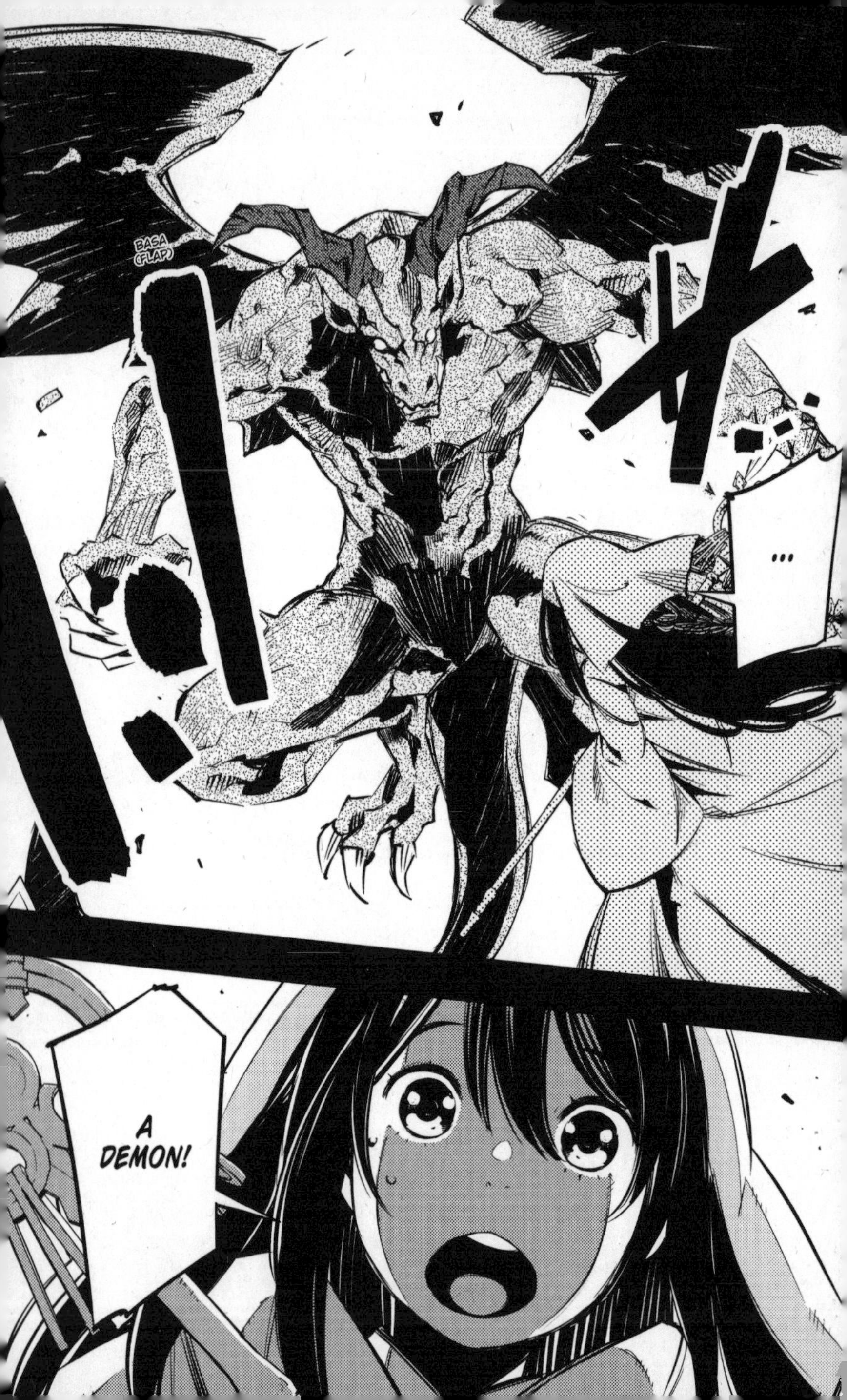
BASA (FLAP)
...
A DEMON!

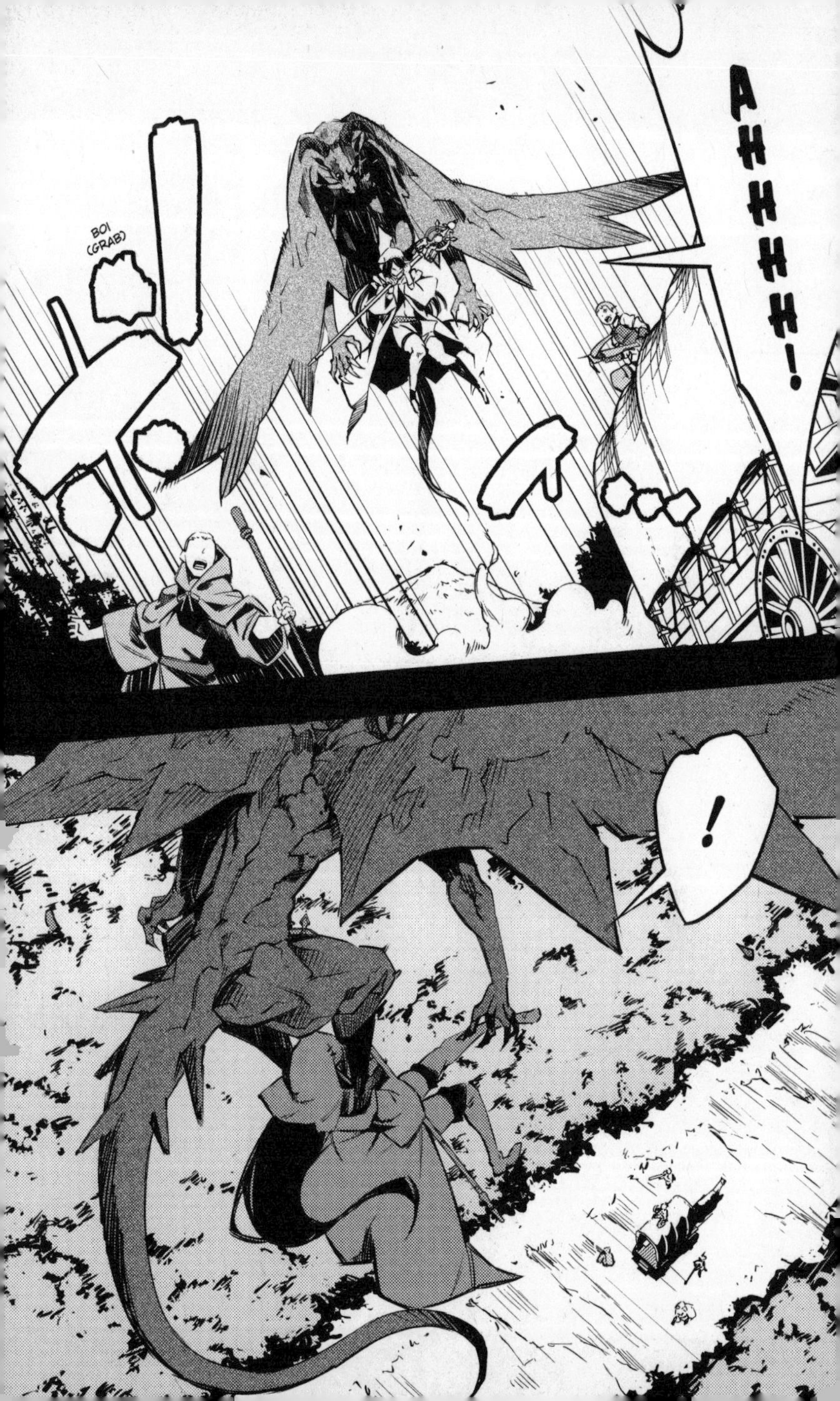
AHHHHH!
BOI
(GRAB)
!

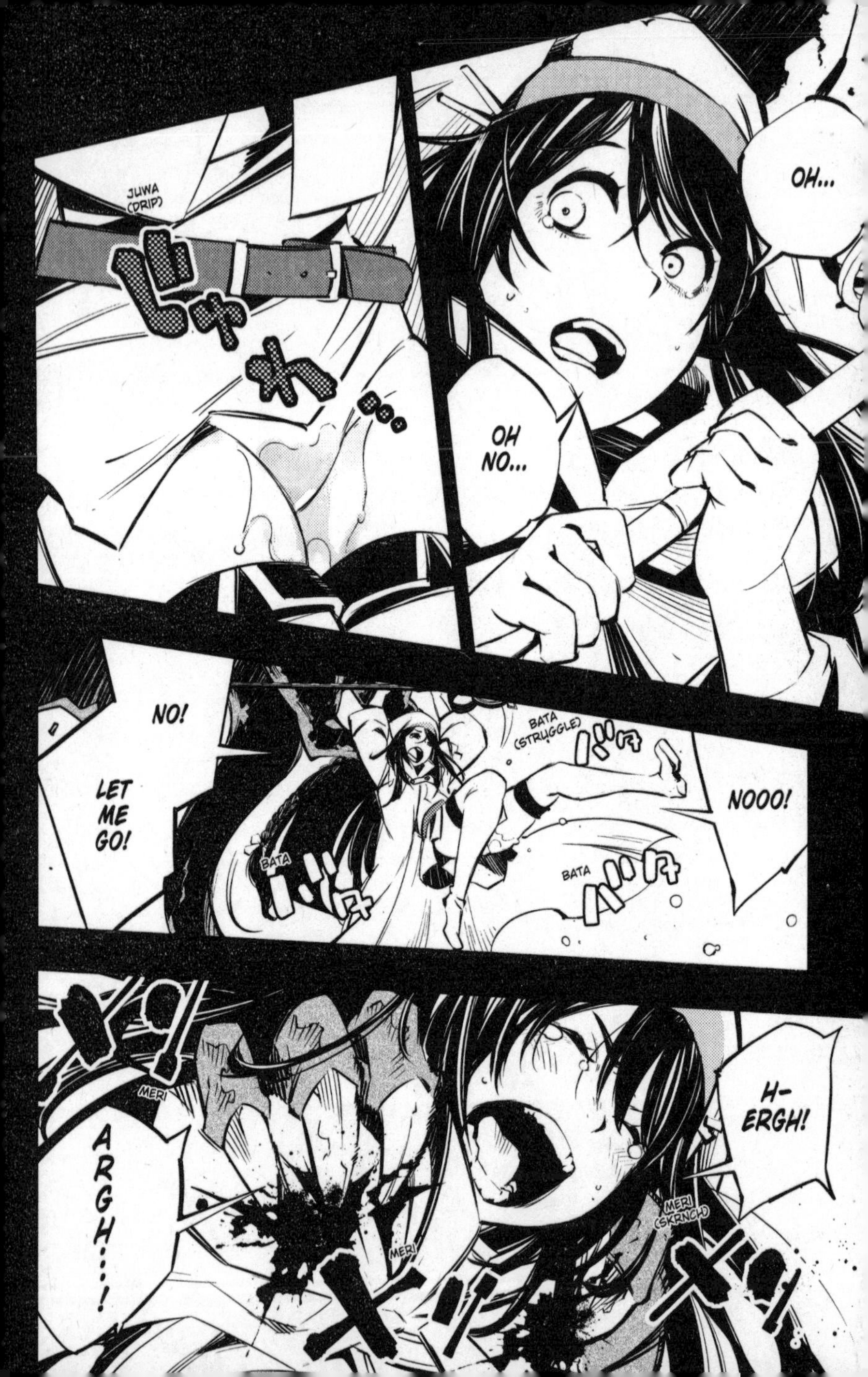
OH...
OH NO...
JUWA (DRIP)
じゅわ...
BATA (STRUGGLE)
NOOO!
NO!
LET ME GO!
BATA
BATA
H-ERGH!
MERI (SKRNCH)
MERI
MERI
ARGH...!

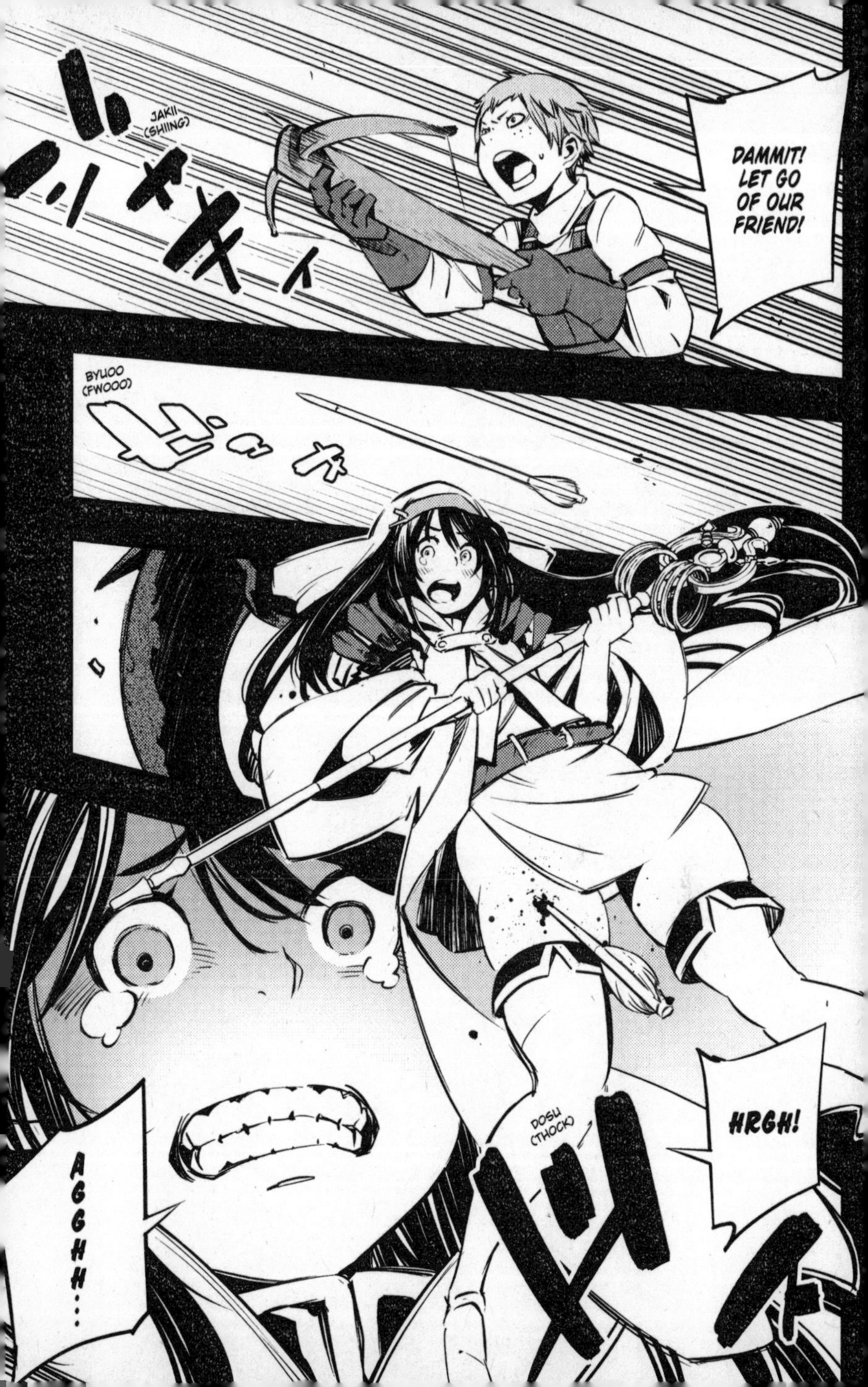
DAMMIT! LET GO OF OUR FRIEND!
JAKII (SHIING)
BYUOO (FWOOO)
HRGH!
DOSU (THOCK)
AGGHH...

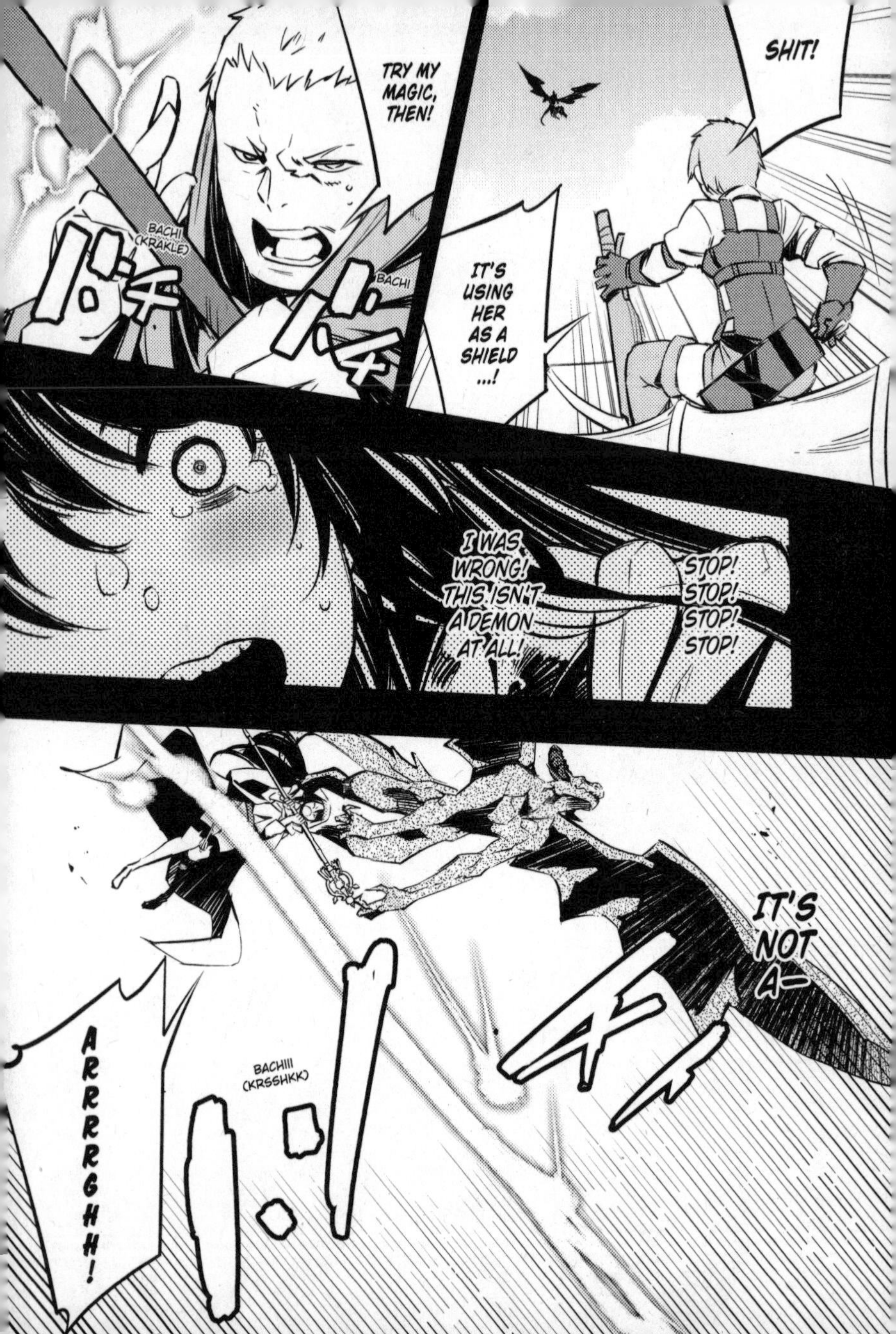
SHIT!
IT'S USING HER AS A SHIELD ...!
TRY MY MAGIC, THEN!
BACHI (KRAKLE)
BACHI
STOP! STOP! STOP! STOP!
I WAS WRONG! THIS ISN'T A DEMON AT ALL!
IT'S NOT A—
BACHIII (KRSSHKK)
ARRRRGHH!

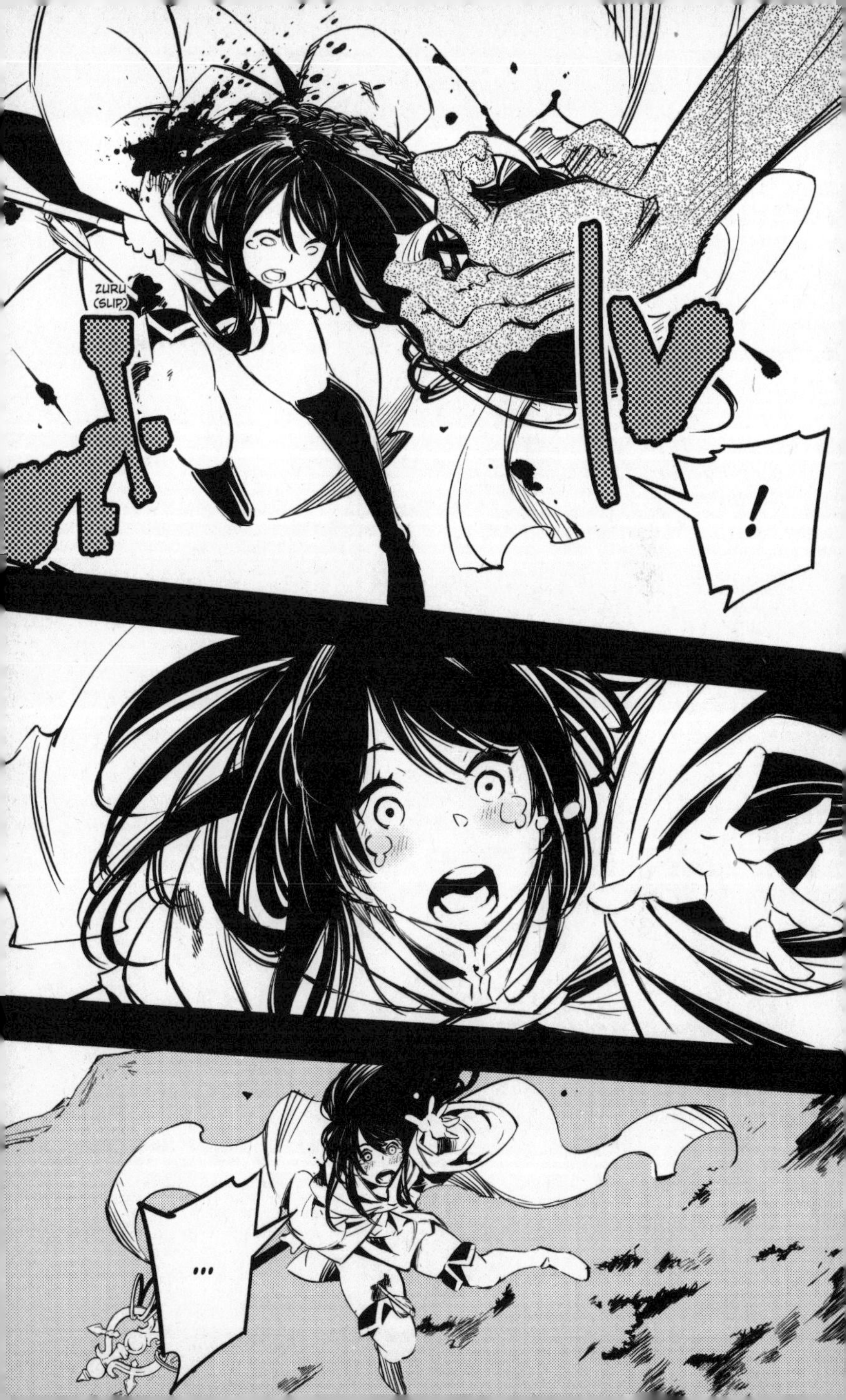
ZURU
(SLIP)
!
...

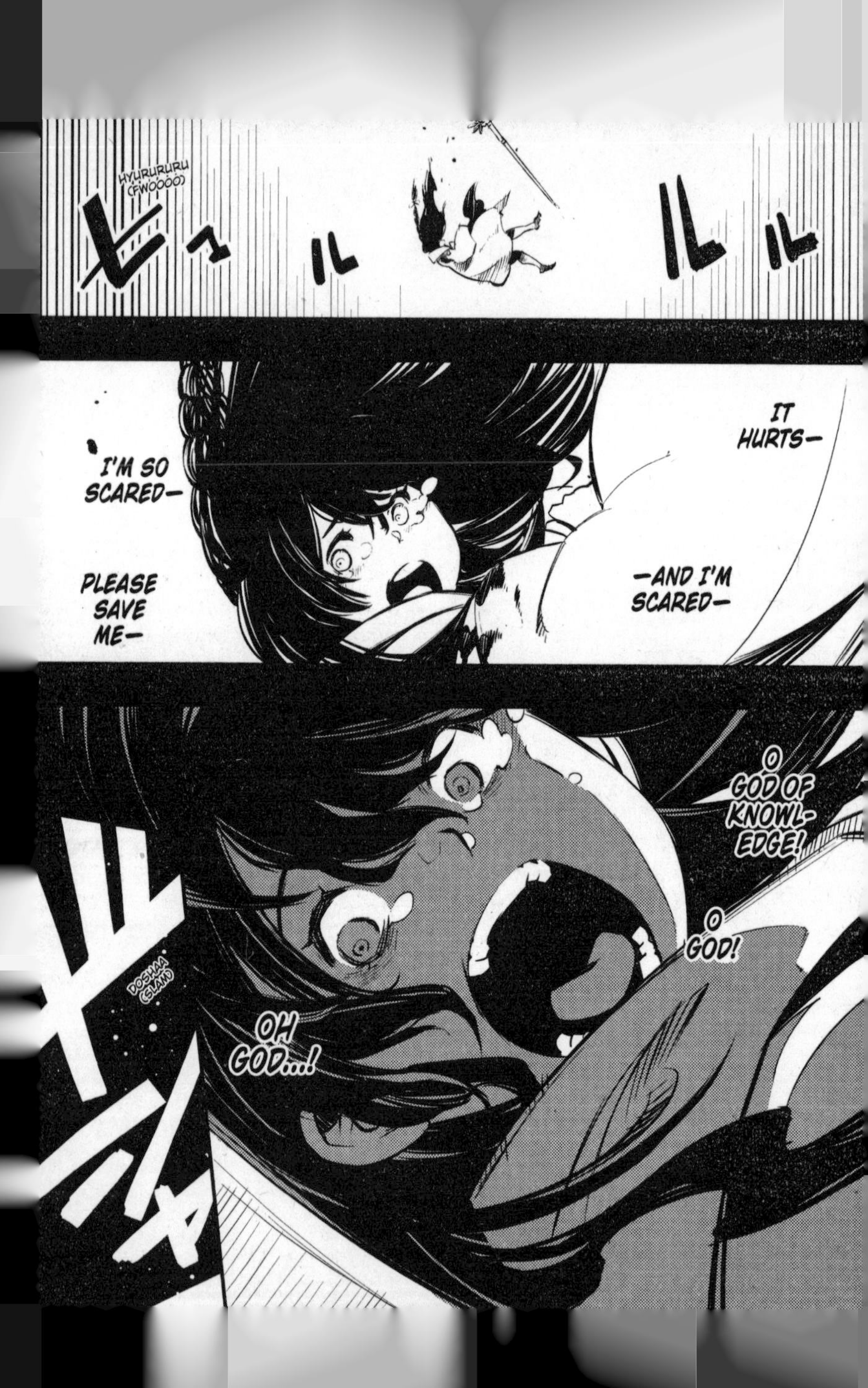
HYURURURU (FWOOOO)
IT HURTS—
—AND I'M SCARED—
I'M SO SCARED—
PLEASE SAVE ME—
O GOD OF KNOWL-EDGE!
O GOD!
OH GOD...!
DOSHAA (SLAM)

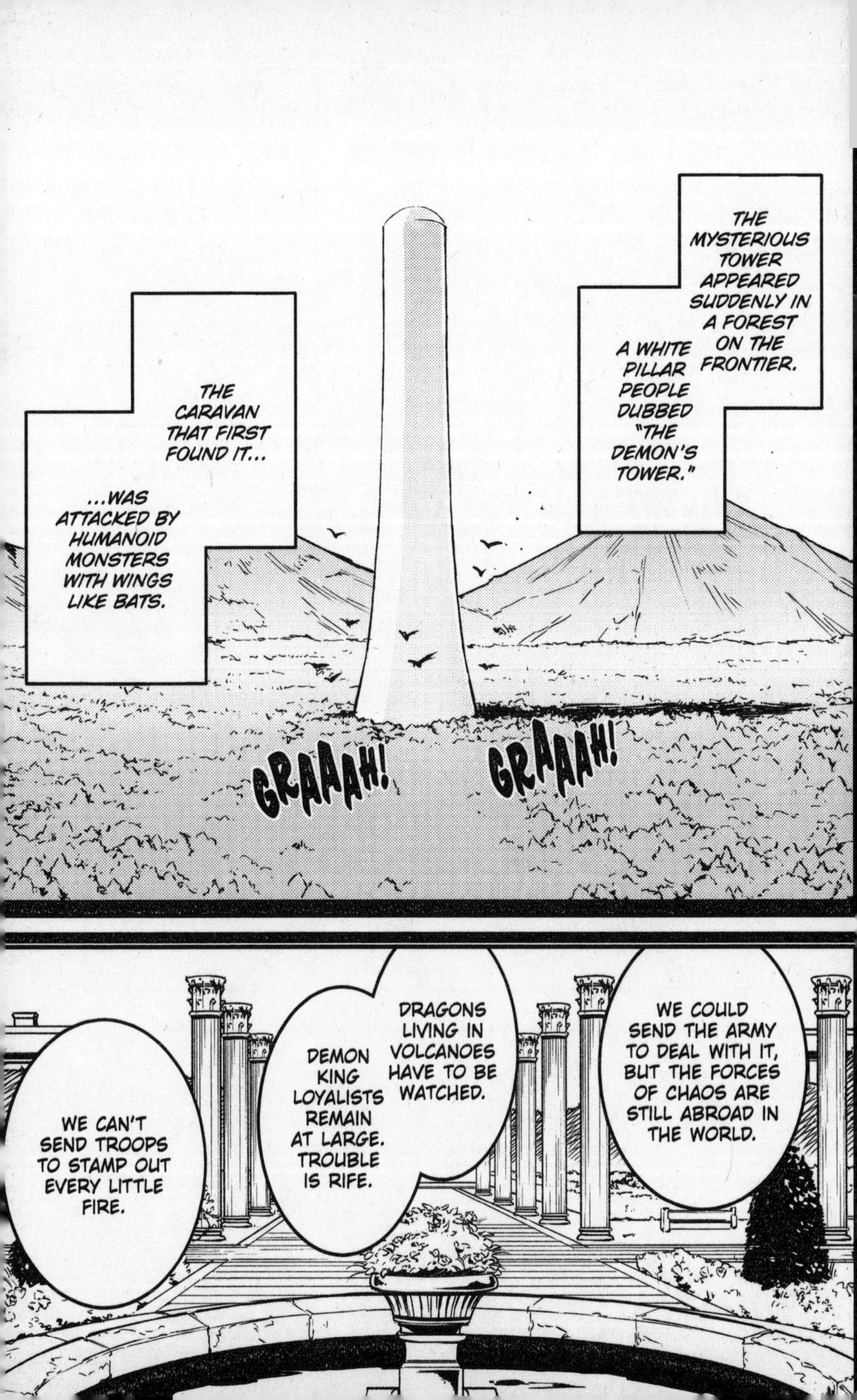
THE MYSTERIOUS TOWER APPEARED SUDDENLY IN A FOREST ON THE FRONTIER.
A WHITE PILLAR PEOPLE DUBBED "THE DEMON'S TOWER."
THE CARAVAN THAT FIRST FOUND IT...
...WAS ATTACKED BY HUMANOID MONSTERS WITH WINGS LIKE BATS.
GRAAAH!
GRAAAH!
WE COULD SEND THE ARMY TO DEAL WITH IT, BUT THE FORCES OF CHAOS ARE STILL ABROAD IN THE WORLD.
DRAGONS LIVING IN VOLCANOES HAVE TO BE WATCHED.
DEMON KING LOYALISTS REMAIN AT LARGE. TROUBLE IS RIFE.
WE CAN'T SEND TROOPS TO STAMP OUT EVERY LITTLE FIRE.

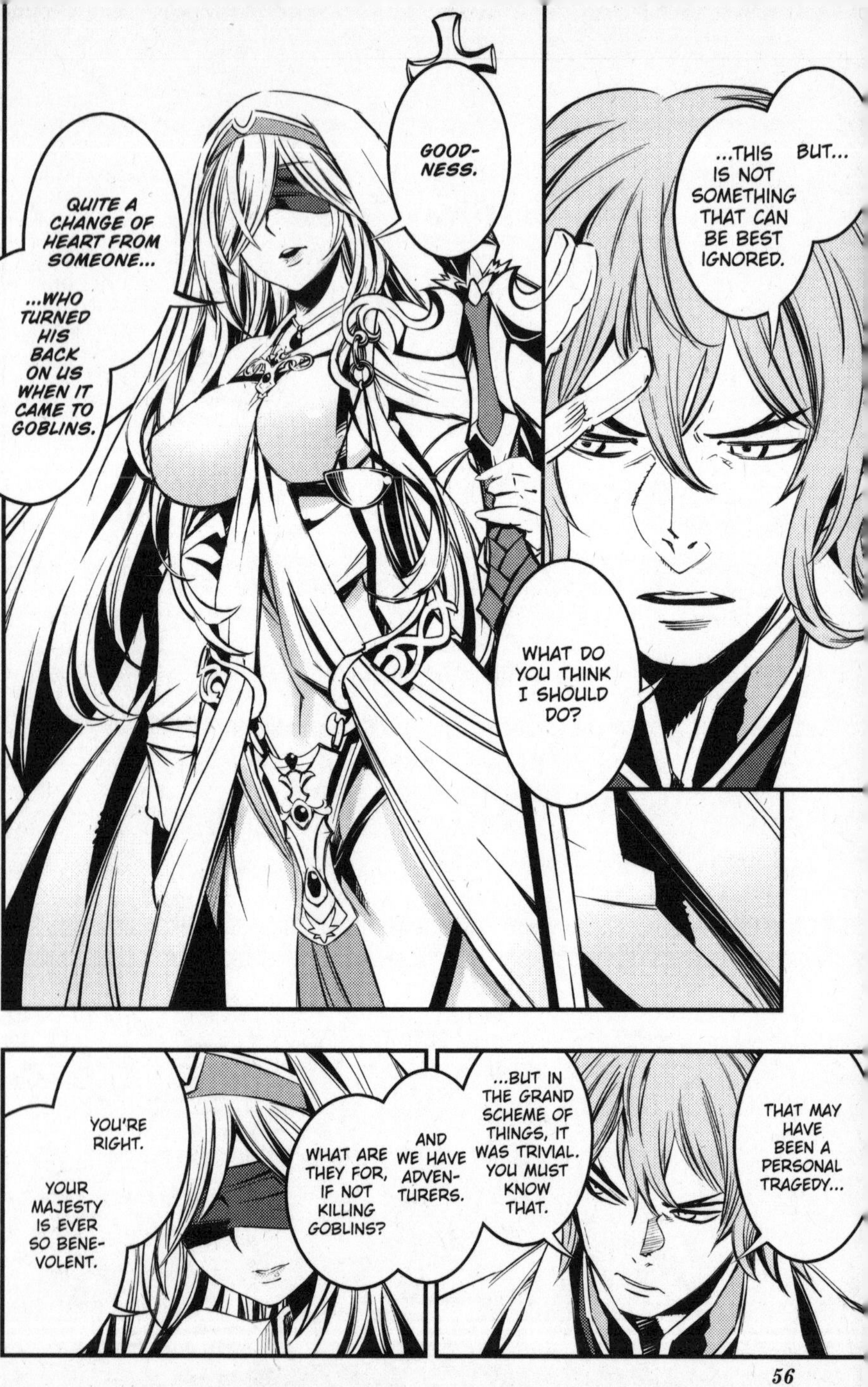
BUT...
...THIS IS NOT SOMETHING THAT CAN BE BEST IGNORED.
WHAT DO YOU THINK I SHOULD DO?
GOODNESS.
QUITE A CHANGE OF HEART FROM SOMEONE...
...WHO TURNED HIS BACK ON US WHEN IT CAME TO GOBLINS.
THAT MAY HAVE BEEN A PERSONAL TRAGEDY...
...BUT IN THE GRAND SCHEME OF THINGS, IT WAS TRIVIAL. YOU MUST KNOW THAT.
AND WE HAVE ADVENTURERS.
WHAT ARE THEY FOR, IF NOT KILLING GOBLINS?
YOU'RE RIGHT.
YOUR MAJESTY IS EVER SO BENEVOLENT.

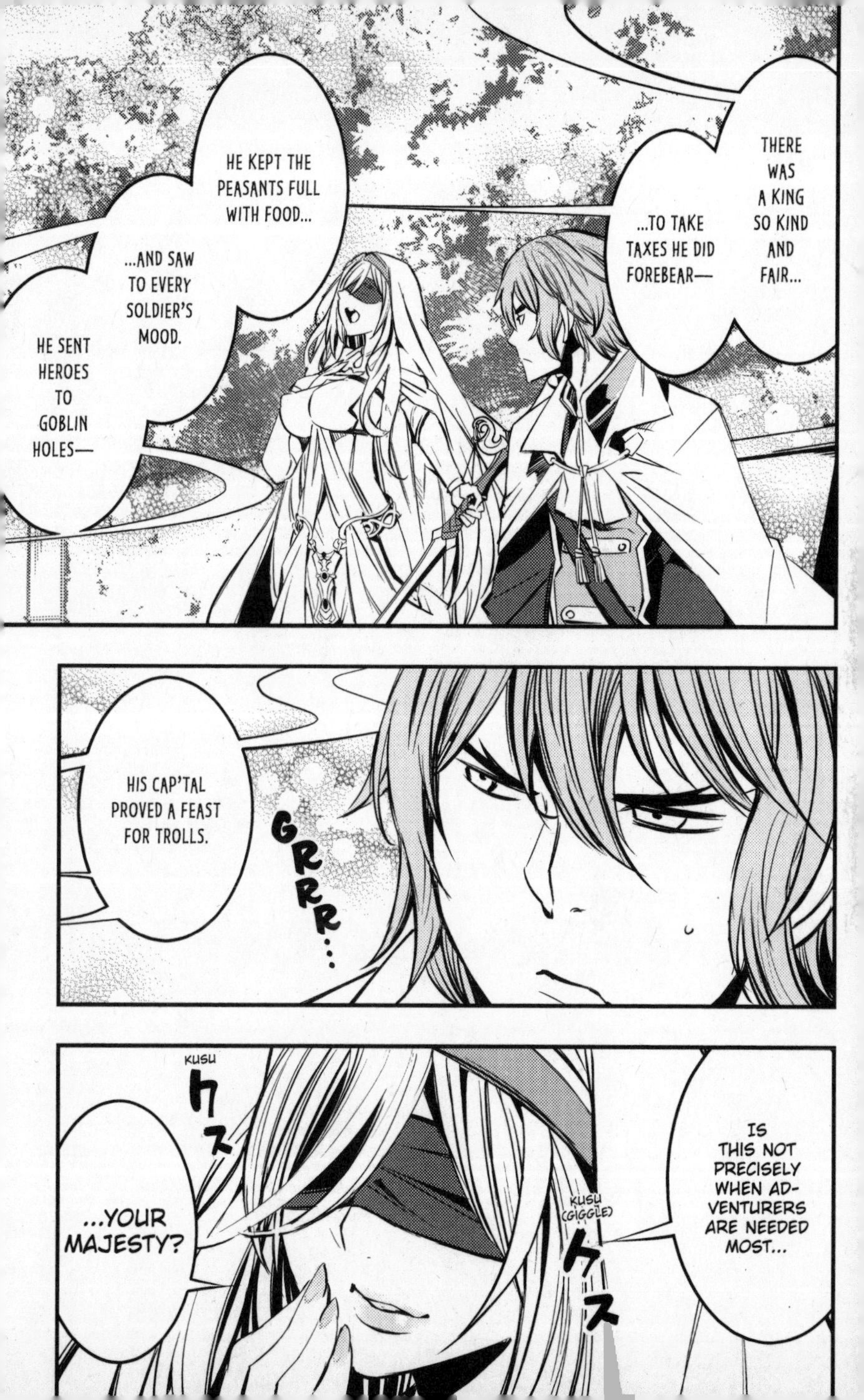
THERE WAS A KING SO KIND AND FAIR...
...TO TAKE TAXES HE DID FOREBEAR—
HE KEPT THE PEASANTS FULL WITH FOOD...
...AND SAW TO EVERY SOLDIER'S MOOD.
HE SENT HEROES TO GOBLIN HOLES—
HIS CAP'TAL PROVED A FEAST FOR TROLLS.
GRRR...
IS THIS NOT PRECISELY WHEN AD-VENTURERS ARE NEEDED MOST...
クス KUSU (GIGGLE)
クス KUSU
...YOUR MAJESTY?

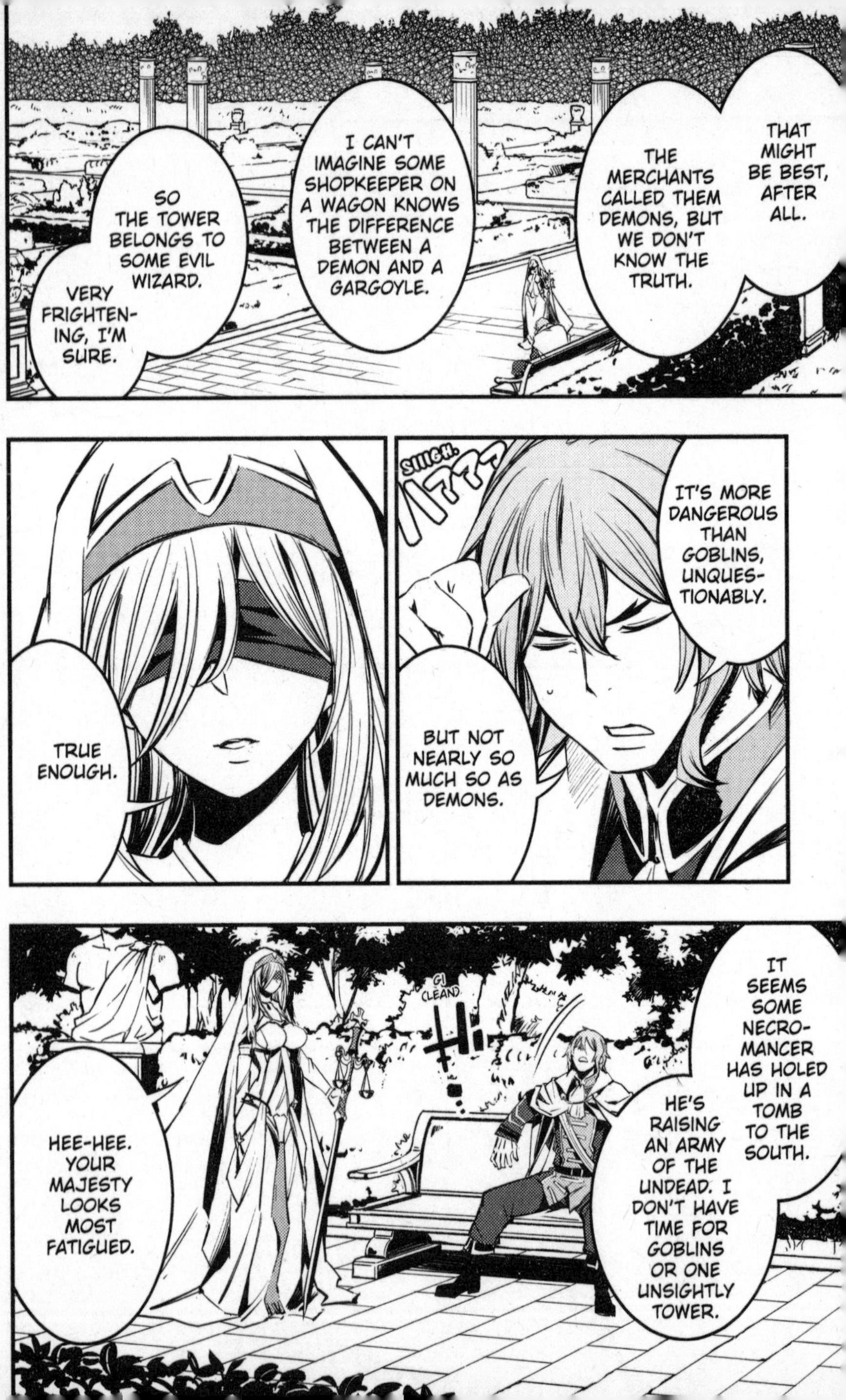
THAT MIGHT BE BEST, AFTER ALL.
THE MERCHANTS CALLED THEM DEMONS, BUT WE DON'T KNOW THE TRUTH.
I CAN'T IMAGINE SOME SHOPKEEPER ON A WAGON KNOWS THE DIFFERENCE BETWEEN A DEMON AND A GARGOYLE.
SO THE TOWER BELONGS TO SOME EVIL WIZARD.
VERY FRIGHTENING, I'M SURE.
SIIIGH.
IT'S MORE DANGEROUS THAN GOBLINS, UNQUESTIONABLY.
BUT NOT NEARLY SO MUCH SO AS DEMONS.
TRUE ENOUGH.
IT SEEMS SOME NECROMANCER HAS HOLED UP IN A TOMB TO THE SOUTH.
HE'S RAISING AN ARMY OF THE UNDEAD. I DON'T HAVE TIME FOR GOBLINS OR ONE UNSIGHTLY TOWER.
GI CLEAND
HEE-HEE. YOUR MAJESTY LOOKS MOST FATIGUED.

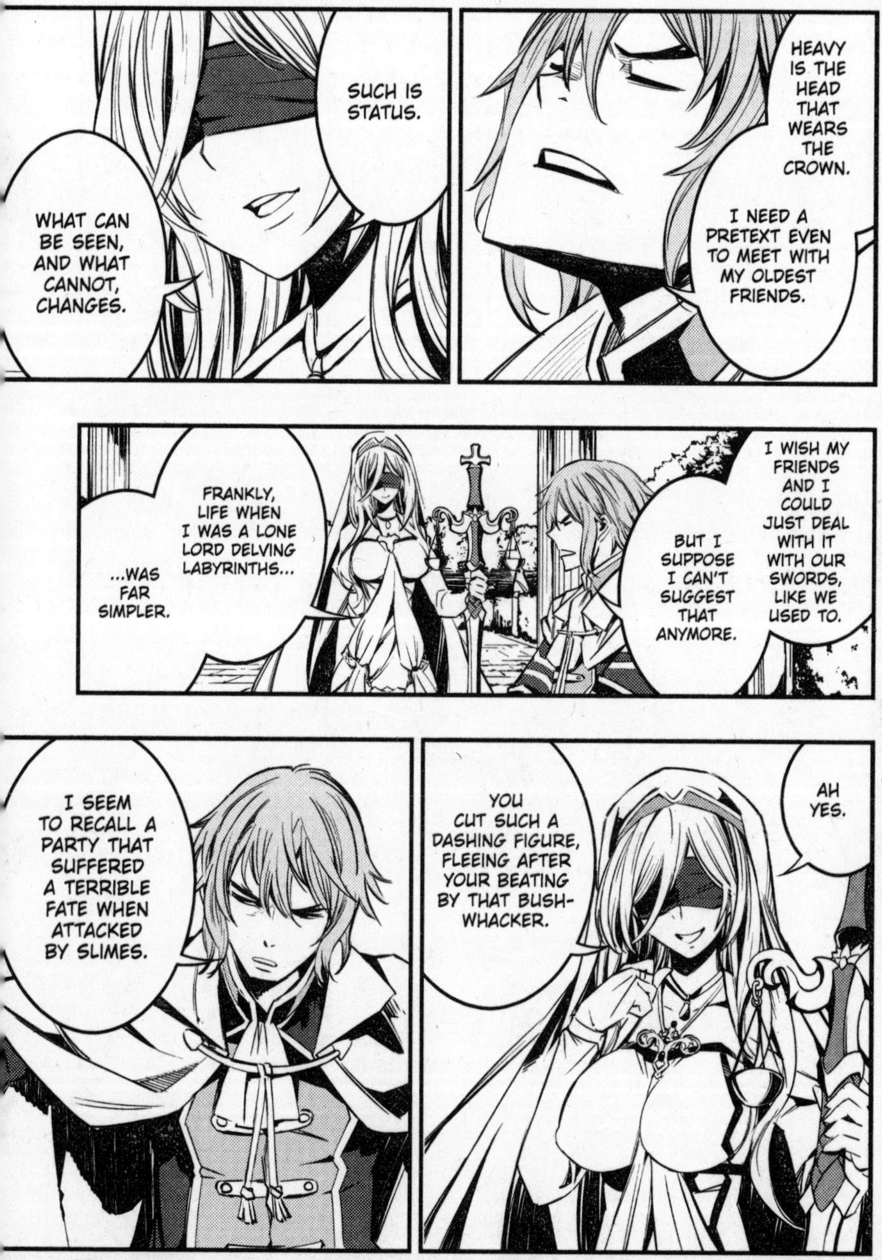
HEAVY IS THE HEAD THAT WEARS THE CROWN.
I NEED A PRETEXT EVEN TO MEET WITH MY OLDEST FRIENDS.
SUCH IS STATUS.
WHAT CAN BE SEEN, AND WHAT CANNOT, CHANGES.
I WISH MY FRIENDS AND I COULD JUST DEAL WITH IT WITH OUR SWORDS, LIKE WE USED TO.
BUT I SUPPOSE I CAN'T SUGGEST THAT ANYMORE.
FRANKLY, LIFE WHEN I WAS A LONE LORD DELVING LABYRINTHS...
...WAS FAR SIMPLER.
AH YES.
YOU CUT SUCH A DASHING FIGURE, FLEEING AFTER YOUR BEATING BY THAT BUSH-WHACKER.
I SEEM TO RECALL A PARTY THAT SUFFERED A TERRIBLE FATE WHEN ATTACKED BY SLIMES.

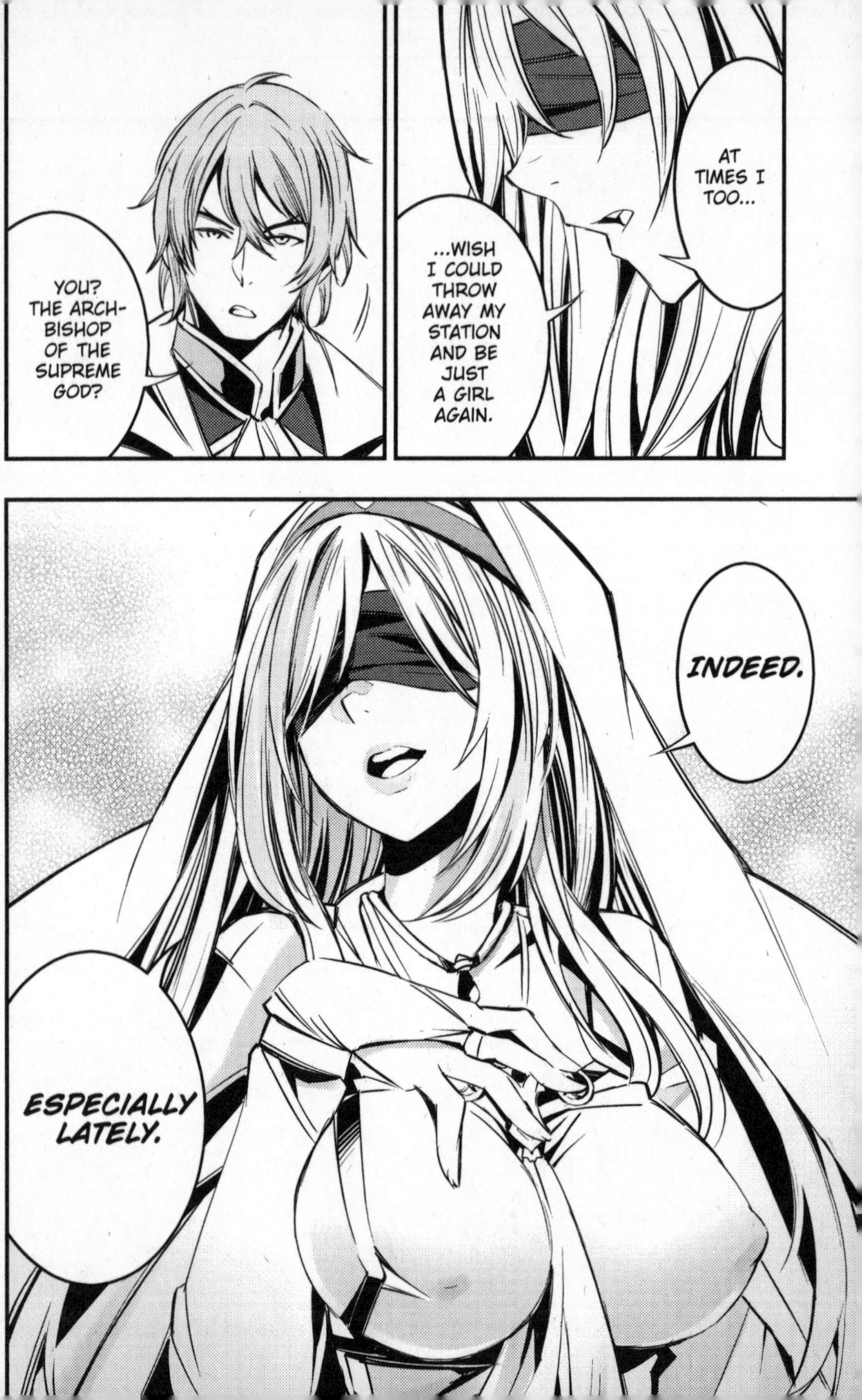
AT TIMES I TOO...
...WISH I COULD THROW AWAY MY STATION AND BE JUST A GIRL AGAIN.
YOU? THE ARCH-BISHOP OF THE SUPREME GOD?
INDEED.
ESPECIALLY LATELY.

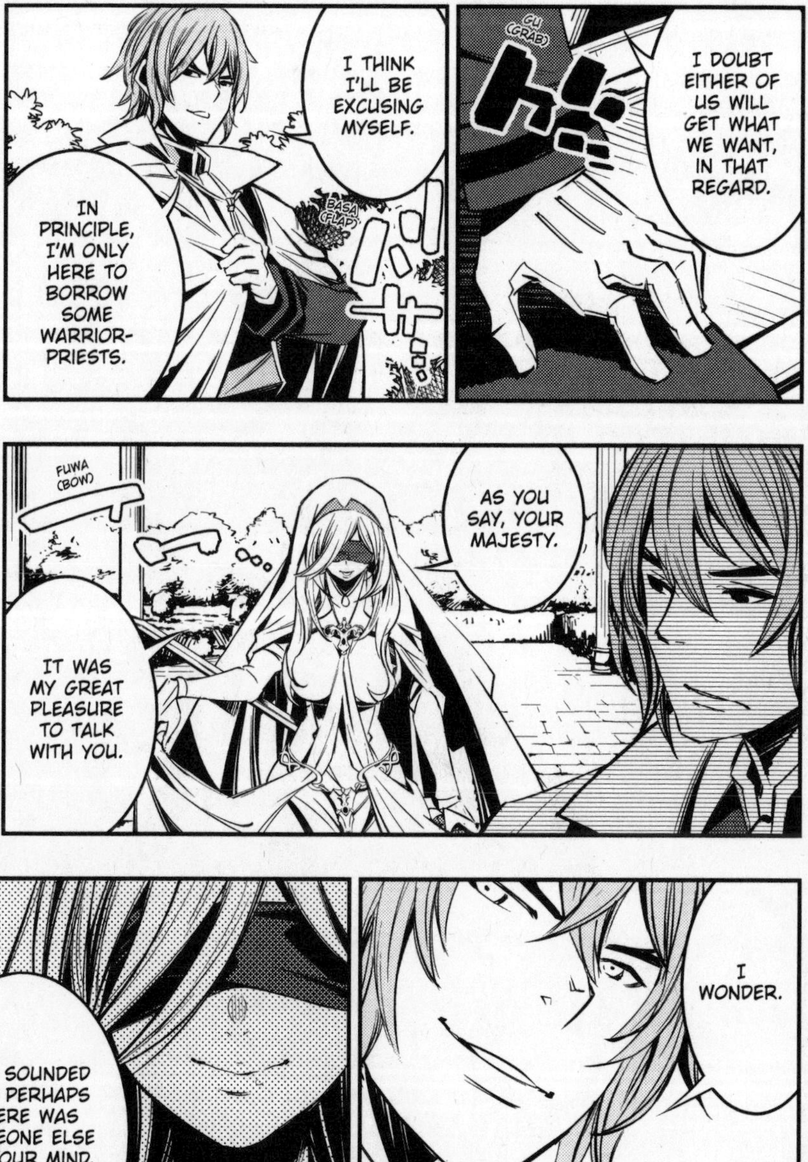
GU (GRAB)
I DOUBT EITHER OF US WILL GET WHAT WE WANT, IN THAT REGARD.
I THINK I'LL BE EXCUSING MYSELF.
BASA (FLAP)
IN PRINCIPLE, I'M ONLY HERE TO BORROW SOME WARRIOR-PRIESTS.
AS YOU SAY, YOUR MAJESTY.
FUWA (BOW)
IT WAS MY GREAT PLEASURE TO TALK WITH YOU.
I WONDER.
YOU SOUNDED LIKE PERHAPS THERE WAS SOMEONE ELSE ON YOUR MIND.

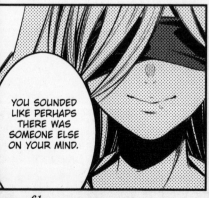

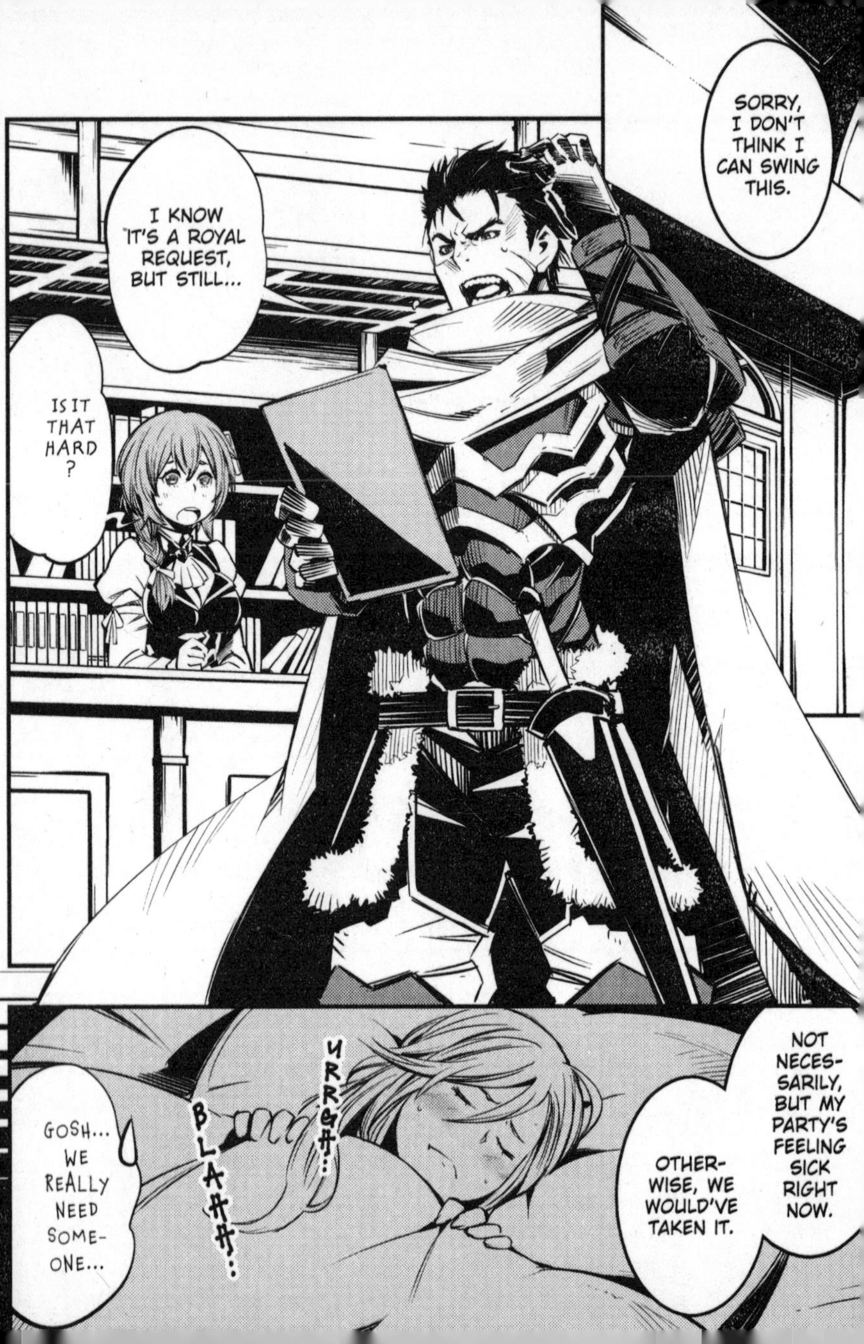
SORRY, I DON'T THINK I CAN SWING THIS.
I KNOW IT'S A ROYAL REQUEST, BUT STILL...
IS IT THAT HARD?
NOT NECES-SARILY, BUT MY PARTY'S FEELING SICK RIGHT NOW.
OTHER-WISE, WE WOULD'VE TAKEN IT.
URRGH...
BLAHH...
GOSH... WE REALLY NEED SOME-ONE...

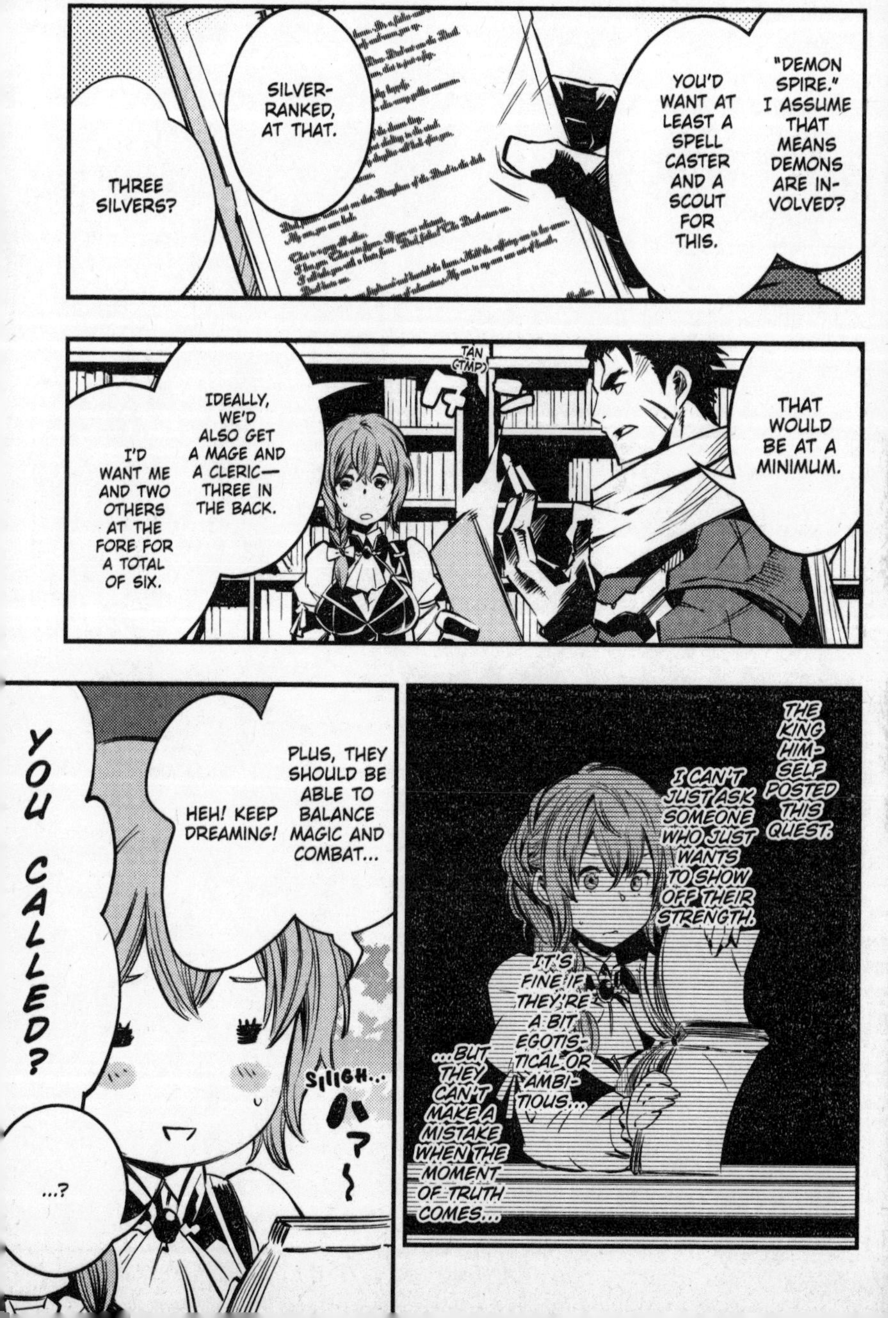
"DEMON SPIRE." I ASSUME THAT MEANS DEMONS ARE INVOLVED?
YOU'D WANT AT LEAST A SPELL CASTER AND A SCOUT FOR THIS.
SILVER-RANKED, AT THAT.
THREE SILVERS?
THAT WOULD BE AT A MINIMUM.
TAN (TMP)
IDEALLY, WE'D ALSO GET A MAGE AND A CLERIC—THREE IN THE BACK.
I'D WANT ME AND TWO OTHERS AT THE FORE FOR A TOTAL OF SIX.
THE KING HIMSELF POSTED THIS QUEST.
I CAN'T JUST ASK SOMEONE WHO JUST WANTS TO SHOW OFF THEIR STRENGTH.
IT'S FINE IF THEY'RE A BIT EGOTISTICAL OR AMBITIOUS...
...BUT THEY CAN'T MAKE A MISTAKE WHEN THE MOMENT OF TRUTH COMES...
PLUS, THEY SHOULD BE ABLE TO BALANCE MAGIC AND COMBAT...
HEH! KEEP DREAMING!
YOU CALLED?
SIIIGH...
...?

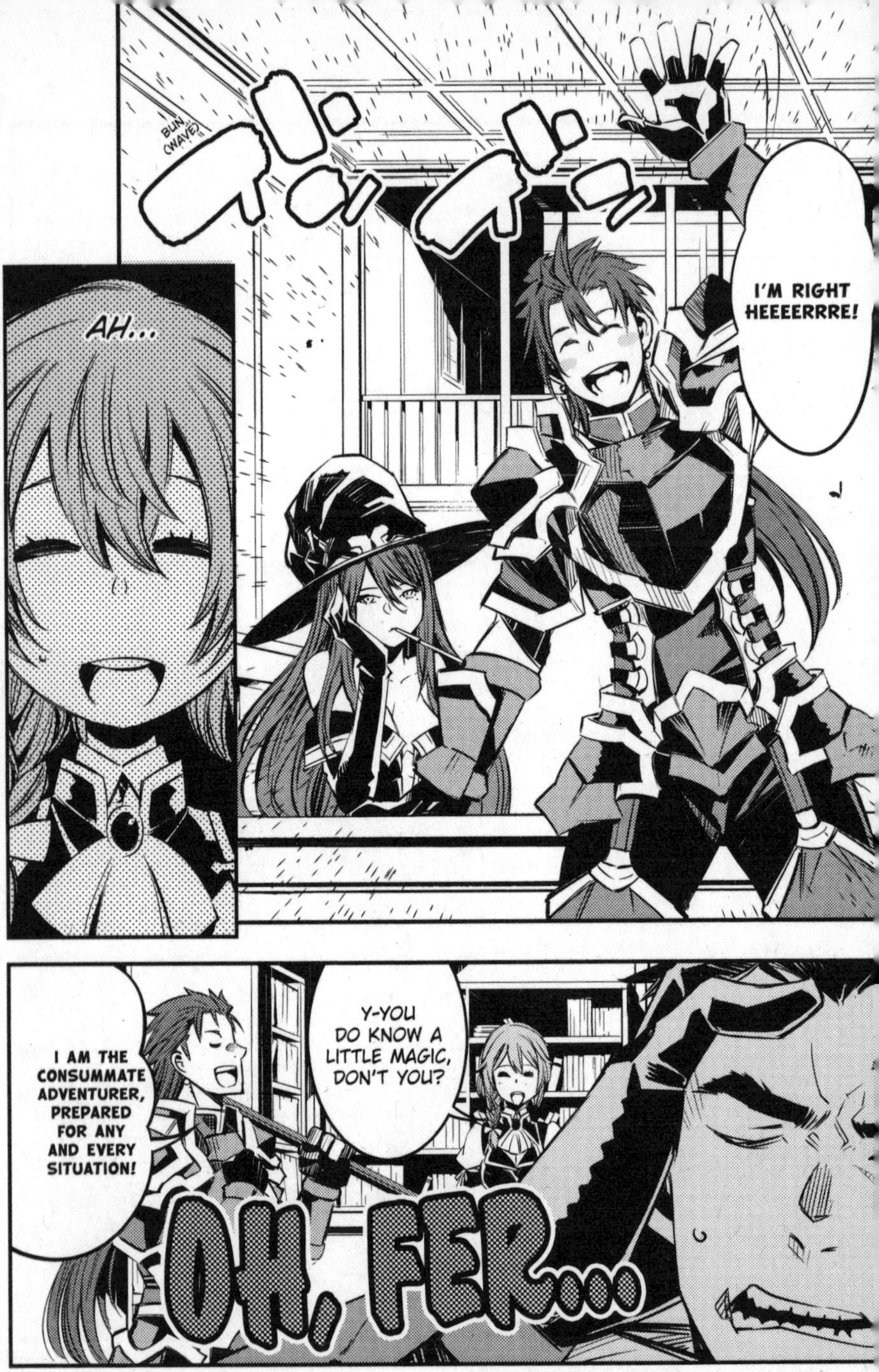
ブン ブン
BUN (WAVE)
I'M RIGHT HEEEERRRE!
AH...
Y-YOU DO KNOW A LITTLE MAGIC, DON'T YOU?
I AM THE CONSUMMATE ADVENTURER, PREPARED FOR ANY AND EVERY SITUATION!
OH, FER...

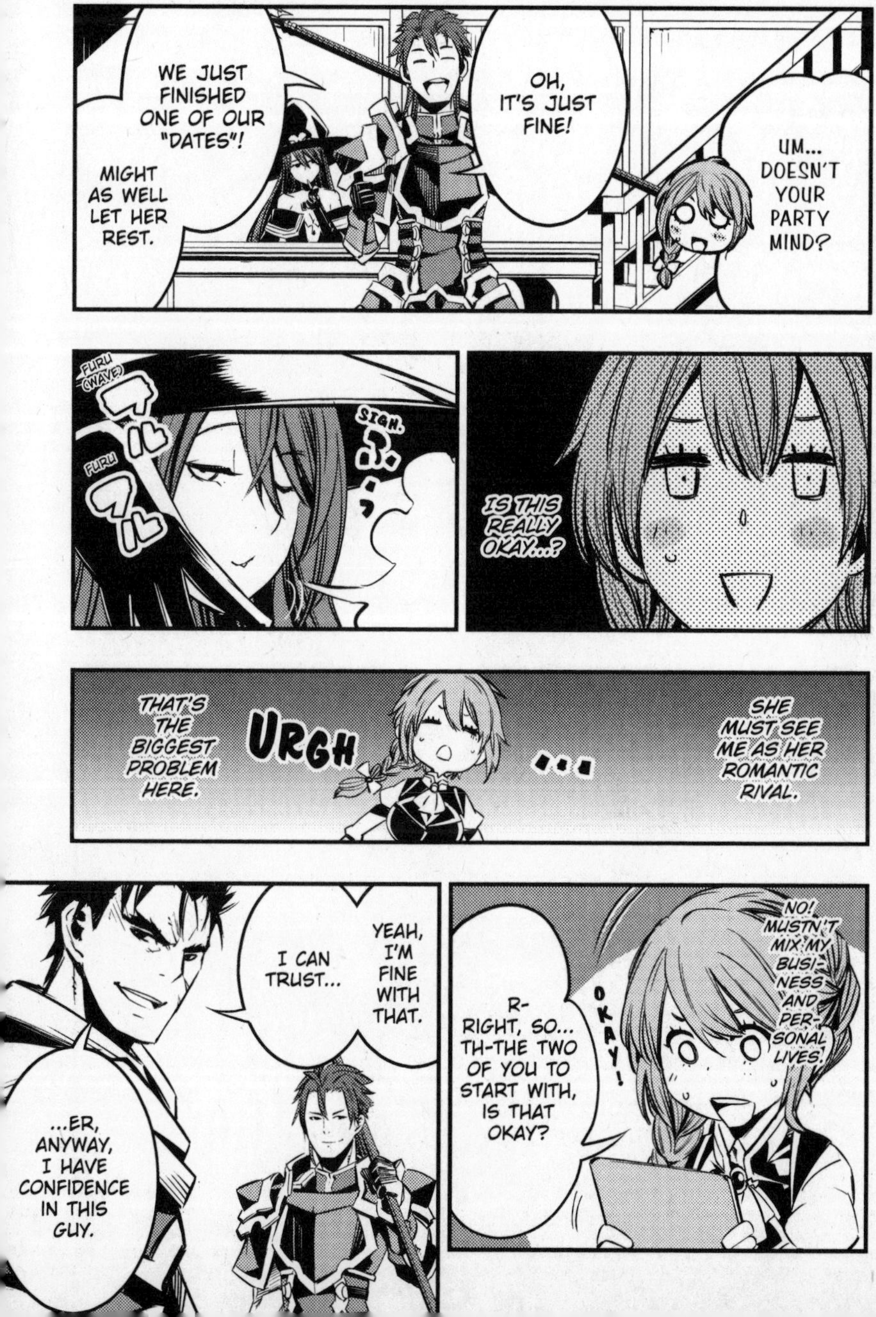
UM... DOESN'T YOUR PARTY MIND?
OH, IT'S JUST FINE!
WE JUST FINISHED ONE OF OUR "DATES"!
MIGHT AS WELL LET HER REST.
IS THIS REALLY OKAY...?
SIGH.
FURU (WAVE)
FURU
SHE MUST SEE ME AS HER ROMANTIC RIVAL.
...
URGH
THAT'S THE BIGGEST PROBLEM HERE.
NO! MUSTN'T MIX MY BUSINESS AND PERSONAL LIVES!
OKAY!
R-RIGHT, SO... TH-THE TWO OF YOU TO START WITH, IS THAT OKAY?
YEAH, I'M FINE WITH THAT.
I CAN TRUST...
...ER, ANYWAY, I HAVE CONFIDENCE IN THIS GUY.

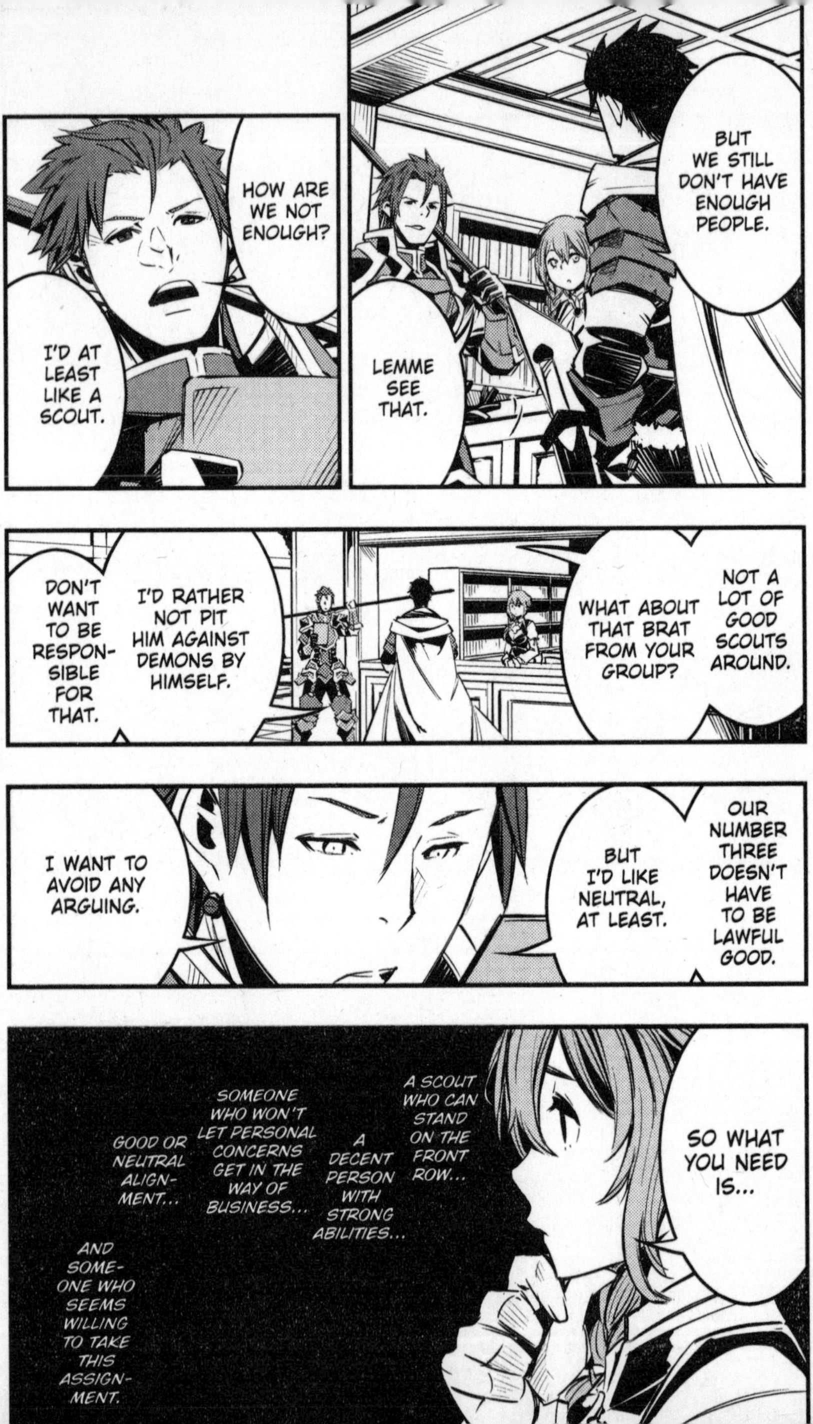
BUT WE STILL DON'T HAVE ENOUGH PEOPLE.
LEMME SEE THAT.
HOW ARE WE NOT ENOUGH?
I'D AT LEAST LIKE A SCOUT.
NOT A LOT OF GOOD SCOUTS AROUND.
WHAT ABOUT THAT BRAT FROM YOUR GROUP?
I'D RATHER NOT PIT HIM AGAINST DEMONS BY HIMSELF.
DON'T WANT TO BE RESPONSIBLE FOR THAT.
OUR NUMBER THREE DOESN'T HAVE TO BE LAWFUL GOOD.
BUT I'D LIKE NEUTRAL, AT LEAST.
I WANT TO AVOID ANY ARGUING.
SO WHAT YOU NEED IS...
A SCOUT WHO CAN STAND ON THE FRONT ROW...
A DECENT PERSON WITH STRONG ABILITIES...
SOMEONE WHO WON'T LET PERSONAL CONCERNS GET IN THE WAY OF BUSINESS...
GOOD OR NEUTRAL ALIGNMENT...
AND SOMEONE WHO SEEMS WILLING TO TAKE THIS ASSIGNMENT.

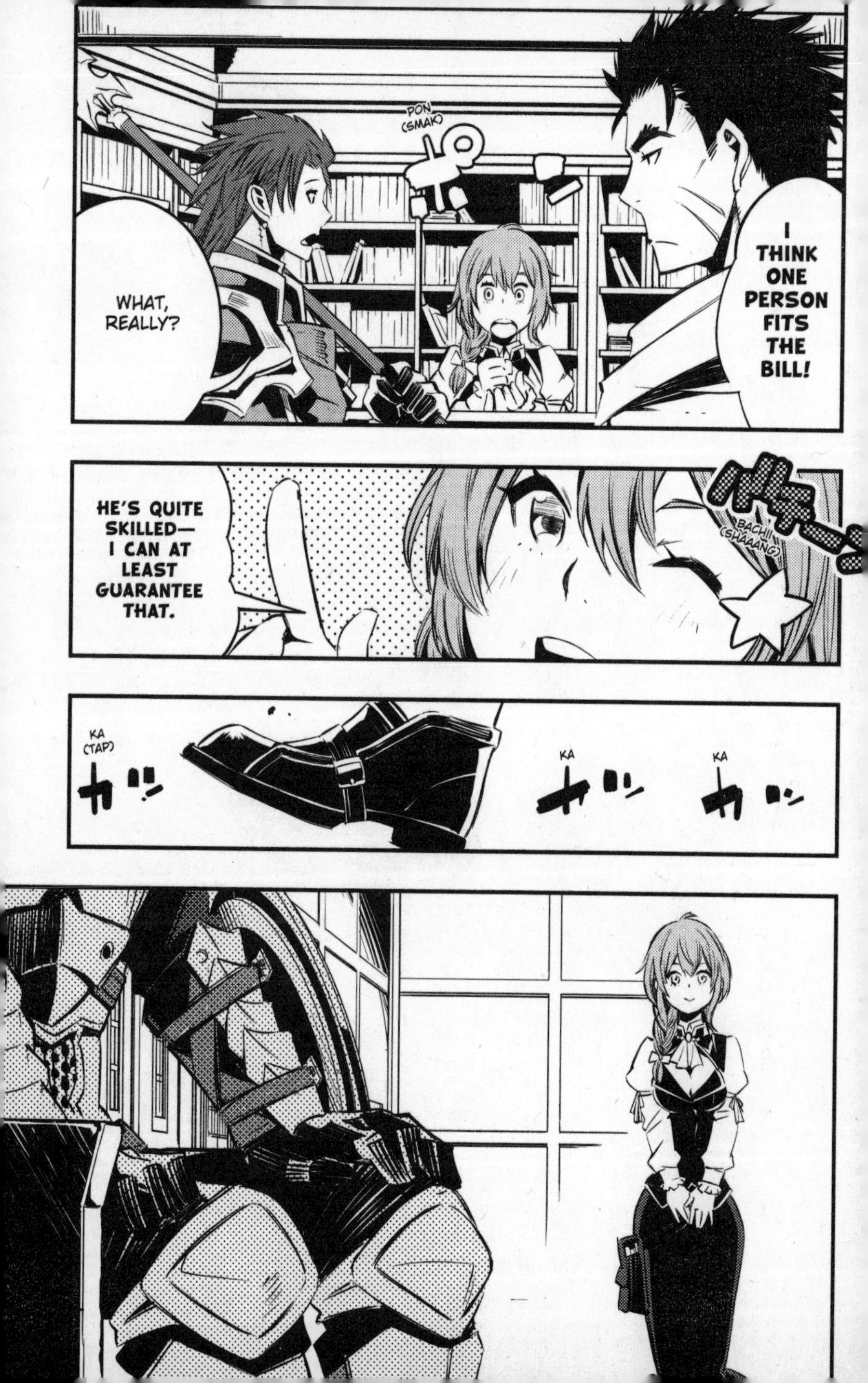
I THINK ONE PERSON FITS THE BILL!
PON (SMAK)
WHAT, REALLY?
BACHI! (SHAAANG)
HE'S QUITE SKILLED— I CAN AT LEAST GUARANTEE THAT.
KA
KA
KA (TAP)

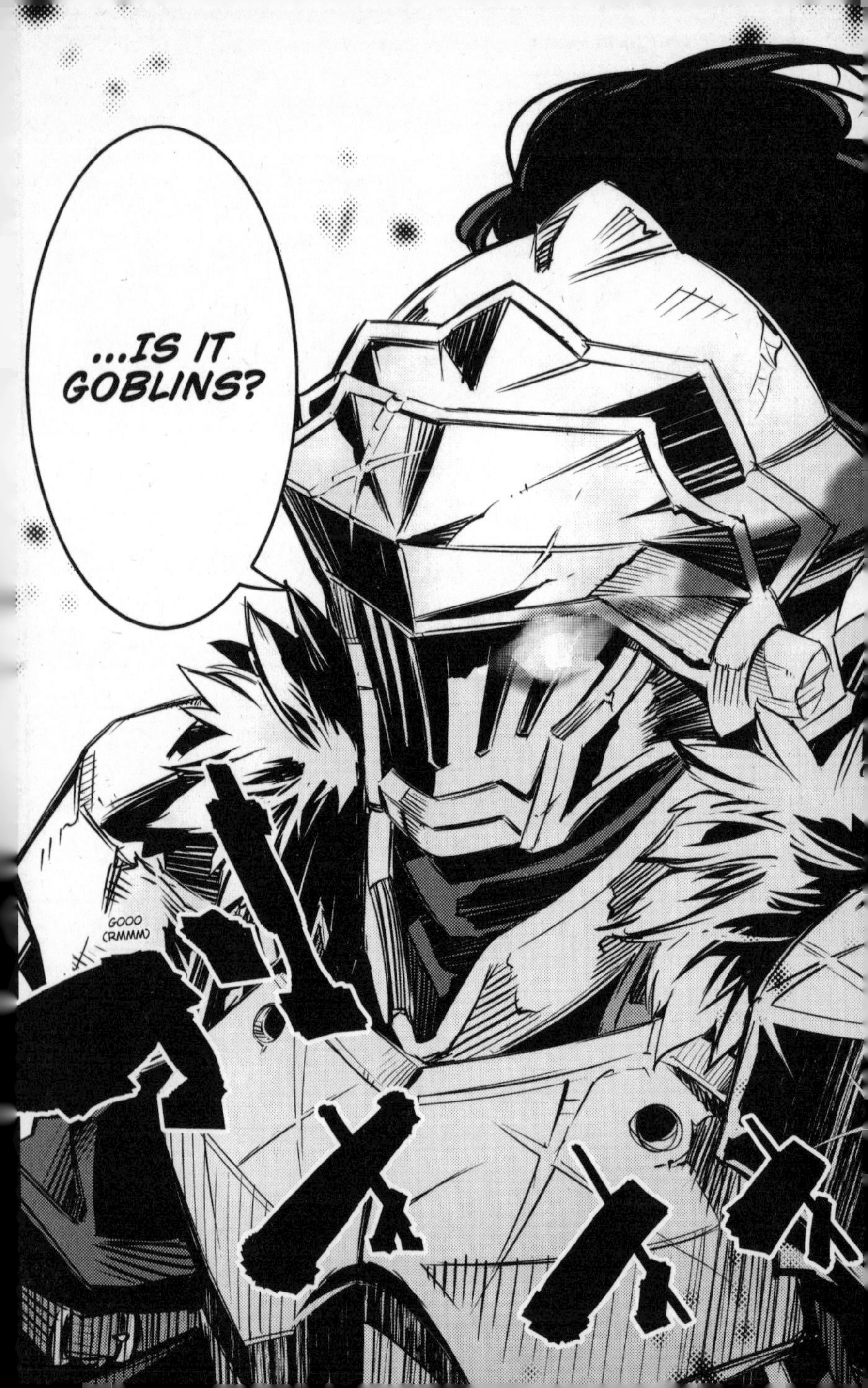
...IS IT GOBLINS?
GOOO (RMMM)

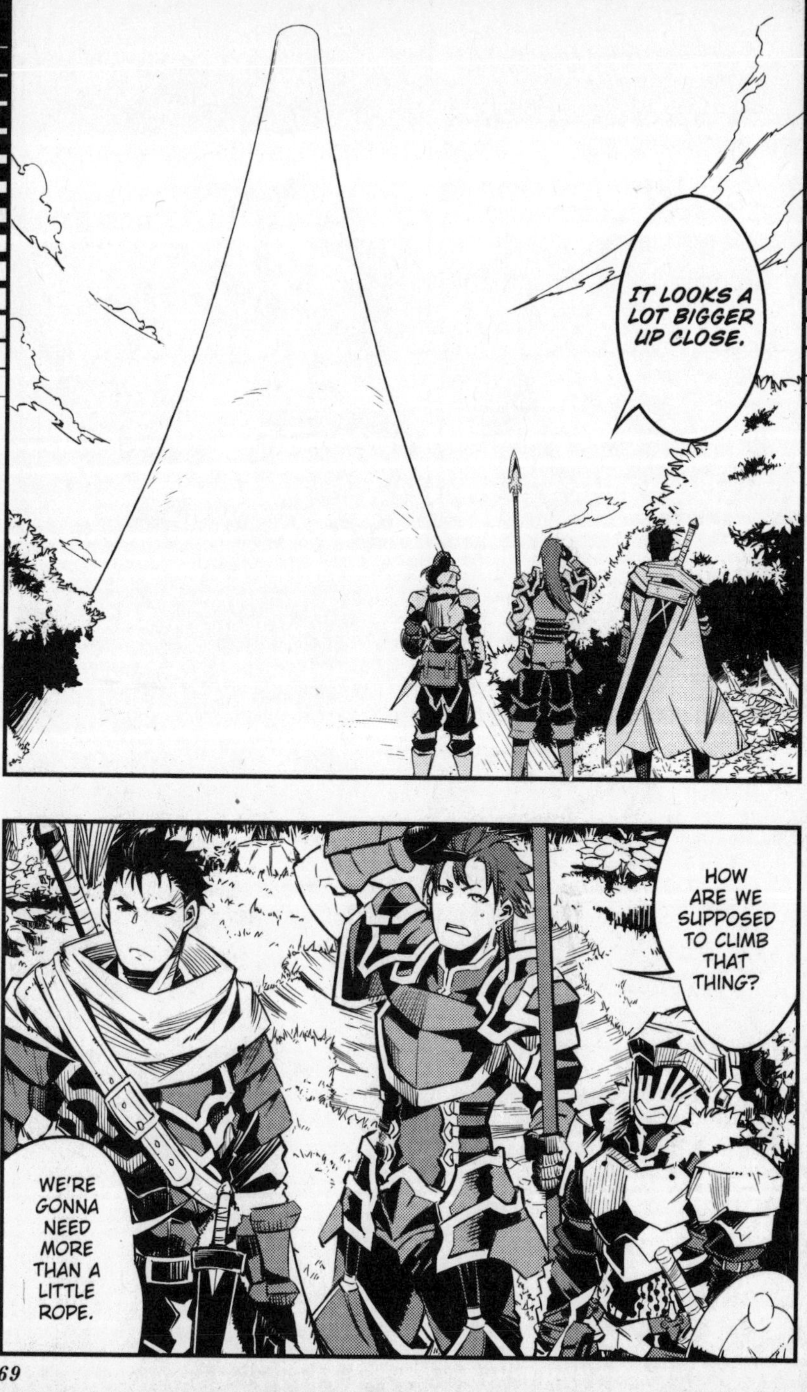
IT LOOKS A LOT BIGGER UP CLOSE.
HOW ARE WE SUPPOSED TO CLIMB THAT THING?
WE'RE GONNA NEED MORE THAN A LITTLE ROPE.

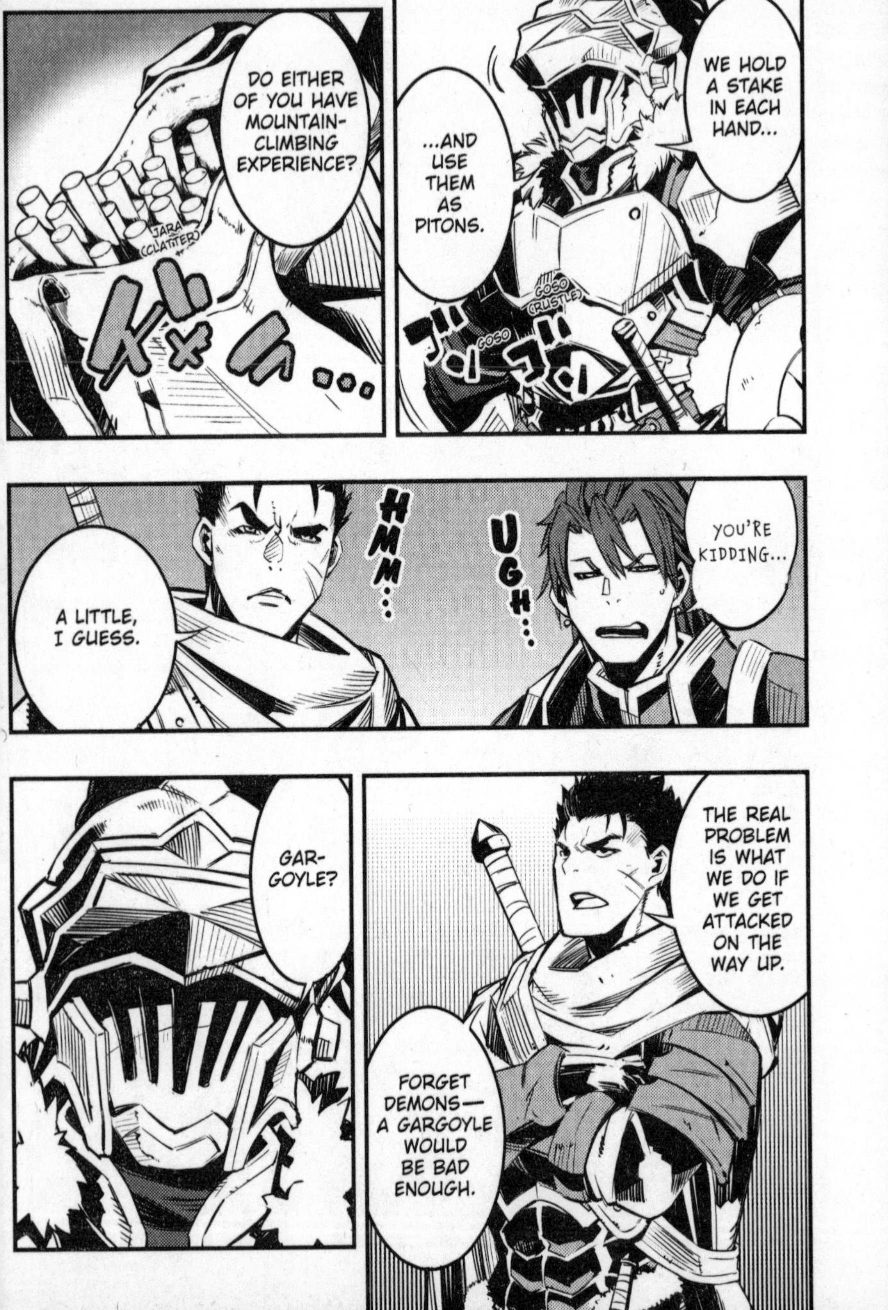
WE HOLD A STAKE IN EACH HAND...
...AND USE THEM AS PITONS.
GOSO (RUSTLE)
GOSO
DO EITHER OF YOU HAVE MOUNTAIN-CLIMBING EXPERIENCE?
JARA (CLATTER)
YOU'RE KIDDING...
UGH...
HMM...
A LITTLE, I GUESS.
THE REAL PROBLEM IS WHAT WE DO IF WE GET ATTACKED ON THE WAY UP.
FORGET DEMONS— A GARGOYLE WOULD BE BAD ENOUGH.
GAR-GOYLE?

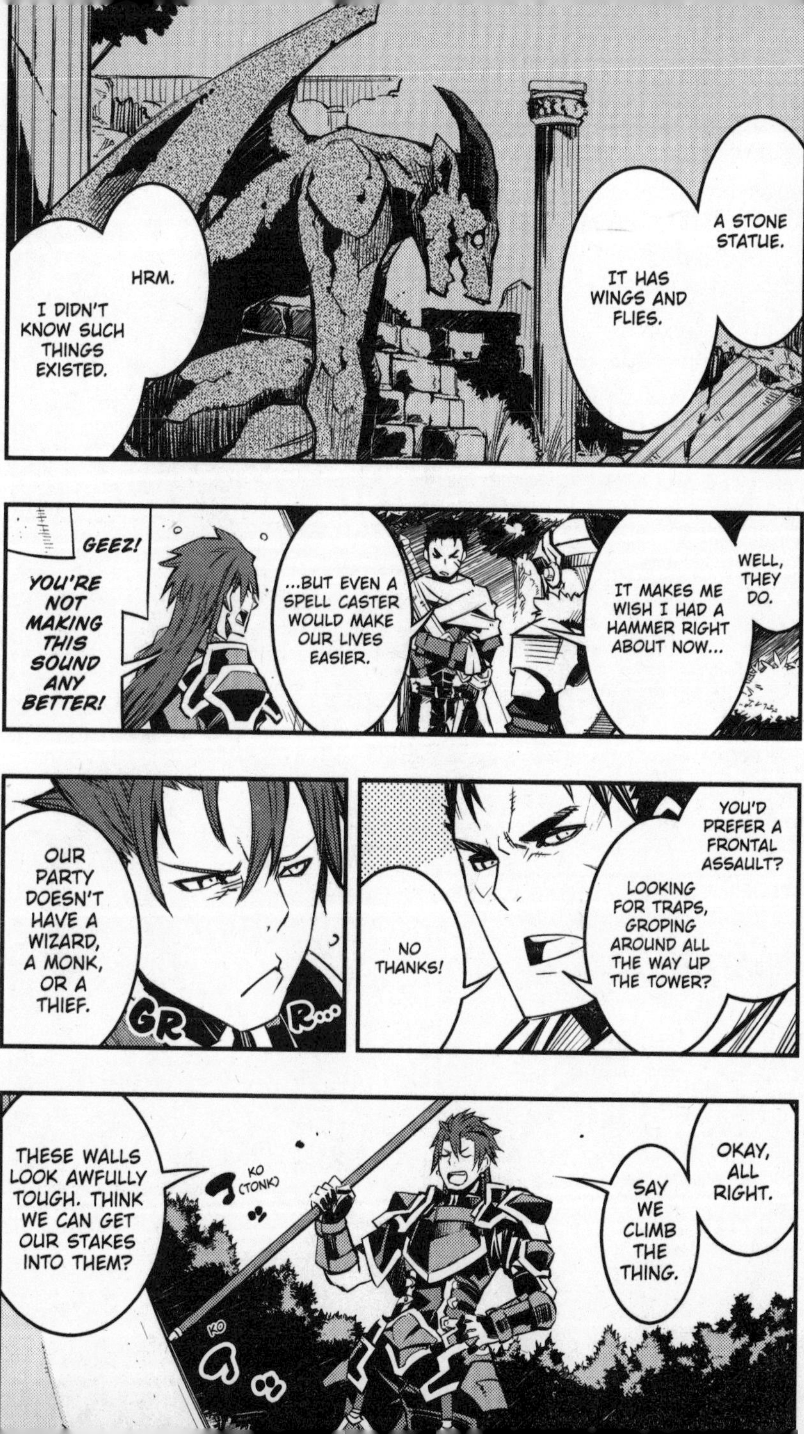
A STONE STATUE.
IT HAS WINGS AND FLIES.
HRM.
I DIDN'T KNOW SUCH THINGS EXISTED.
WELL, THEY DO.
IT MAKES ME WISH I HAD A HAMMER RIGHT ABOUT NOW...
...BUT EVEN A SPELL CASTER WOULD MAKE OUR LIVES EASIER.
GEEZ!
YOU'RE NOT MAKING THIS SOUND ANY BETTER!
YOU'D PREFER A FRONTAL ASSAULT?
LOOKING FOR TRAPS, GROPING AROUND ALL THE WAY UP THE TOWER?
NO THANKS!
OUR PARTY DOESN'T HAVE A WIZARD, A MONK, OR A THIEF.
GR
R...
OKAY, ALL RIGHT.
SAY WE CLIMB THE THING.
KO (TONK)
THESE WALLS LOOK AWFULLY TOUGH. THINK WE CAN GET OUR STAKES INTO THEM?
KO

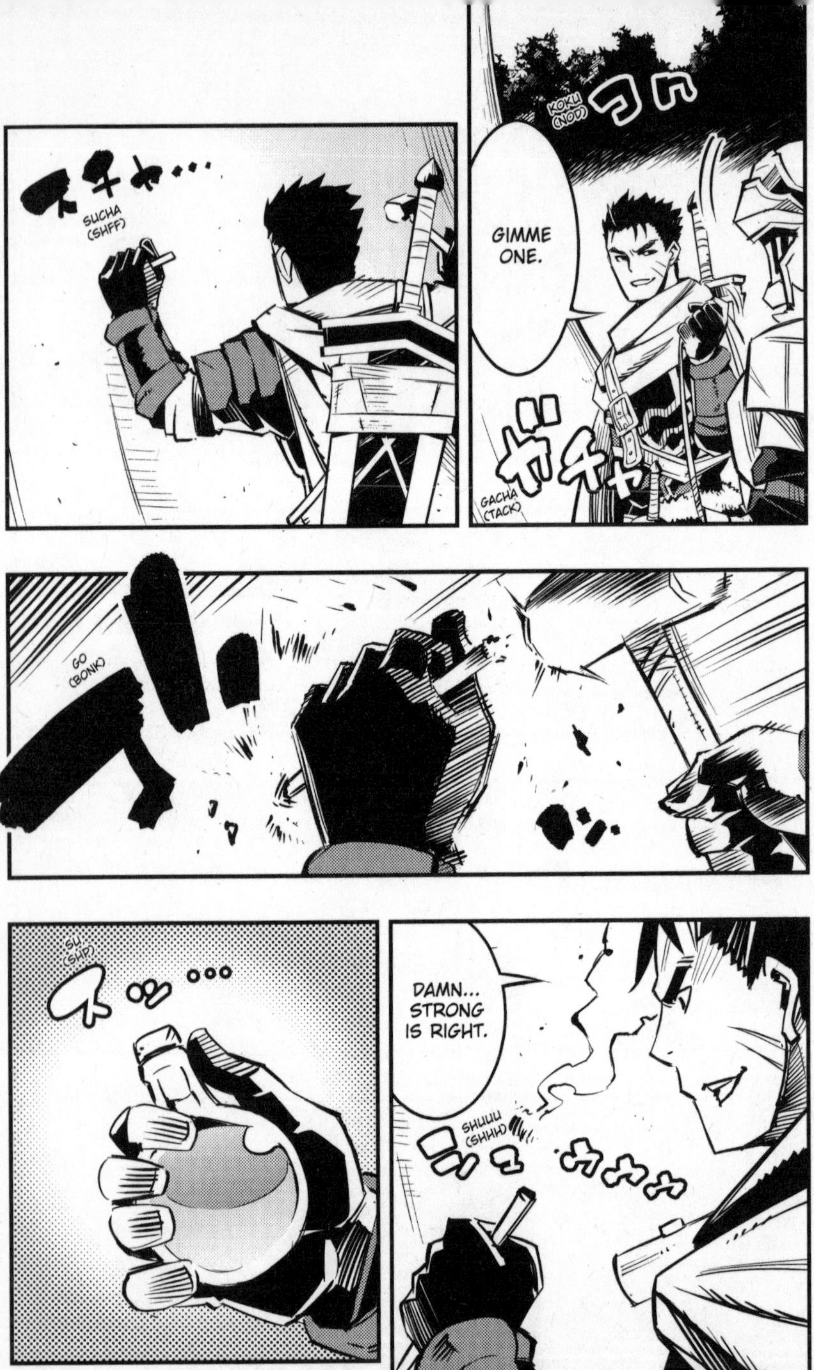
KOKU (NOD)
GIMME ONE.
GACHA (TACK)
SUCHA (SHFF)
GO (BONK)
DAMN... STRONG IS RIGHT.
SHUUU (SHHH)
SU (SHP)

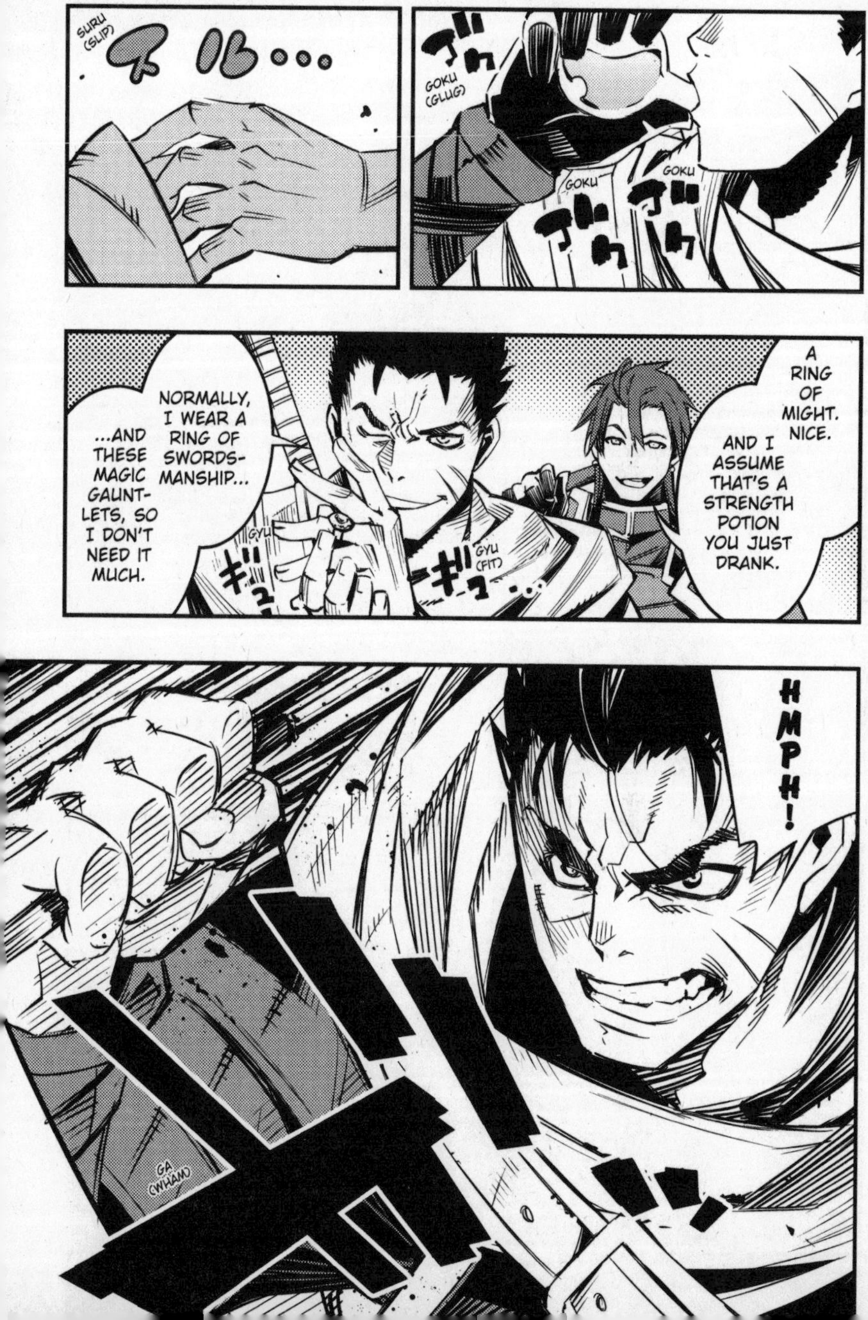
GOKU (GLUG)
GOKU
GOKU
SURU (SLIP)
A RING OF MIGHT. NICE.
AND I ASSUME THAT'S A STRENGTH POTION YOU JUST DRANK.
GYU (FIT)
NORMALLY, I WEAR A RING OF SWORDS-MANSHIP...
GYU
...AND THESE MAGIC GAUNT-LETS, SO I DON'T NEED IT MUCH.
HMPH!
GA (WHAM)

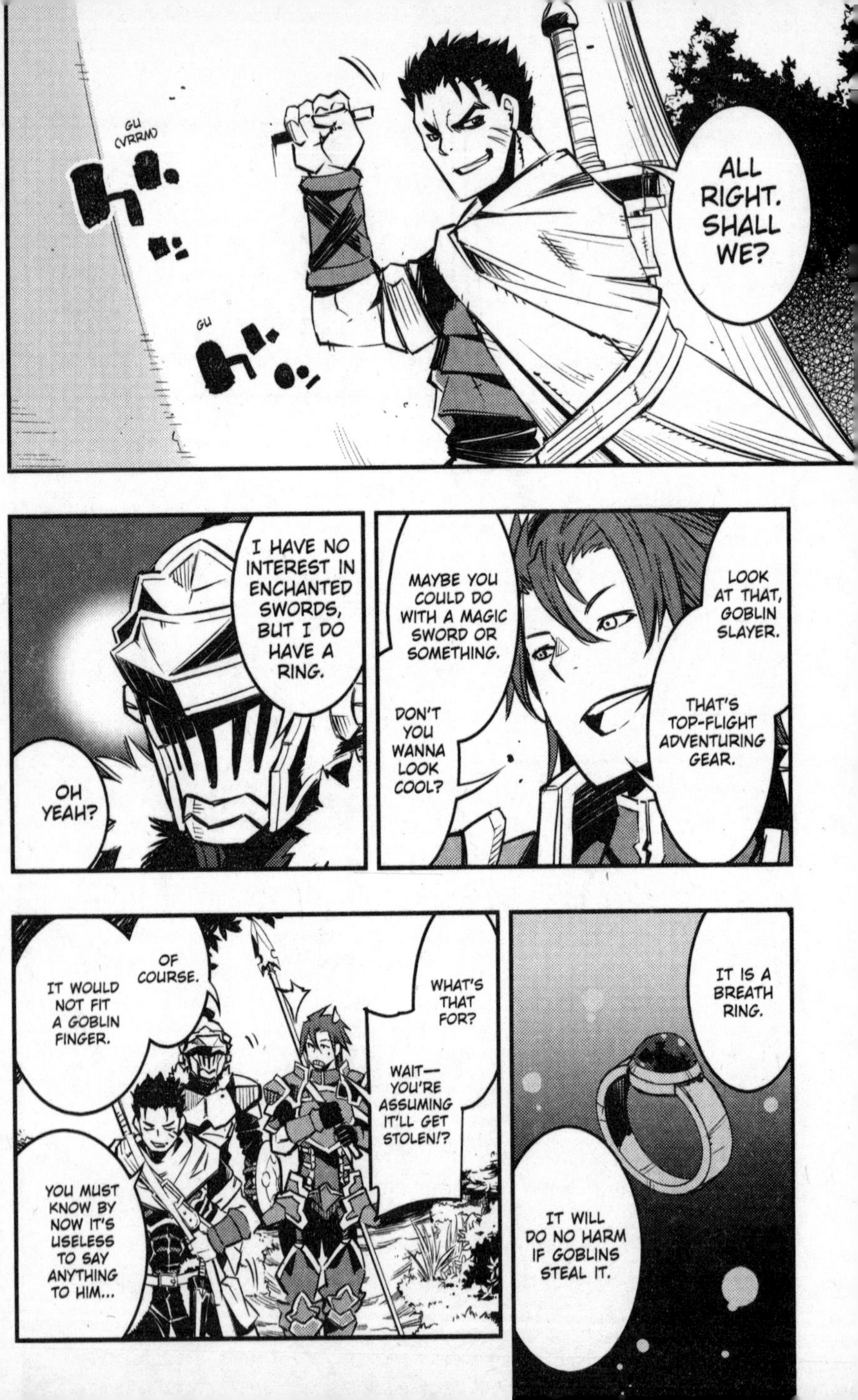
ALL RIGHT. SHALL WE?
GU (VRRM)
GU
LOOK AT THAT, GOBLIN SLAYER.
THAT'S TOP-FLIGHT ADVENTURING GEAR.
MAYBE YOU COULD DO WITH A MAGIC SWORD OR SOMETHING.
DON'T YOU WANNA LOOK COOL?
I HAVE NO INTEREST IN ENCHANTED SWORDS, BUT I DO HAVE A RING.
OH YEAH?
IT IS A BREATH RING.
IT WILL DO NO HARM IF GOBLINS STEAL IT.
WHAT'S THAT FOR?
WAIT— YOU'RE ASSUMING IT'LL GET STOLEN!?
OF COURSE.
IT WOULD NOT FIT A GOBLIN FINGER.
YOU MUST KNOW BY NOW IT'S USELESS TO SAY ANYTHING TO HIM...

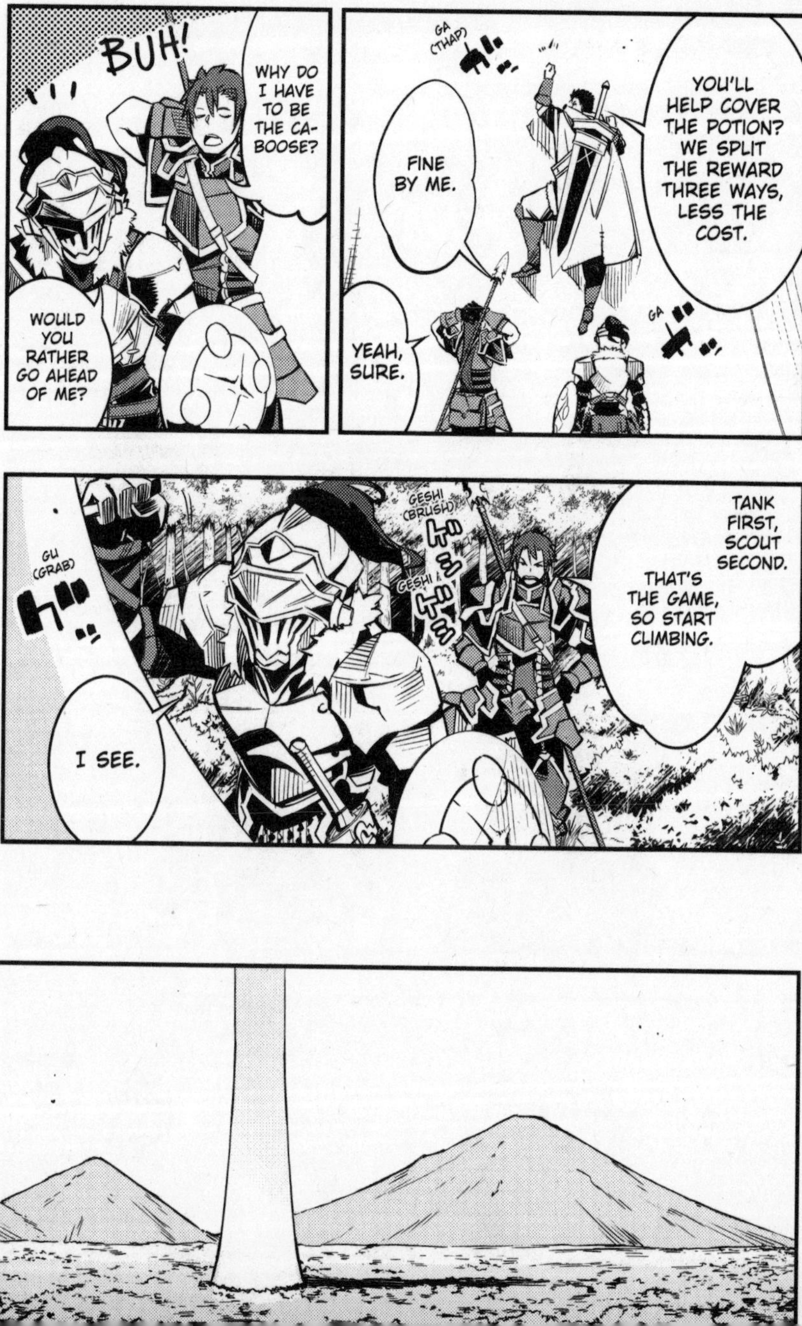
YOU'LL HELP COVER THE POTION? WE SPLIT THE REWARD THREE WAYS, LESS THE COST.
GA (THAP)
FINE BY ME.
YEAH, SURE.
GA
BUH!
WHY DO I HAVE TO BE THE CA-BOOSE?
WOULD YOU RATHER GO AHEAD OF ME?
TANK FIRST, SCOUT SECOND.
THAT'S THE GAME, SO START CLIMBING.
GESHI (BRUSH)
GESHI
GU (GRAB)
I SEE.

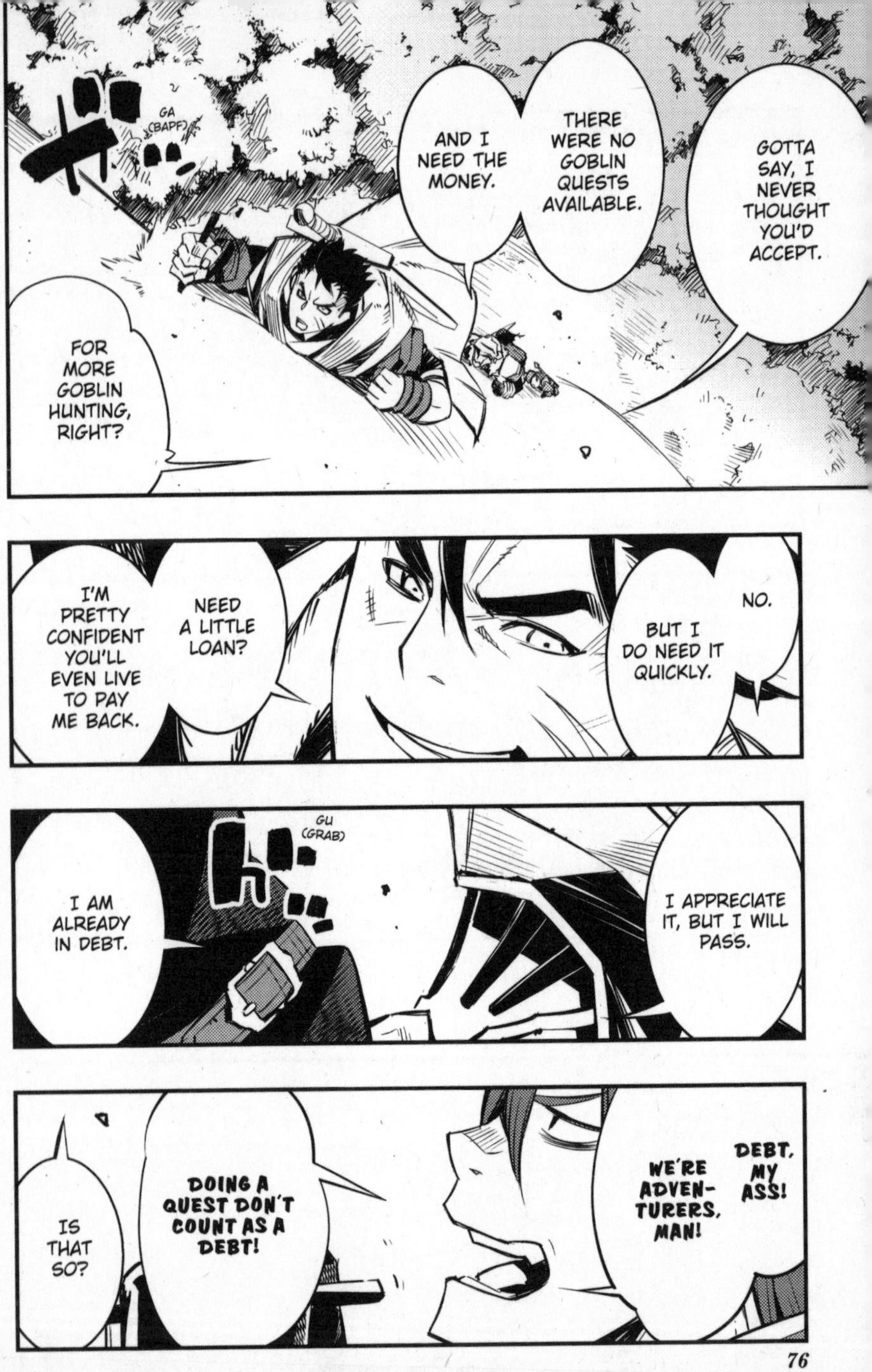
GOTTA SAY, I NEVER THOUGHT YOU'D ACCEPT.
THERE WERE NO GOBLIN QUESTS AVAILABLE.
AND I NEED THE MONEY.
GA (BAPF)
FOR MORE GOBLIN HUNTING, RIGHT?
NO.
BUT I DO NEED IT QUICKLY.
NEED A LITTLE LOAN?
I'M PRETTY CONFIDENT YOU'LL EVEN LIVE TO PAY ME BACK.
I APPRECIATE IT, BUT I WILL PASS.
GU (GRAB)
I AM ALREADY IN DEBT.
DEBT, MY ASS!
WE'RE ADVEN-TURERS, MAN!
DOING A QUEST DON'T COUNT AS A DEBT!
IS THAT SO?

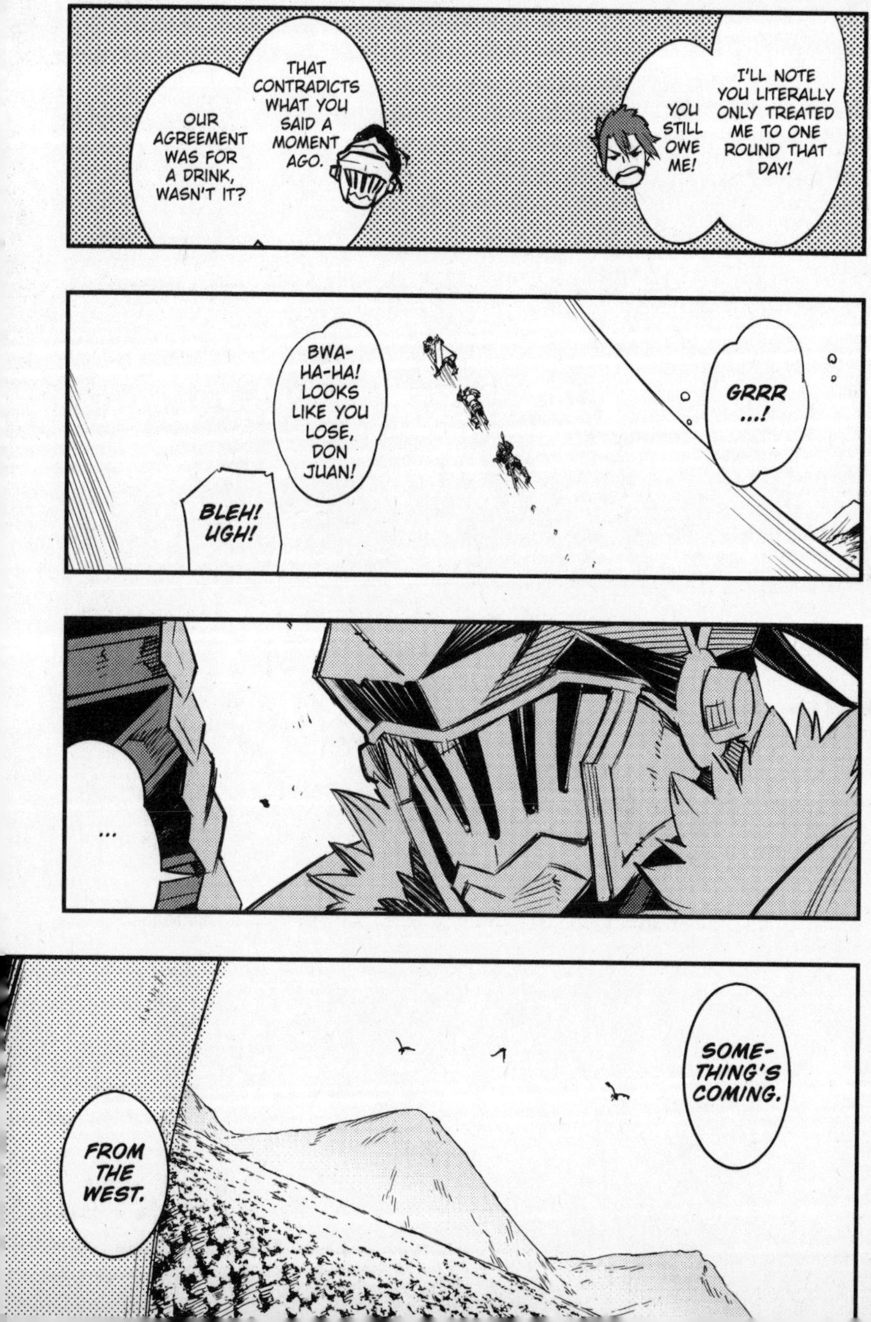
I'LL NOTE YOU LITERALLY ONLY TREATED ME TO ONE ROUND THAT DAY!
YOU STILL OWE ME!
THAT CONTRADICTS WHAT YOU SAID A MOMENT AGO.
OUR AGREEMENT WAS FOR A DRINK, WASN'T IT?
GRRR ...!
BWA-HA-HA! LOOKS LIKE YOU LOSE, DON JUAN!
BLEH! UGH!
...
SOME-THING'S COMING.
FROM THE WEST.

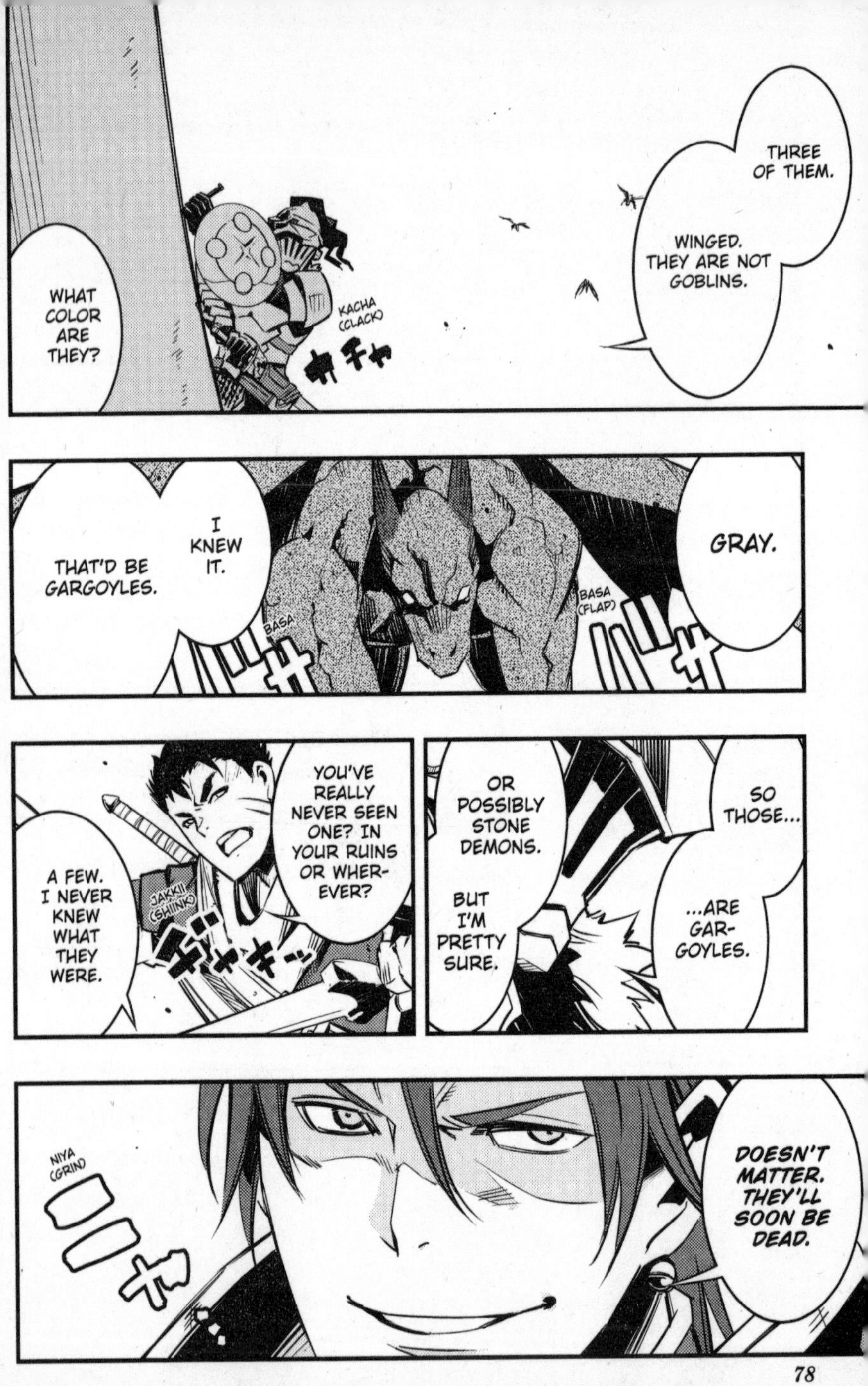
THREE OF THEM.
WINGED. THEY ARE NOT GOBLINS.
KACHA (CLACK)
WHAT COLOR ARE THEY?
GRAY.
BASA (FLAP)
BASA
I KNEW IT.
THAT'D BE GARGOYLES.
SO THOSE...
...ARE GAR-GOYLES.
OR POSSIBLY STONE DEMONS.
BUT I'M PRETTY SURE.
YOU'VE REALLY NEVER SEEN ONE? IN YOUR RUINS OR WHER-EVER?
JAKKII (SHIINK)
A FEW. I NEVER KNEW WHAT THEY WERE.
DOESN'T MATTER. THEY'LL SOON BE DEAD.
NIYA (GRIN)

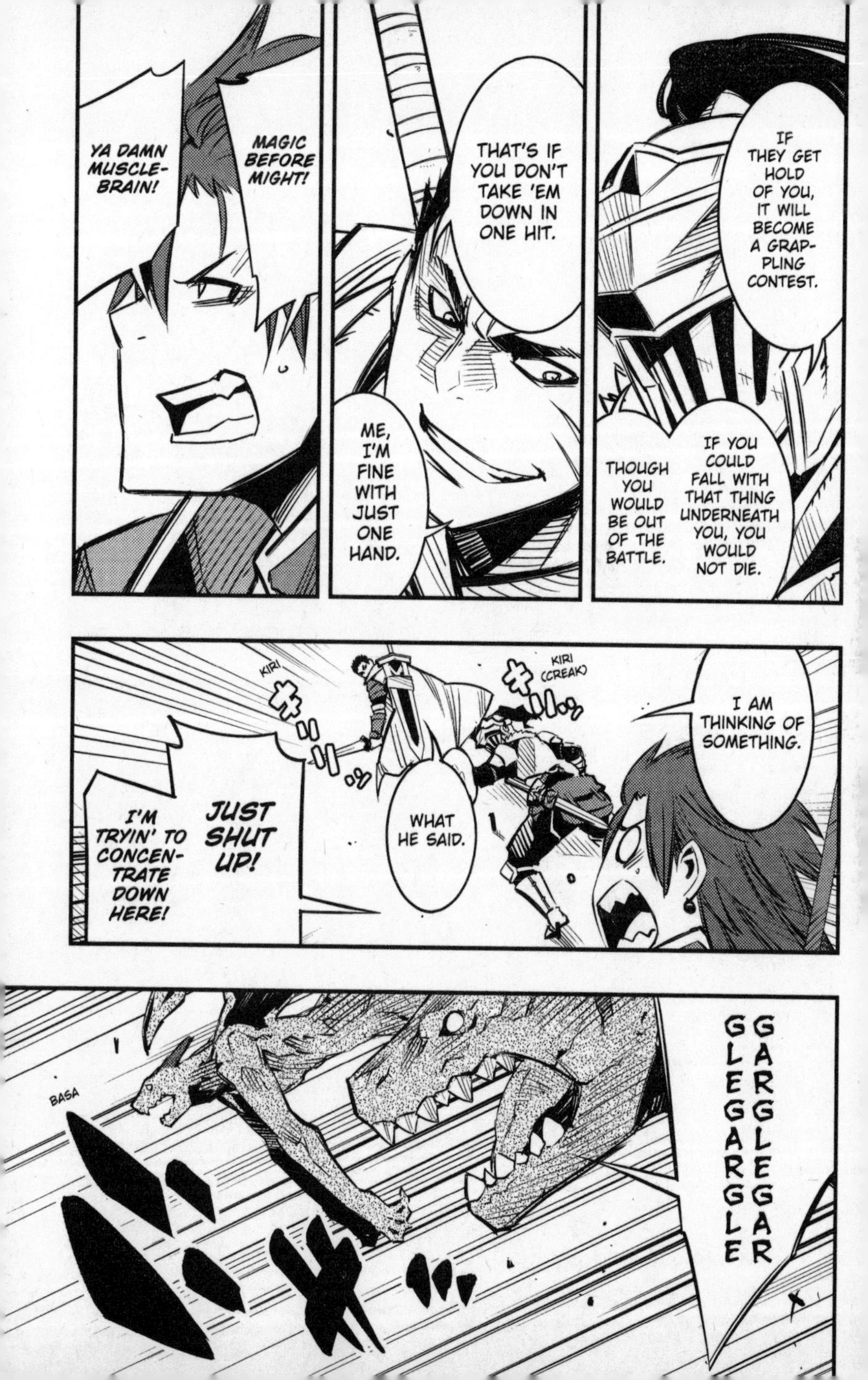
IF THEY GET HOLD OF YOU, IT WILL BECOME A GRAPPLING CONTEST.
IF YOU COULD FALL WITH THAT THING UNDERNEATH YOU, YOU WOULD NOT DIE.
THOUGH YOU WOULD BE OUT OF THE BATTLE.
THAT'S IF YOU DON'T TAKE 'EM DOWN IN ONE HIT.
ME, I'M FINE WITH JUST ONE HAND.
MAGIC BEFORE MIGHT!
YA DAMN MUSCLE-BRAIN!
I AM THINKING OF SOMETHING.
KIRI (CREAK)
WHAT HE SAID.
KIRI
JUST SHUT UP!
I'M TRYIN' TO CONCENTRATE DOWN HERE!
GARGLEGAR
GLEGARGLE
BASA

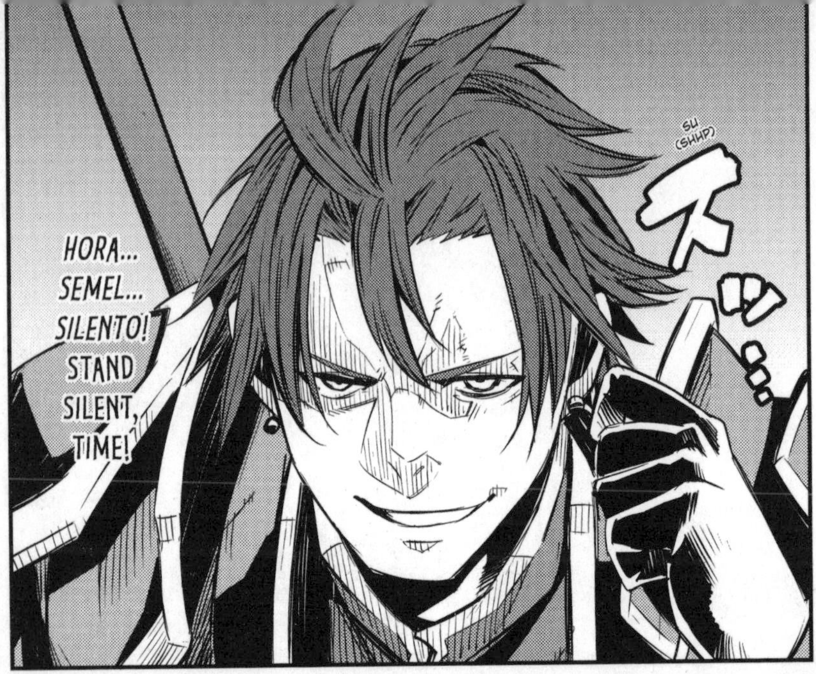
SU
(SHHP)
HORA... SEMEL... SILENTO! STAND SILENT, TIME!
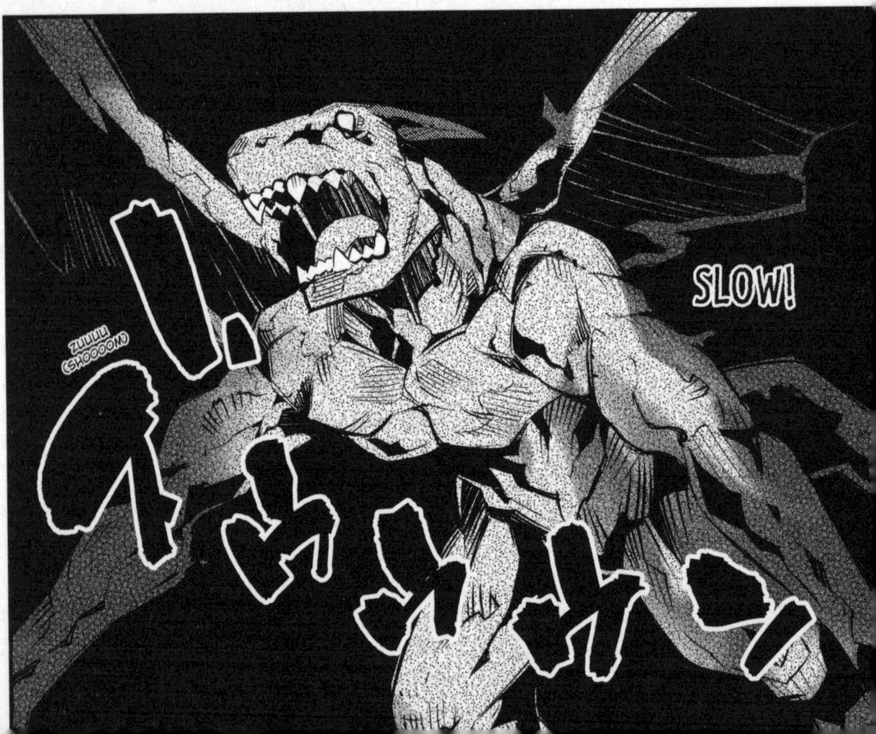
SLOW!
ZUUUU
(SHOOOOM)

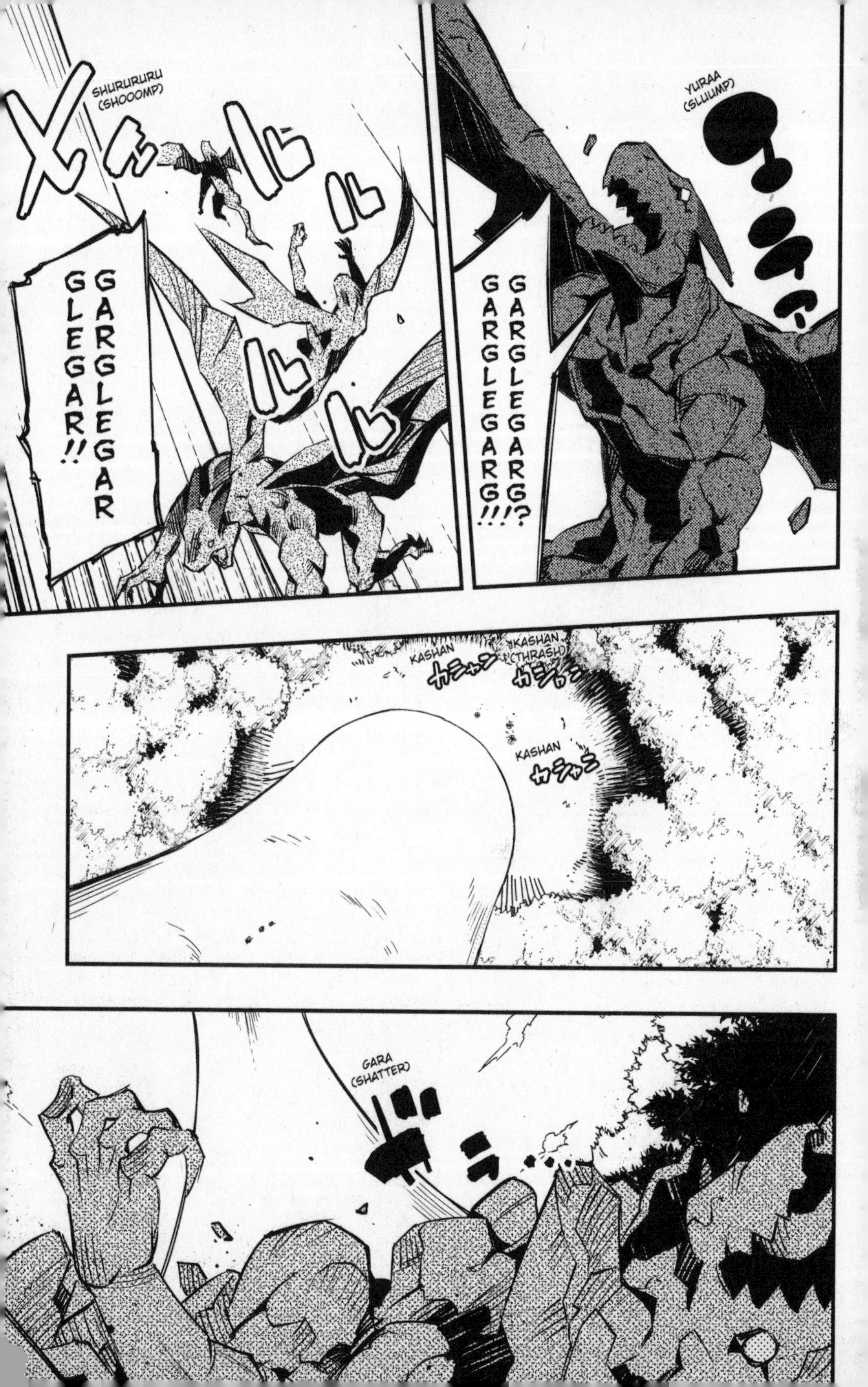
YURAA (SLUUMP)
GARGLEGARG!?
GARGLEGARG!!!
SHURURURU (SHOOOMP)
GARGLEGAR
GLEGAR!!
KASHAN (THRASH)
KASHAN
KASHAN
...
GARA (SHATTER)

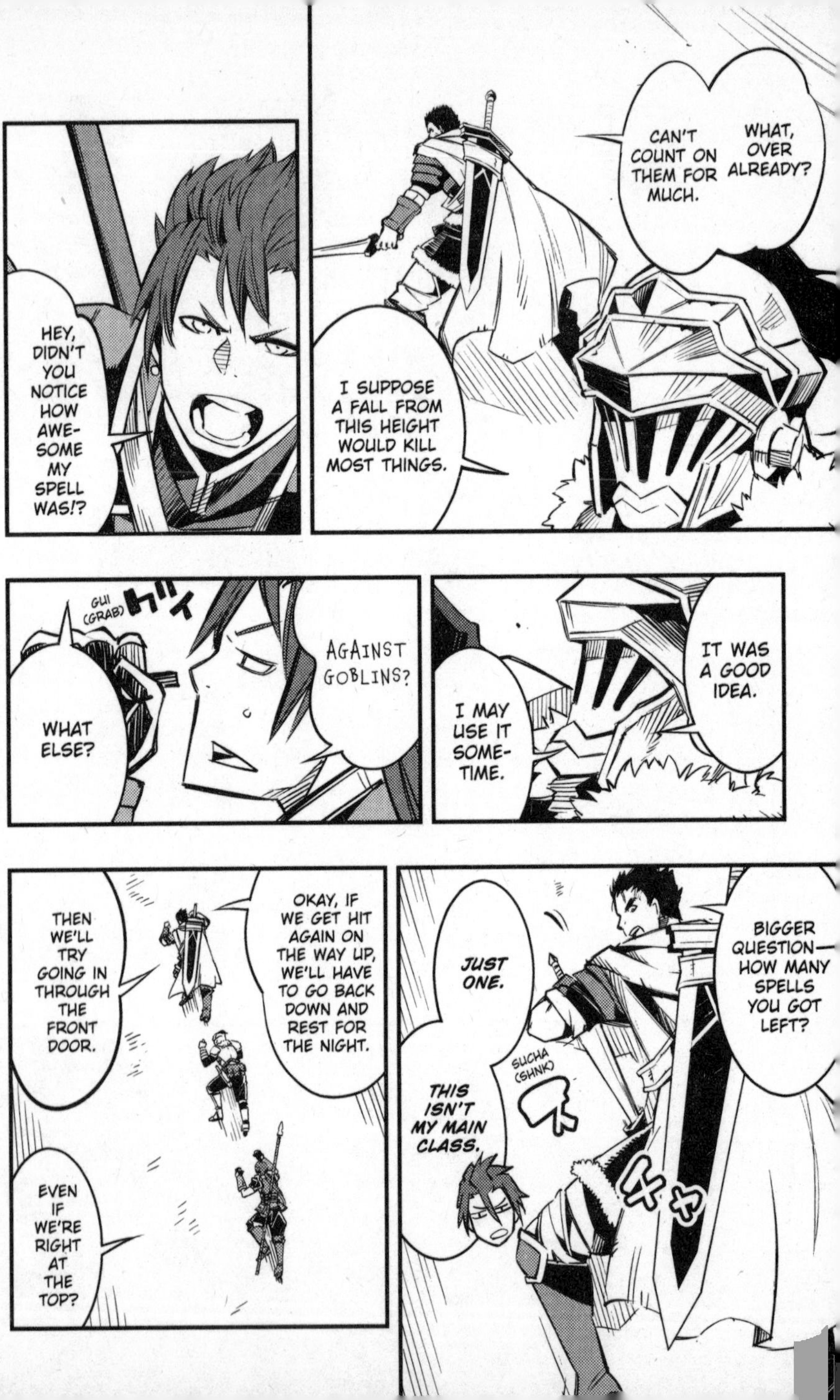
WHAT, OVER ALREADY?
CAN'T COUNT ON THEM FOR MUCH.
I SUPPOSE A FALL FROM THIS HEIGHT WOULD KILL MOST THINGS.
HEY, DIDN'T YOU NOTICE HOW AWE-SOME MY SPELL WAS!?
IT WAS A GOOD IDEA.
I MAY USE IT SOME-TIME.
AGAINST GOBLINS?
GUI (GRAB)
WHAT ELSE?
BIGGER QUESTION—HOW MANY SPELLS YOU GOT LEFT?
JUST ONE.
SUCHA (SHNK)
THIS ISN'T MY MAIN CLASS.
OKAY, IF WE GET HIT AGAIN ON THE WAY UP, WE'LL HAVE TO GO BACK DOWN AND REST FOR THE NIGHT.
THEN WE'LL TRY GOING IN THROUGH THE FRONT DOOR.
EVEN IF WE'RE RIGHT AT THE TOP?

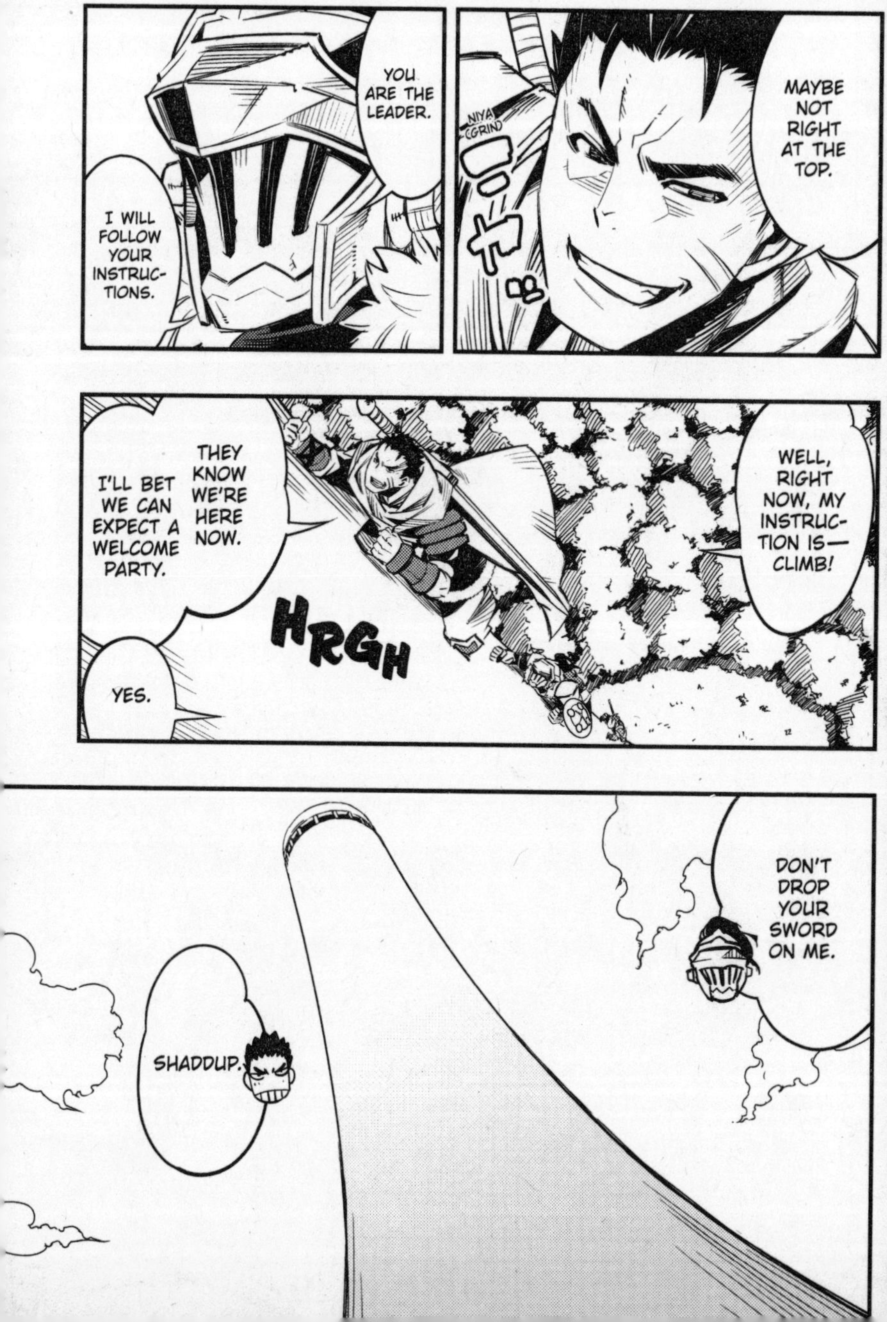
MAYBE NOT RIGHT AT THE TOP.
NIYA (GRIN)
YOU ARE THE LEADER.
I WILL FOLLOW YOUR INSTRUCTIONS.
WELL, RIGHT NOW, MY INSTRUCTION IS— CLIMB!
THEY KNOW WE'RE HERE NOW.
I'LL BET WE CAN EXPECT A WELCOME PARTY.
HRGH
YES.
DON'T DROP YOUR SWORD ON ME.
SHADDUP.

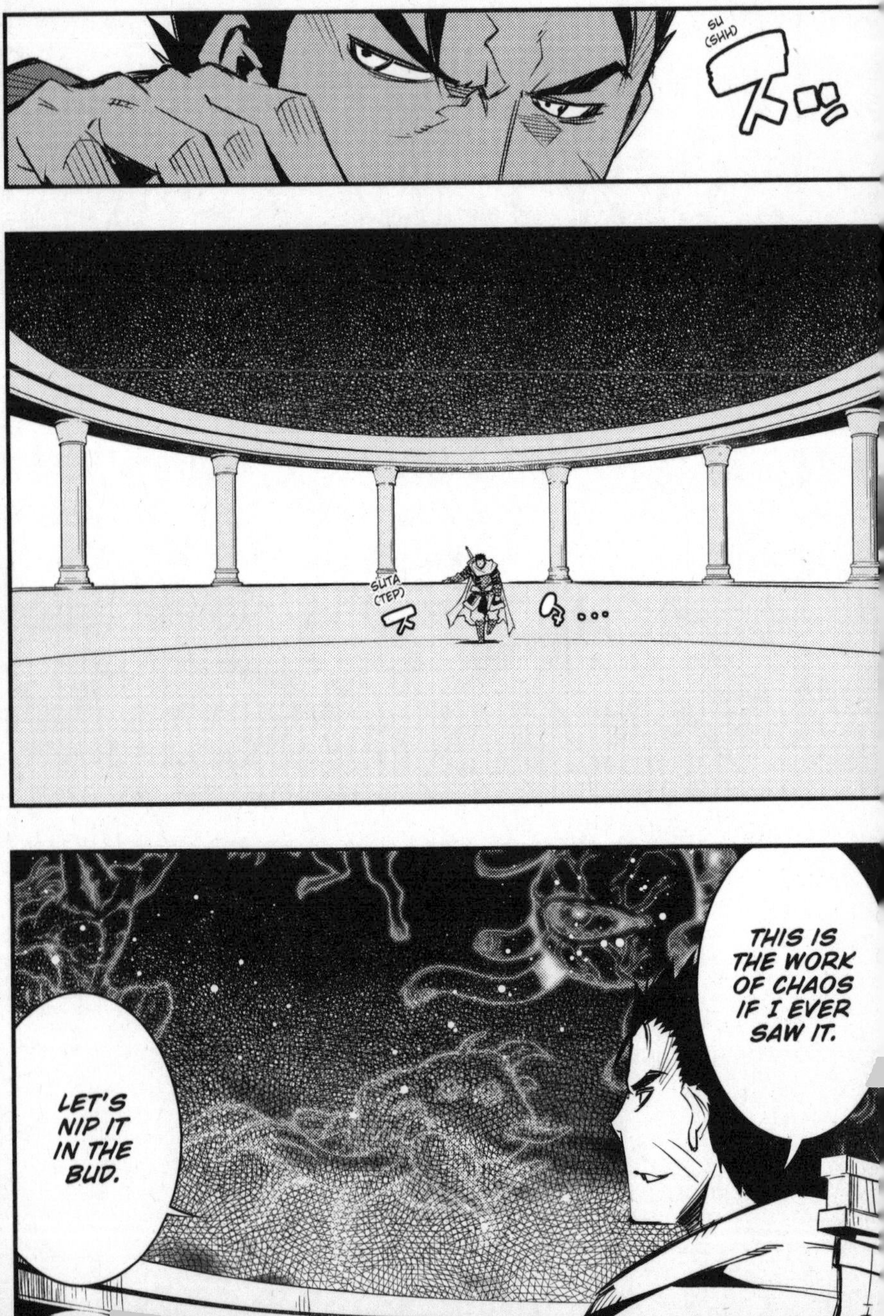
SU (SHH)
SUTA (TEP)
THIS IS THE WORK OF CHAOS IF I EVER SAW IT.
LET'S NIP IT IN THE BUD.

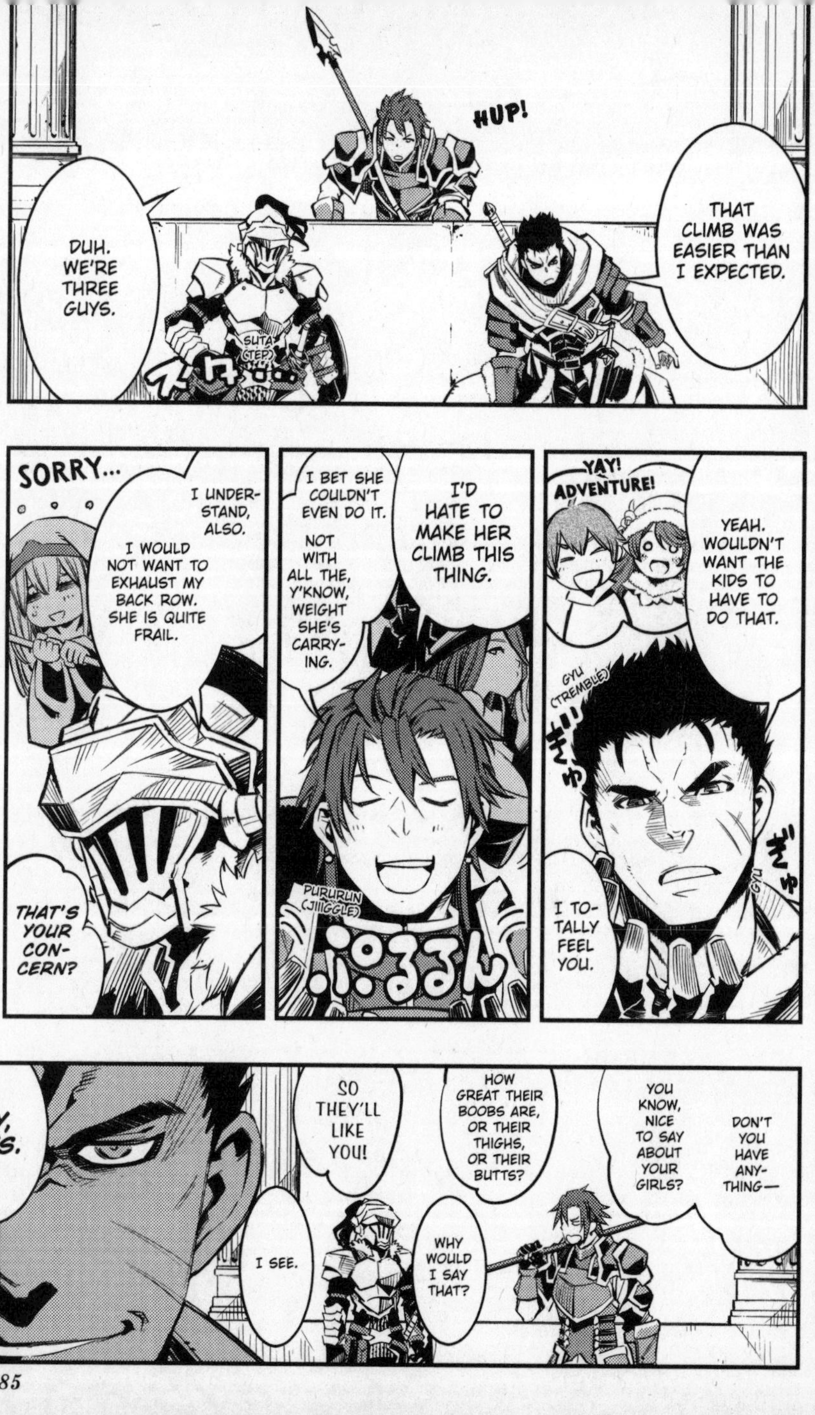
HUP!
THAT CLIMB WAS EASIER THAN I EXPECTED.
DUH. WE'RE THREE GUYS.
SUTA (TEP)
YAY! ADVENTURE!
YEAH. WOULDN'T WANT THE KIDS TO HAVE TO DO THAT.
GYU (TREMBLE)
I TO-TALLY FEEL YOU.
I'D HATE TO MAKE HER CLIMB THIS THING.
I BET SHE COULDN'T EVEN DO IT.
NOT WITH ALL THE, Y'KNOW, WEIGHT SHE'S CARRY-ING.
PURURUN (JIIIGGLE)
I UNDER-STAND, ALSO.
I WOULD NOT WANT TO EXHAUST MY BACK ROW. SHE IS QUITE FRAIL.
SORRY...
THAT'S YOUR CON-CERN?
DON'T YOU HAVE ANY-THING—
YOU KNOW, NICE TO SAY ABOUT YOUR GIRLS?
HOW GREAT THEIR BOOBS ARE, OR THEIR THIGHS, OR THEIR BUTTS?
SO THEY'LL LIKE YOU!
WHY WOULD I SAY THAT?
I SEE.
HEY, BOYS.

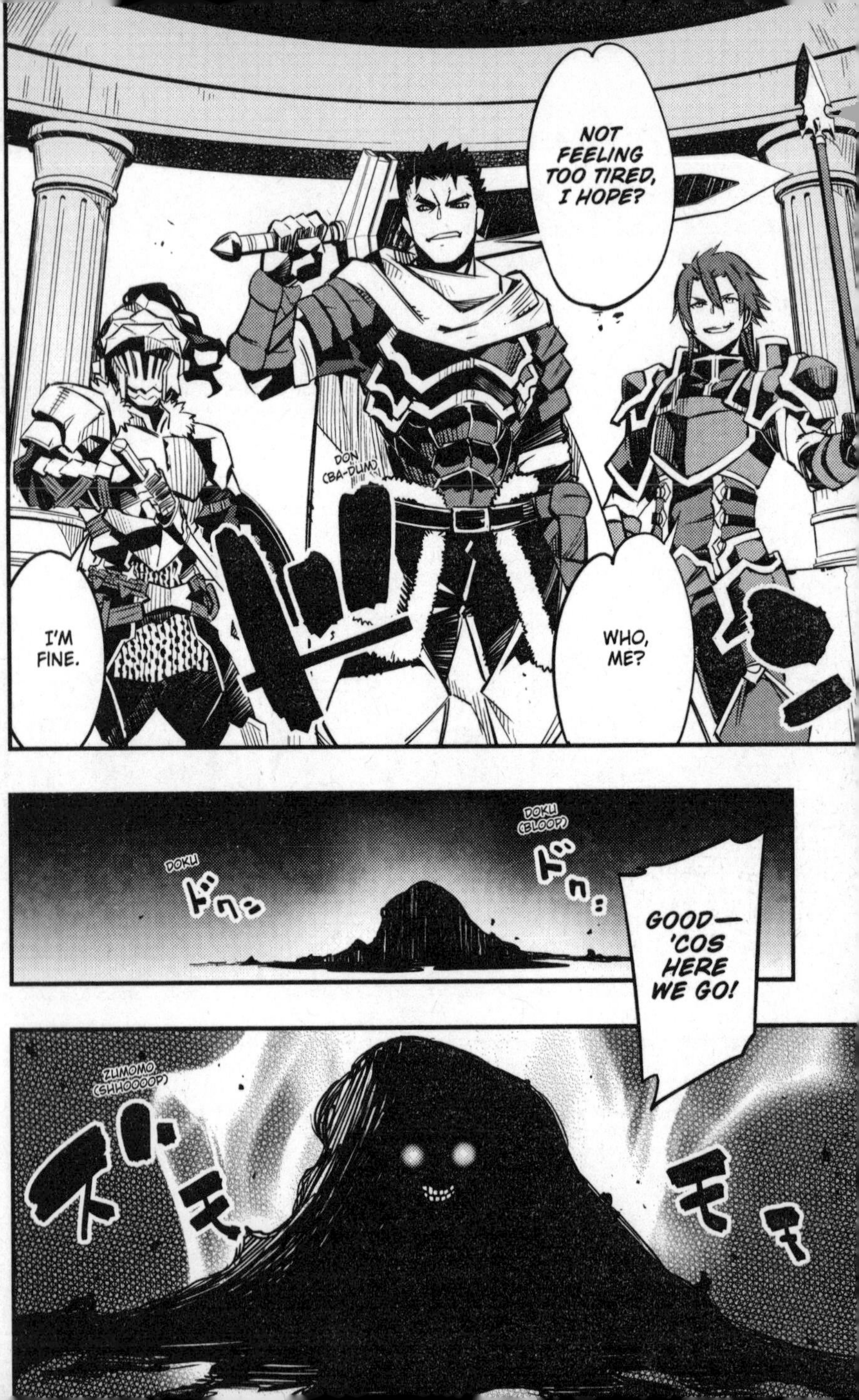
NOT FEELING TOO TIRED, I HOPE?
DON (BA-DUM)
WHO, ME?
I'M FINE.
DOKU (BLOOP)
DOKU
GOOD— 'COS HERE WE GO!
ZUMOMO (SHHOOOOP)

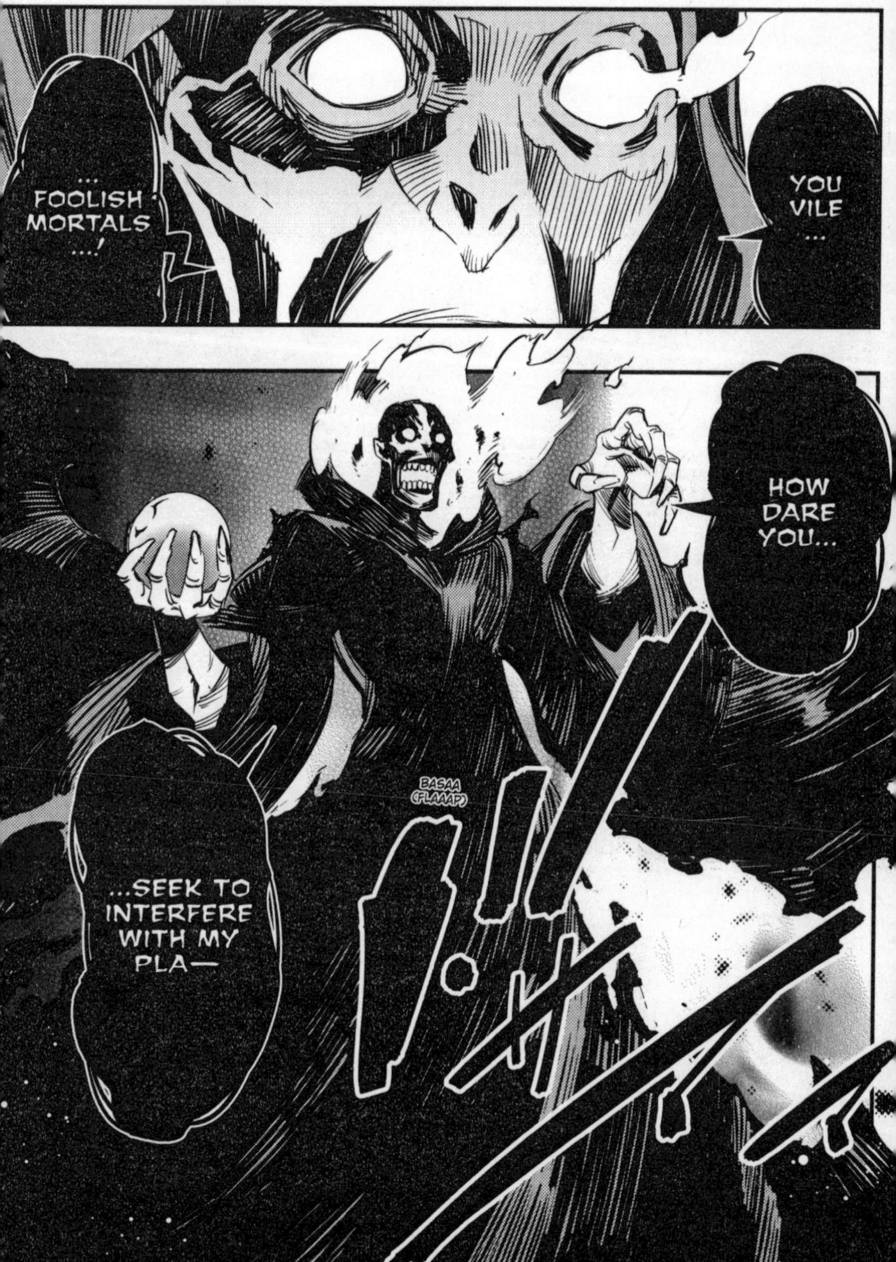
YOU VILE ...
... FOOLISH MORTALS ...!
HOW DARE YOU...
BASAA (FLAAAP)
...SEEK TO INTERFERE WITH MY PLA—

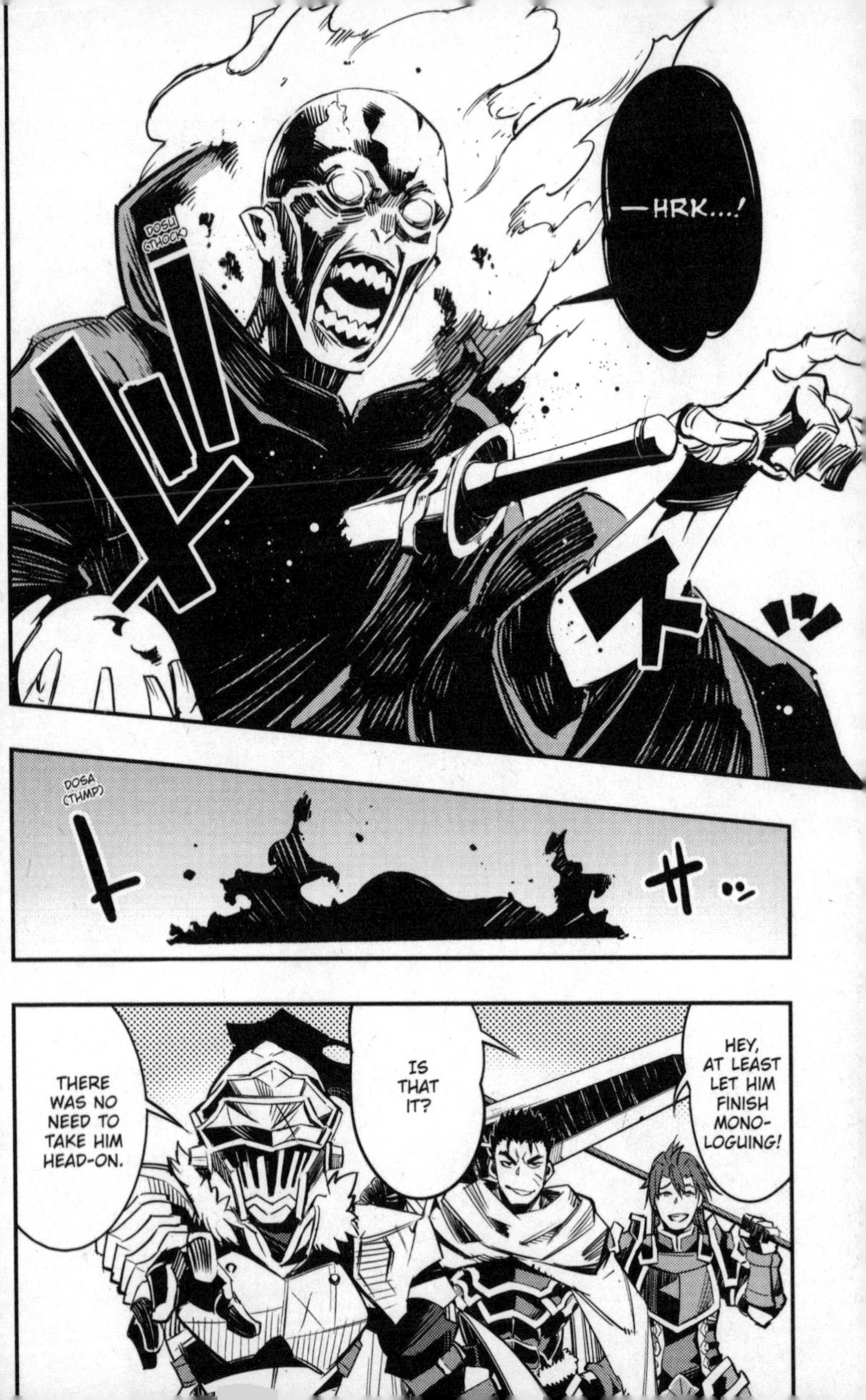
—HRK...!
DOSU (THOCK)
DOSA (THMP)
HEY, AT LEAST LET HIM FINISH MONO-LOGUING!
IS THAT IT?
THERE WAS NO NEED TO TAKE HIM HEAD-ON.

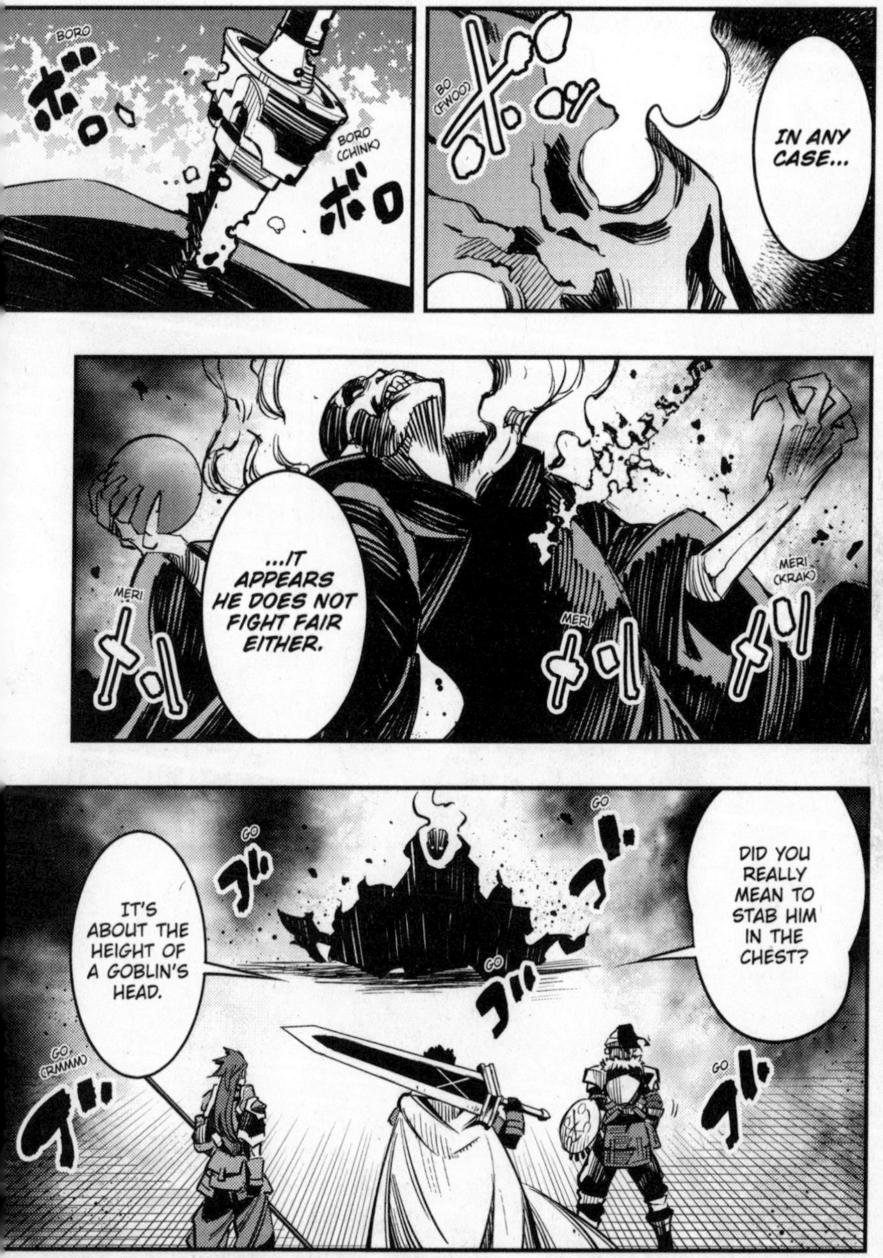
BO (FWOO)
IN ANY CASE...
BORO
BORO (CHINK)
MERI (KRAK)
MERI
...IT APPEARS HE DOES NOT FIGHT FAIR EITHER.
MERI
GO
DID YOU REALLY MEAN TO STAB HIM IN THE CHEST?
GO
GO
GO
IT'S ABOUT THE HEIGHT OF A GOBLIN'S HEAD.
GO (RMMM)

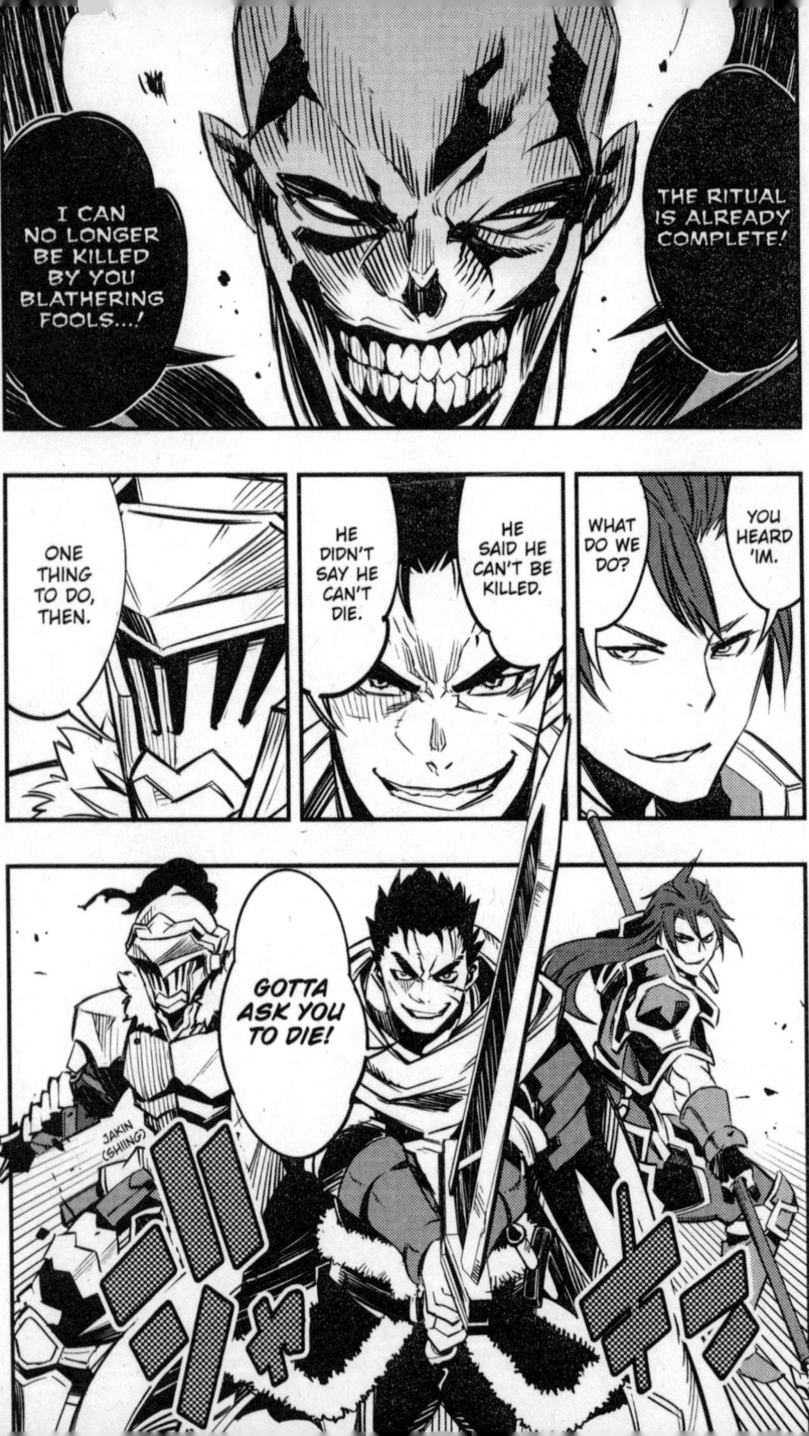
THE RITUAL IS ALREADY COMPLETE!
I CAN NO LONGER BE KILLED BY YOU BLATHERING FOOLS...!
YOU HEARD 'IM.
WHAT DO WE DO?
HE SAID HE CAN'T BE KILLED.
HE DIDN'T SAY HE CAN'T DIE.
ONE THING TO DO, THEN.
GOTTA ASK YOU TO DIE!
JAKIN (SHIING)

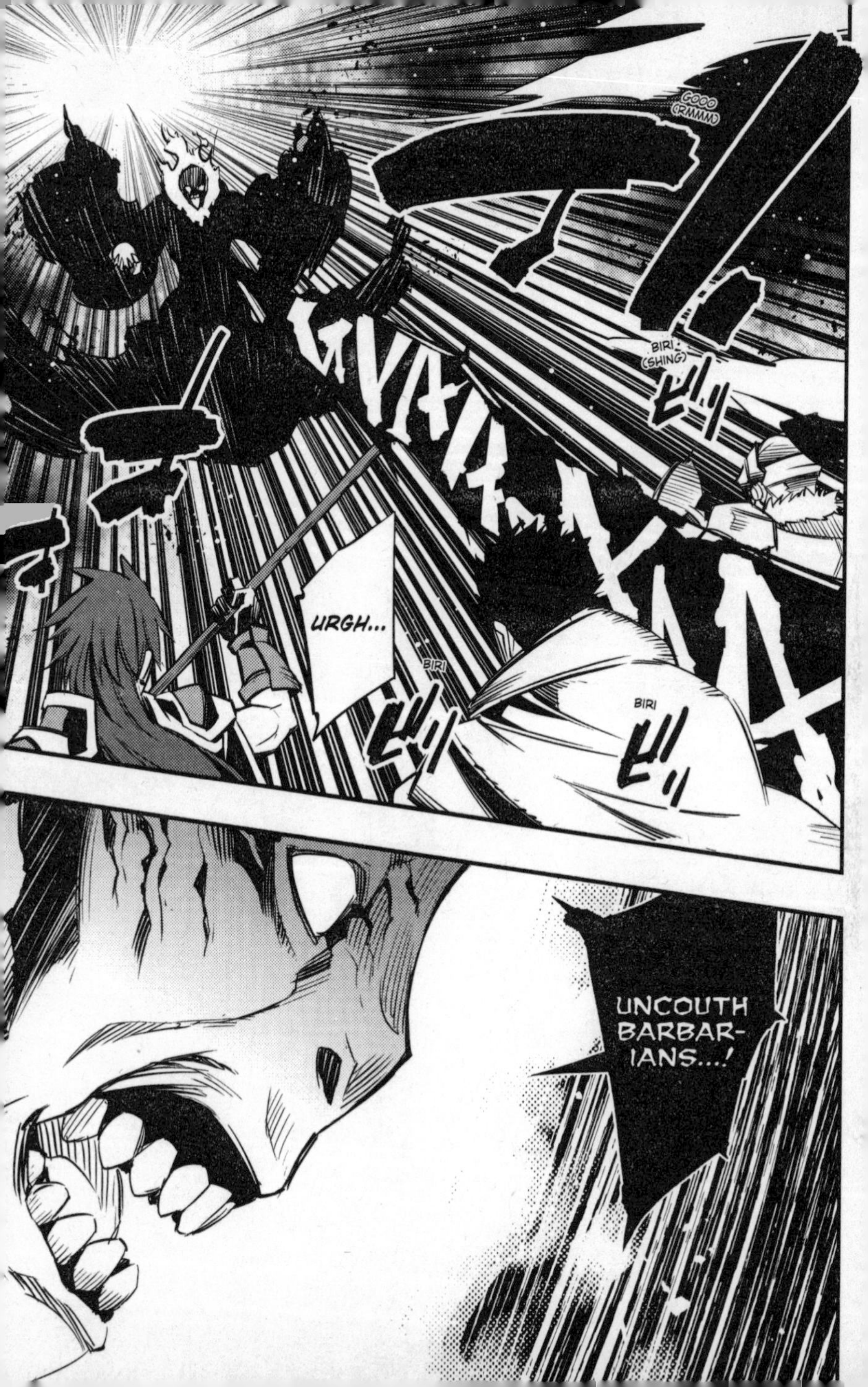
GOOO (RMMM)
BIRI (SHING)
BIRI
URGH...
BIRI
UNCOUTH BARBAR-IANS...!

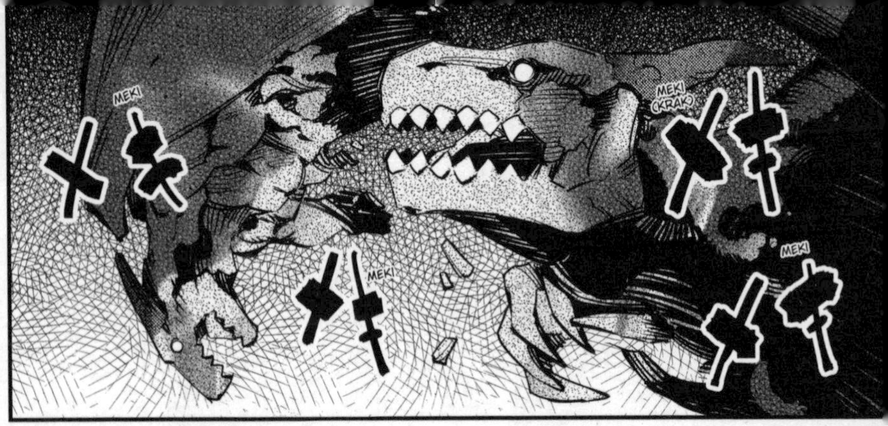
MEKI (KRAK)
MEKI
MEKI
MEKI

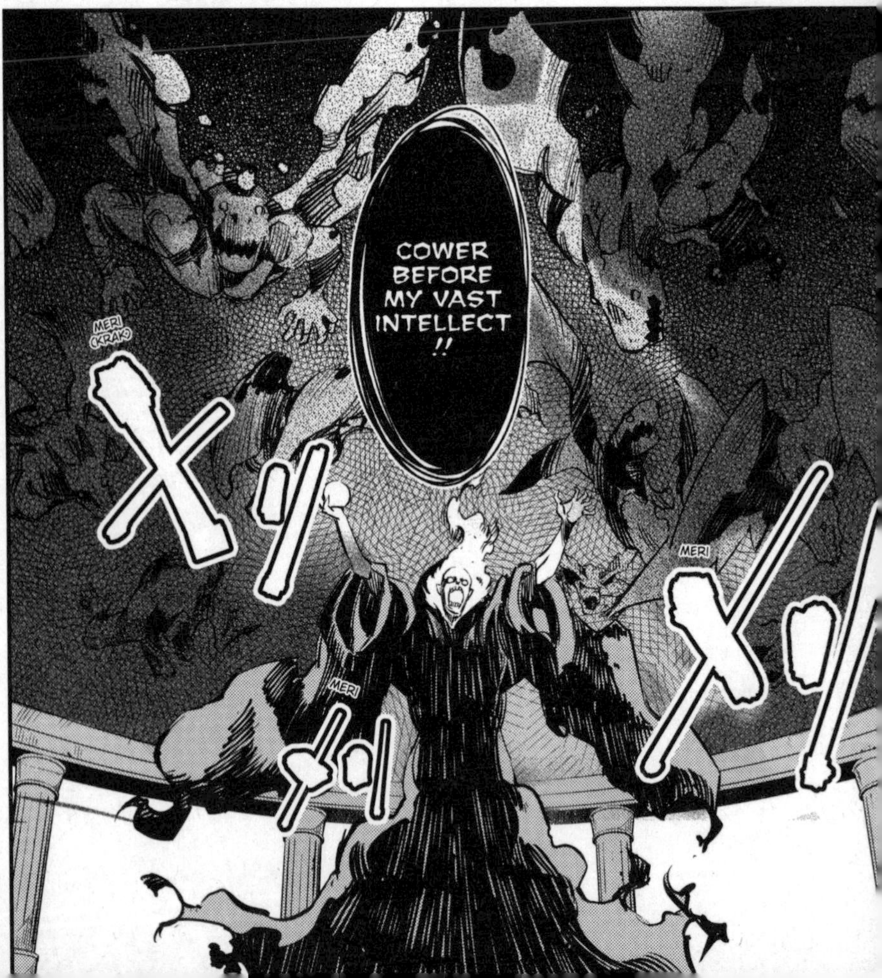
COWER BEFORE MY VAST INTELLECT!!
MERI (KRAK)
MERI
MERI

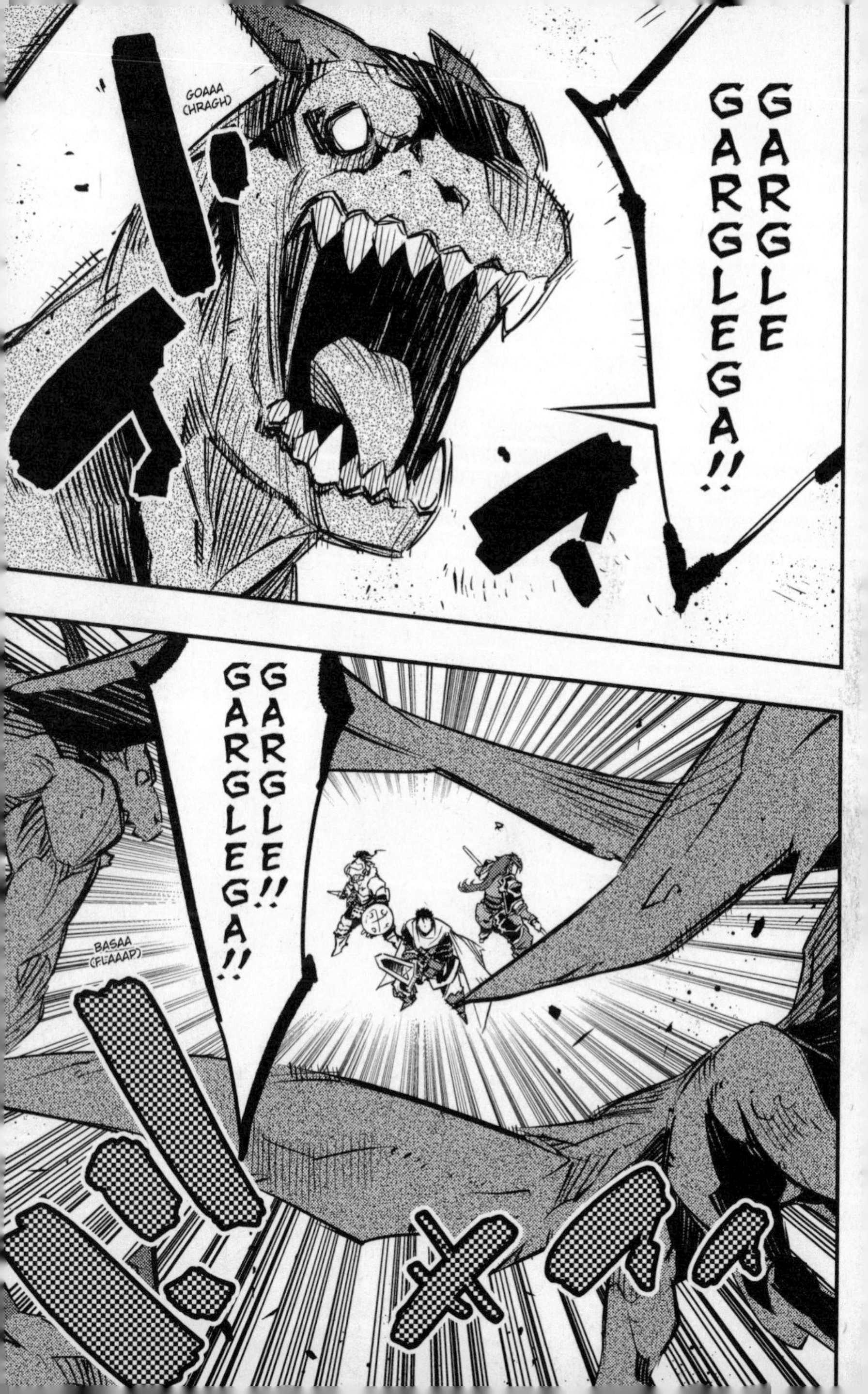
GARGLE GARGLEGA!!
GOAAA (HRAGH)
GARGLE!! GARGLEGA!!
BASAA (FLAAAP)

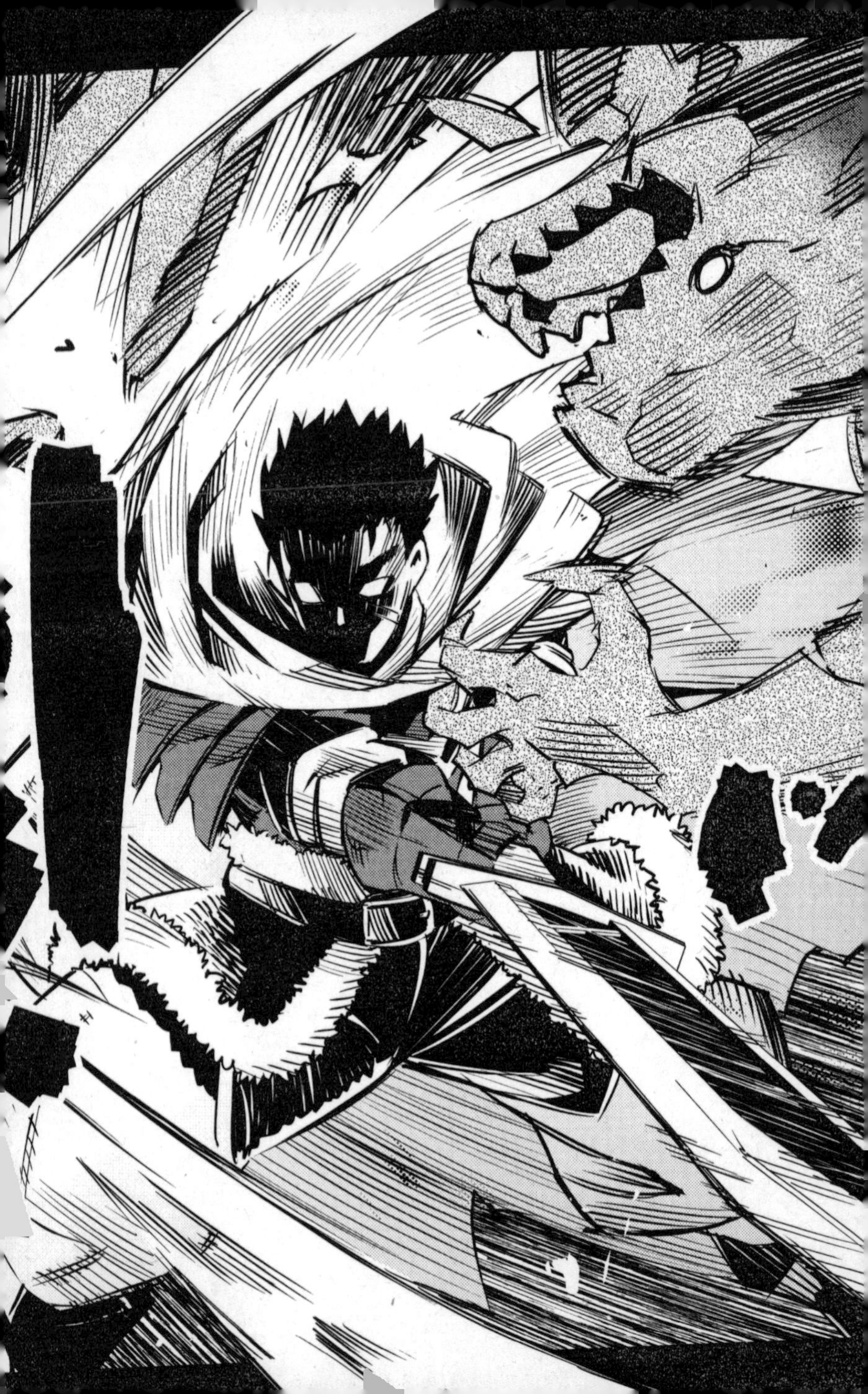

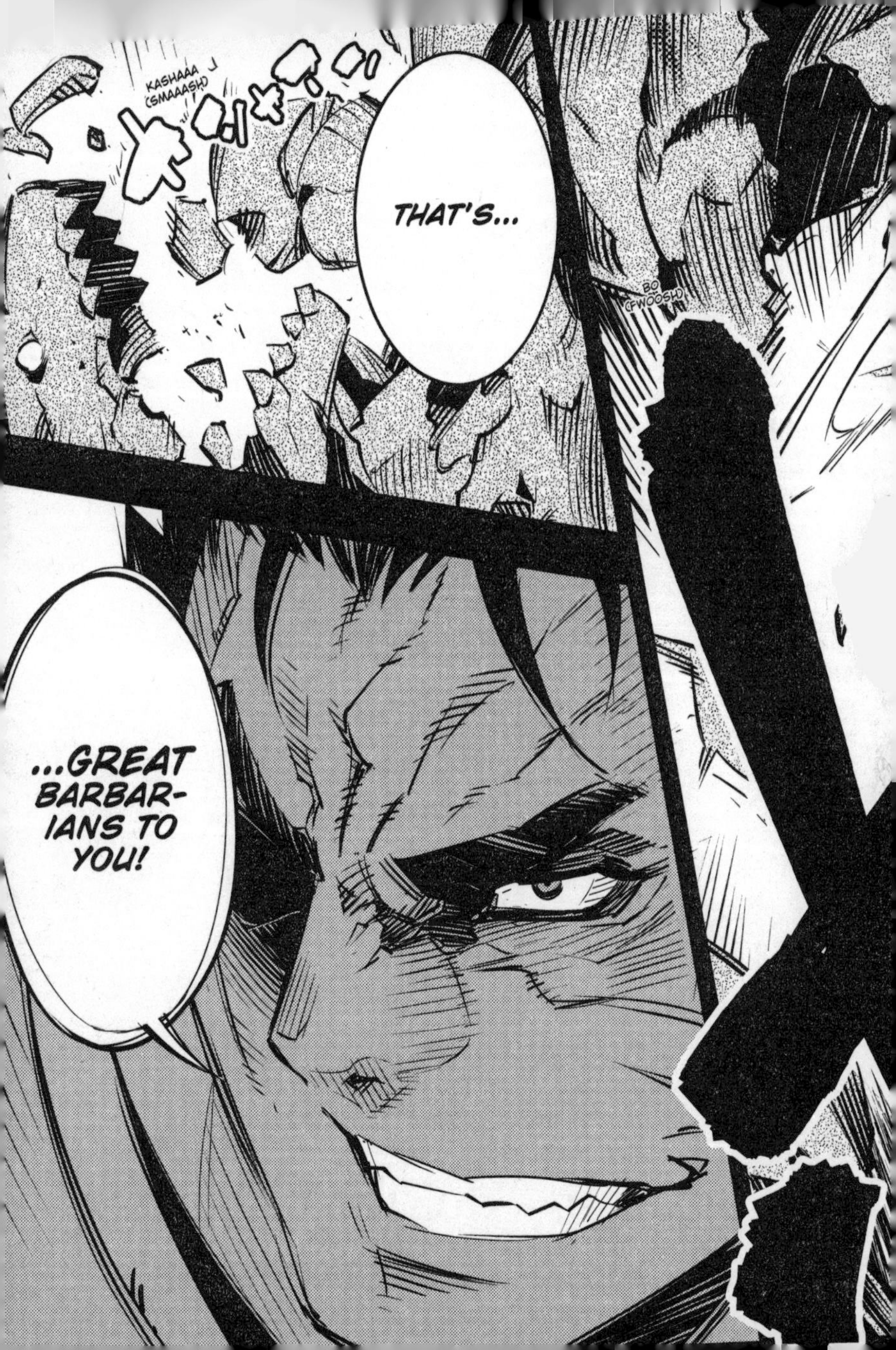
BO (FWOOSH)
KASHAAA (SMAAASH)
THAT'S...
...GREAT BARBARIANS TO YOU!

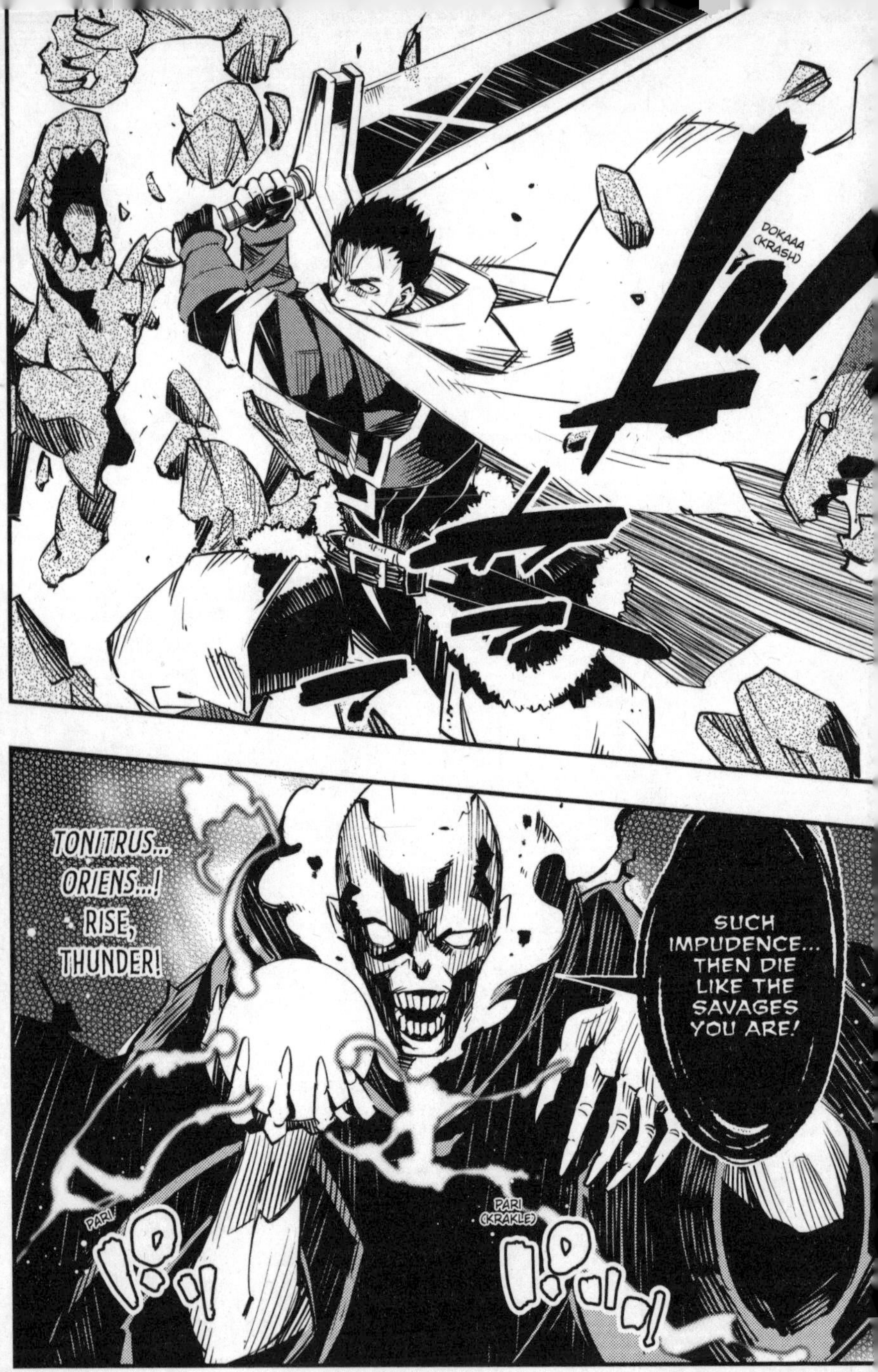
DOKAAA (KRASH)
SUCH IMPUDENCE... THEN DIE LIKE THE SAVAGES YOU ARE!
TONITRUS... ORIENS...! RISE, THUNDER!
PARI (KRAKLE)
PARI

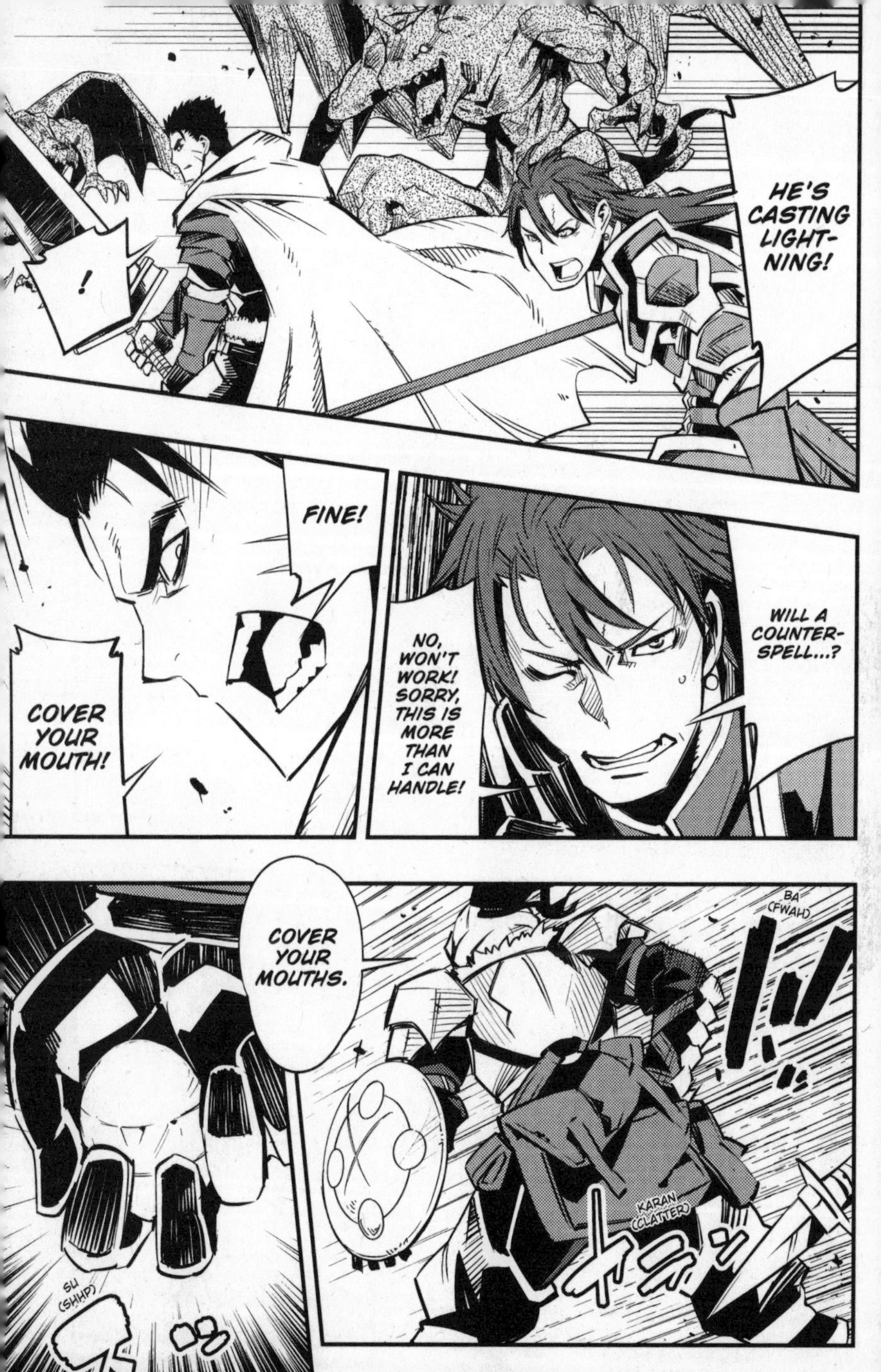
HE'S CASTING LIGHT-NING!
!
WILL A COUNTER-SPELL...?
NO, WON'T WORK! SORRY, THIS IS MORE THAN I CAN HANDLE!
FINE!
COVER YOUR MOUTH!
BA (FWAH)
!!
KARAN (CLATTER)
COVER YOUR MOUTHS.
SU (SHHP)

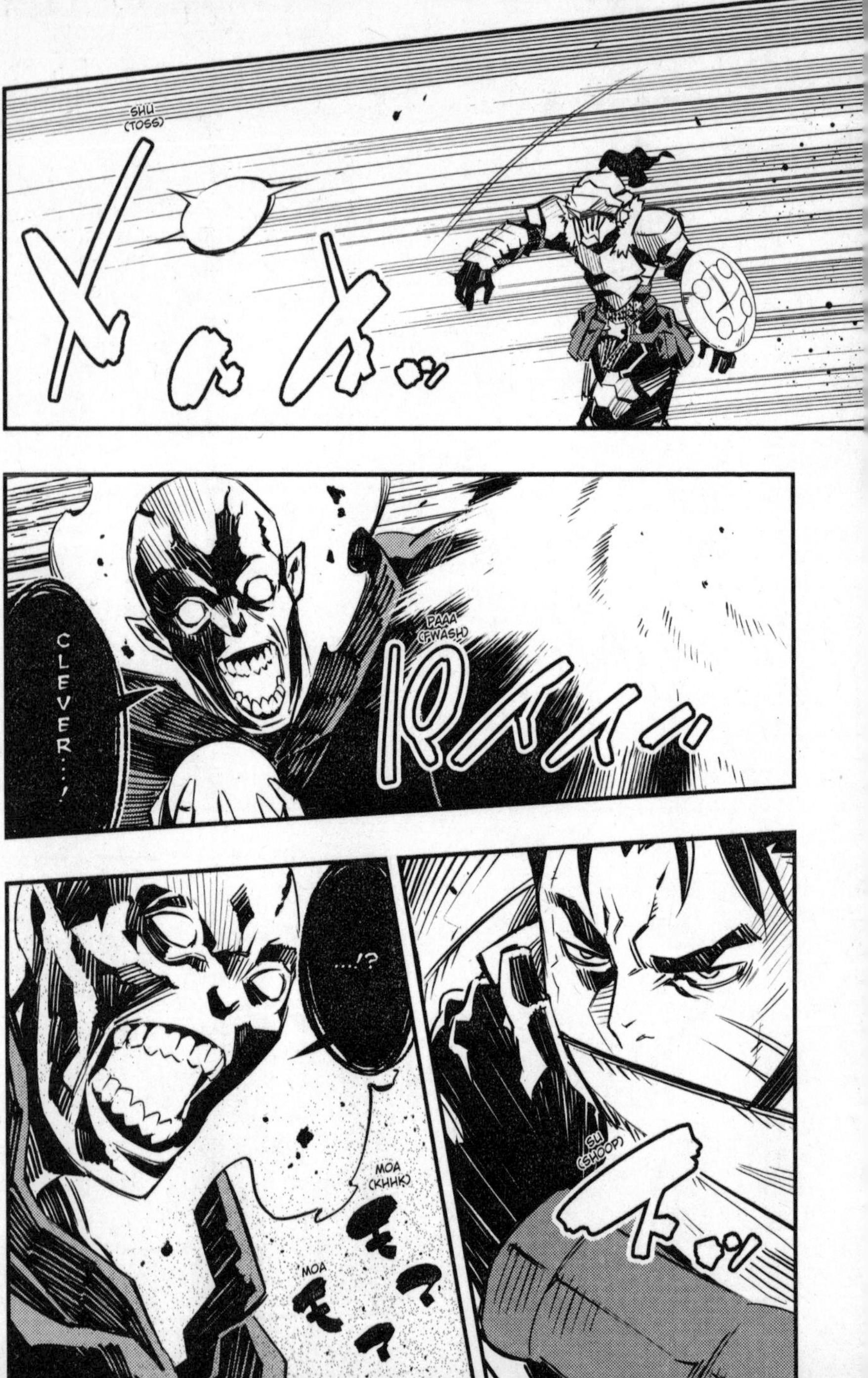
SHU (TOSS)
PAAA (FWASH)
CLEVER...!
SU (SHOOP)
...!?
MOA (KHHK)
MOA

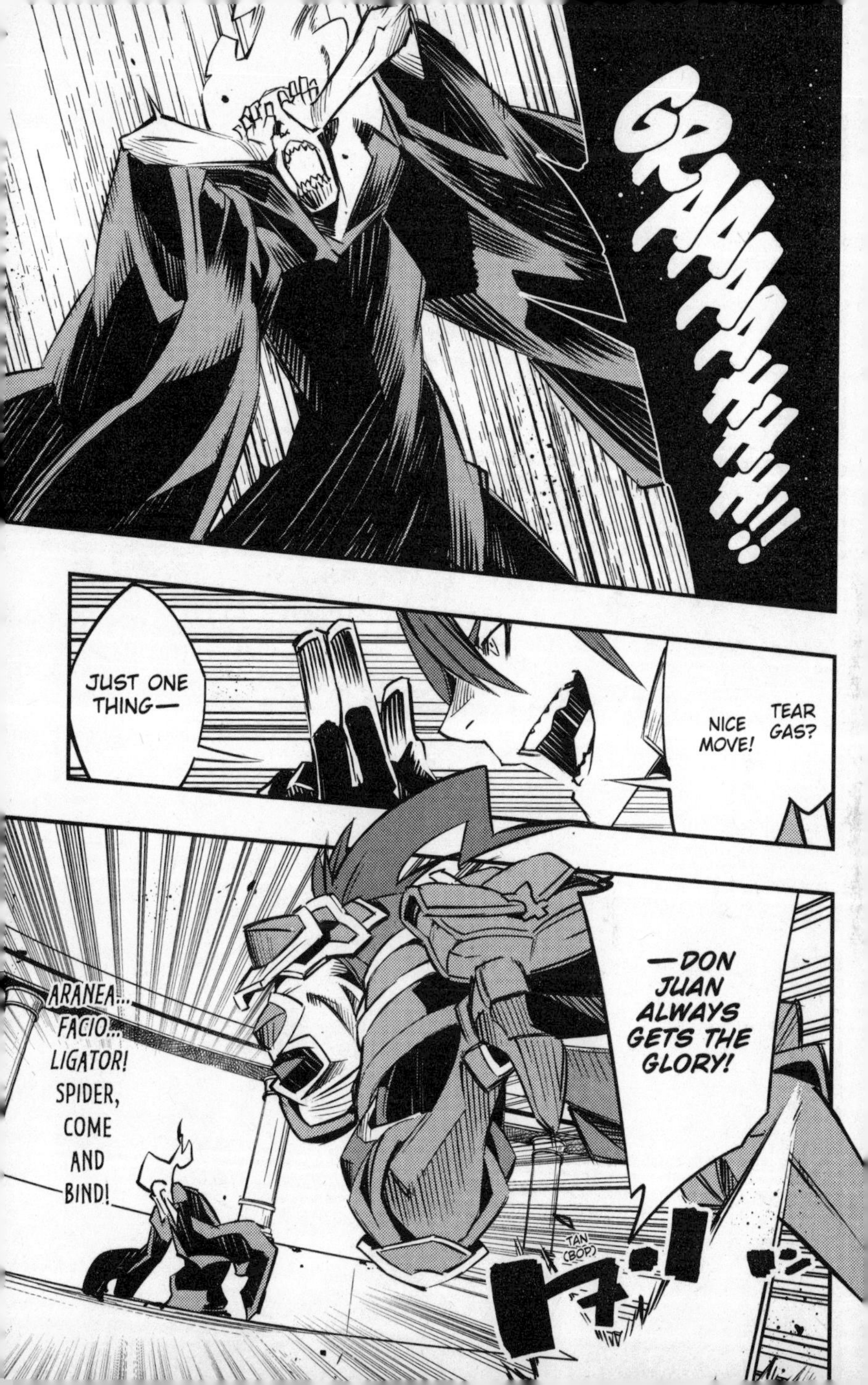
GRAAAHHH!!!
TEAR GAS?
NICE MOVE!
JUST ONE THING—
—DON JUAN ALWAYS GETS THE GLORY!
TAN (BOP)
ARANEA... FACIO... LIGATOR! SPIDER, COME AND BIND!

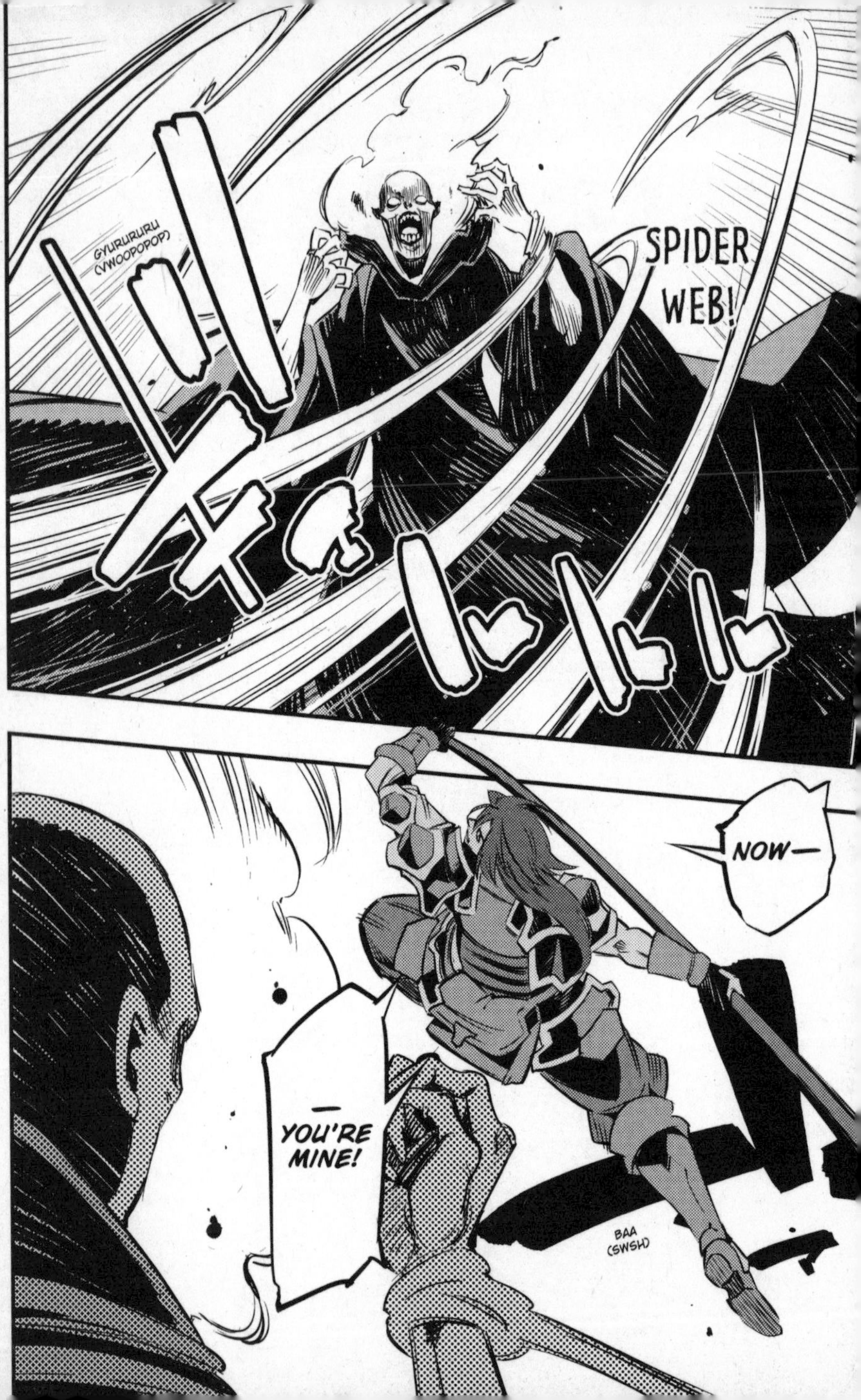
SPIDER WEB!
GYURURURU (VWOOPOPOP)
NOW—
—YOU'RE MINE!
BAA (SWSH)

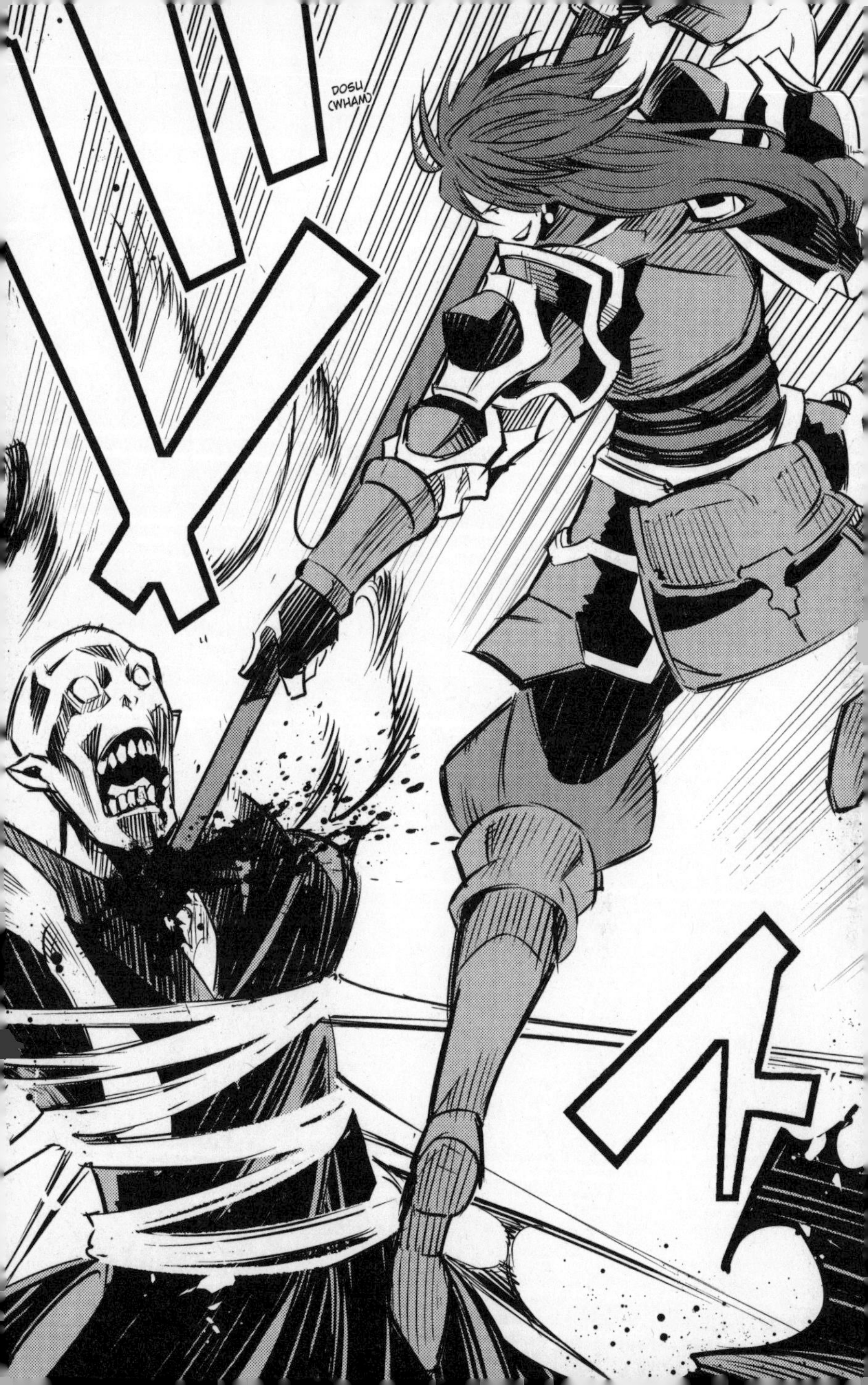
DOSU
(WHAM)

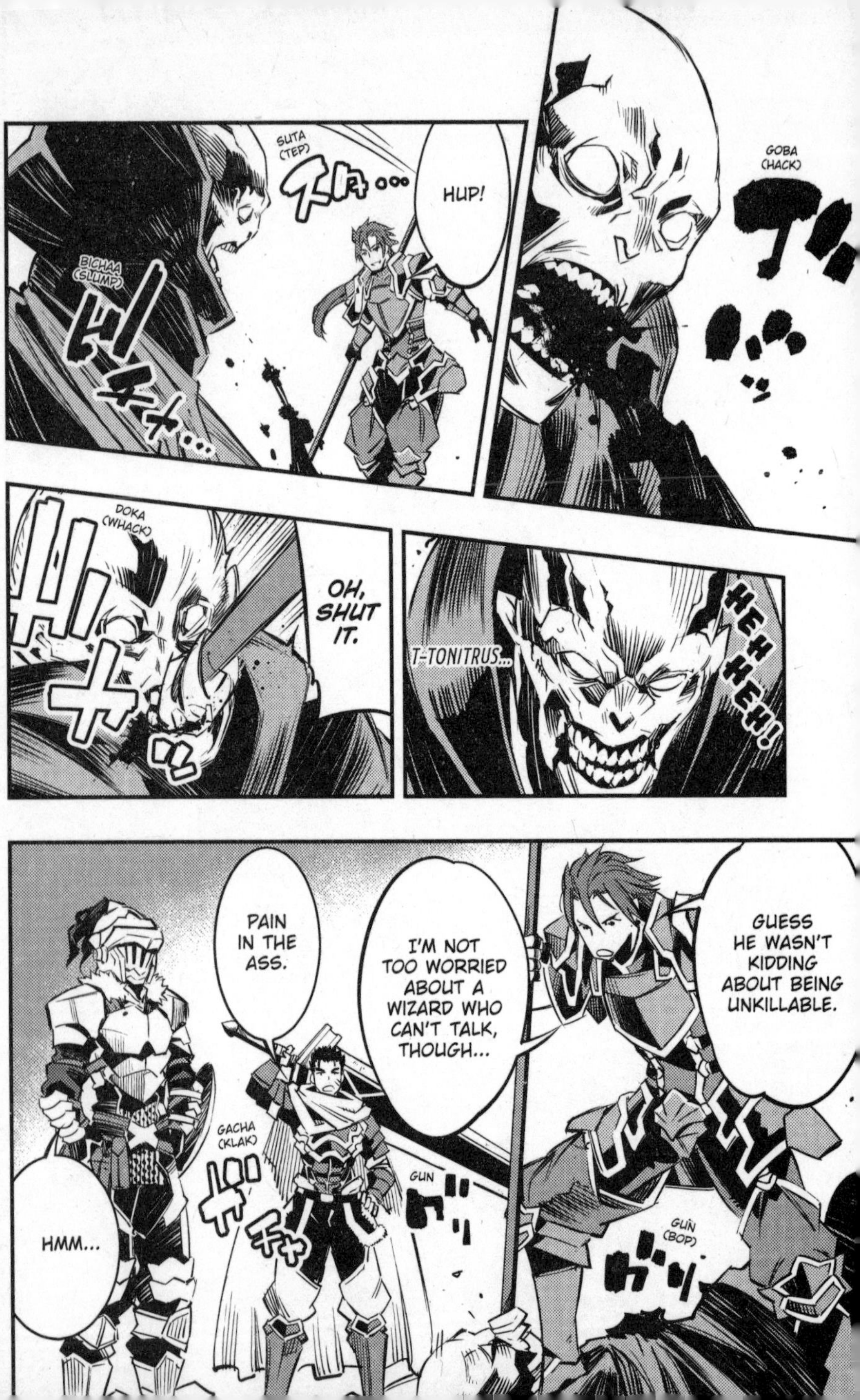
GOBA (HACK)
HUP!
SUTA (TEP)
BICHAA (SLUMP)
HEH HEH HEH!
T-TONITRUS...
OH, SHUT IT.
DOKA (WHACK)
GUESS HE WASN'T KIDDING ABOUT BEING UNKILLABLE.
I'M NOT TOO WORRIED ABOUT A WIZARD WHO CAN'T TALK, THOUGH...
PAIN IN THE ASS.
GUN (BOP)
GUN
GACHA (KLAK)
HMM...

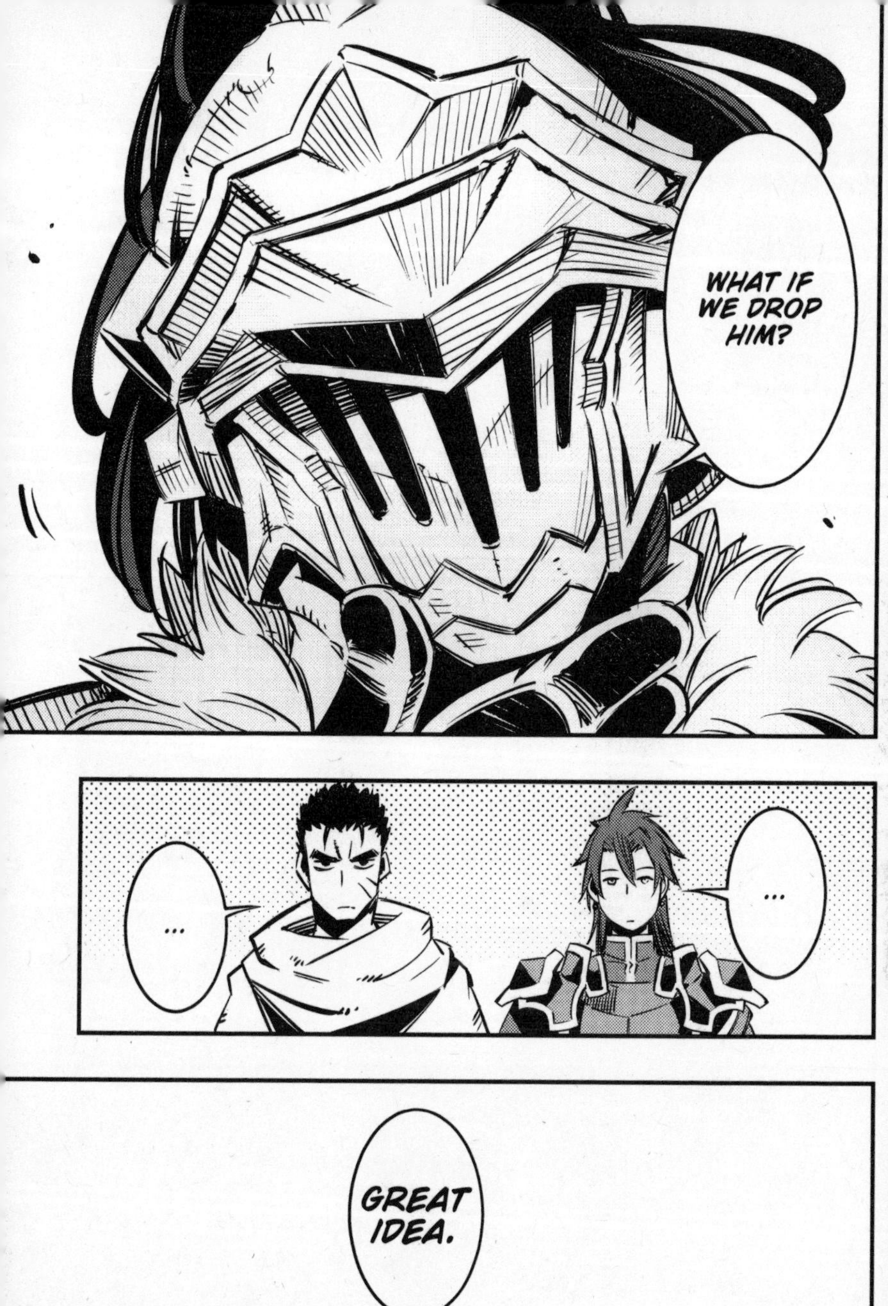
WHAT IF WE DROP HIM?
...
...
GREAT IDEA.

DOKA
(BONK)

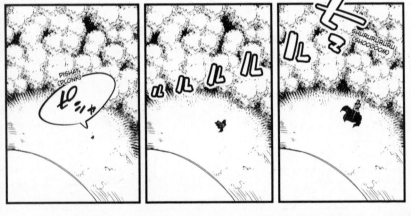

PISHA
(PLONK)

SHURURURURU
(SHOOOOOM)

HUH.
DEAD AS A
DOORNAIL.

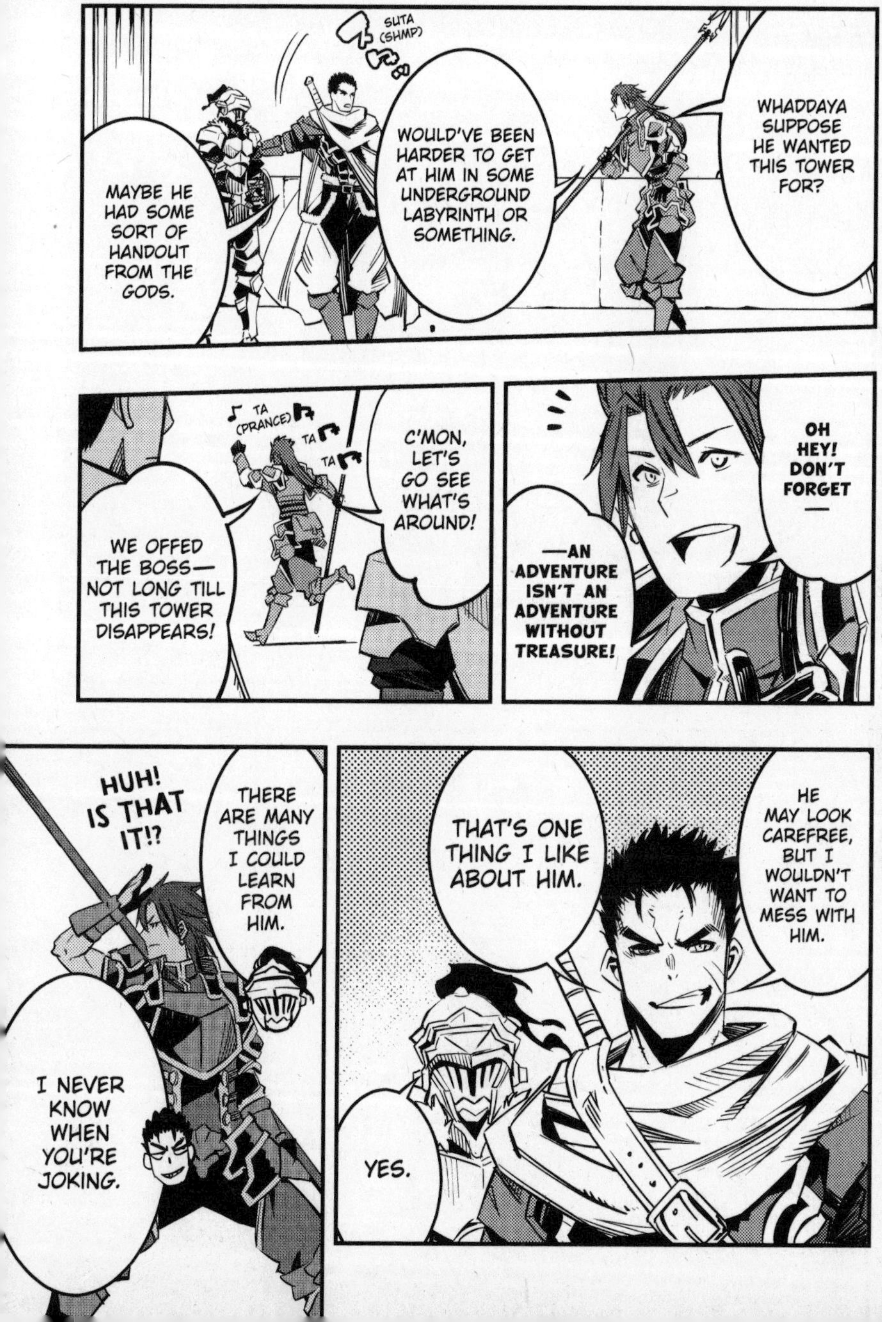
WHADDAYA SUPPOSE HE WANTED THIS TOWER FOR?
SUTA (SHMP)
WOULD'VE BEEN HARDER TO GET AT HIM IN SOME UNDERGROUND LABYRINTH OR SOMETHING.
MAYBE HE HAD SOME SORT OF HANDOUT FROM THE GODS.
OH HEY! DON'T FORGET—
—AN ADVENTURE ISN'T AN ADVENTURE WITHOUT TREASURE!
C'MON, LET'S GO SEE WHAT'S AROUND!
TA (PRANCE)
TA
TA
WE OFFED THE BOSS— NOT LONG TILL THIS TOWER DISAPPEARS!
HE MAY LOOK CAREFREE, BUT I WOULDN'T WANT TO MESS WITH HIM.
THAT'S ONE THING I LIKE ABOUT HIM.
YES.
THERE ARE MANY THINGS I COULD LEARN FROM HIM.
HUH! IS THAT IT!?
I NEVER KNOW WHEN YOU'RE JOKING.

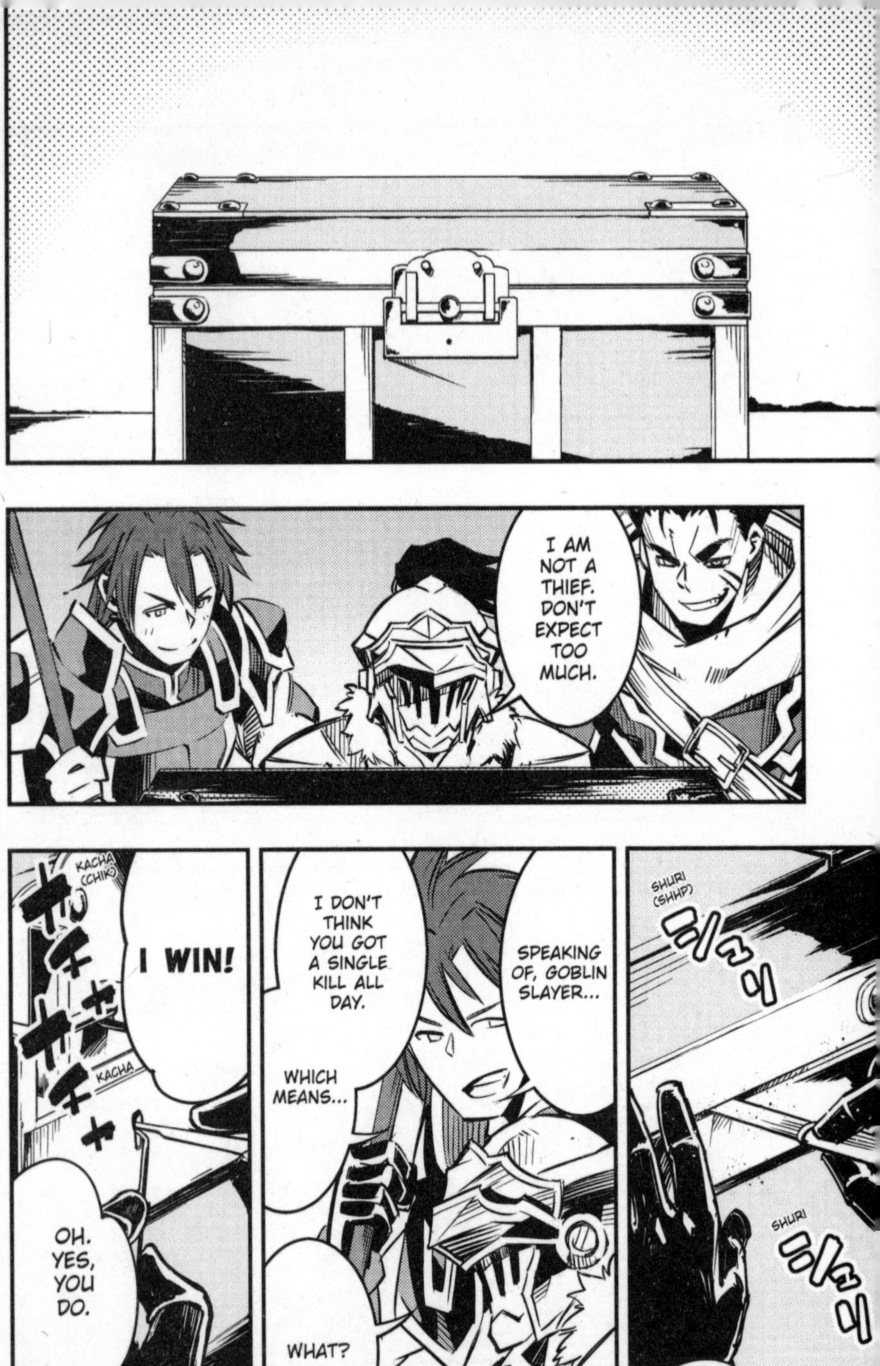
I AM NOT A THIEF. DON'T EXPECT TOO MUCH.
SHURI (SHHP)
SHURI
SPEAKING OF, GOBLIN SLAYER...
I DON'T THINK YOU GOT A SINGLE KILL ALL DAY.
WHICH MEANS...
WHAT?
KACHA (CHIK)
I WIN!
KACHA
OH. YES, YOU DO.

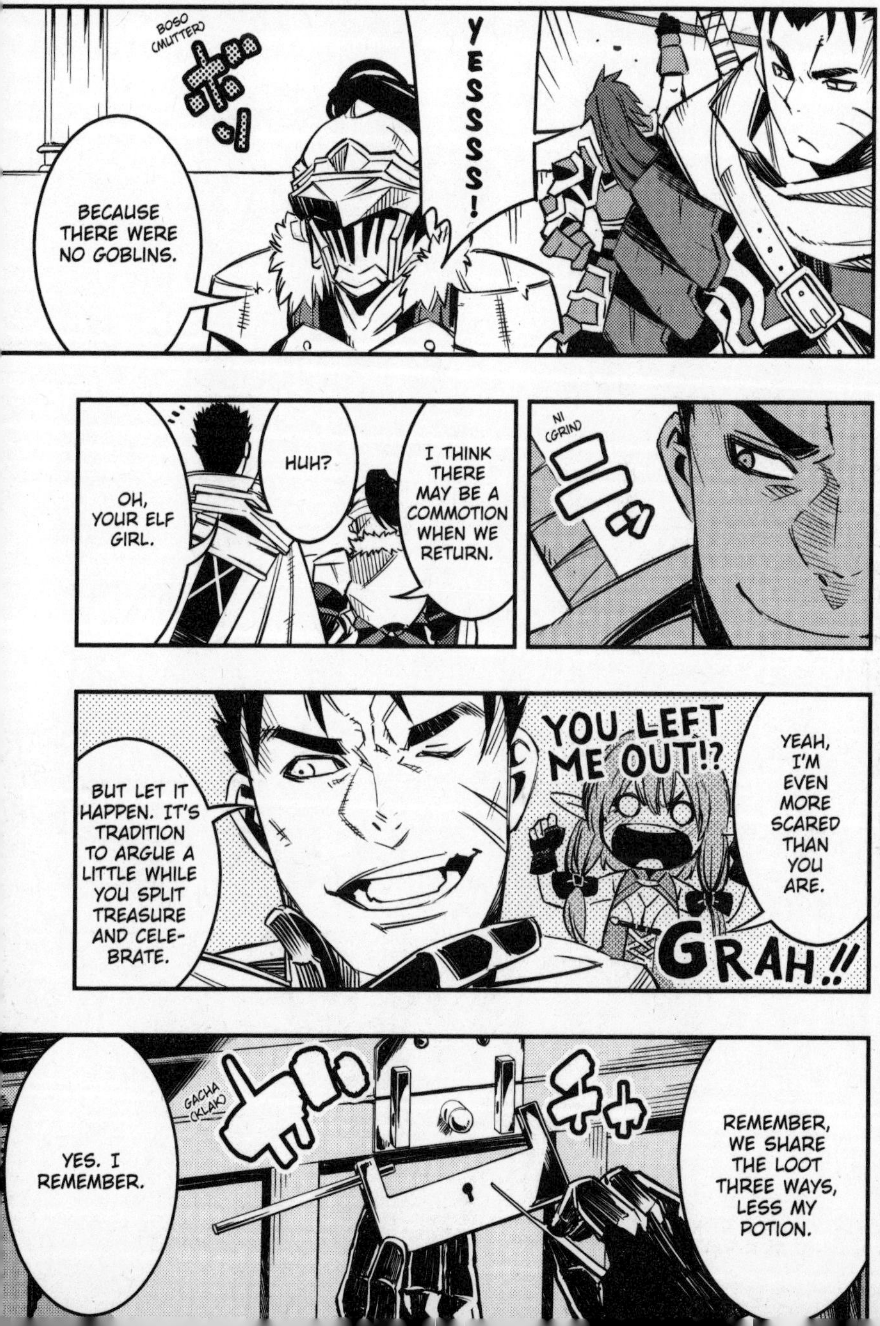
YESSSS!
BOSO (MUTTER)
BECAUSE THERE WERE NO GOBLINS.
NI (GRIND)
I THINK THERE MAY BE A COMMOTION WHEN WE RETURN.
HUH?
...
OH, YOUR ELF GIRL.
YEAH, I'M EVEN MORE SCARED THAN YOU ARE.
YOU LEFT ME OUT!?
GRAH!!
BUT LET IT HAPPEN. IT'S TRADITION TO ARGUE A LITTLE WHILE YOU SPLIT TREASURE AND CELE-BRATE.
REMEMBER, WE SHARE THE LOOT THREE WAYS, LESS MY POTION.
GACHA (KLAK)
YES. I REMEMBER.

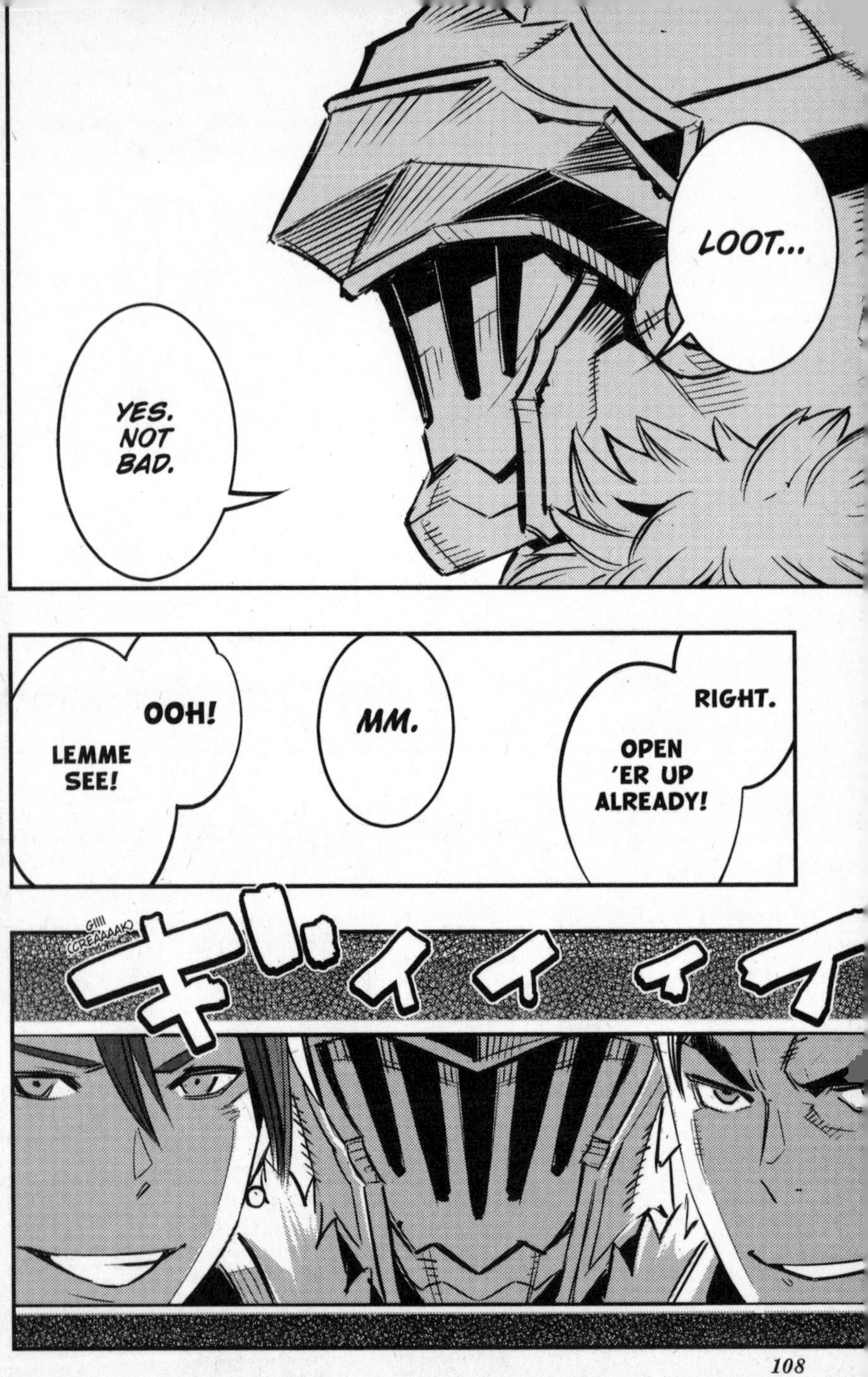
LOOT...
YES. NOT BAD.
RIGHT. OPEN 'ER UP ALREADY!
MM.
OOH! LEMME SEE!
GIIII (CREAAAAK)

Chapter 7:
Of the Second Time the Necromancer's Plans Were Upset

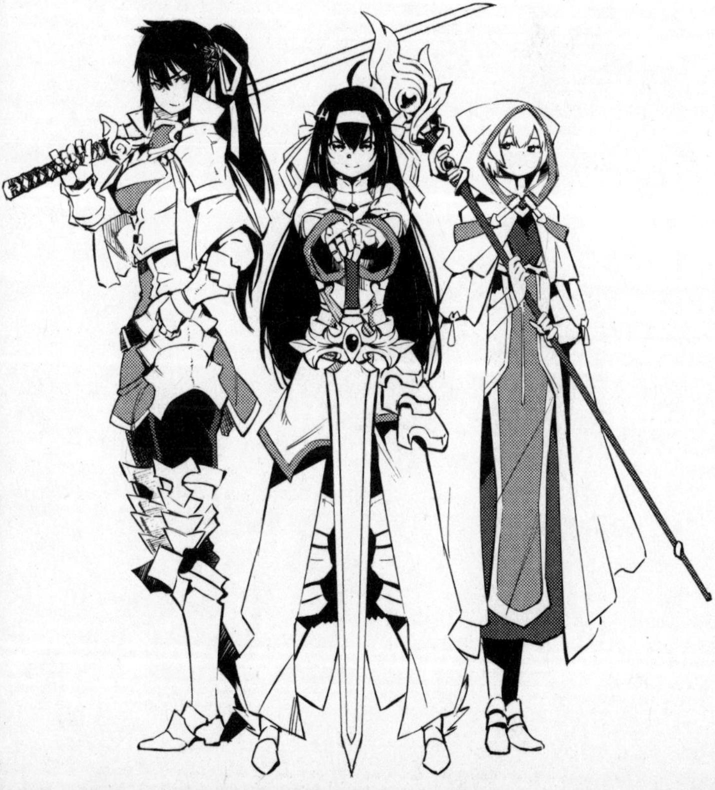

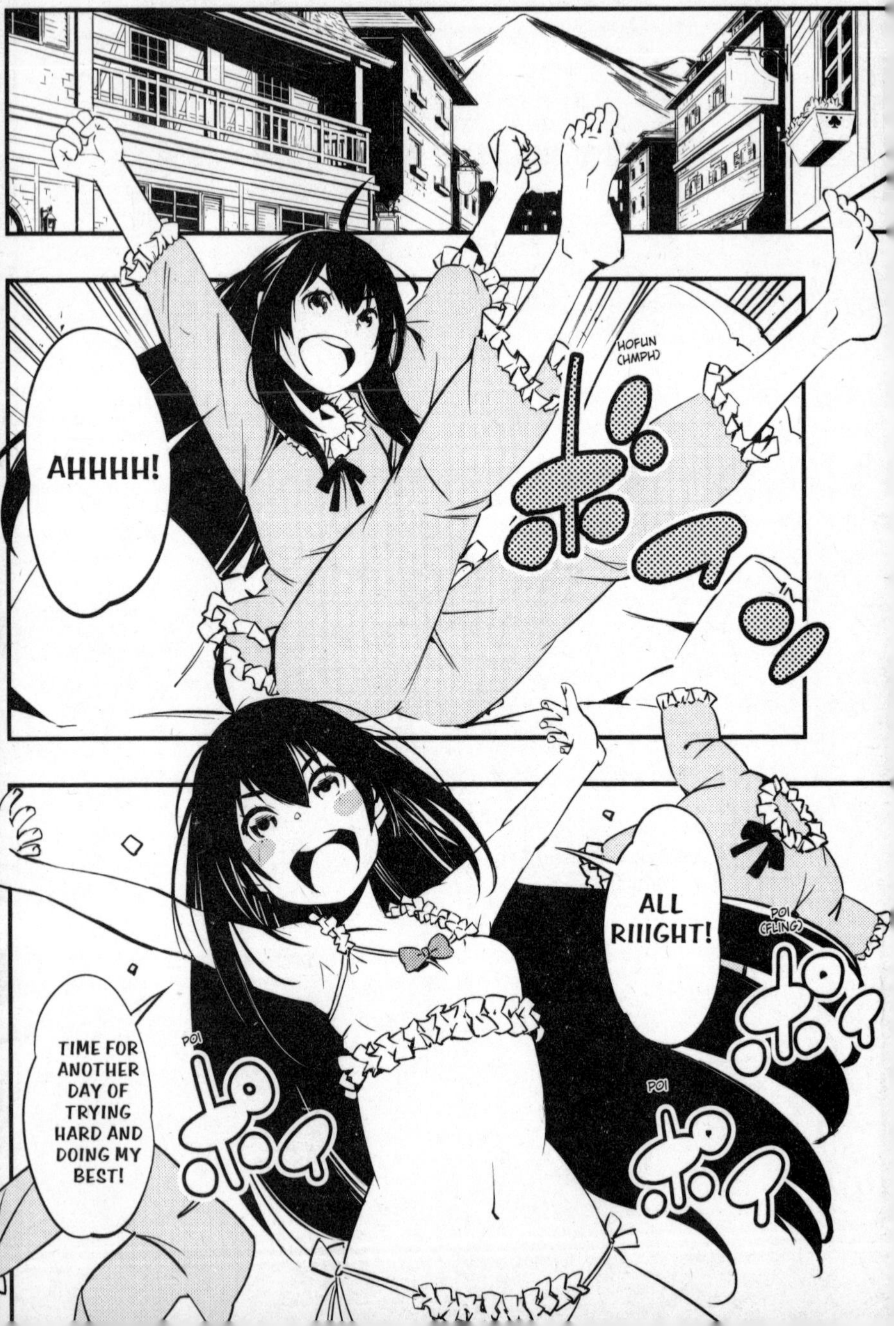
HOFUN (HMPH)
AHHHH!
ALL RIIIGHT!
POI (FLING)
POI
TIME FOR ANOTHER DAY OF TRYING HARD AND DOING MY BEST!
POI

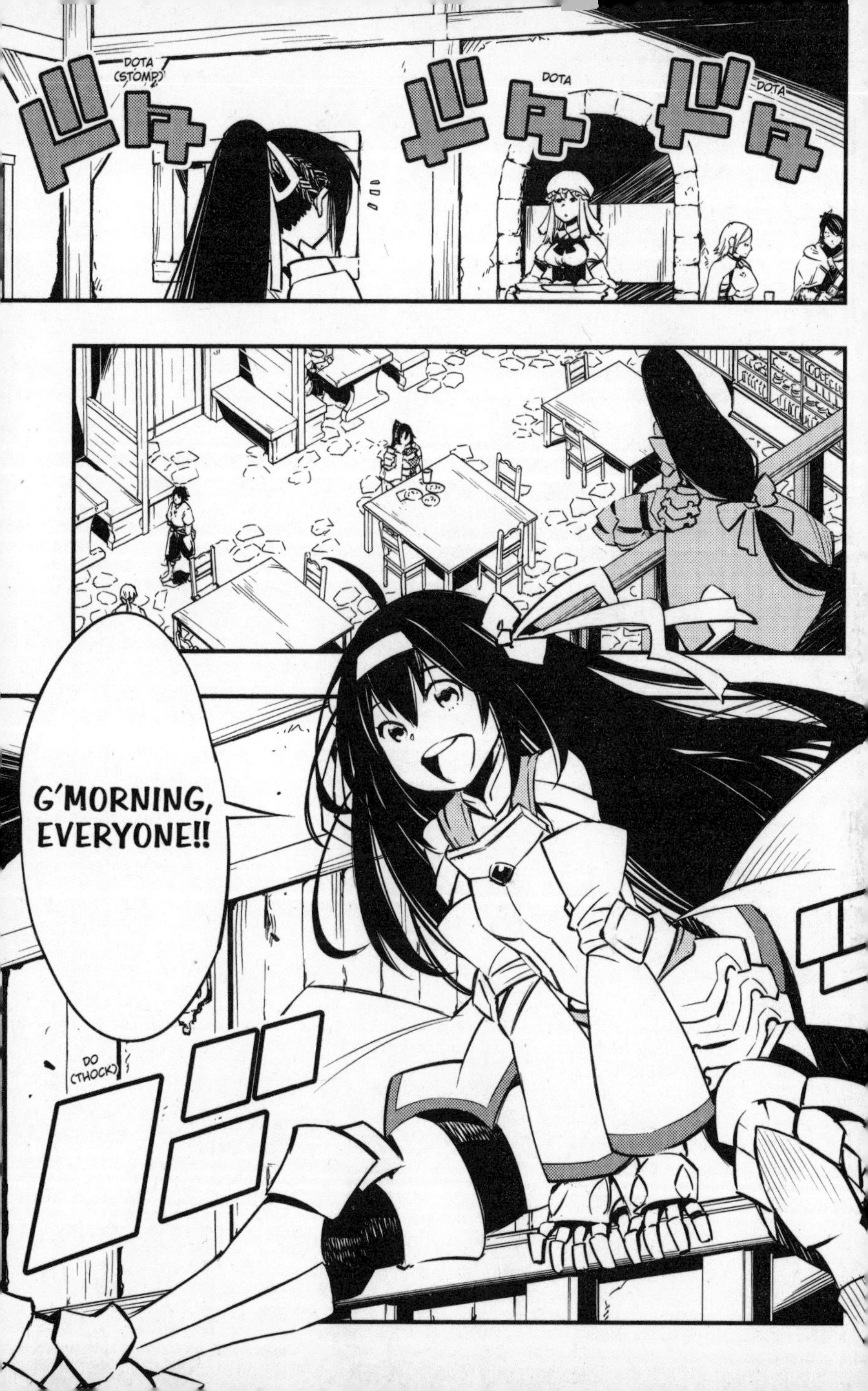
DOTA
DOTA
DOTA (STOMP)
G'MORNING, EVERYONE!!
DO (THOCK)

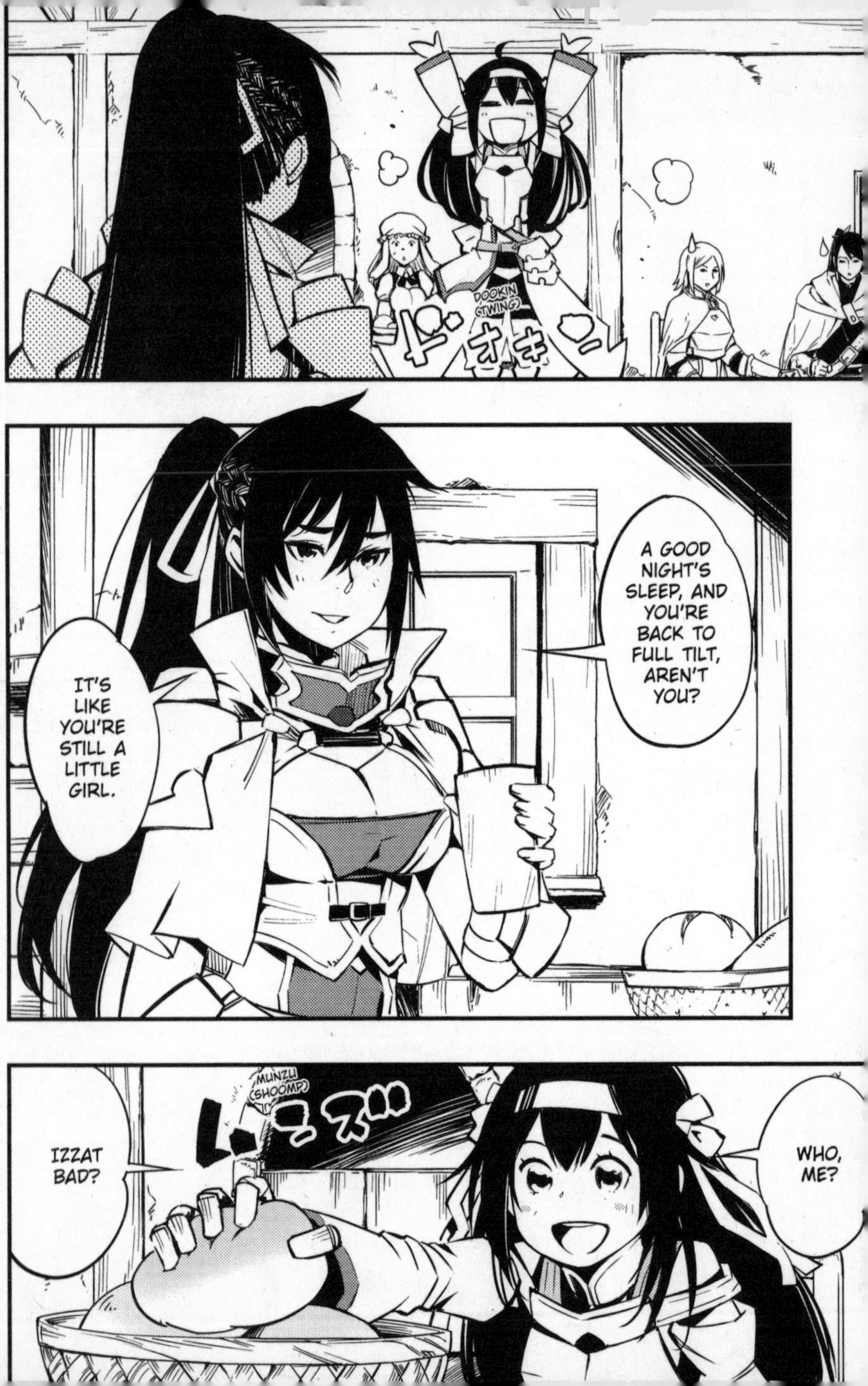
DOOKIN (TWING)
A GOOD NIGHT'S SLEEP, AND YOU'RE BACK TO FULL TILT, AREN'T YOU?
IT'S LIKE YOU'RE STILL A LITTLE GIRL.
WHO, ME?
MUNZU (SHOOMP)
IZZAT BAD?

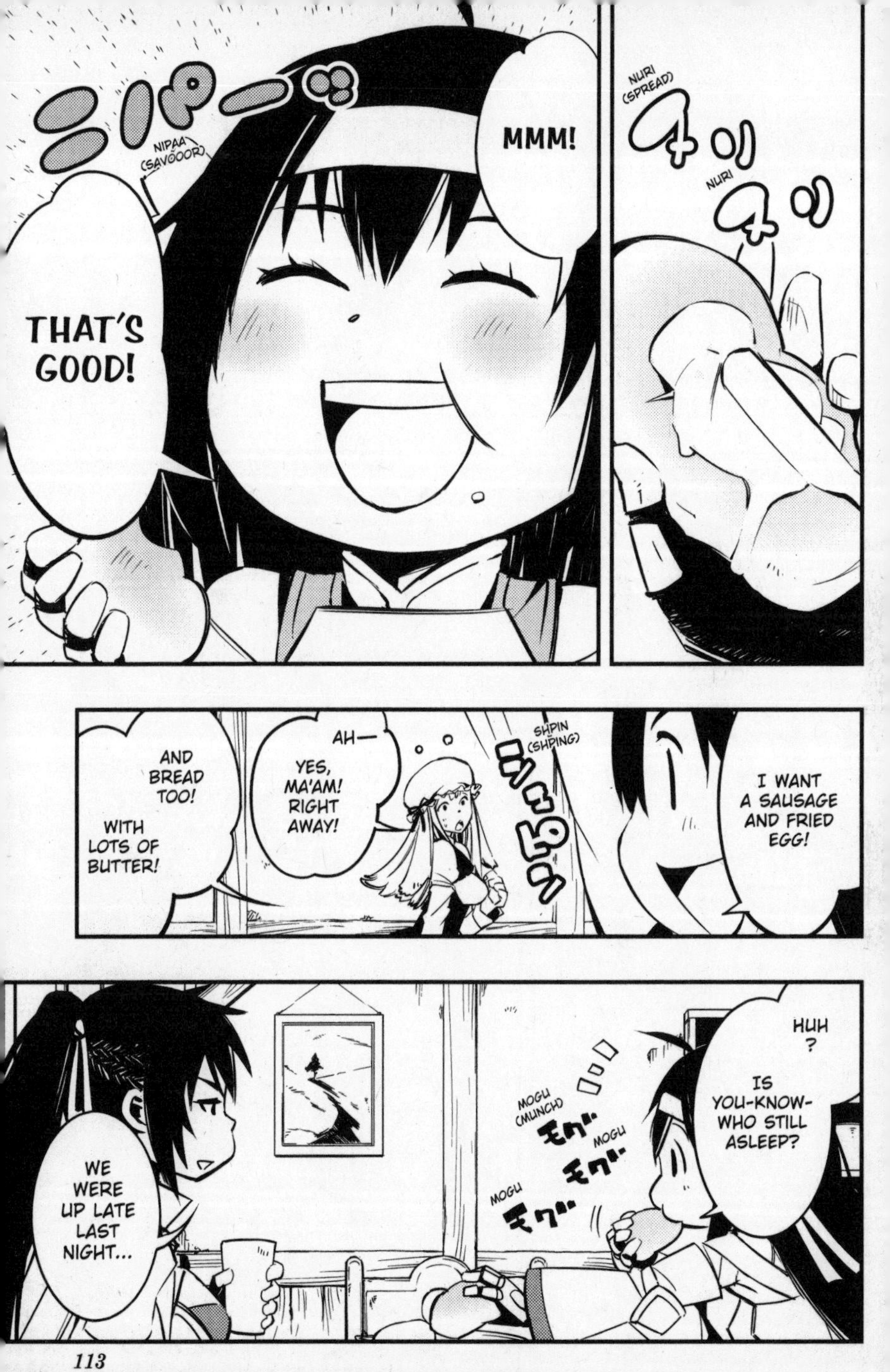
NURI (SPREAD)
NURI
MMM!
NIPAA (SAVOOOR)
THAT'S GOOD!
I WANT A SAUSAGE AND FRIED EGG!
SHPIN (SHPING)
AH—
YES, MA'AM! RIGHT AWAY!
AND BREAD TOO!
WITH LOTS OF BUTTER!
HUH?
IS YOU-KNOW-WHO STILL ASLEEP?
MOGU (MUNCH)
MOGU
MOGU
WE WERE UP LATE LAST NIGHT...

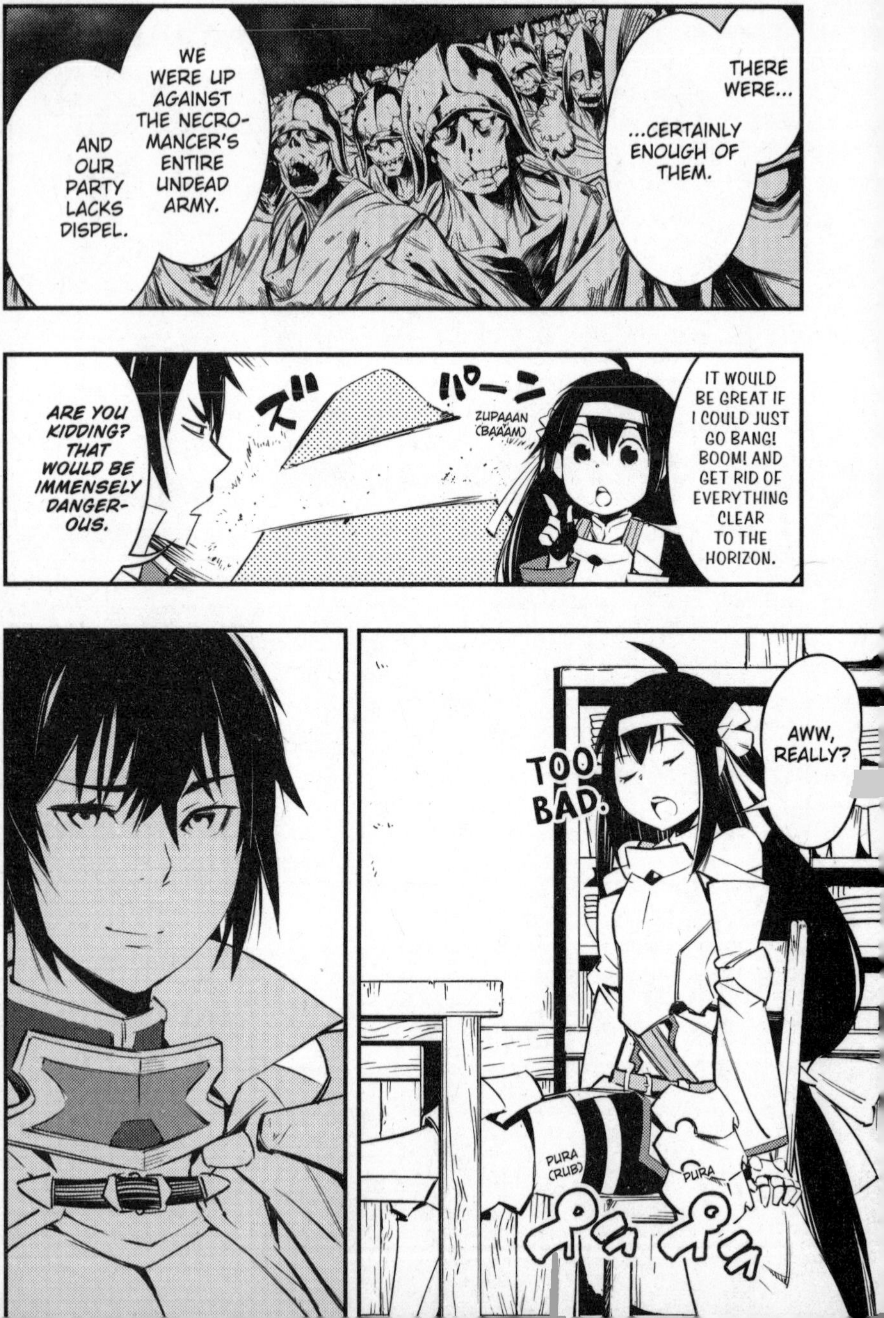
THERE WERE...
...CERTAINLY ENOUGH OF THEM.
WE WERE UP AGAINST THE NECROMANCER'S ENTIRE UNDEAD ARMY.
AND OUR PARTY LACKS DISPEL.
IT WOULD BE GREAT IF I COULD JUST GO BANG! BOOM! AND GET RID OF EVERYTHING CLEAR TO THE HORIZON.
ズパーン
ZUPAAAN (BAAAM)
ARE YOU KIDDING? THAT WOULD BE IMMENSELY DANGER-OUS.
AWW, REALLY?
TOO BAD.
PURA (RUB)
PURA

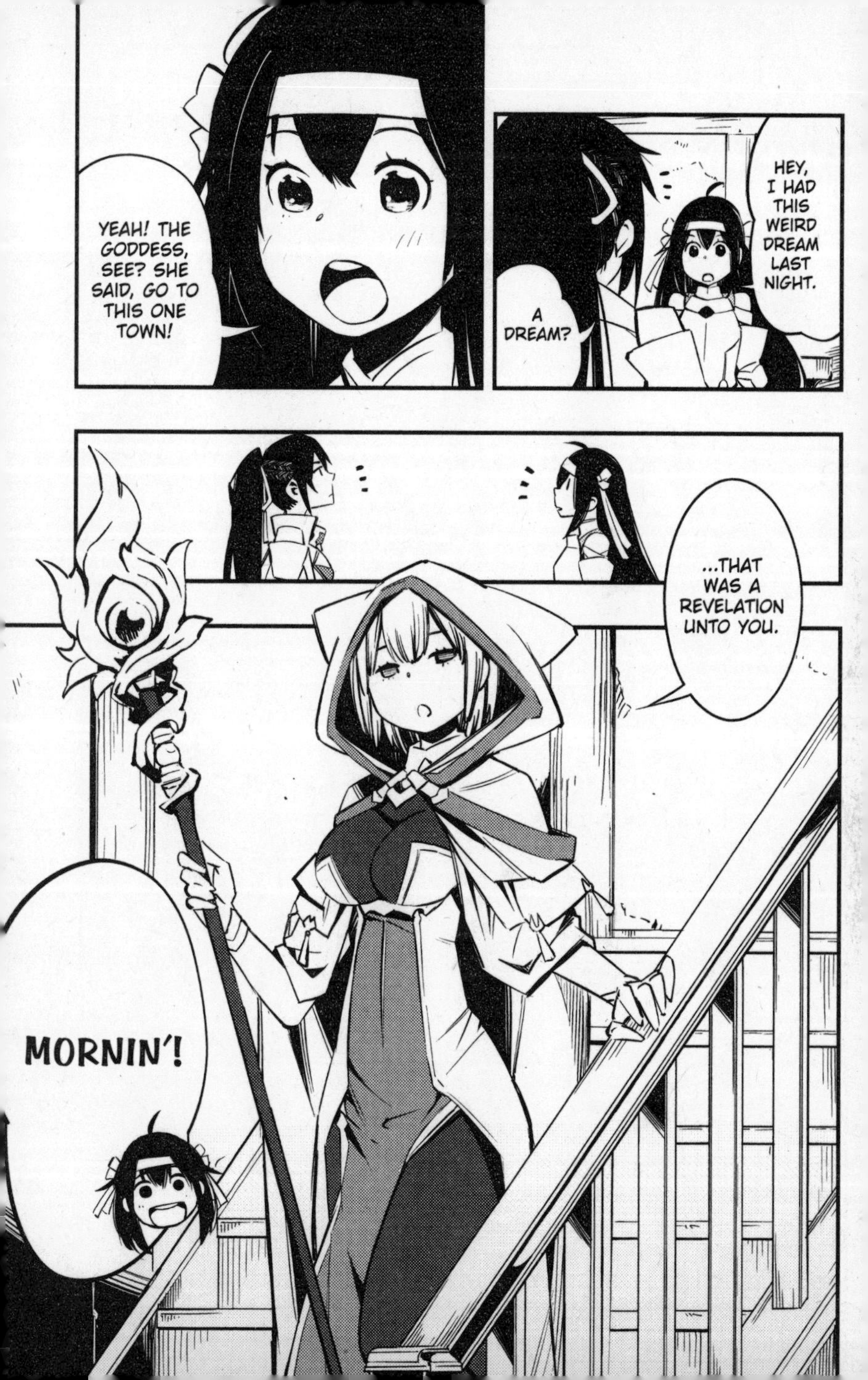
HEY, I HAD THIS WEIRD DREAM LAST NIGHT.
A DREAM?
YEAH! THE GODDESS, SEE? SHE SAID, GO TO THIS ONE TOWN!
...THAT WAS A REVELATION UNTO YOU.
MORNIN'!

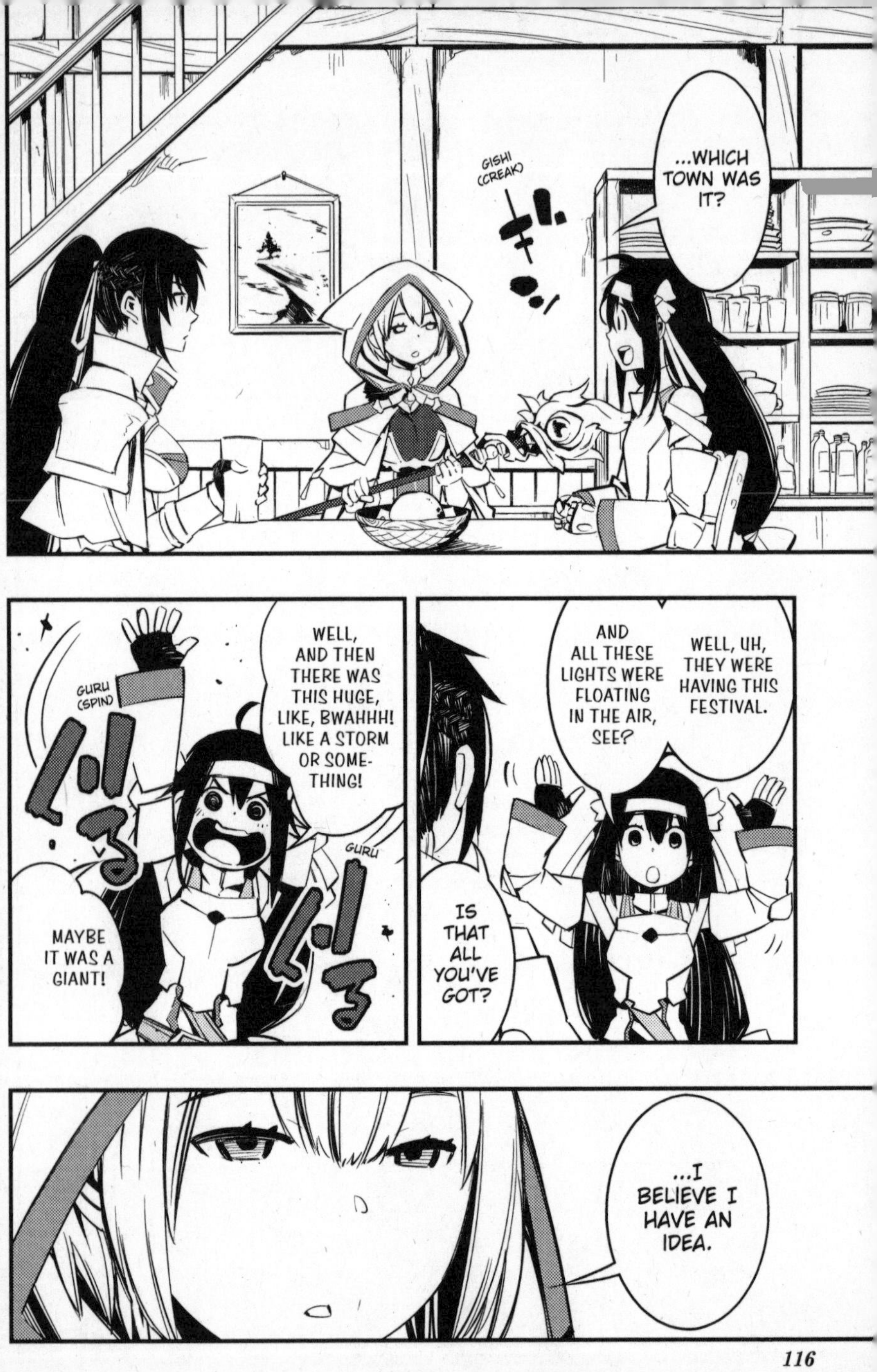
...WHICH TOWN WAS IT?
GISHI (CREAK)
WELL, UH, THEY WERE HAVING THIS FESTIVAL.
AND ALL THESE LIGHTS WERE FLOATING IN THE AIR, SEE?
IS THAT ALL YOU'VE GOT?
WELL, AND THEN THERE WAS THIS HUGE, LIKE, BWAHHH! LIKE A STORM OR SOME-THING!
GURU (SPIN)
GURU
MAYBE IT WAS A GIANT!
...I BELIEVE I HAVE AN IDEA.

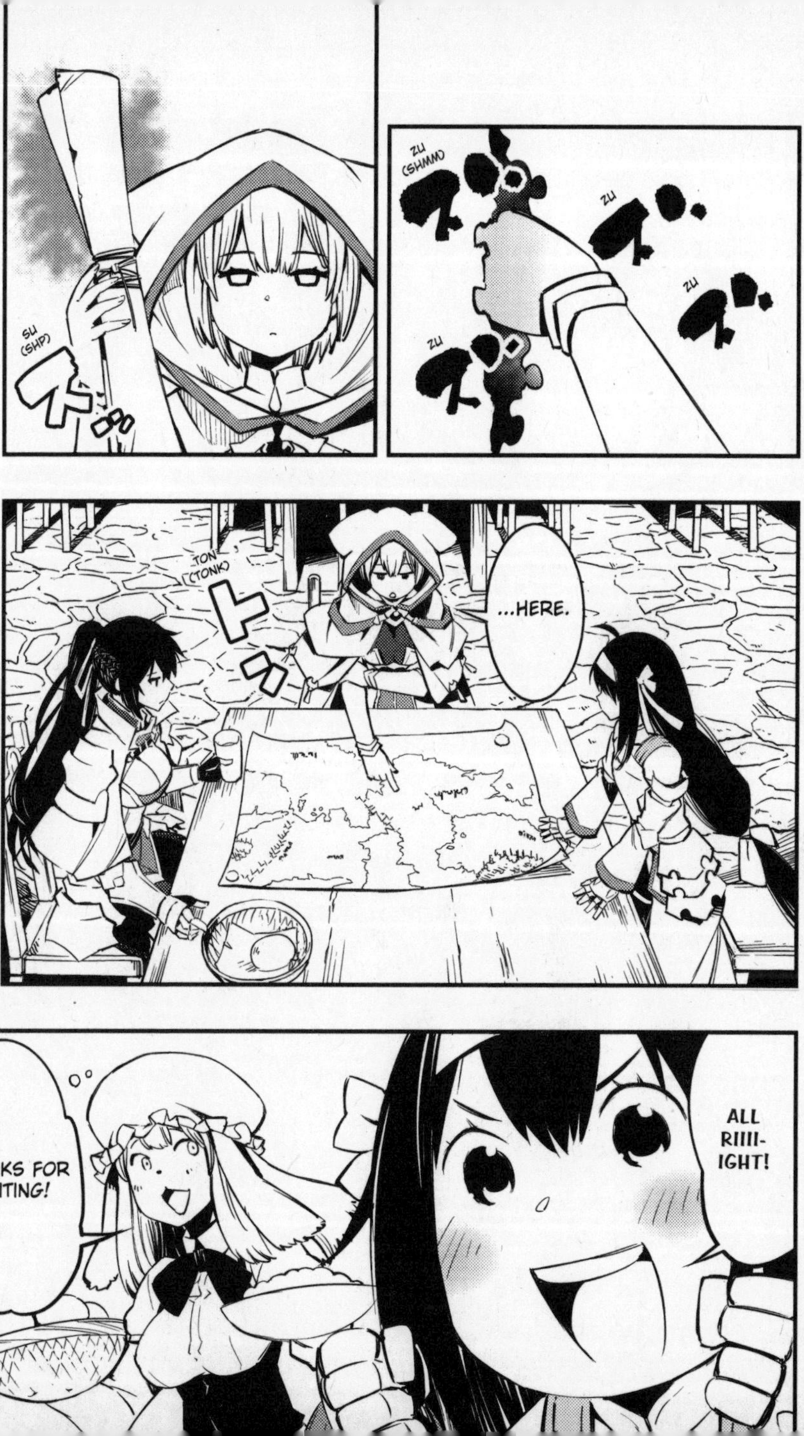
ZU (SHMM)
ZU
ZU
ZU
SU (SHP)
TON (TONK)
...HERE.
ALL RIIII-IGHT!
THANKS FOR WAITING!

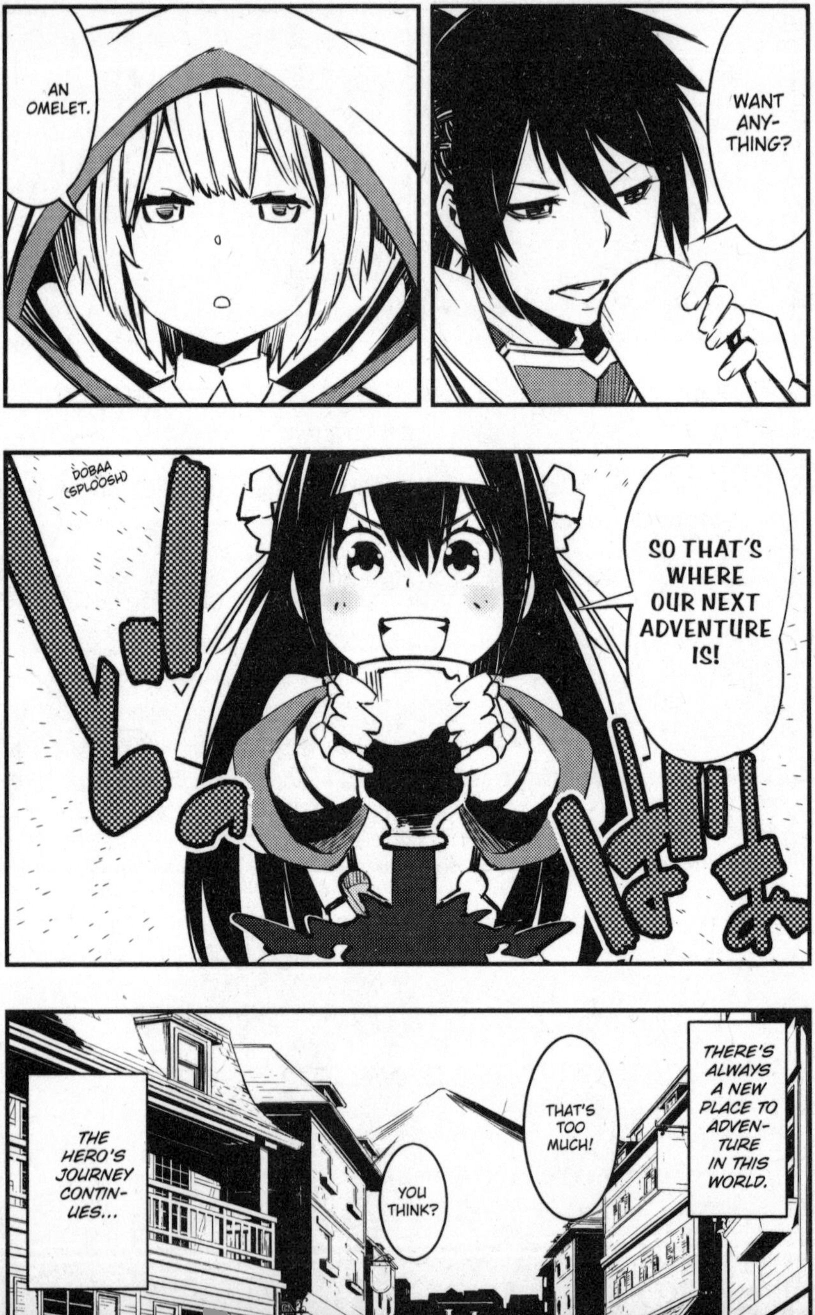
WANT ANY-THING?
AN OMELET.
SO THAT'S WHERE OUR NEXT ADVENTURE IS!
DOBAA (SPLOOSH)
THERE'S ALWAYS A NEW PLACE TO ADVEN-TURE IN THIS WORLD.
THAT'S TOO MUCH!
YOU THINK?
THE HERO'S JOURNEY CONTIN-UES...

Chapter 8:
Of an Elf's Lazy Day Off

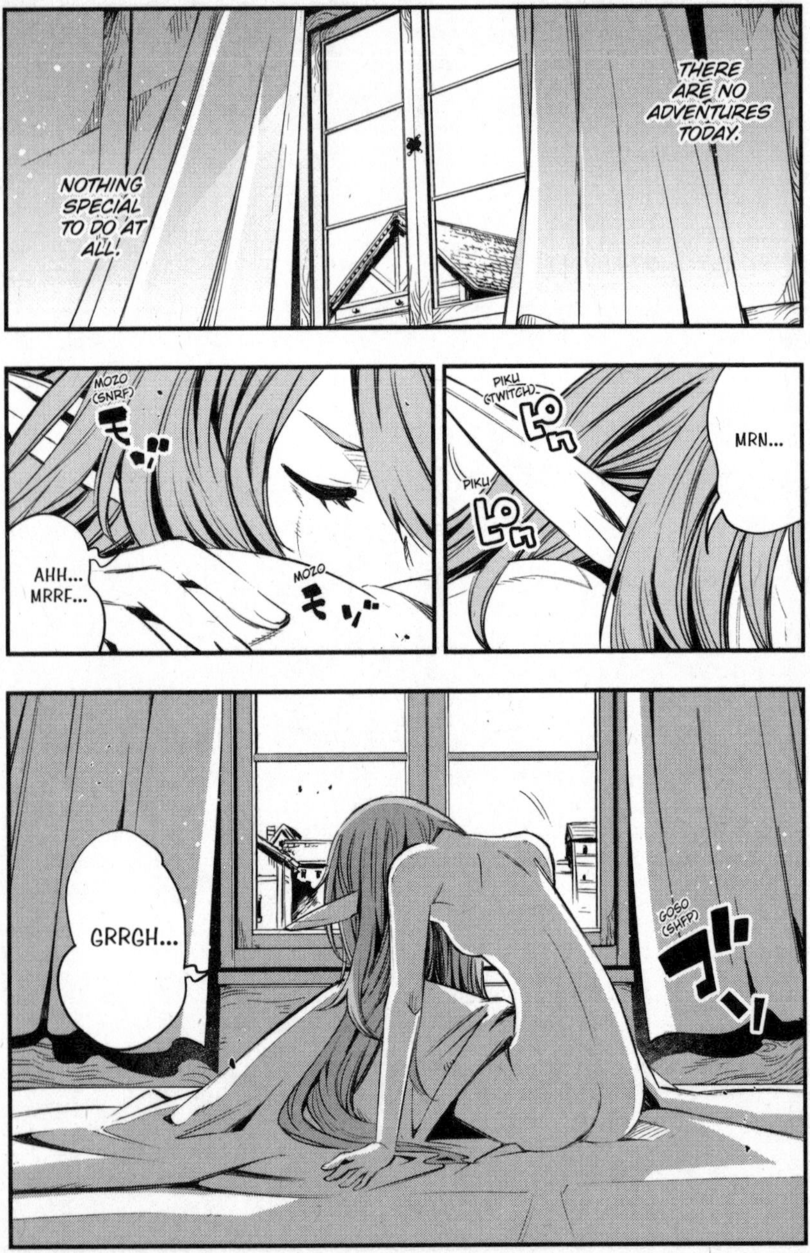
THERE ARE NO ADVENTURES TODAY.
NOTHING SPECIAL TO DO AT ALL!
MRN...
PIKU (TWITCH)
ピクッ
PIKU
ピクッ
MOZO (SNRF)
モゾ
AHH... MRRF...
MOZO
モゾ
GOSO (SHFF)
ゴソッ
GRRGH...

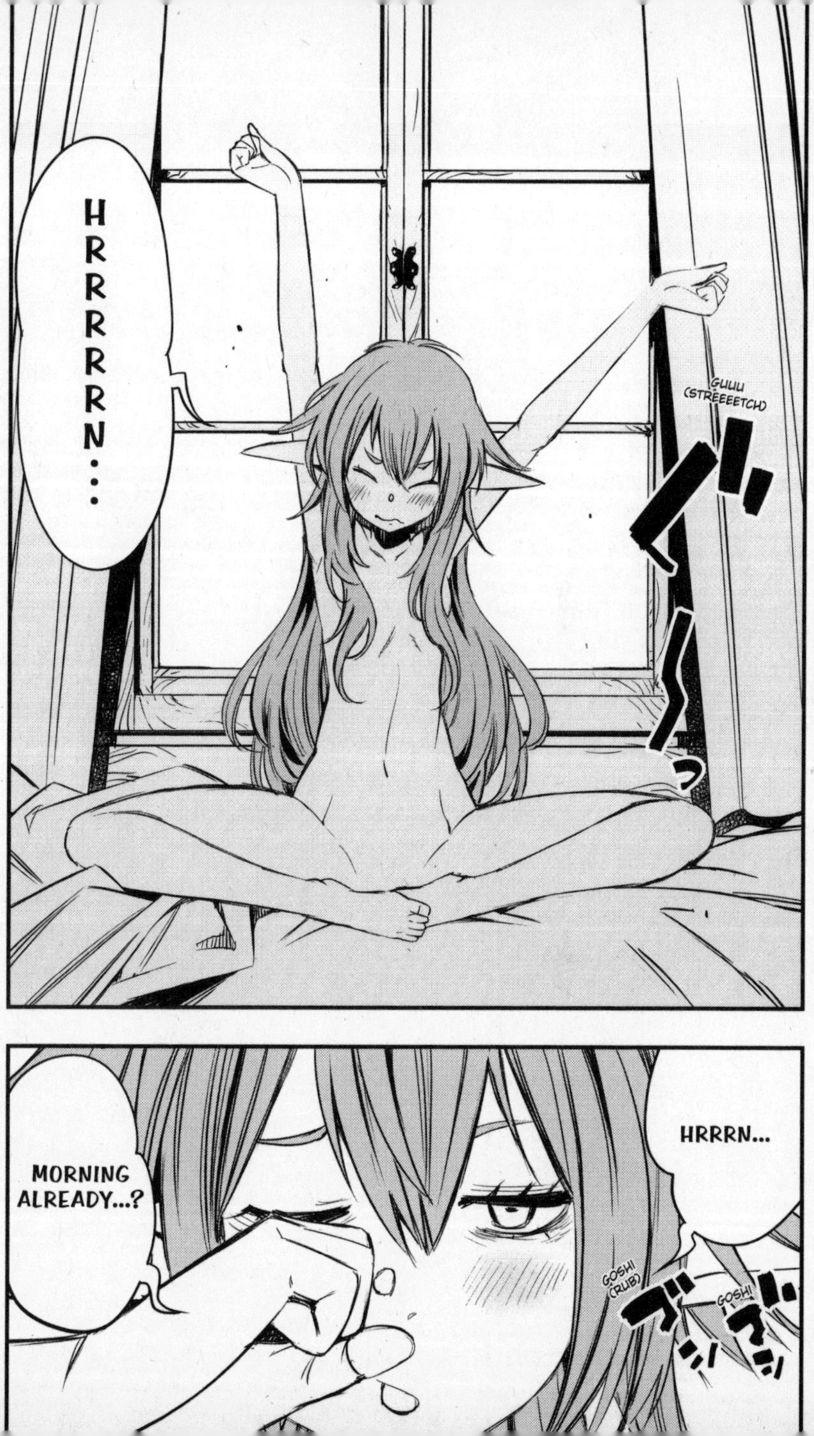
HRRRRRRN...
GUUU (STREEEETCH)
HRRRN...
GOSHI (RUB)
GOSHI
MORNING ALREADY...?

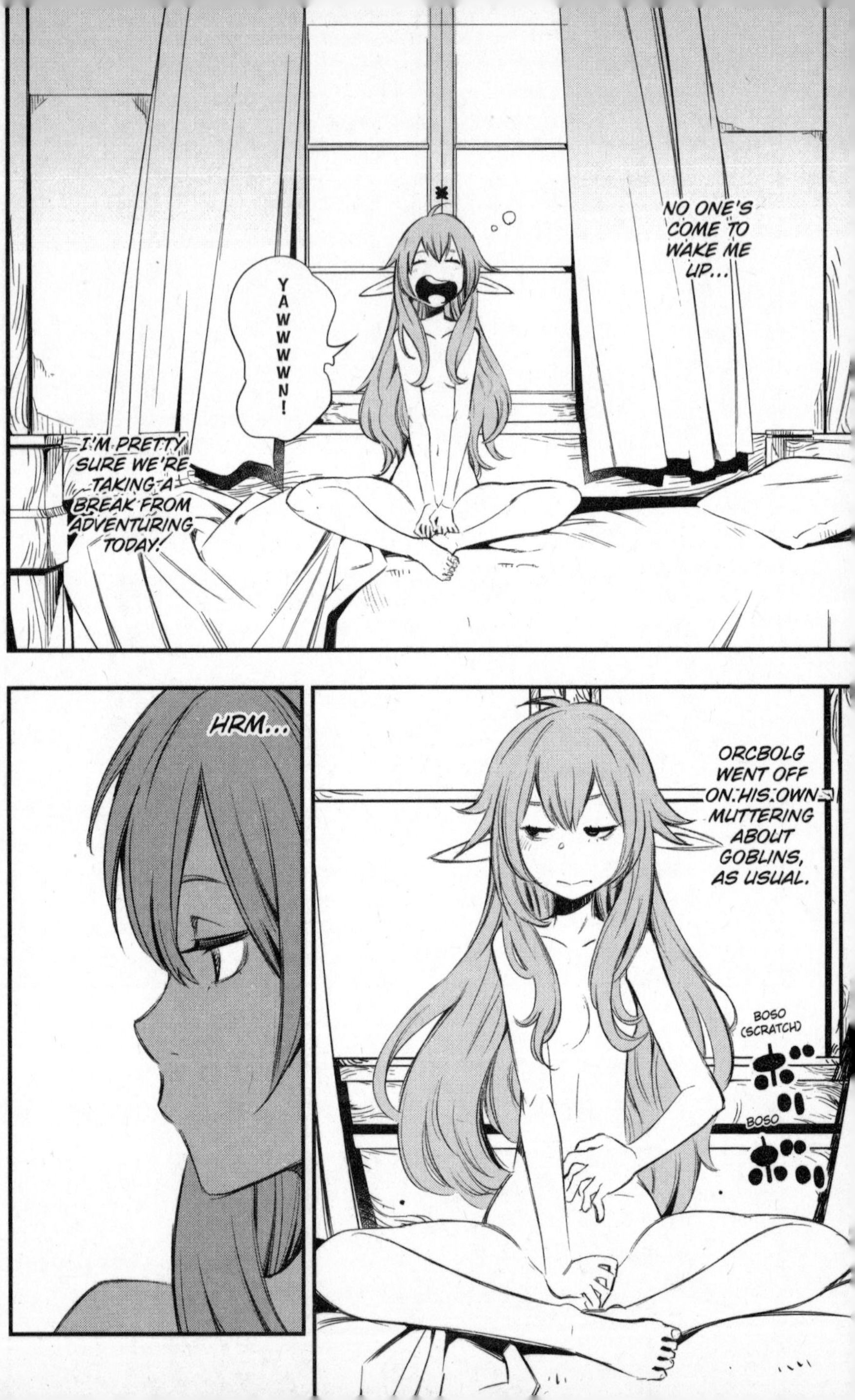
NO ONE'S COME TO WAKE ME UP...
YAWWWWN!
I'M PRETTY SURE WE'RE TAKING A BREAK FROM ADVENTURING TODAY!
ORCBOLG WENT OFF ON HIS OWN, MUTTERING ABOUT GOBLINS, AS USUAL.
BOSO (SCRATCH)
BOSO
HRM...

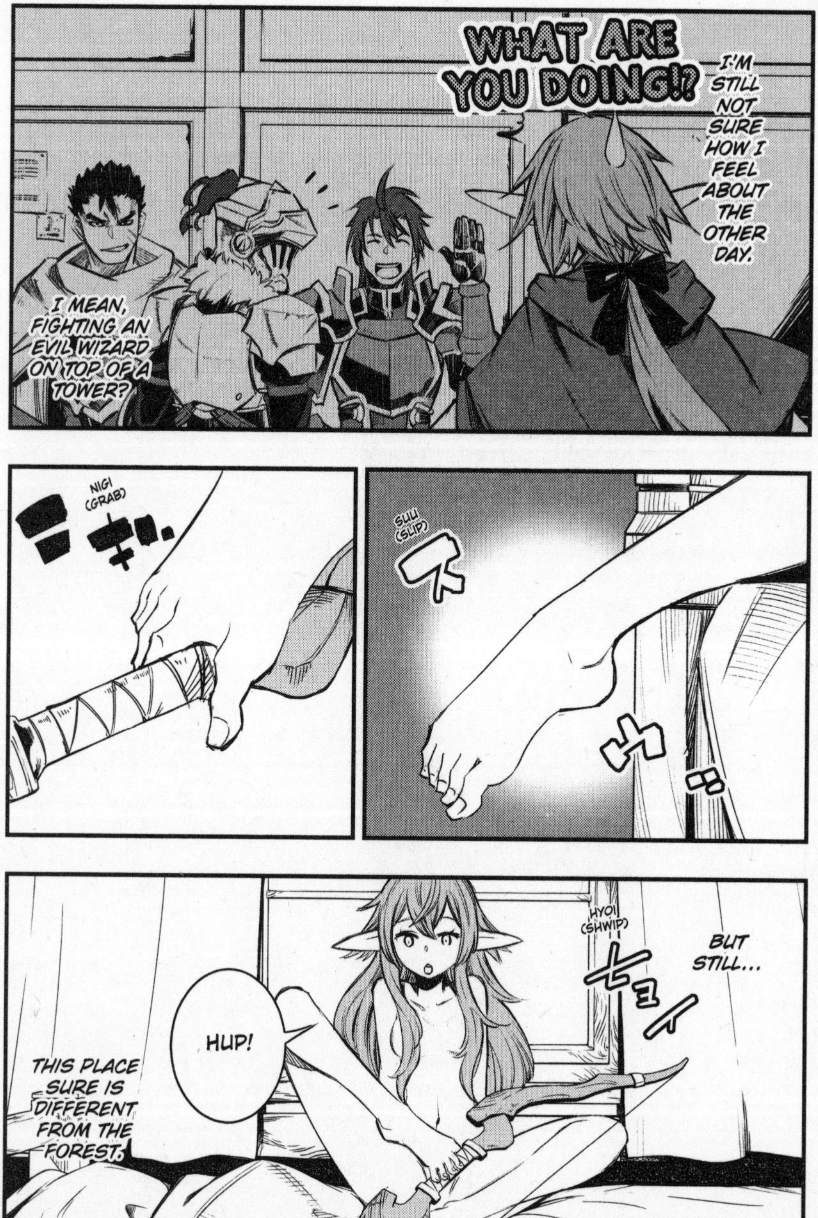
I'M STILL NOT SURE HOW I FEEL ABOUT THE OTHER DAY.
WHAT ARE YOU DOING!?
I MEAN, FIGHTING AN EVIL WIZARD ON TOP OF A TOWER?
SUU (SLIP)
NIGI (GRAB)
HYOI (SHWIP)
BUT STILL...
HUP!
THIS PLACE SURE IS DIFFERENT FROM THE FOREST.

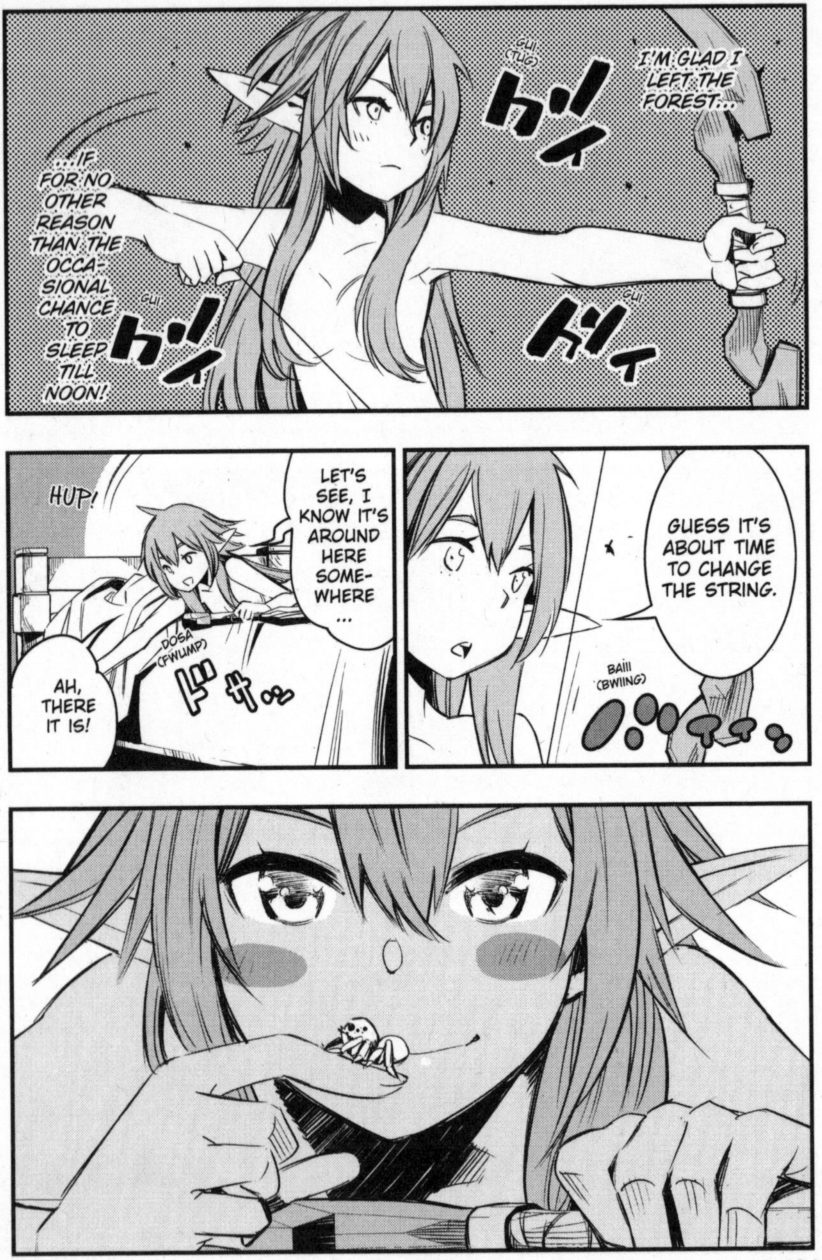
I'M GLAD I LEFT THE FOREST...
GUI (TUG)
GUI
...IF FOR NO OTHER REASON THAN THE OCCA-SIONAL CHANCE TO SLEEP TILL NOON!
GUI
GUESS IT'S ABOUT TIME TO CHANGE THE STRING.
BAIII (BWIING)
LET'S SEE, I KNOW IT'S AROUND HERE SOME-WHERE ...
HUP!
DOSA (FWUMP)
AH, THERE IT IS!

TSUI!!
(SHWEE)

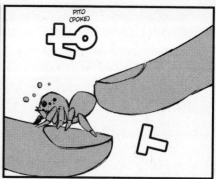

PITO
(POKE)

TSUI!!

TSUI!!

TSUI!!

TSUI!!

KURI
(TWIST)

KURI

KURI

KURI

THINK THAT'S PLENTY.

THANKS!

SU
(SET)

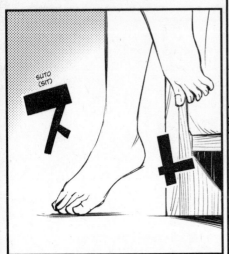

SUTO
(SIT)

THAT'LL DO.

KURU
(TWIRL)

KURU

♪

KACHA
(SHK)

KACHA

GYU
(TUG)

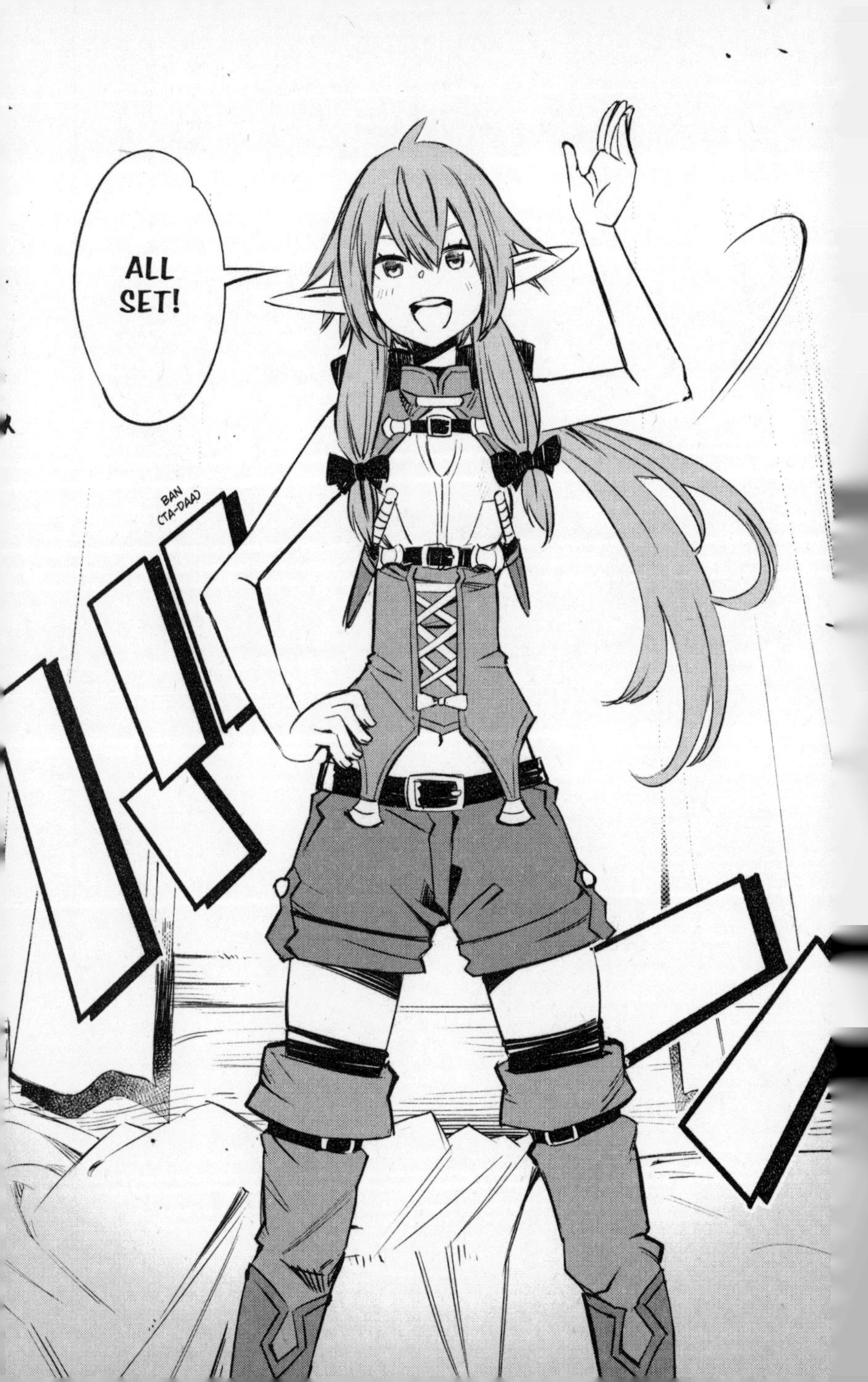
ALL SET!
BAN (TA-DAA)

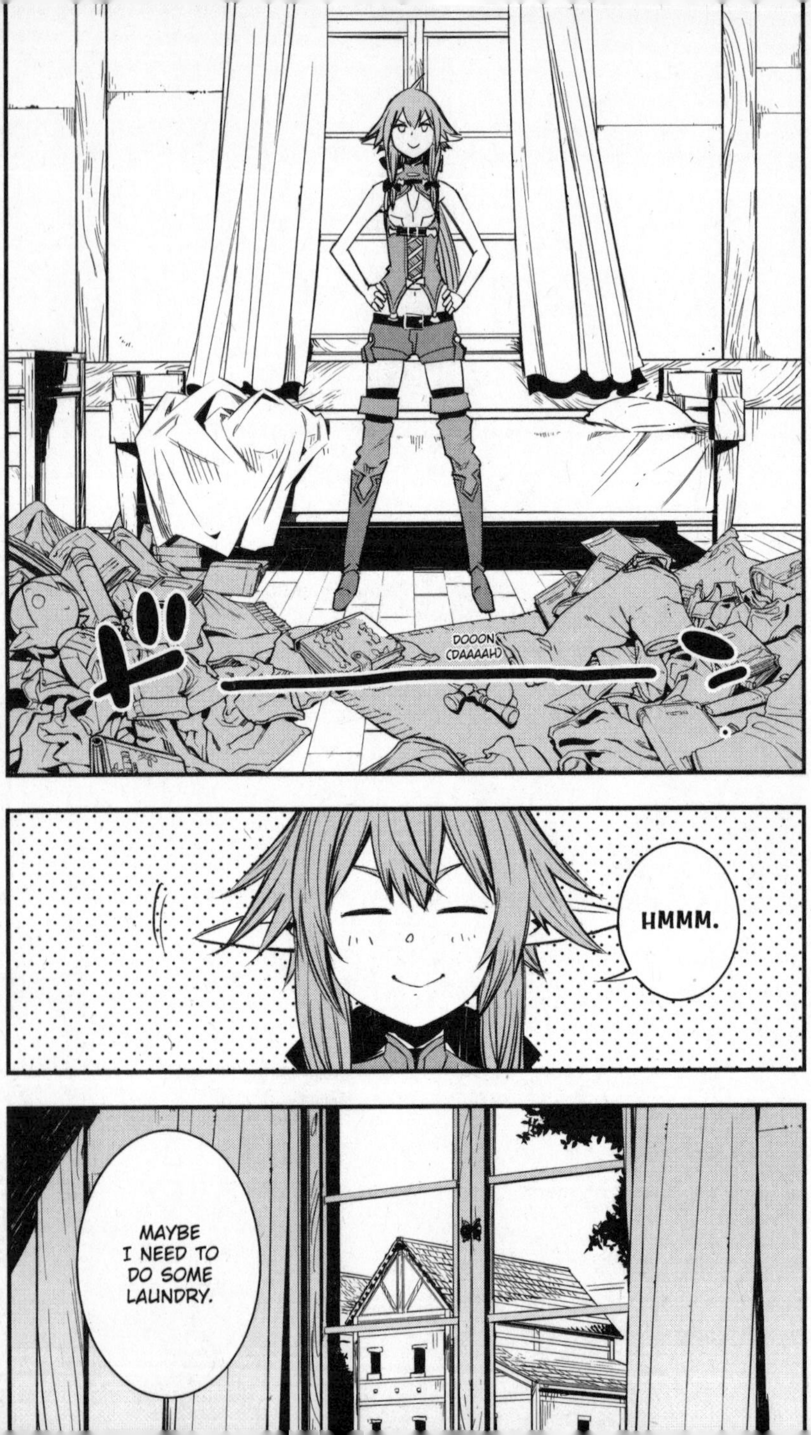
DOOON (DAAAAH)
HMMM.
MAYBE I NEED TO DO SOME LAUNDRY.

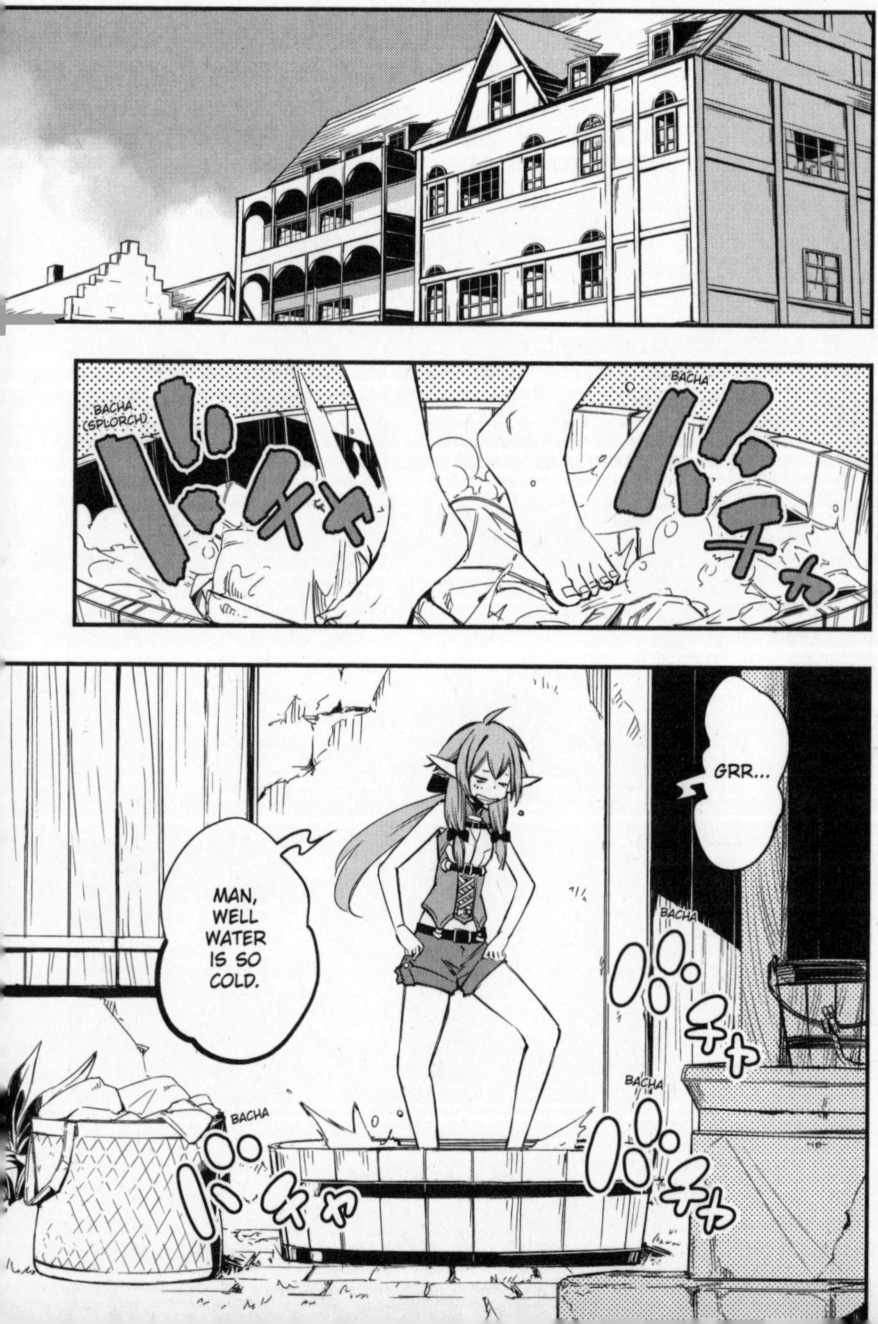
BACHA
バチャ
BACHA (SPLORCH)
バチャ
GRR...
BACHA
バチャ
BACHA
バチャ
MAN, WELL WATER IS SO COLD.
BACHA
バチャ

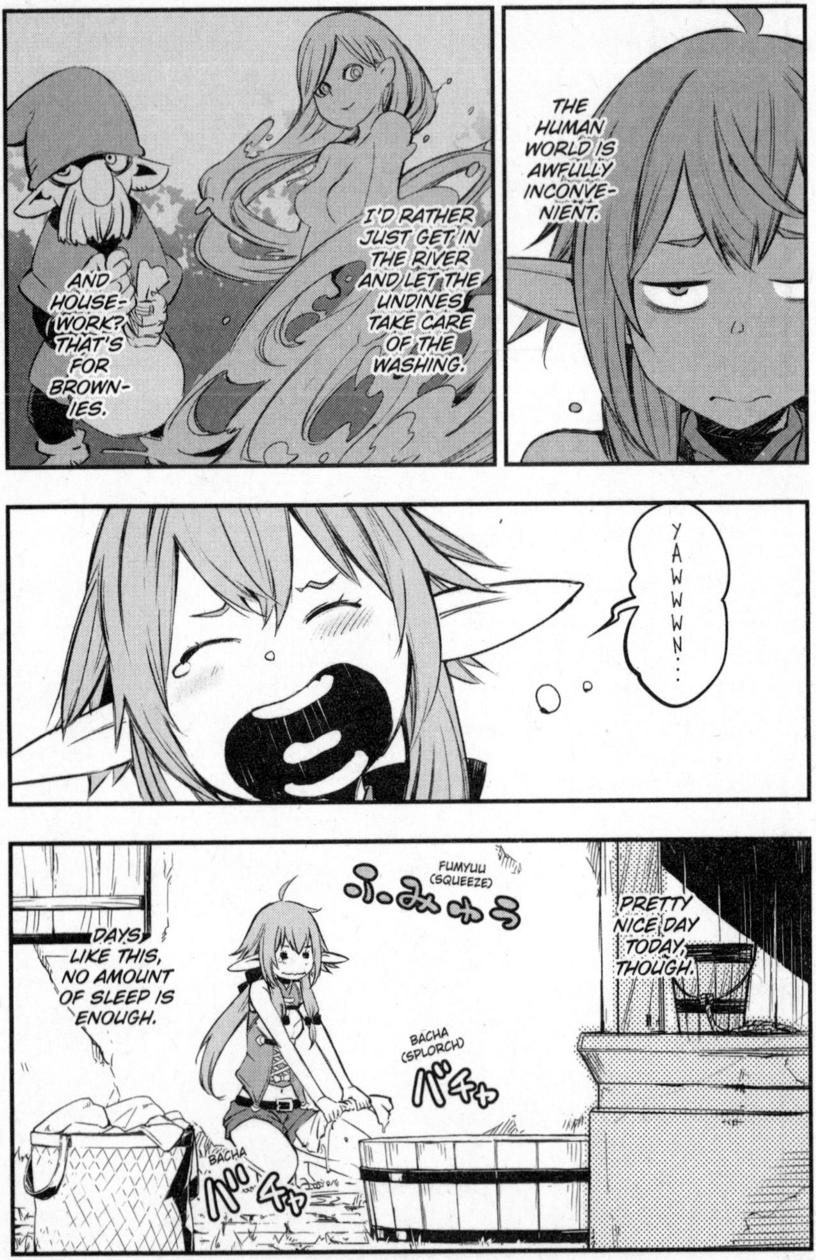
THE HUMAN WORLD IS AWFULLY INCONVENIENT.
I'D RATHER JUST GET IN THE RIVER AND LET THE UNDINES TAKE CARE OF THE WASHING.
AND HOUSEWORK? THAT'S FOR BROWNIES.
YAWWWN...
PRETTY NICE DAY TODAY, THOUGH.
FUMYUU (SQUEEZE)
DAYS LIKE THIS, NO AMOUNT OF SLEEP IS ENOUGH.
BACHA (SPLORCH)
BACHA

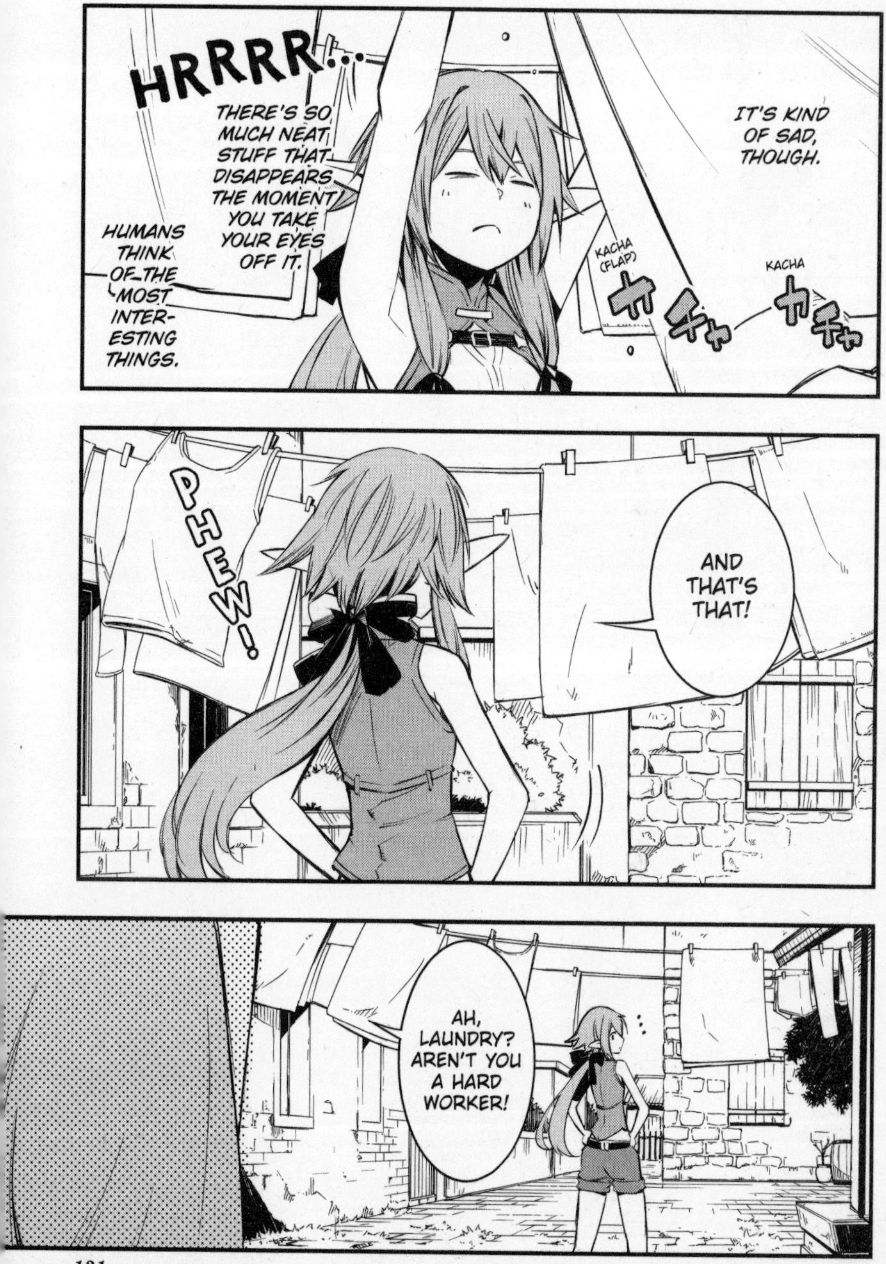
IT'S KIND OF SAD, THOUGH.
KACHA
KACHA (FLAP)
HRRRR!...
THERE'S SO MUCH NEAT STUFF THAT DISAPPEARS THE MOMENT YOU TAKE YOUR EYES OFF IT.
HUMANS THINK OF THE MOST INTERESTING THINGS.
AND THAT'S THAT!
PHEW!
AH, LAUNDRY? AREN'T YOU A HARD WORKER!

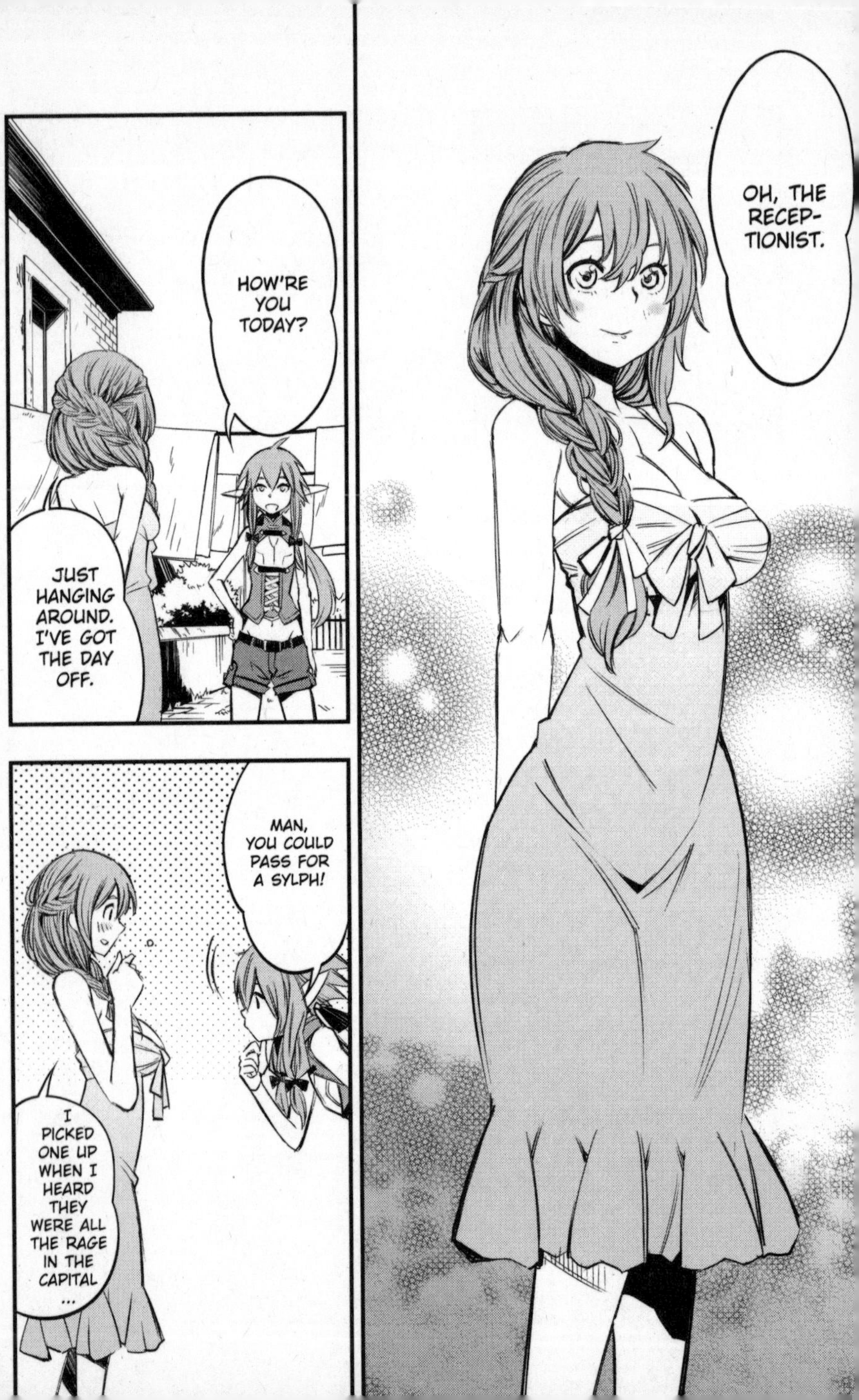
OH, THE RECEPTIONIST.
HOW'RE YOU TODAY?
JUST HANGING AROUND. I'VE GOT THE DAY OFF.
MAN, YOU COULD PASS FOR A SYLPH!
I PICKED ONE UP WHEN I HEARD THEY WERE ALL THE RAGE IN THE CAPITAL...

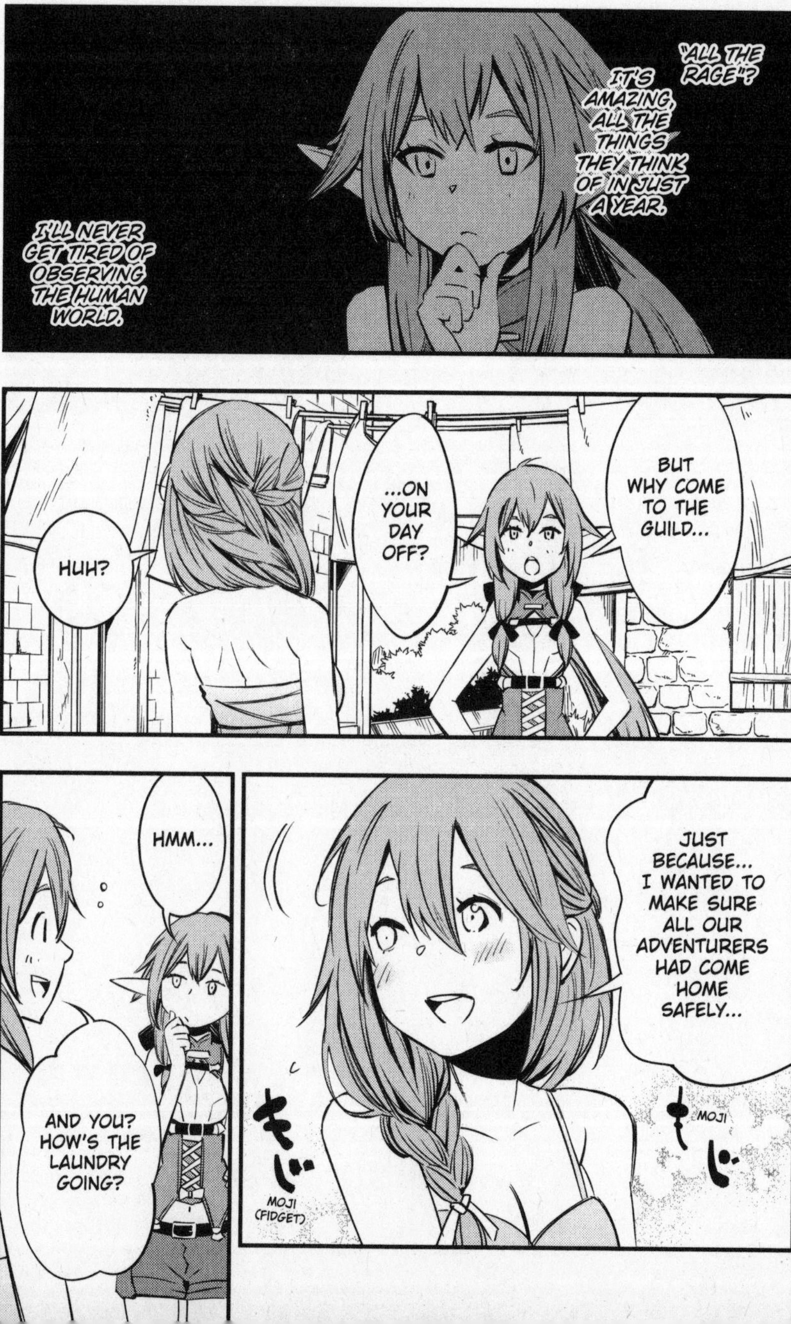
"ALL THE RAGE"?
IT'S AMAZING, ALL THE THINGS THEY THINK OF IN JUST A YEAR.
I'LL NEVER GET TIRED OF OBSERVING THE HUMAN WORLD.
BUT WHY COME TO THE GUILD...
...ON YOUR DAY OFF?
HUH?
JUST BECAUSE... I WANTED TO MAKE SURE ALL OUR ADVENTURERS HAD COME HOME SAFELY...
MOJI
MOJI (FIDGET)
HMM...
AND YOU? HOW'S THE LAUNDRY GOING?

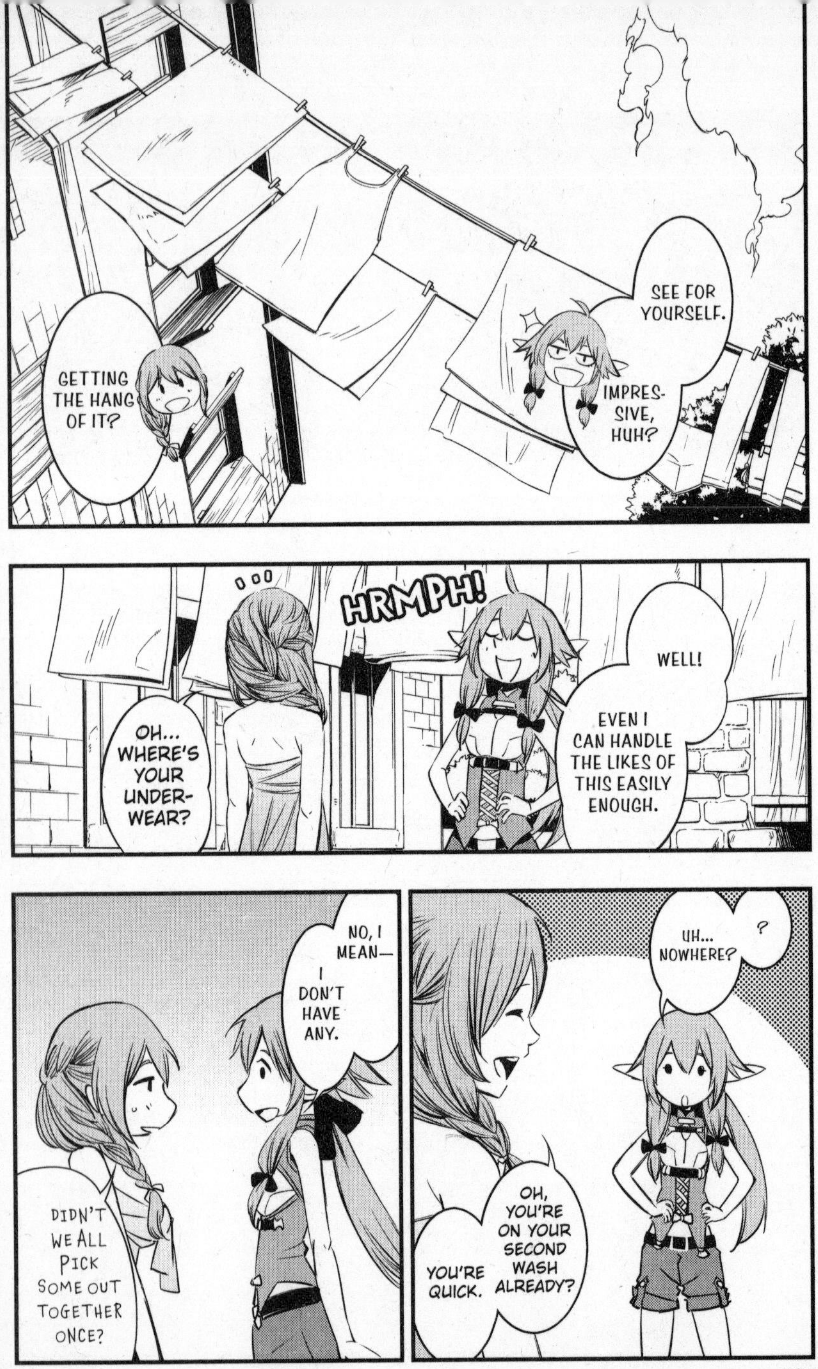
SEE FOR YOURSELF.
IMPRESSIVE, HUH?
GETTING THE HANG OF IT?
WELL!
EVEN I CAN HANDLE THE LIKES OF THIS EASILY ENOUGH.
HRMPH!
OH... WHERE'S YOUR UNDERWEAR?
?
UH... NOWHERE?
OH, YOU'RE ON YOUR SECOND WASH ALREADY?
YOU'RE QUICK.
NO, I MEAN—
I DON'T HAVE ANY.
DIDN'T WE ALL PICK SOME OUT TOGETHER ONCE?

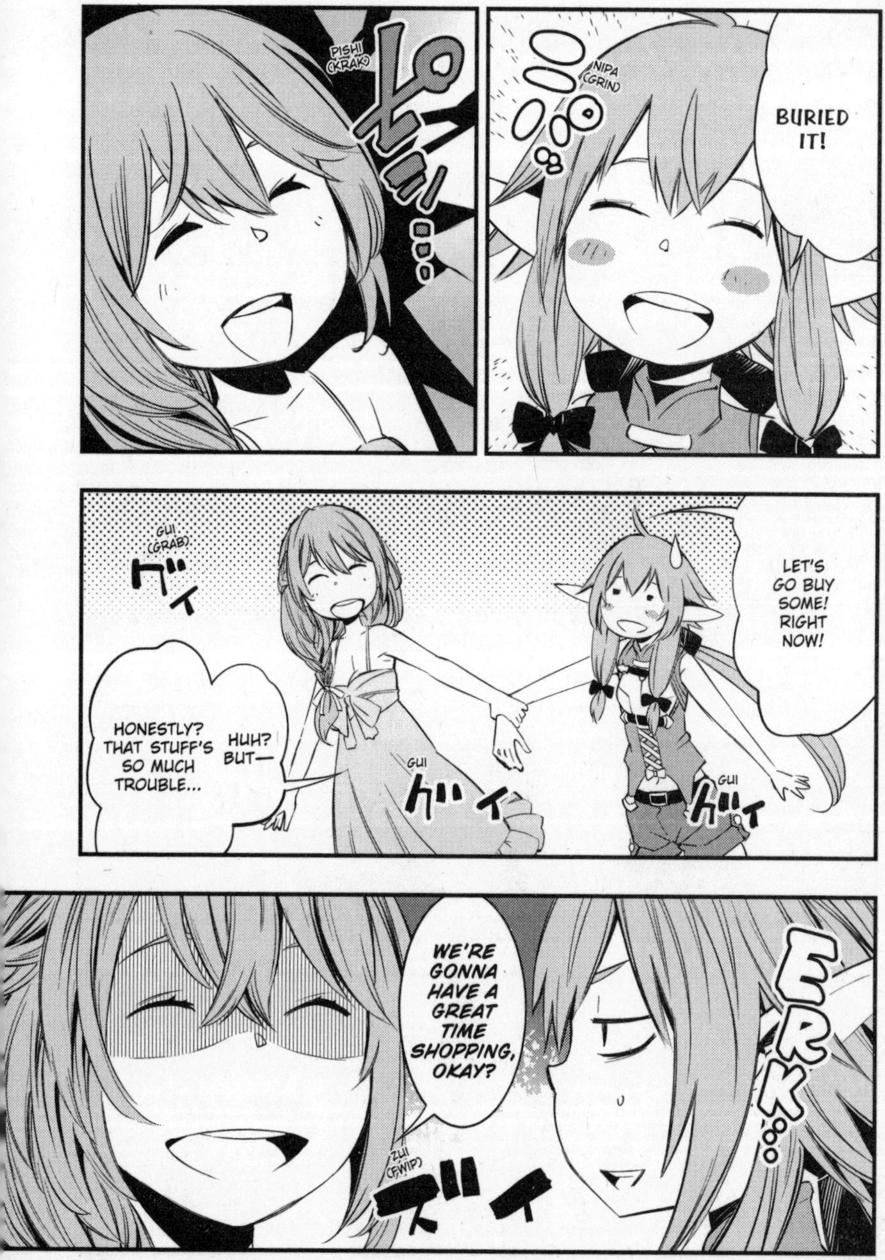
NIPA (GRIN)
BURIED IT!
PISHI (KRAK)
LET'S GO BUY SOME! RIGHT NOW!
GUI
GUI
HUH? BUT—
HONESTLY? THAT STUFF'S SO MUCH TROUBLE...
GUI (GRAB)
ERK...
WE'RE GONNA HAVE A GREAT TIME SHOPPING, OKAY?
ZUI (FWIP)

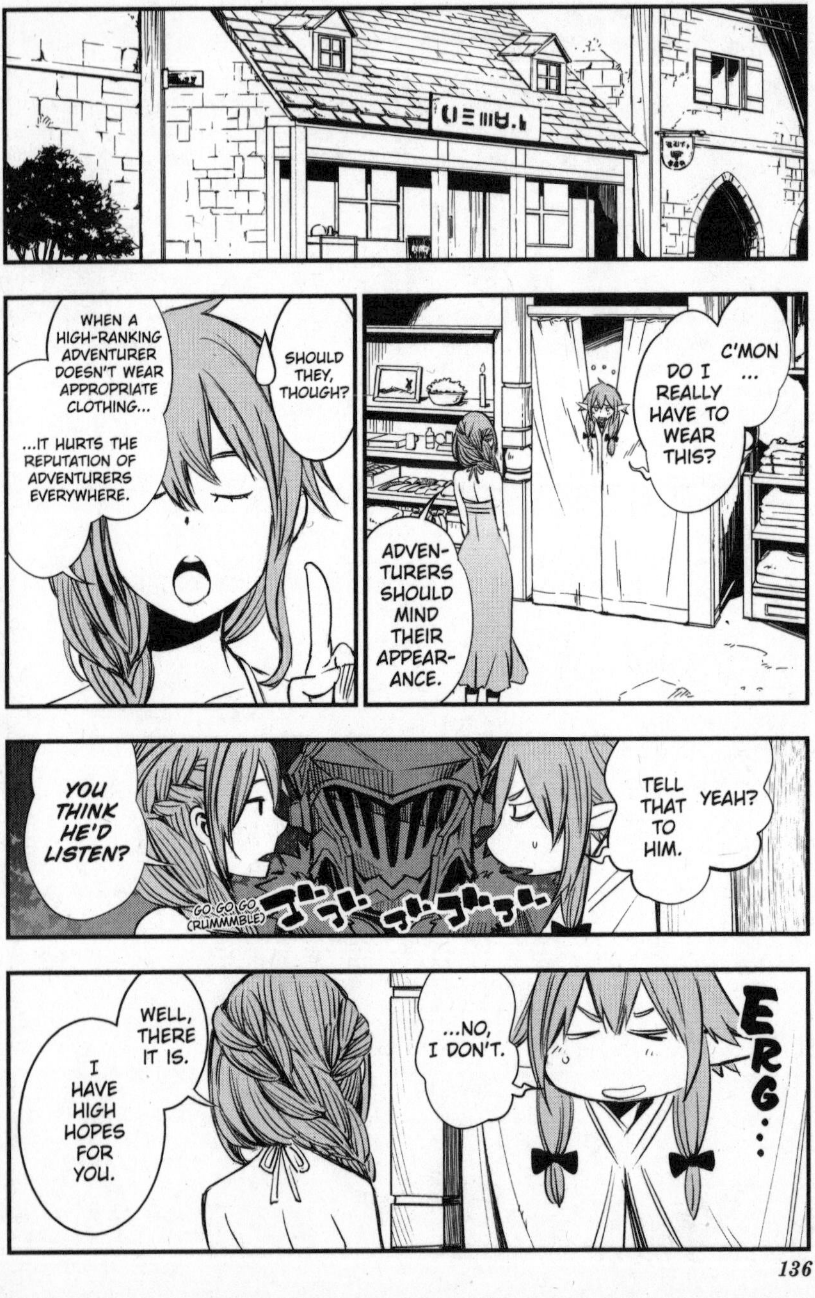
C'MON ... DO I REALLY HAVE TO WEAR THIS?
ADVENTURERS SHOULD MIND THEIR APPEARANCE.
SHOULD THEY, THOUGH?
WHEN A HIGH-RANKING ADVENTURER DOESN'T WEAR APPROPRIATE CLOTHING...
...IT HURTS THE REPUTATION OF ADVENTURERS EVERYWHERE.
TELL THAT TO HIM. YEAH?
GO GO GO (RUMMMBLE)
YOU THINK HE'D LISTEN?
ERG...
...NO, I DON'T.
WELL, THERE IT IS.
I HAVE HIGH HOPES FOR YOU.

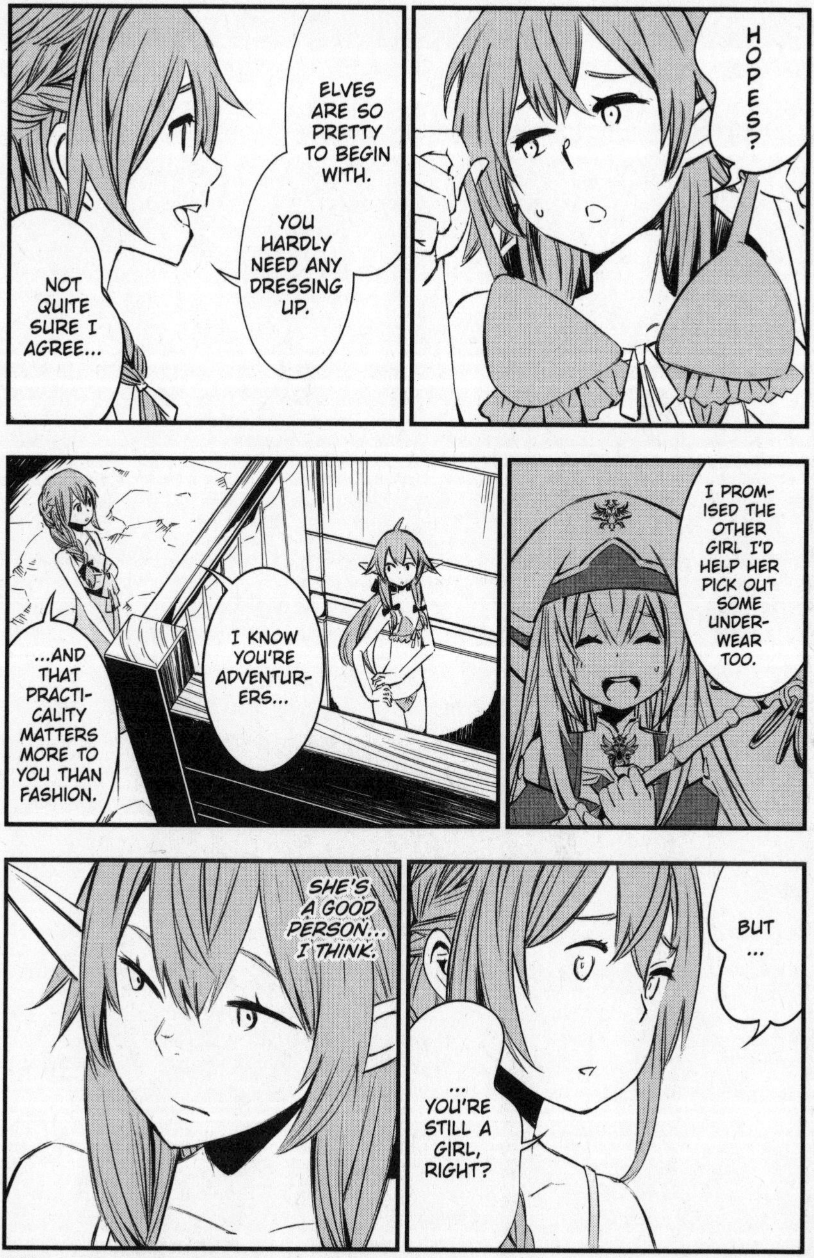
HOPES?
ELVES ARE SO PRETTY TO BEGIN WITH.
YOU HARDLY NEED ANY DRESSING UP.
NOT QUITE SURE I AGREE...
I PROMISED THE OTHER GIRL I'D HELP HER PICK OUT SOME UNDERWEAR TOO.
I KNOW YOU'RE ADVENTURERS...
...AND THAT PRACTICALITY MATTERS MORE TO YOU THAN FASHION.
BUT ...
... YOU'RE STILL A GIRL, RIGHT?
SHE'S A GOOD PERSON... I THINK.

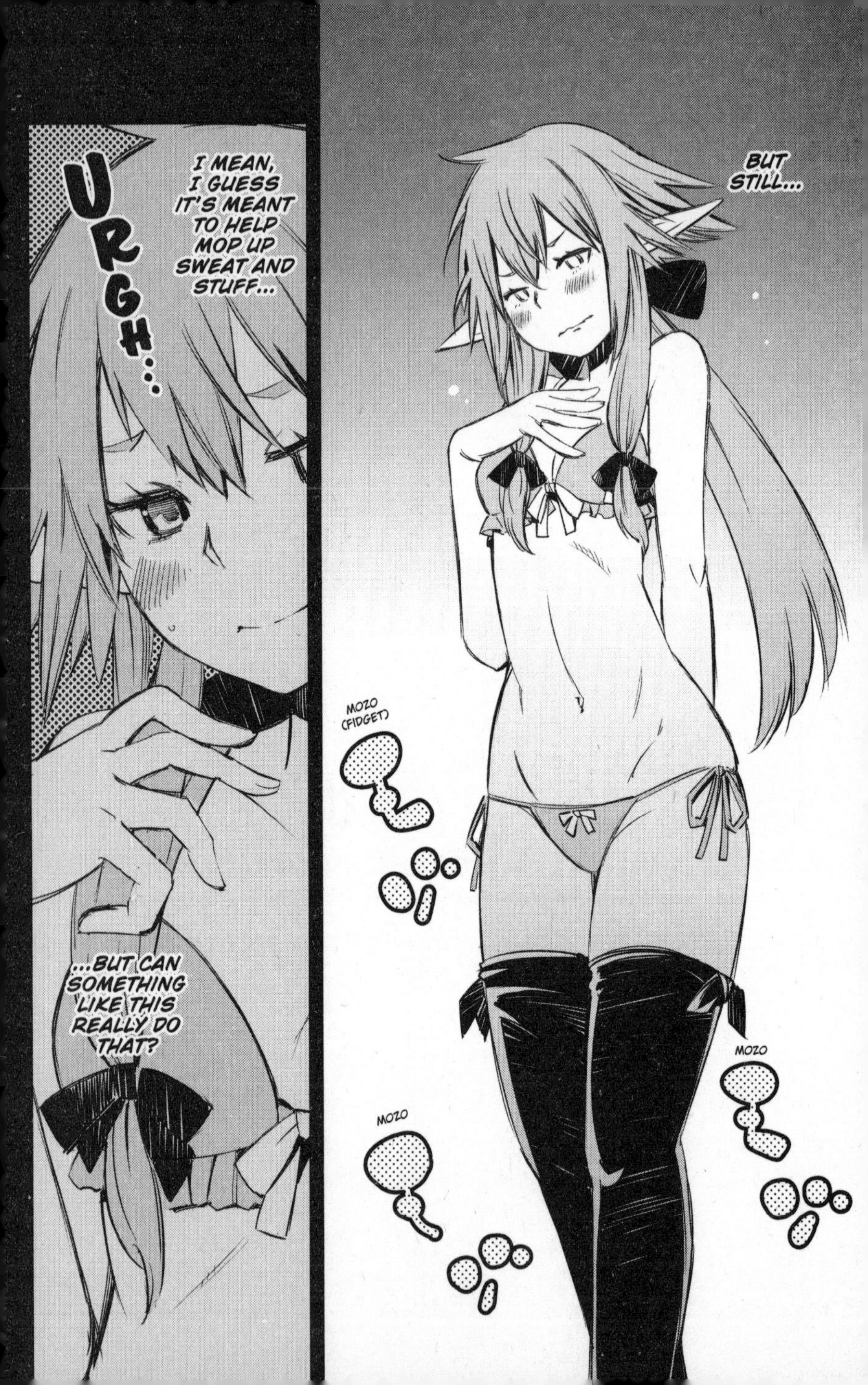
BUT STILL...
MOZO (FIDGET)
MOZO
MOZO
I MEAN, I GUESS IT'S MEANT TO HELP MOP UP SWEAT AND STUFF...
URGH...
...BUT CAN SOMETHING LIKE THIS REALLY DO THAT?

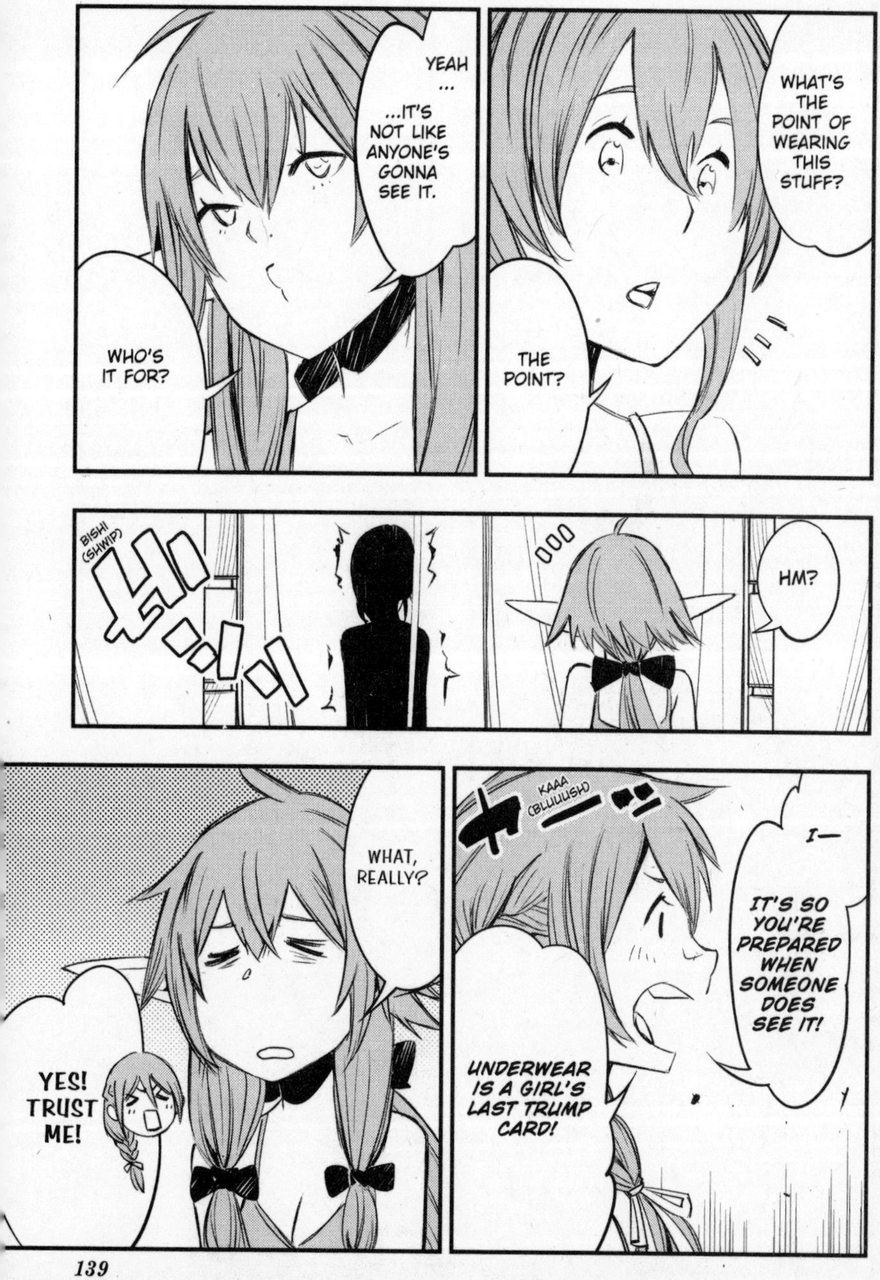
WHAT'S THE POINT OF WEARING THIS STUFF?
THE POINT?
YEAH ...
...IT'S NOT LIKE ANYONE'S GONNA SEE IT.
WHO'S IT FOR?
HM?
BISHI (SHWIP)
KAAA (BLUUUSH)
I—
IT'S SO YOU'RE PREPARED WHEN SOMEONE DOES SEE IT!
UNDERWEAR IS A GIRL'S LAST TRUMP CARD!
WHAT, REALLY?
YES! TRUST ME!

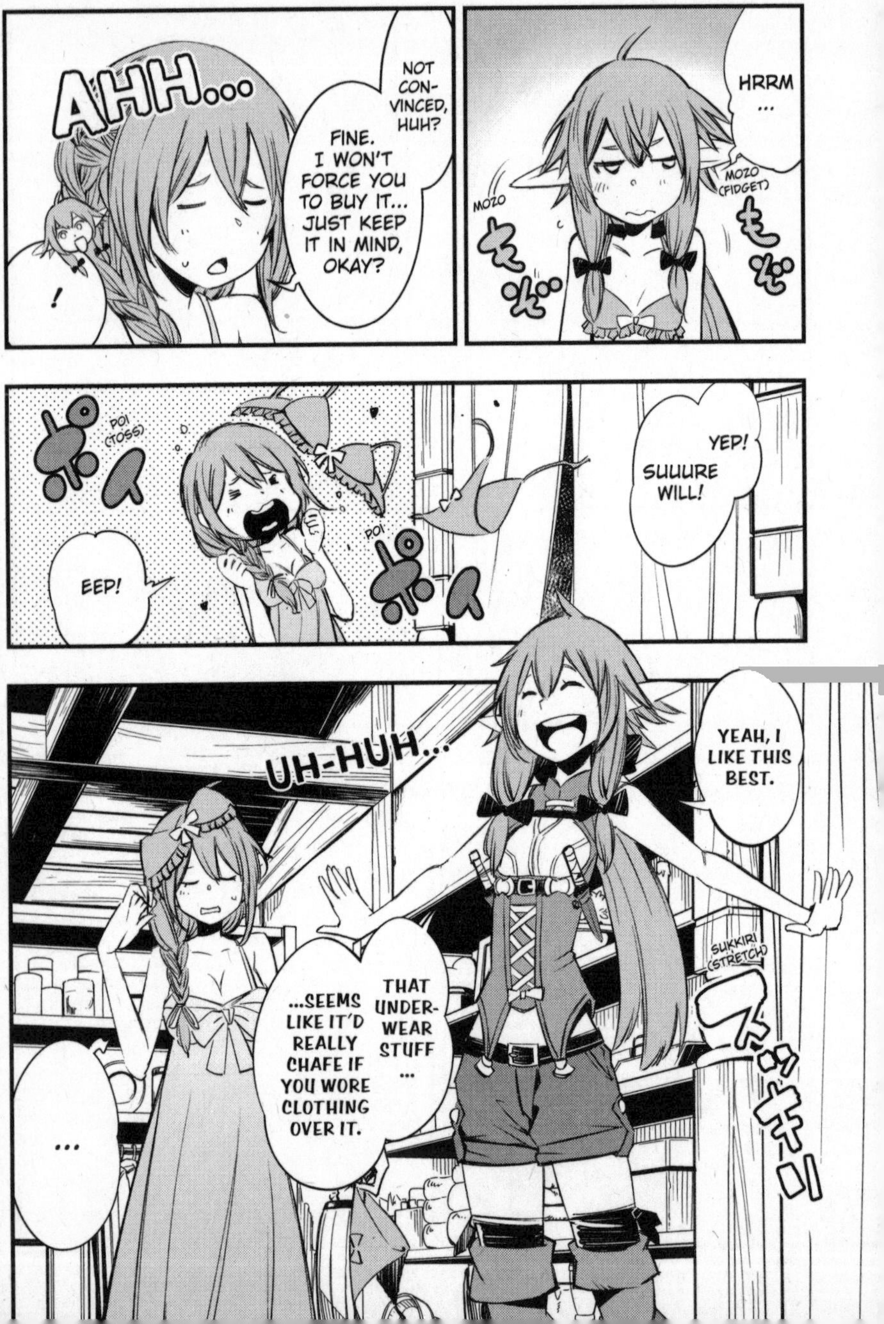
HRRM ...
MOZO (FIDGET)
MOZO
NOT CON-VINCED, HUH?
FINE. I WON'T FORCE YOU TO BUY IT... JUST KEEP IT IN MIND, OKAY?
AHH...
!
YEP! SUUURE WILL!
POI
POI (TOSS)
EEP!
YEAH, I LIKE THIS BEST.
SUKKIRI (STRETCH)
UH-HUH...
THAT UNDER-WEAR STUFF ...
...SEEMS LIKE IT'D REALLY CHAFE IF YOU WORE CLOTHING OVER IT.
...

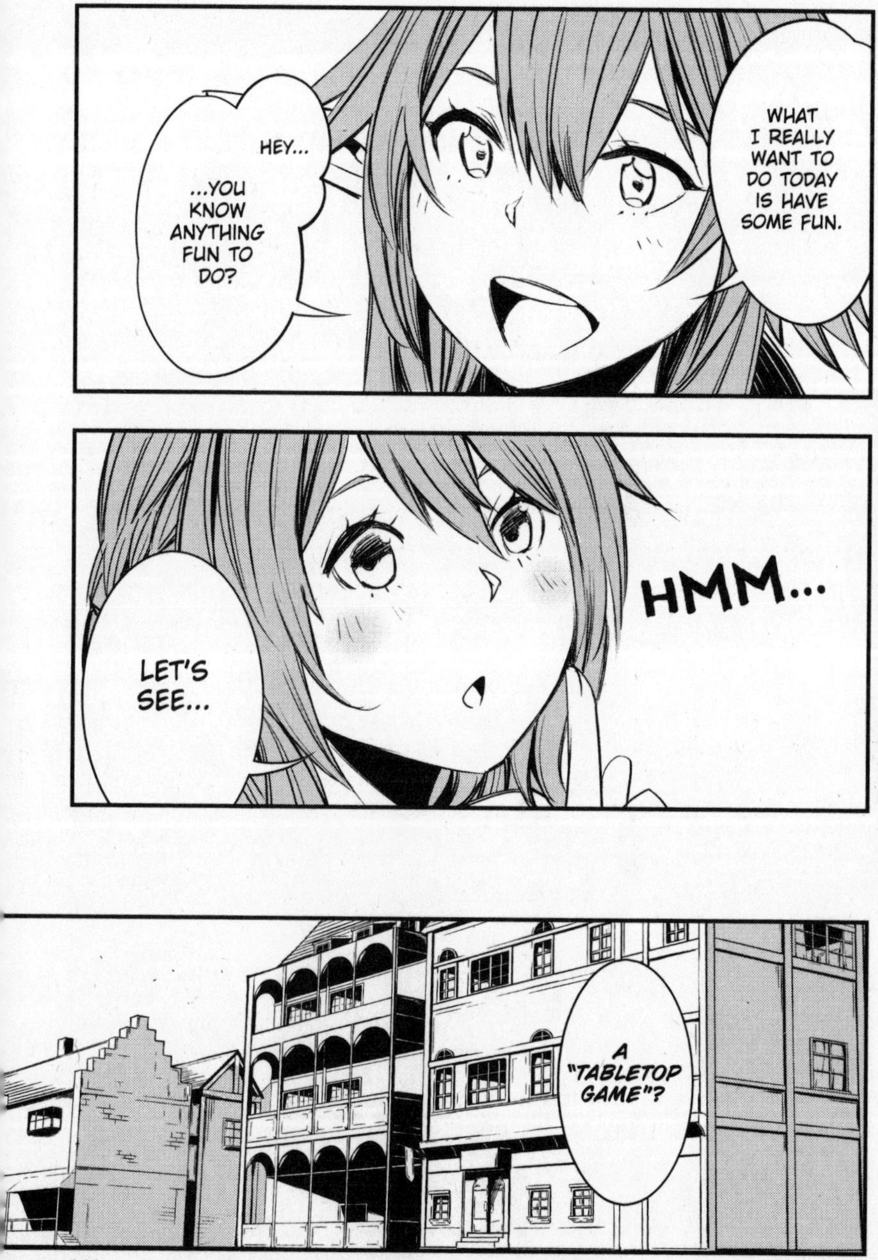
WHAT I REALLY WANT TO DO TODAY IS HAVE SOME FUN.
HEY...
...YOU KNOW ANYTHING FUN TO DO?
HMM...
LET'S SEE...
A "TABLETOP GAME"?

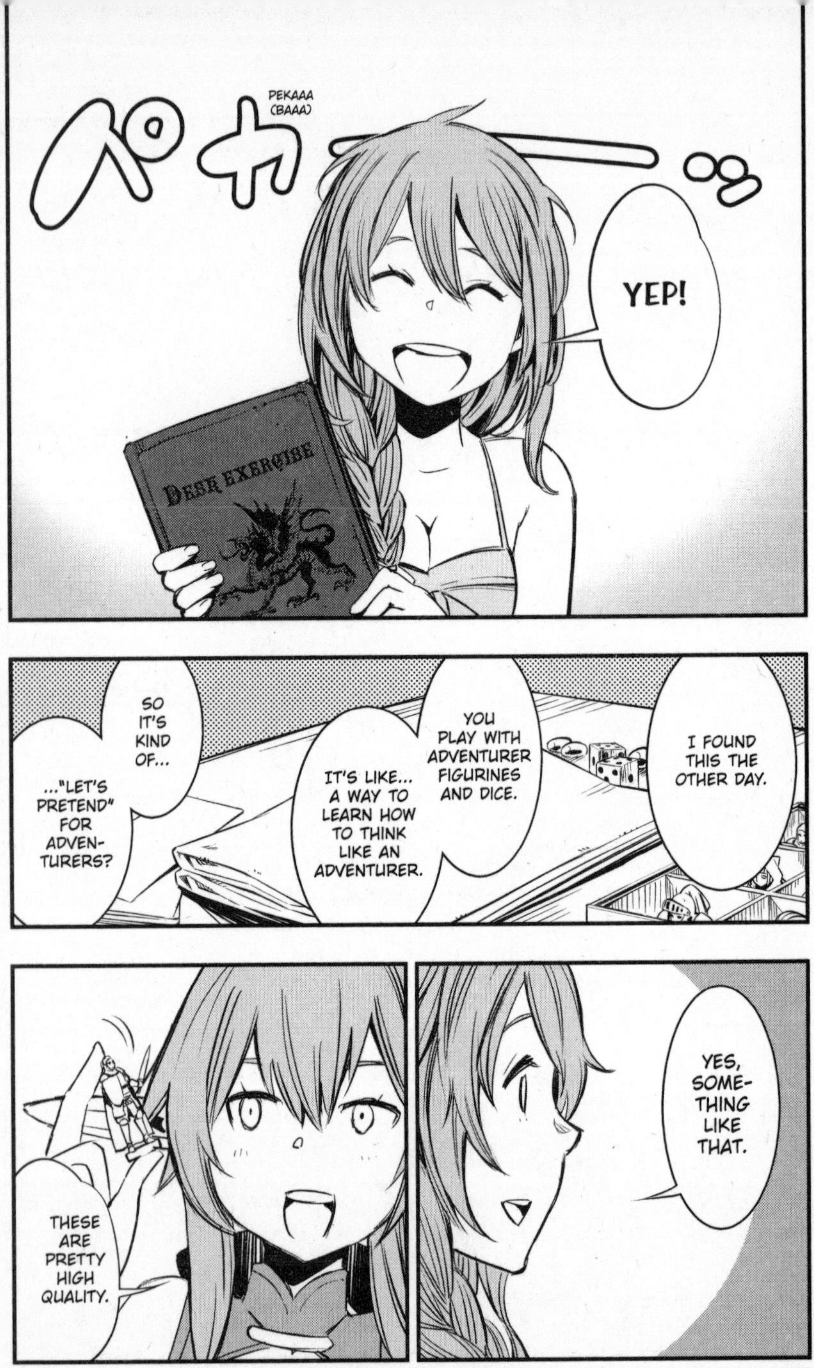
PEKAAA (BAAA)
YEP!
DESK EXERCISE
I FOUND THIS THE OTHER DAY.
YOU PLAY WITH ADVENTURER FIGURINES AND DICE.
IT'S LIKE... A WAY TO LEARN HOW TO THINK LIKE AN ADVENTURER.
SO IT'S KIND OF...
..."LET'S PRETEND" FOR ADVEN-TURERS?
YES, SOME-THING LIKE THAT.
THESE ARE PRETTY HIGH QUALITY.

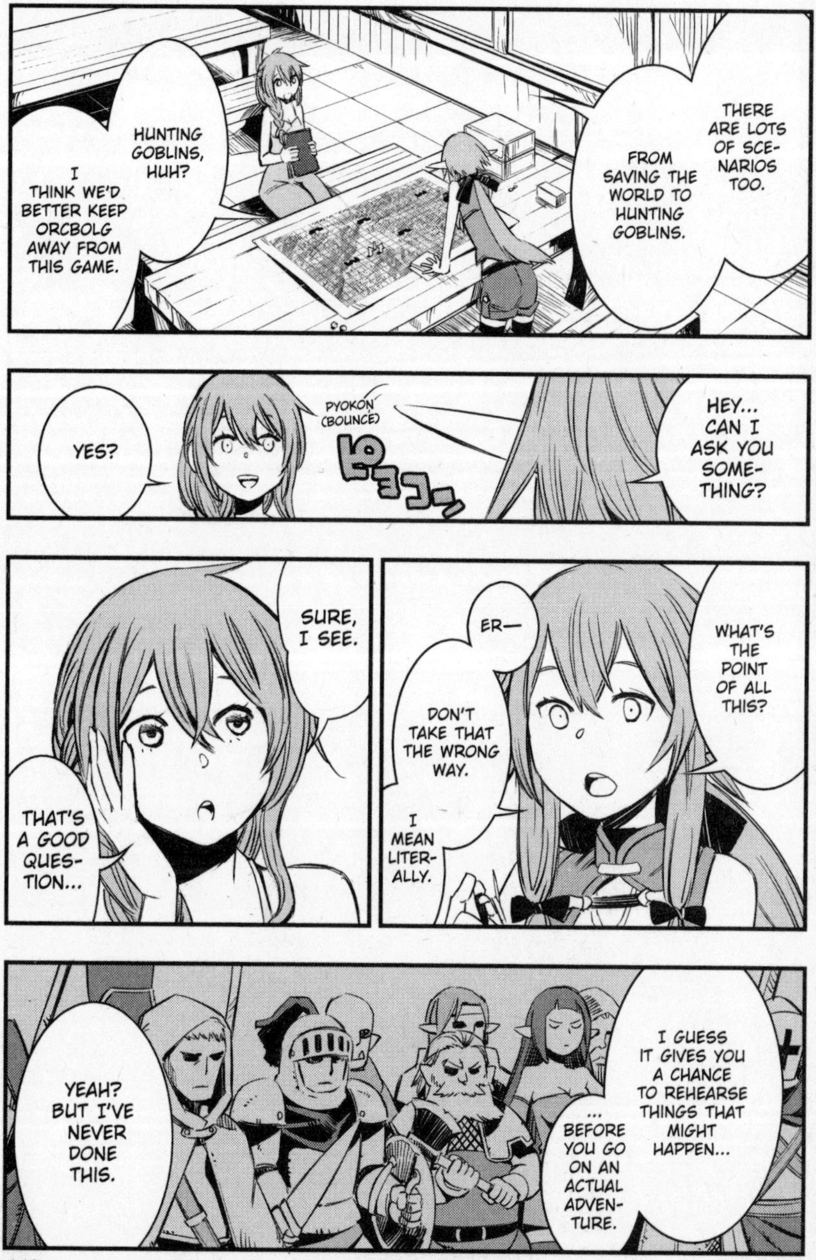
THERE ARE LOTS OF SCE-NARIOS TOO.
FROM SAVING THE WORLD TO HUNTING GOBLINS.
HUNTING GOBLINS, HUH?
I THINK WE'D BETTER KEEP ORCBOLG AWAY FROM THIS GAME.
HEY... CAN I ASK YOU SOME-THING?
PYOKON (BOUNCE)
YES?
WHAT'S THE POINT OF ALL THIS?
ER—
DON'T TAKE THAT THE WRONG WAY.
I MEAN LITER-ALLY.
SURE, I SEE.
THAT'S A GOOD QUES-TION...
I GUESS IT GIVES YOU A CHANCE TO REHEARSE THINGS THAT MIGHT HAPPEN...
...BEFORE YOU GO ON AN ACTUAL ADVEN-TURE.
YEAH? BUT I'VE NEVER DONE THIS.

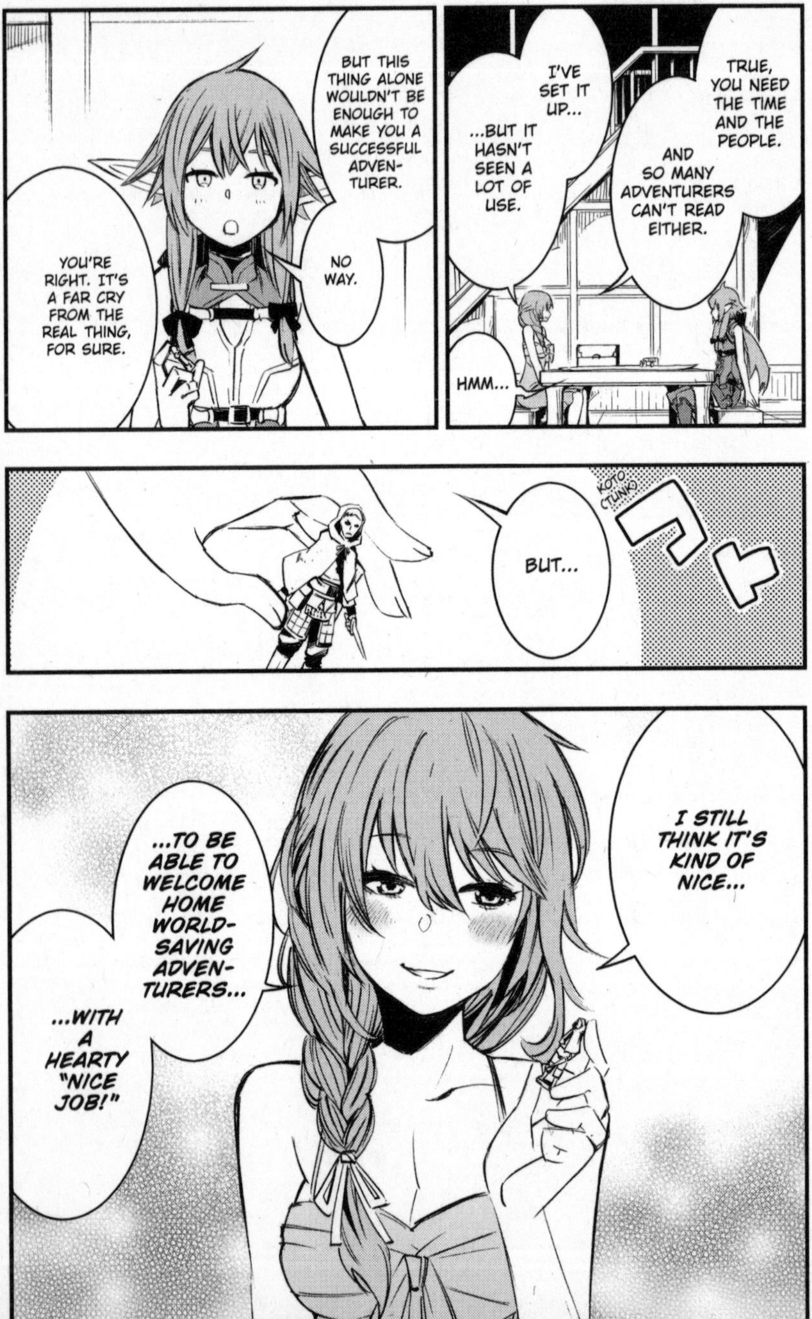
TRUE, YOU NEED THE TIME AND THE PEOPLE.
AND SO MANY ADVENTURERS CAN'T READ EITHER.
I'VE SET IT UP...
...BUT IT HASN'T SEEN A LOT OF USE.
HMM...
BUT THIS THING ALONE WOULDN'T BE ENOUGH TO MAKE YOU A SUCCESSFUL ADVEN-TURER.
NO WAY.
YOU'RE RIGHT. IT'S A FAR CRY FROM THE REAL THING, FOR SURE.
KOTO (TUNK)
BUT...
I STILL THINK IT'S KIND OF NICE...
...TO BE ABLE TO WELCOME HOME WORLD-SAVING ADVEN-TURERS...
...WITH A HEARTY "NICE JOB!"

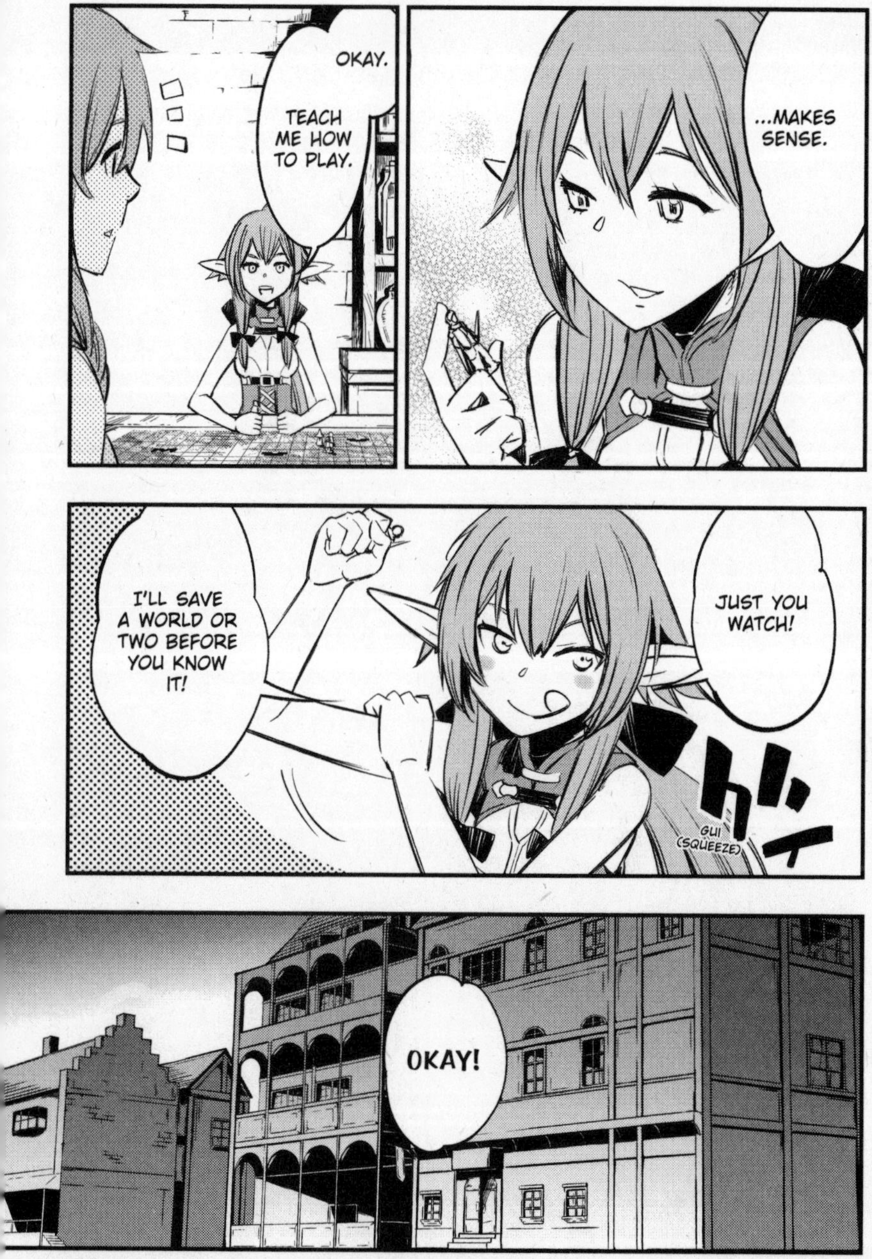
...MAKES SENSE.
OKAY.
TEACH ME HOW TO PLAY.
JUST YOU WATCH!
I'LL SAVE A WORLD OR TWO BEFORE YOU KNOW IT!
GUI (SQUEEZE)
OKAY!

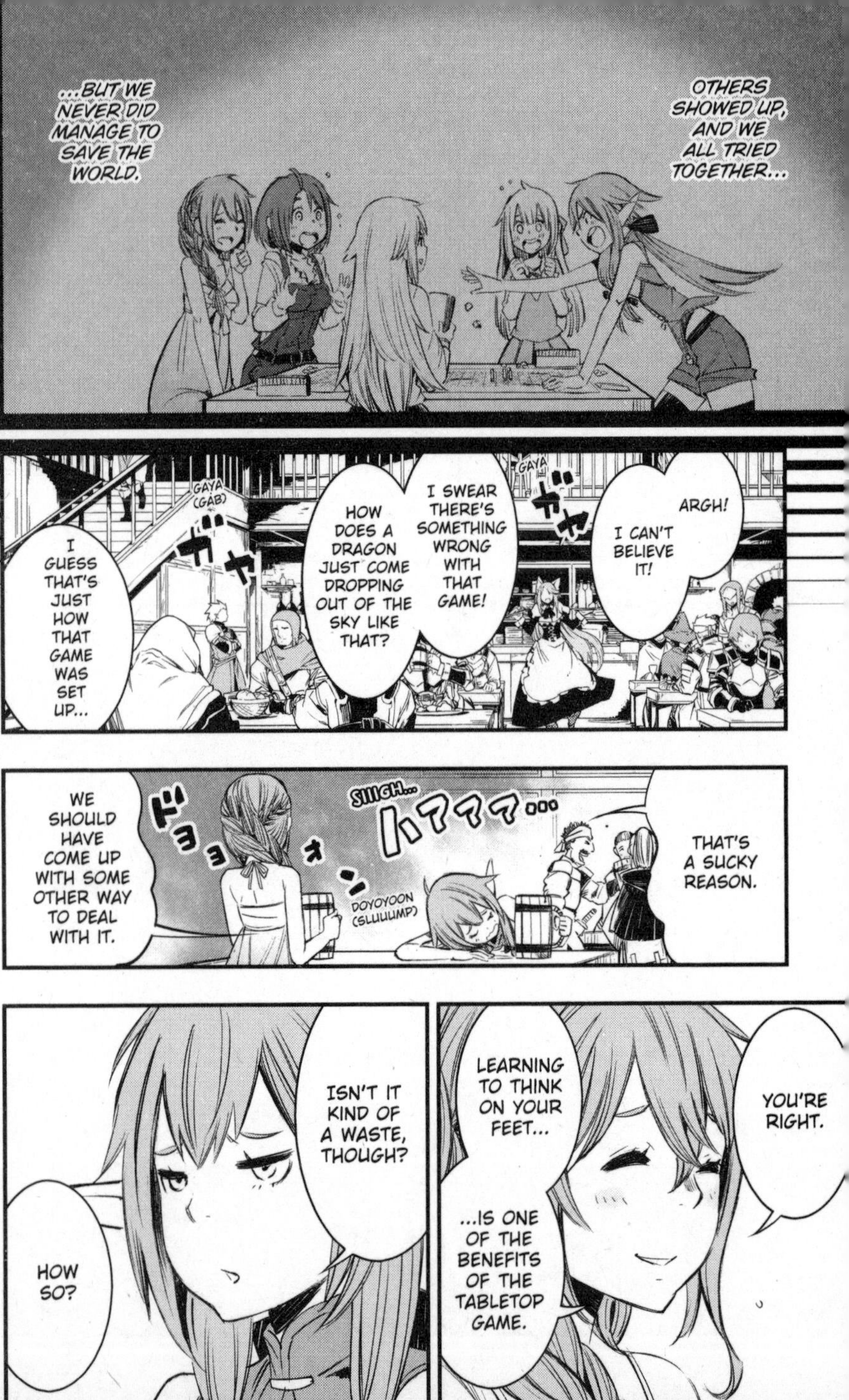
OTHERS SHOWED UP, AND WE ALL TRIED TOGETHER...
...BUT WE NEVER DID MANAGE TO SAVE THE WORLD.
ARGH!
I CAN'T BELIEVE IT!
GAYA
ガヤ
I SWEAR THERE'S SOMETHING WRONG WITH THAT GAME!
HOW DOES A DRAGON JUST COME DROPPING OUT OF THE SKY LIKE THAT?
GAYA (GAB)
ガヤ
I GUESS THAT'S JUST HOW THAT GAME WAS SET UP...
THAT'S A SUCKY REASON.
SIIIGH...
ハァァァ...
DOYOYOON (SLUUUMP)
ドョョォン
WE SHOULD HAVE COME UP WITH SOME OTHER WAY TO DEAL WITH IT.
YOU'RE RIGHT.
LEARNING TO THINK ON YOUR FEET...
...IS ONE OF THE BENEFITS OF THE TABLETOP GAME.
ISN'T IT KIND OF A WASTE, THOUGH?
HOW SO?

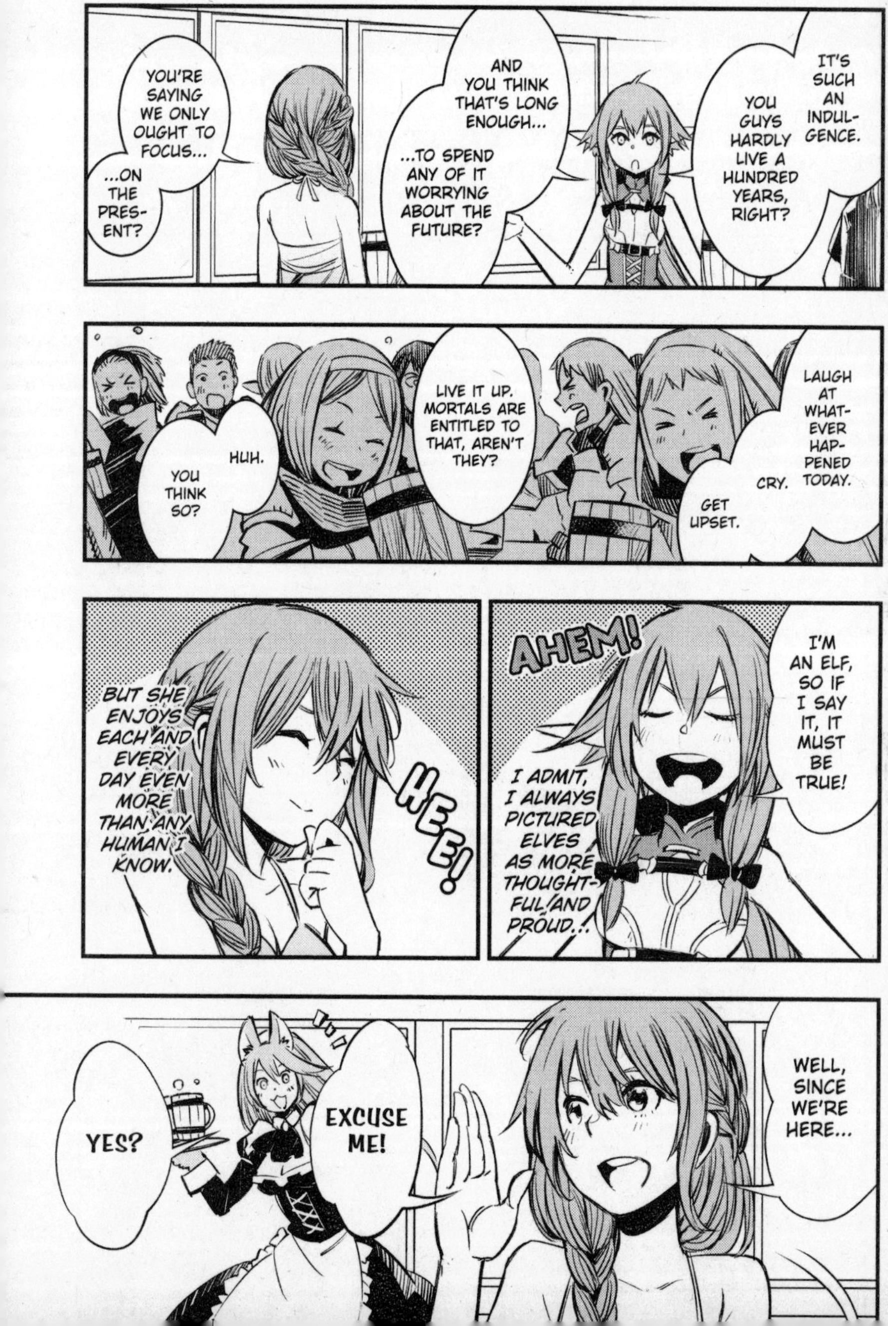
IT'S SUCH AN INDULGENCE.
YOU GUYS HARDLY LIVE A HUNDRED YEARS, RIGHT?
AND YOU THINK THAT'S LONG ENOUGH...
...TO SPEND ANY OF IT WORRYING ABOUT THE FUTURE?
YOU'RE SAYING WE ONLY OUGHT TO FOCUS...
...ON THE PRESENT?
LAUGH AT WHATEVER HAPPENED TODAY.
CRY.
GET UPSET.
LIVE IT UP. MORTALS ARE ENTITLED TO THAT, AREN'T THEY?
HUH.
YOU THINK SO?
AHEM!
I'M AN ELF, SO IF I SAY IT, IT MUST BE TRUE!
I ADMIT, I ALWAYS PICTURED ELVES AS MORE THOUGHTFUL AND PROUD...
HEE!
BUT SHE ENJOYS EACH AND EVERY DAY EVEN MORE THAN ANY HUMAN I KNOW.
WELL, SINCE WE'RE HERE...
EXCUSE ME!
YES?

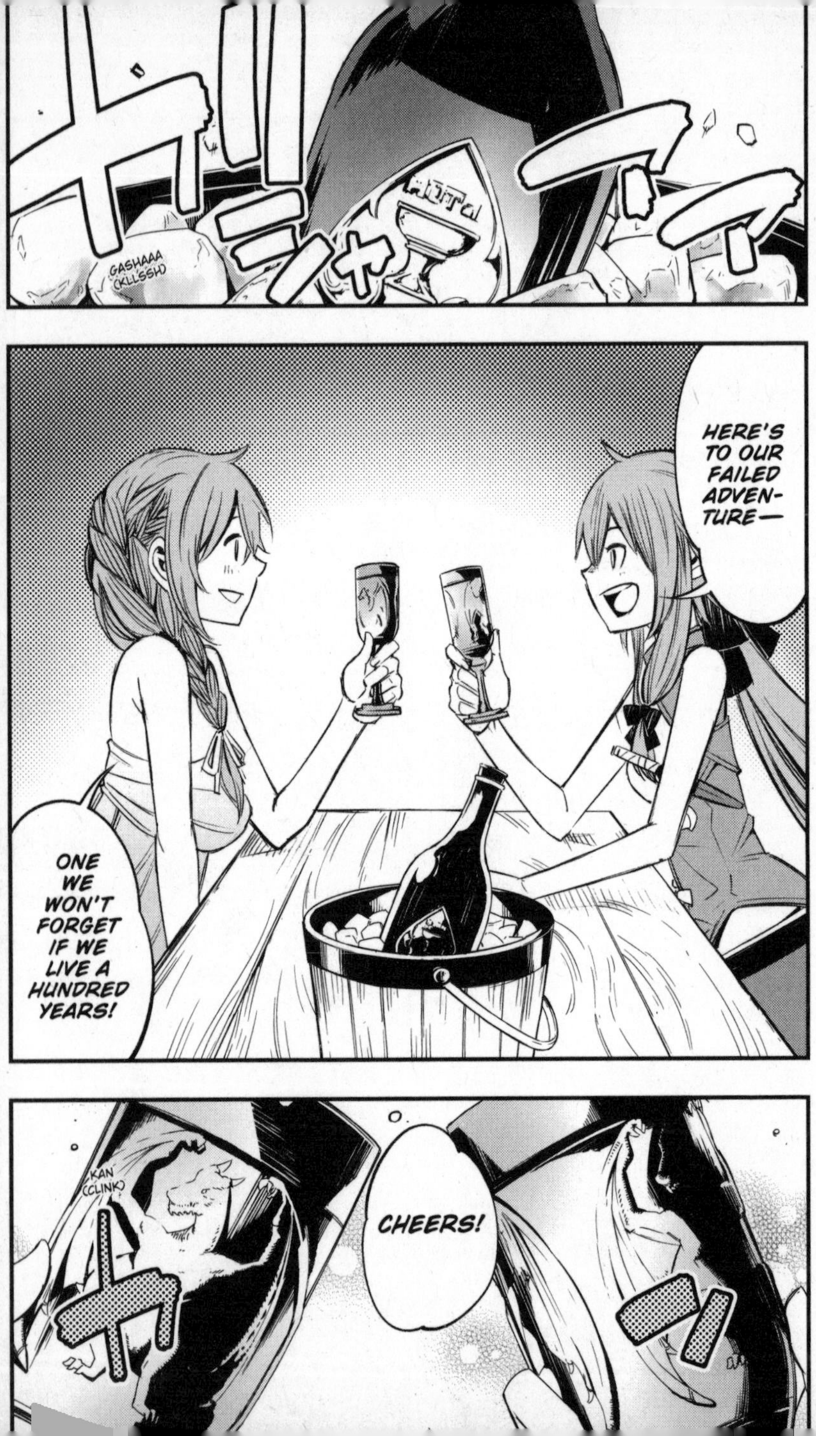
GASHAAA (KLLSSH)
HERE'S TO OUR FAILED ADVENTURE—
ONE WE WON'T FORGET IF WE LIVE A HUNDRED YEARS!
KAN (CLINK)
CHEERS!

Chapter 9:
Of the Three of Them,
Some Months Ago

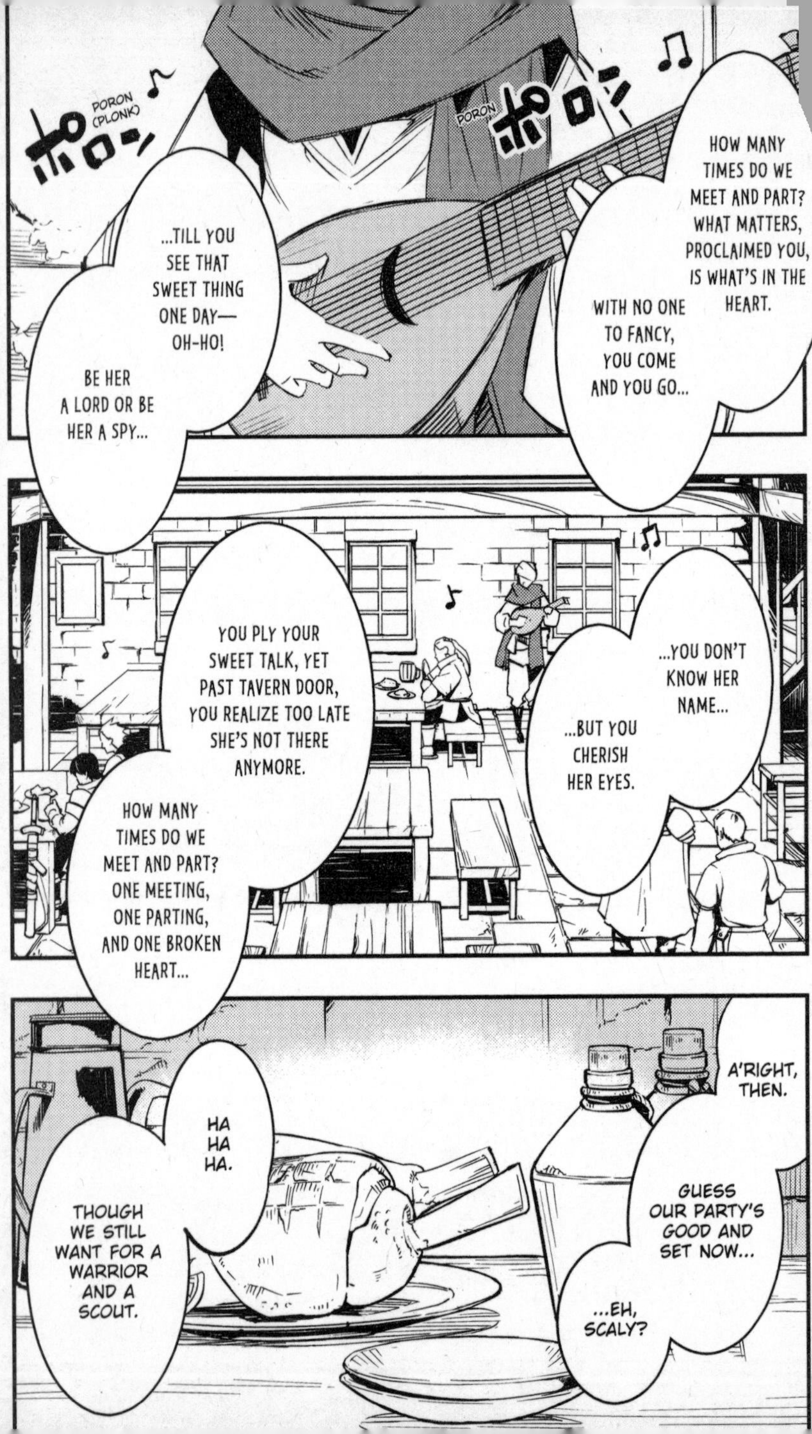
ポロン
PORON
HOW MANY TIMES DO WE MEET AND PART? WHAT MATTERS, PROCLAIMED YOU, IS WHAT'S IN THE HEART.
WITH NO ONE TO FANCY, YOU COME AND YOU GO...
ポロン
PORON (PLONK)
...TILL YOU SEE THAT SWEET THING ONE DAY—OH-HO!
BE HER A LORD OR BE HER A SPY...
...YOU DON'T KNOW HER NAME...
...BUT YOU CHERISH HER EYES.
YOU PLY YOUR SWEET TALK, YET PAST TAVERN DOOR, YOU REALIZE TOO LATE SHE'S NOT THERE ANYMORE.
HOW MANY TIMES DO WE MEET AND PART? ONE MEETING, ONE PARTING, AND ONE BROKEN HEART...
A'RIGHT, THEN.
GUESS OUR PARTY'S GOOD AND SET NOW...
...EH, SCALY?
HA HA HA.
THOUGH WE STILL WANT FOR A WARRIOR AND A SCOUT.

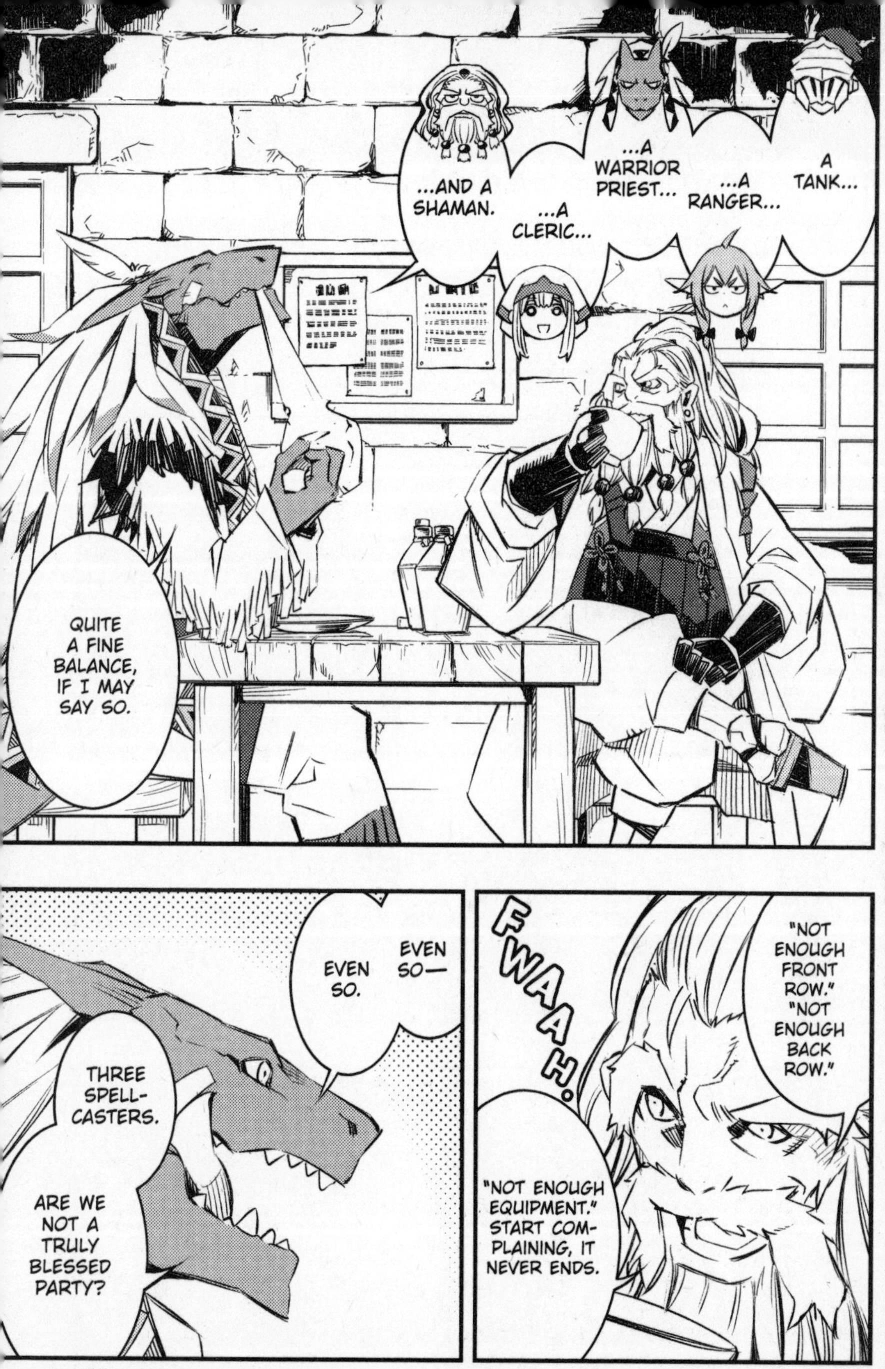
A TANK...
...A RANGER...
...A WARRIOR PRIEST...
...A CLERIC...
...AND A SHAMAN.
QUITE A FINE BALANCE, IF I MAY SAY SO.
"NOT ENOUGH FRONT ROW." "NOT ENOUGH BACK ROW."
FWAAH.
"NOT ENOUGH EQUIPMENT." START COMPLAINING, IT NEVER ENDS.
EVEN SO—
EVEN SO.
THREE SPELL-CASTERS.
ARE WE NOT A TRULY BLESSED PARTY?

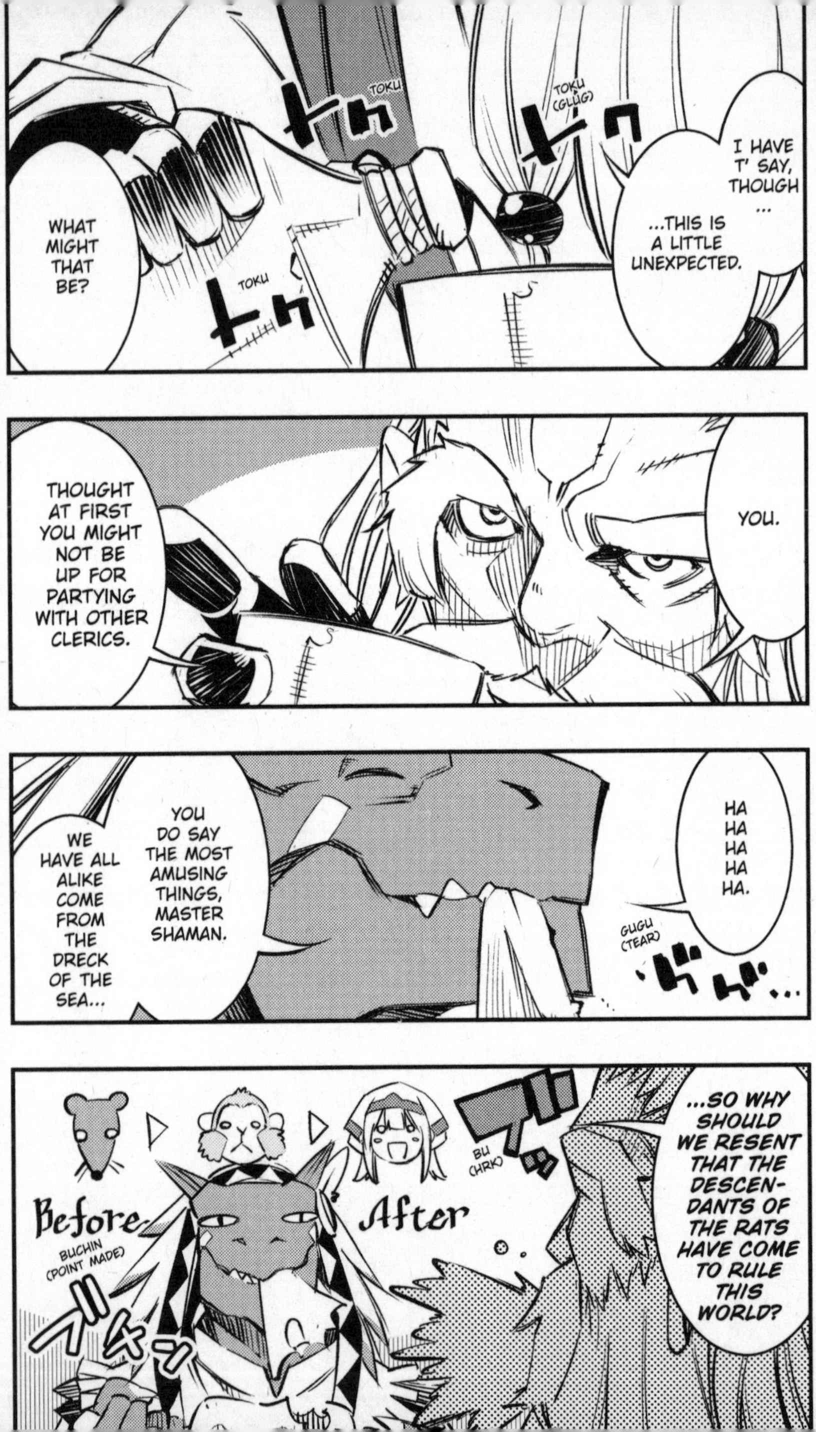
I HAVE T' SAY, THOUGH ...
TOKU (GLUG)
...THIS IS A LITTLE UNEXPECTED.
TOKU
TOKU
WHAT MIGHT THAT BE?
YOU.
THOUGHT AT FIRST YOU MIGHT NOT BE UP FOR PARTYING WITH OTHER CLERICS.
HA HA HA HA HA.
GUGU (TEAR)
YOU DO SAY THE MOST AMUSING THINGS, MASTER SHAMAN.
WE HAVE ALL ALIKE COME FROM THE DRECK OF THE SEA...
...SO WHY SHOULD WE RESENT THAT THE DESCEN-DANTS OF THE RATS HAVE COME TO RULE THIS WORLD?
BU (HRK)
After
Before
BUCHIN (POINT MADE)

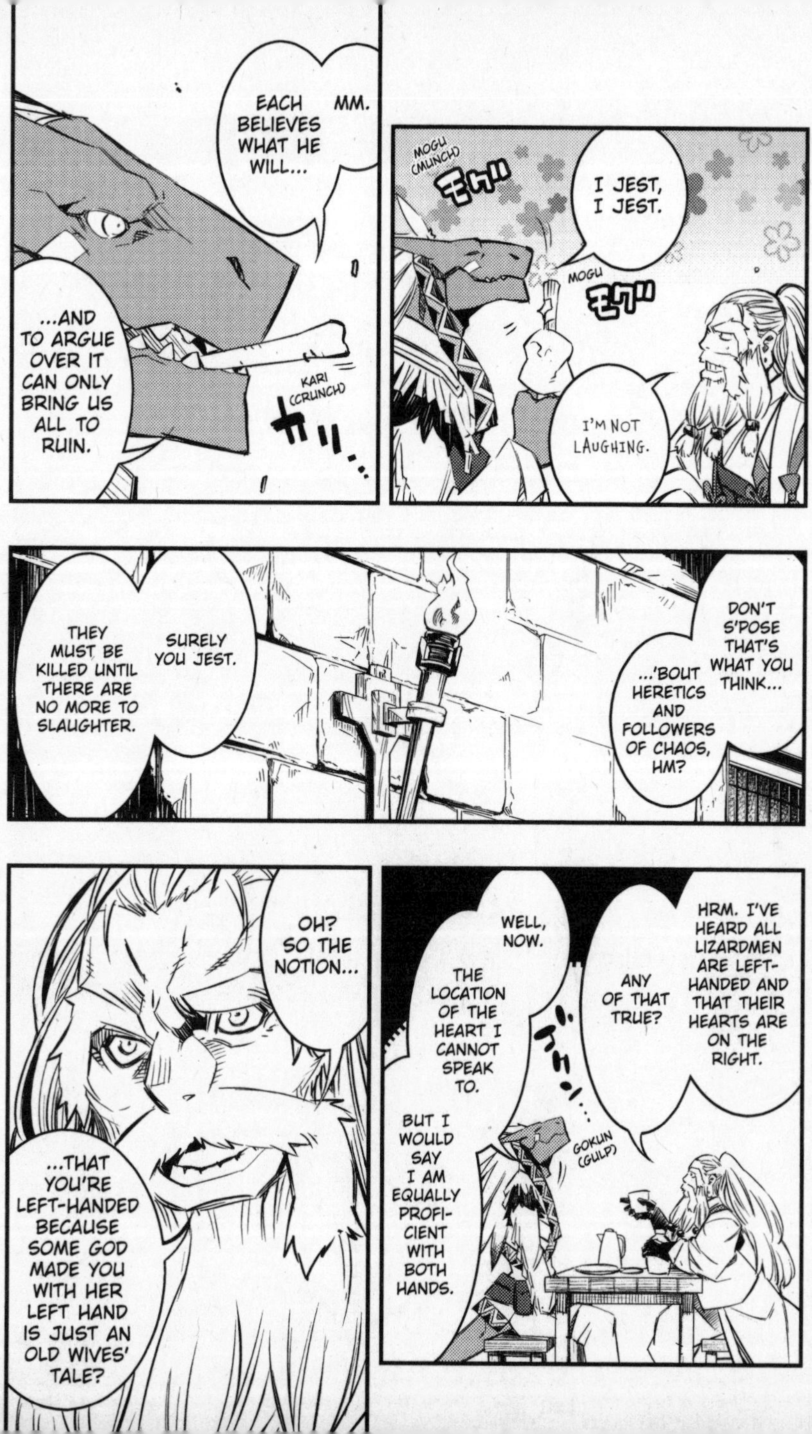
I JEST, I JEST.
MOGU (MUNCH)
MOGU
I'M NOT LAUGHING.
MM.
EACH BELIEVES WHAT HE WILL...
...AND TO ARGUE OVER IT CAN ONLY BRING US ALL TO RUIN.
KARI (CRUNCH)
DON'T S'POSE THAT'S WHAT YOU THINK...
...'BOUT HERETICS AND FOLLOWERS OF CHAOS, HM?
SURELY YOU JEST.
THEY MUST BE KILLED UNTIL THERE ARE NO MORE TO SLAUGHTER.
HRM. I'VE HEARD ALL LIZARDMEN ARE LEFT-HANDED AND THAT THEIR HEARTS ARE ON THE RIGHT.
ANY OF THAT TRUE?
GOKUN (GULP)
WELL, NOW.
THE LOCATION OF THE HEART I CANNOT SPEAK TO.
BUT I WOULD SAY I AM EQUALLY PROFI-CIENT WITH BOTH HANDS.
OH? SO THE NOTION...
...THAT YOU'RE LEFT-HANDED BECAUSE SOME GOD MADE YOU WITH HER LEFT HAND IS JUST AN OLD WIVES' TALE?

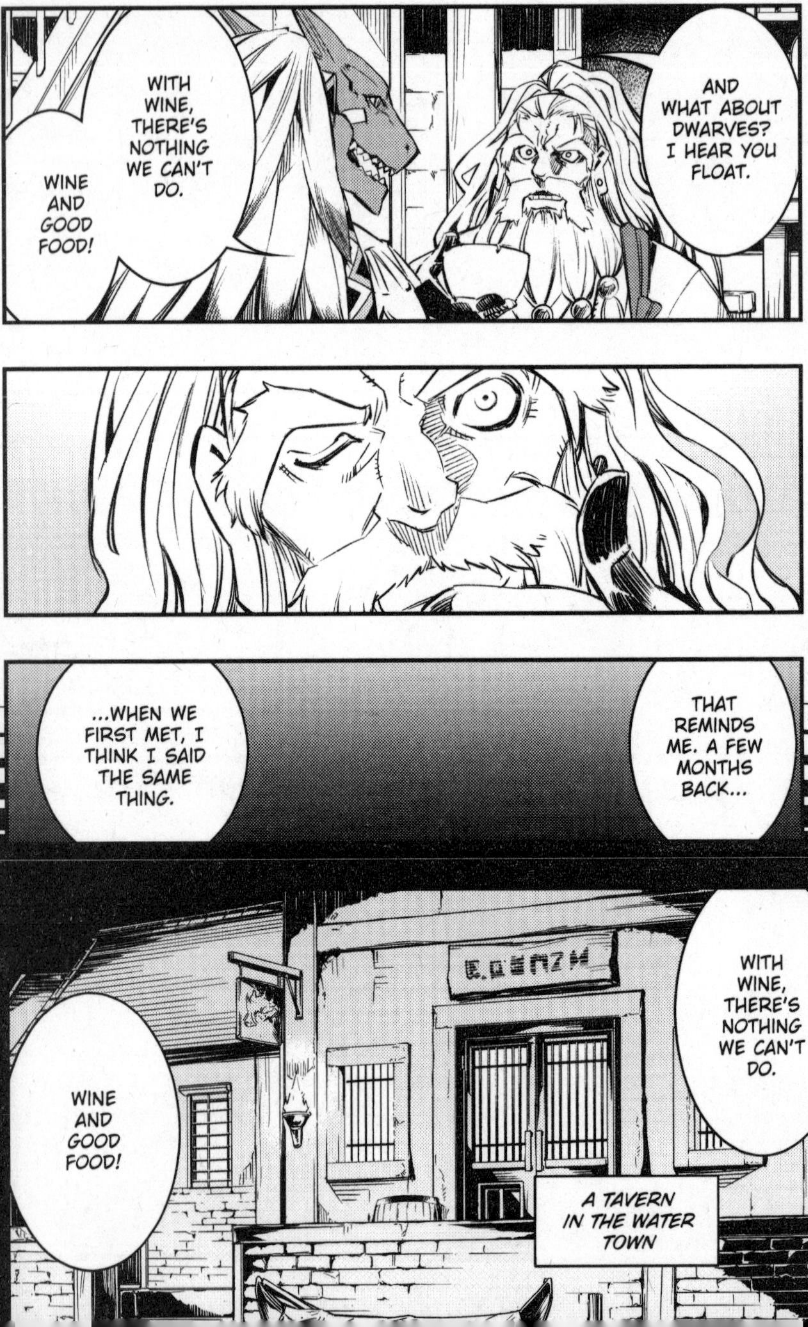
AND WHAT ABOUT DWARVES? I HEAR YOU FLOAT.
WITH WINE, THERE'S NOTHING WE CAN'T DO.
WINE AND GOOD FOOD!
THAT REMINDS ME. A FEW MONTHS BACK...
...WHEN WE FIRST MET, I THINK I SAID THE SAME THING.
WITH WINE, THERE'S NOTHING WE CAN'T DO.
A TAVERN IN THE WATER TOWN
WINE AND GOOD FOOD!

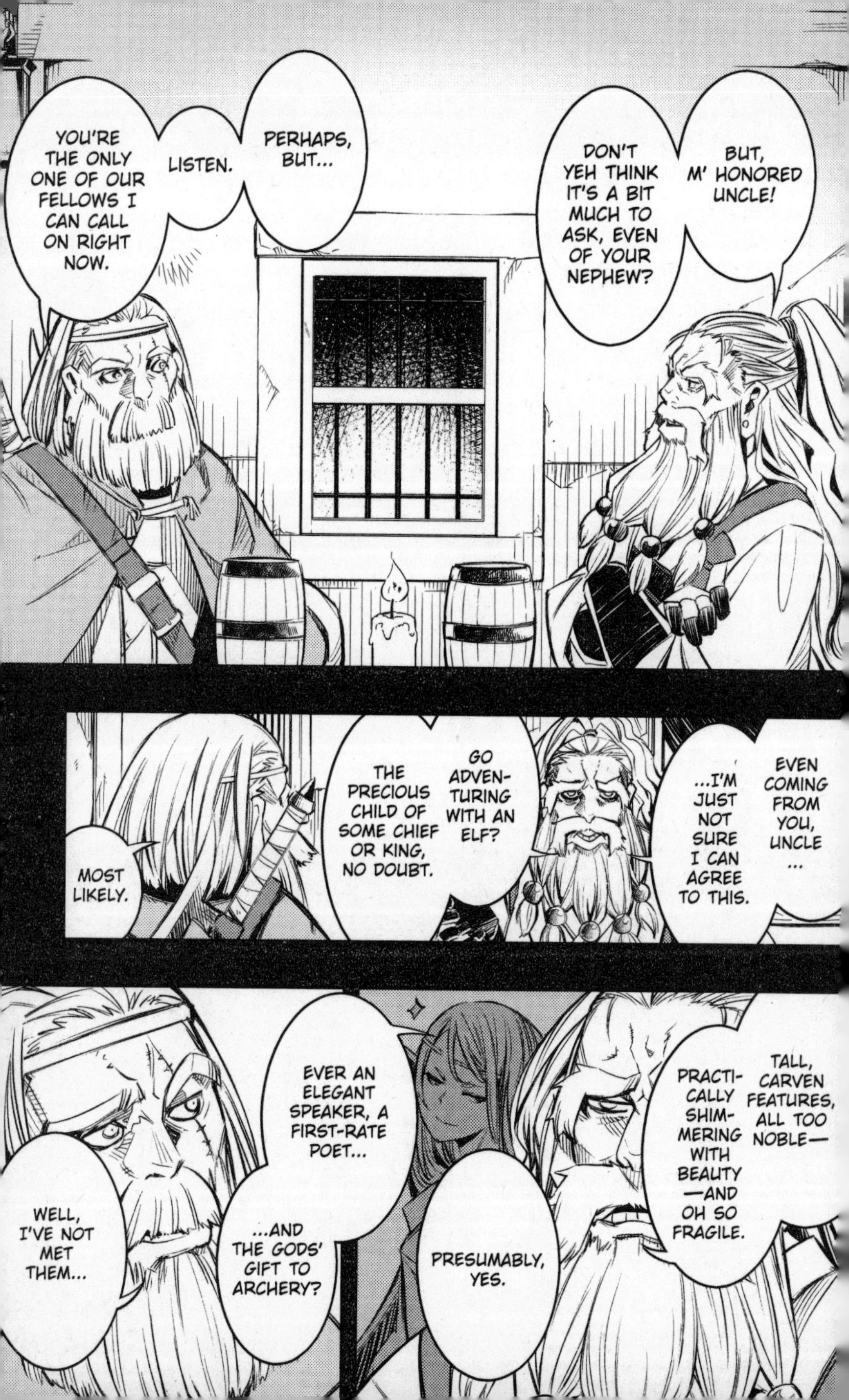
BUT, M' HONORED UNCLE!
DON'T YEH THINK IT'S A BIT MUCH TO ASK, EVEN OF YOUR NEPHEW?
PERHAPS, BUT...
LISTEN.
YOU'RE THE ONLY ONE OF OUR FELLOWS I CAN CALL ON RIGHT NOW.
EVEN COMING FROM YOU, UNCLE...
...I'M JUST NOT SURE I CAN AGREE TO THIS.
GO ADVENTURING WITH AN ELF?
THE PRECIOUS CHILD OF SOME CHIEF OR KING, NO DOUBT.
MOST LIKELY.
TALL, CARVEN FEATURES, ALL TOO NOBLE—
PRACTICALLY SHIMMERING WITH BEAUTY—AND OH SO FRAGILE.
PRESUMABLY, YES.
EVER AN ELEGANT SPEAKER, A FIRST-RATE POET...
...AND THE GODS' GIFT TO ARCHERY?
WELL, I'VE NOT MET THEM...

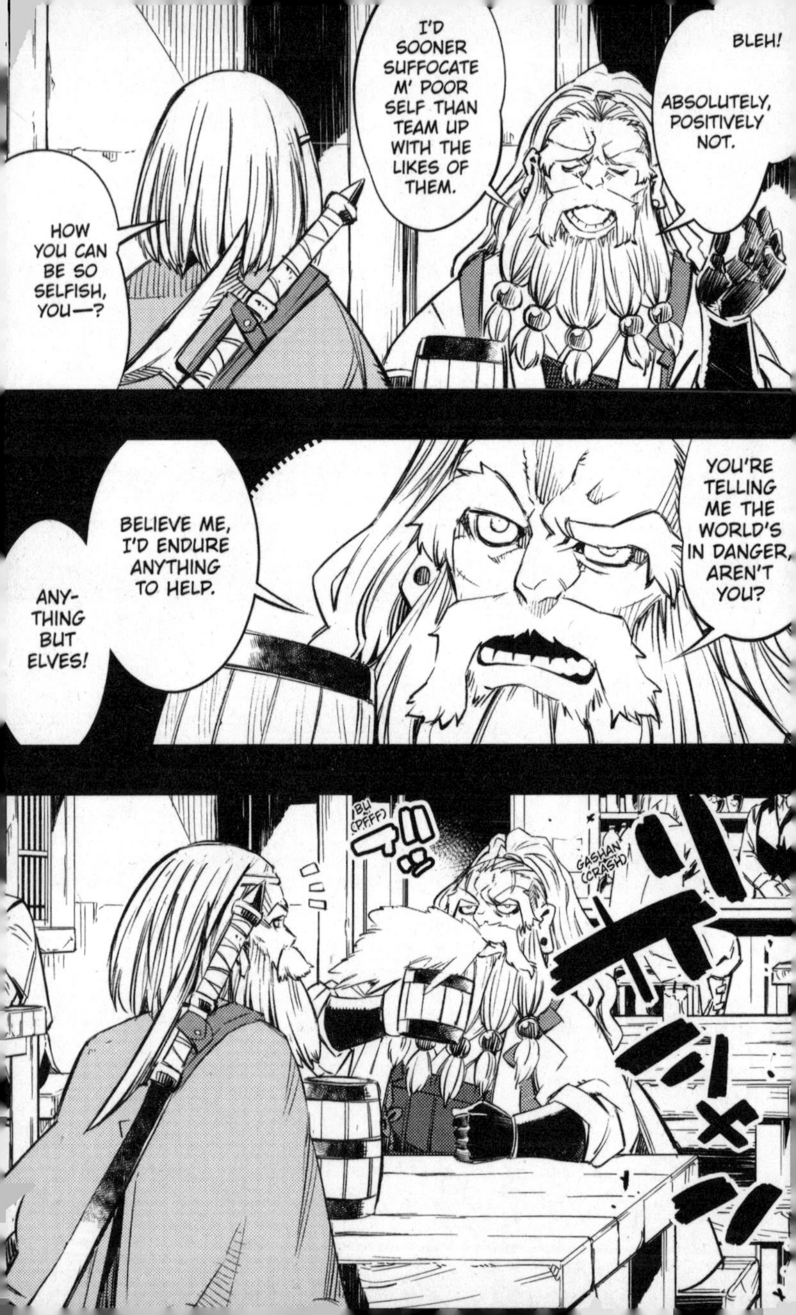
BLEH!
ABSOLUTELY, POSITIVELY NOT.
I'D SOONER SUFFOCATE M' POOR SELF THAN TEAM UP WITH THE LIKES OF THEM.
HOW YOU CAN BE SO SELFISH, YOU—?
YOU'RE TELLING ME THE WORLD'S IN DANGER, AREN'T YOU?
BELIEVE ME, I'D ENDURE ANYTHING TO HELP.
ANY-THING BUT ELVES!
GASHAN (CRASH)
BU (PFFF)

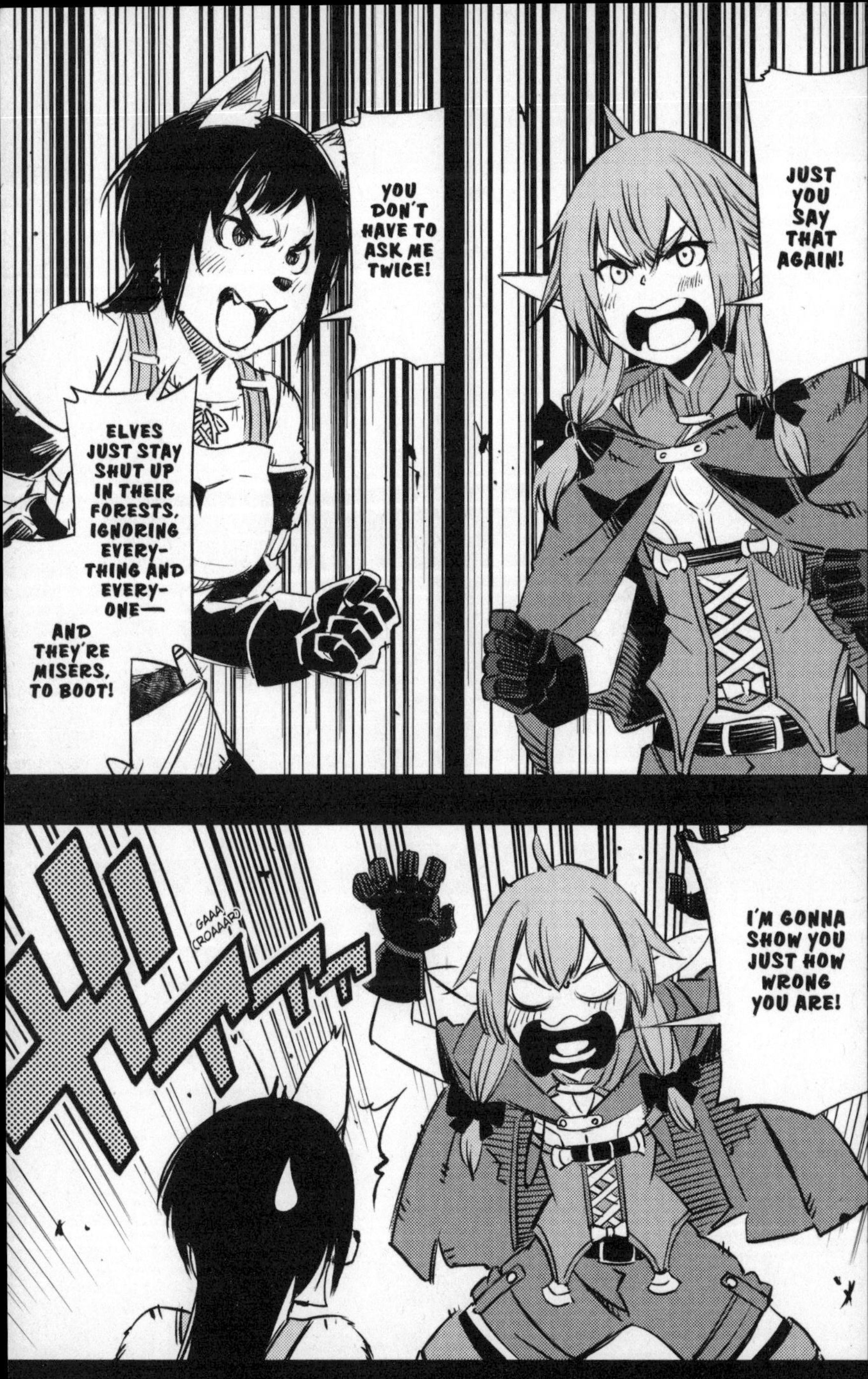
JUST YOU SAY THAT AGAIN!
YOU DON'T HAVE TO ASK ME TWICE!
ELVES JUST STAY SHUT UP IN THEIR FORESTS, IGNORING EVERY-THING AND EVERY-ONE—
AND THEY'RE MISERS, TO BOOT!
I'M GONNA SHOW YOU JUST HOW WRONG YOU ARE!
GAAA (ROAAAR)

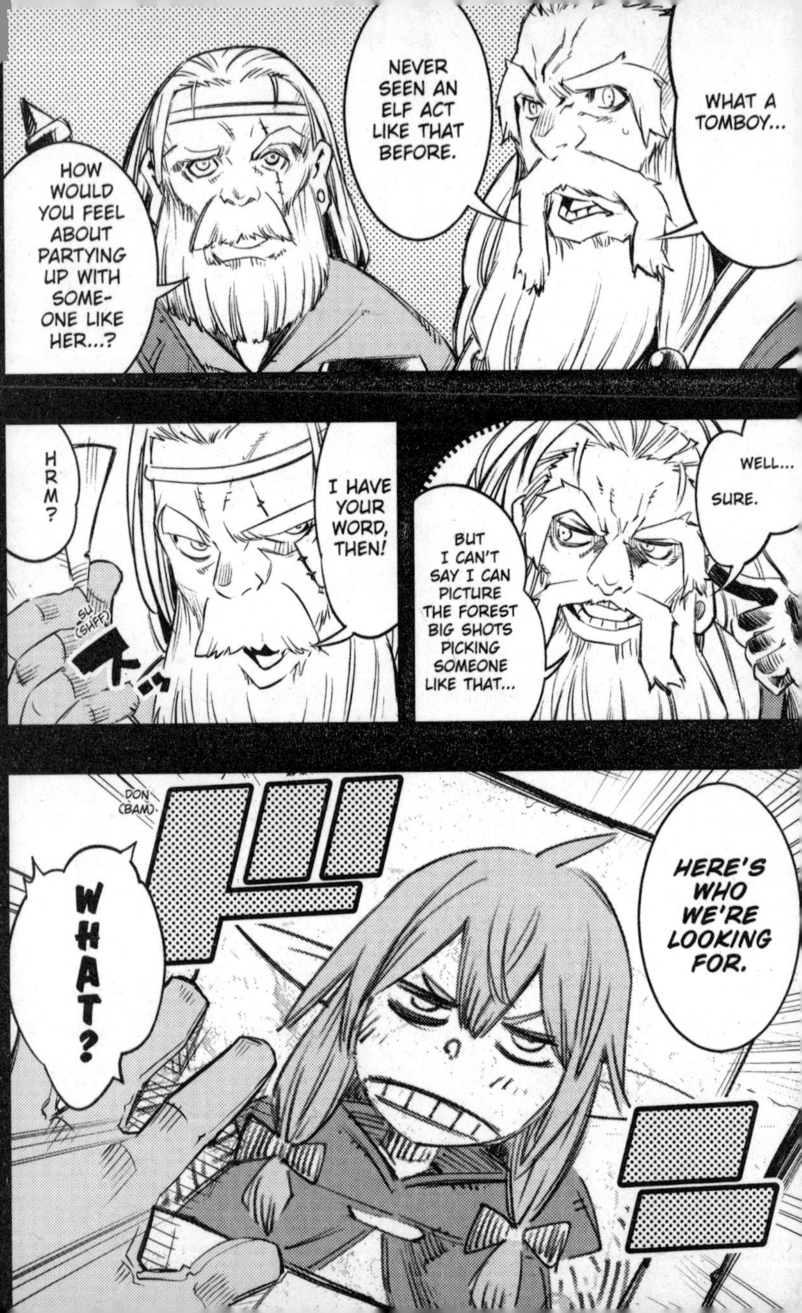
WHAT A TOMBOY...
NEVER SEEN AN ELF ACT LIKE THAT BEFORE.
HOW WOULD YOU FEEL ABOUT PARTYING UP WITH SOME-ONE LIKE HER...?
WELL...
SURE.
BUT I CAN'T SAY I CAN PICTURE THE FOREST BIG SHOTS PICKING SOMEONE LIKE THAT...
I HAVE YOUR WORD, THEN!
HRM?
SU (SHFF)
DON (BAM)
HERE'S WHO WE'RE LOOKING FOR.
WHAT?

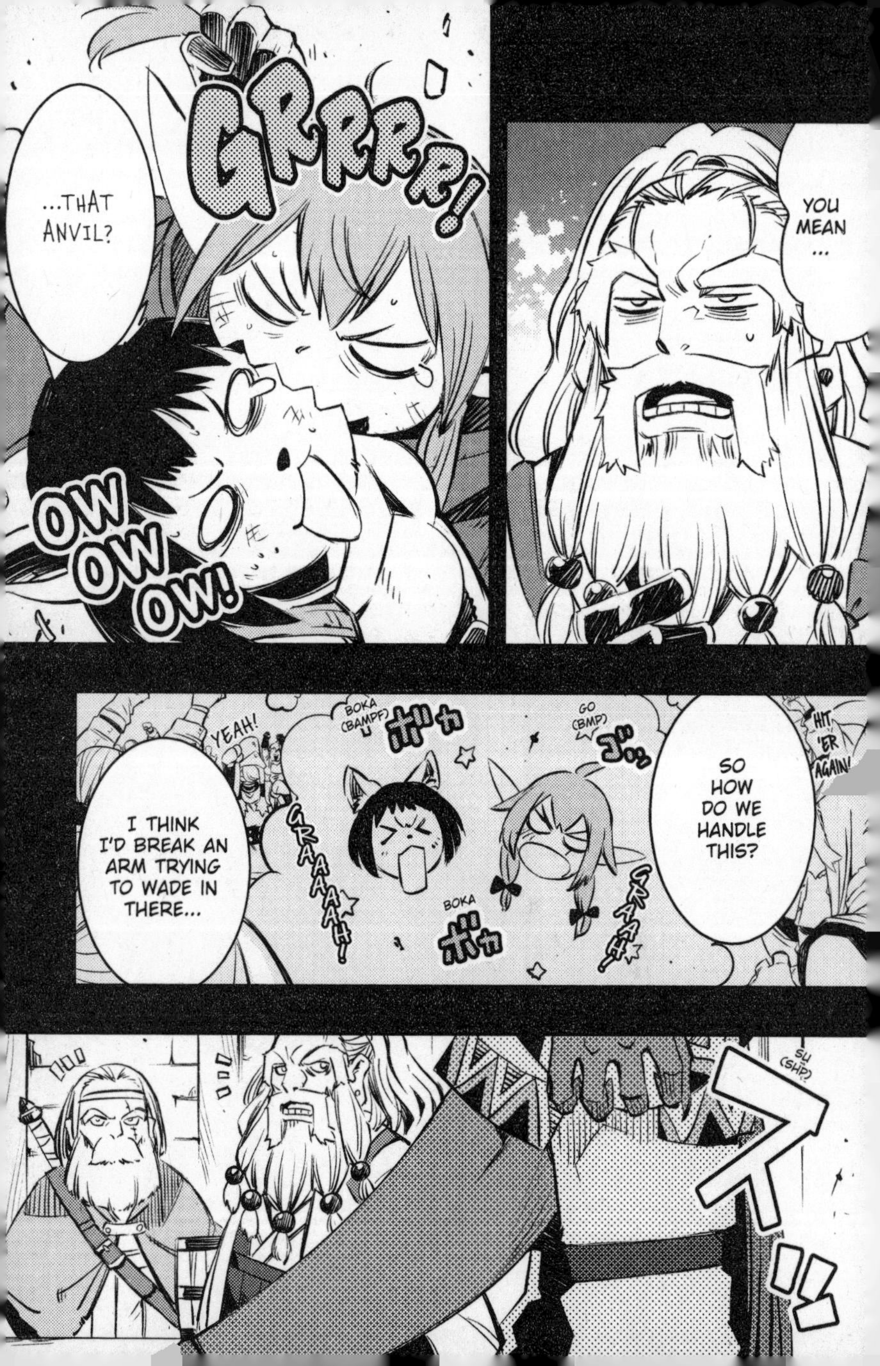
YOU MEAN ...
GRRRR!
...THAT ANVIL?
OW OW OW!
HIT 'ER AGAIN!
SO HOW DO WE HANDLE THIS?
GO (BMP)
ゴッ
GRAAH!
BOKA (BAMPF)
ボカ
YEAH!
GRAAAAAH!
BOKA
ボカ
I THINK I'D BREAK AN ARM TRYING TO WADE IN THERE...
SU (SHP)
ス
!!

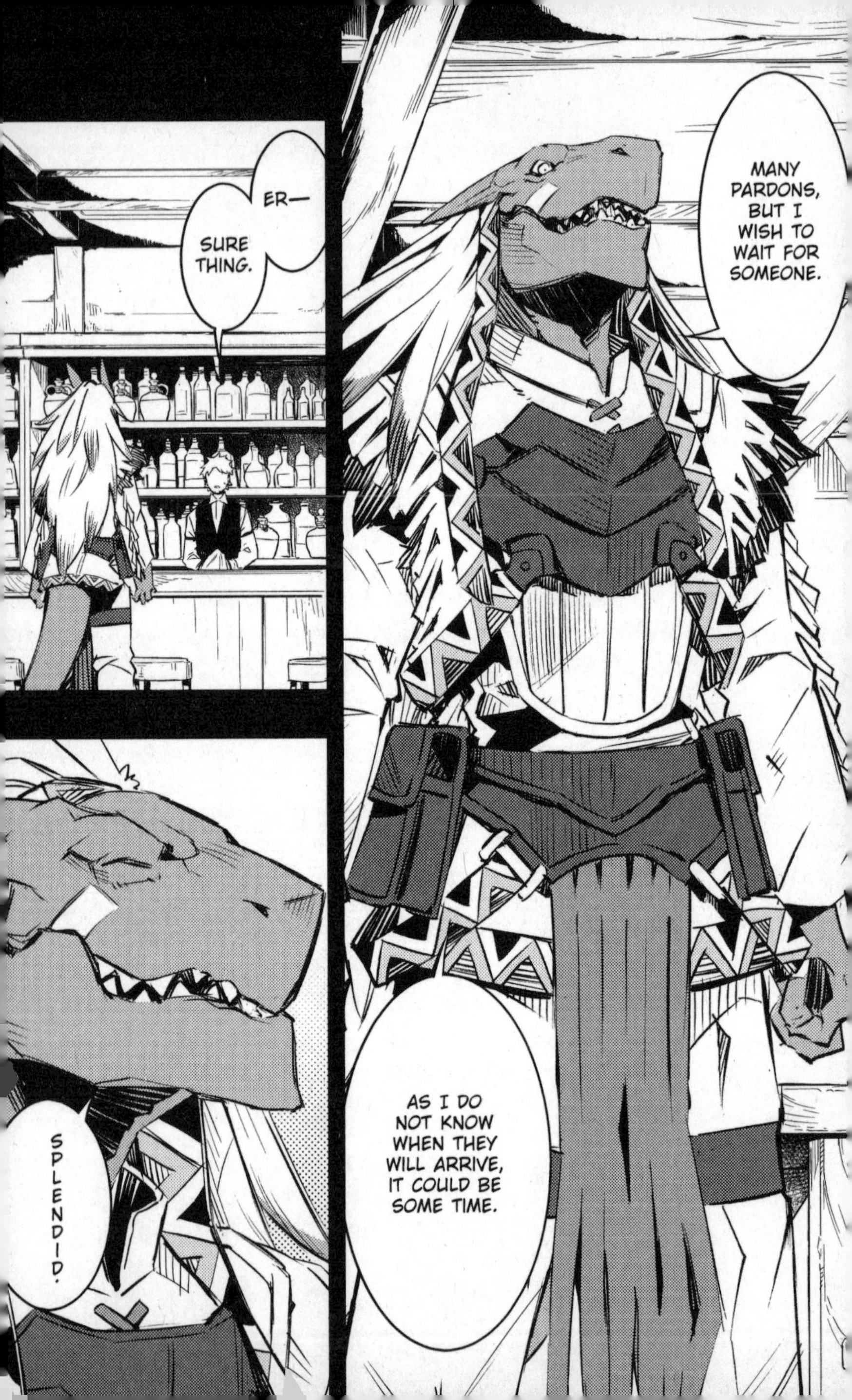
MANY PARDONS, BUT I WISH TO WAIT FOR SOMEONE.
AS I DO NOT KNOW WHEN THEY WILL ARRIVE, IT COULD BE SOME TIME.
ER—
SURE THING.
SPLENDID.

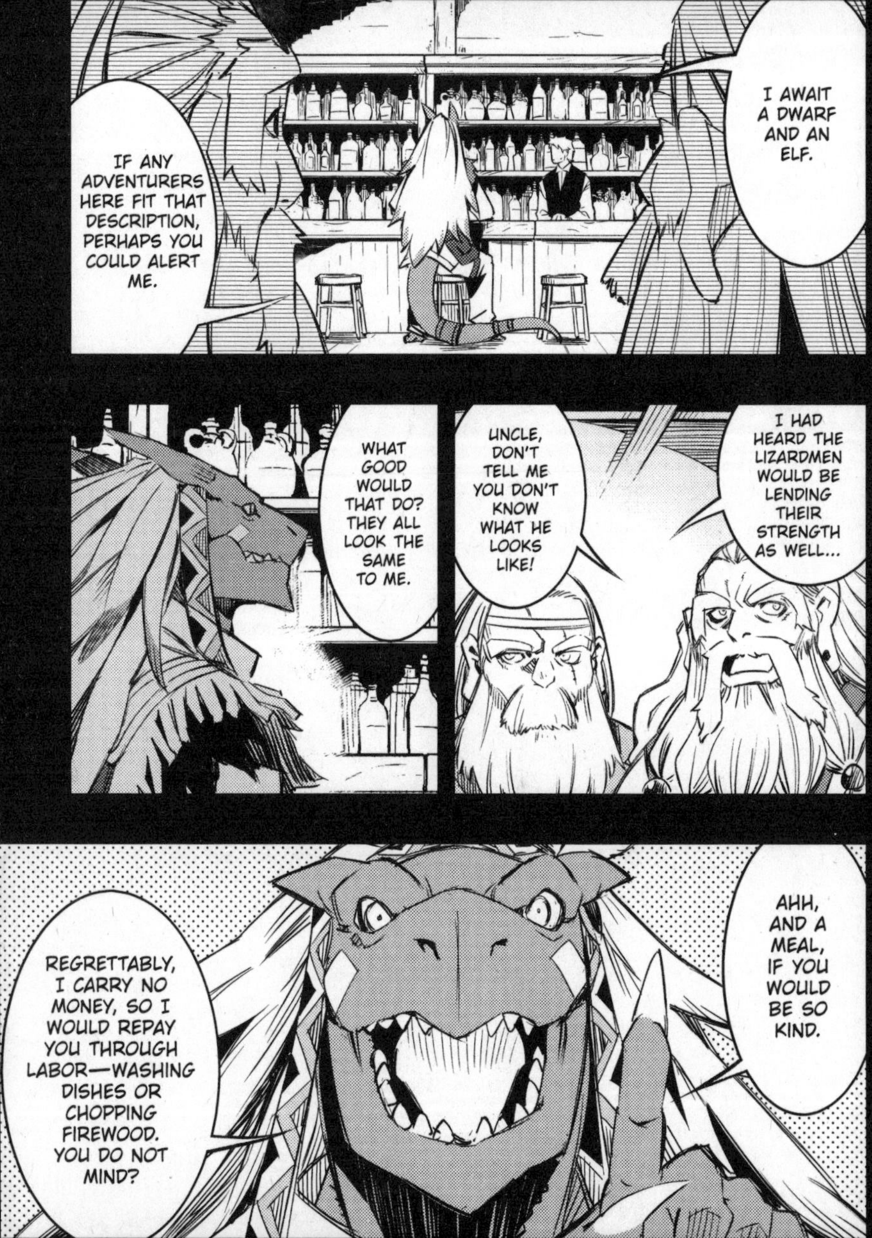
I AWAIT A DWARF AND AN ELF.
IF ANY ADVENTURERS HERE FIT THAT DESCRIPTION, PERHAPS YOU COULD ALERT ME.
I HAD HEARD THE LIZARDMEN WOULD BE LENDING THEIR STRENGTH AS WELL...
UNCLE, DON'T TELL ME YOU DON'T KNOW WHAT HE LOOKS LIKE!
WHAT GOOD WOULD THAT DO? THEY ALL LOOK THE SAME TO ME.
AHH, AND A MEAL, IF YOU WOULD BE SO KIND.
REGRETTABLY, I CARRY NO MONEY, SO I WOULD REPAY YOU THROUGH LABOR—WASHING DISHES OR CHOPPING FIREWOOD. YOU DO NOT MIND?

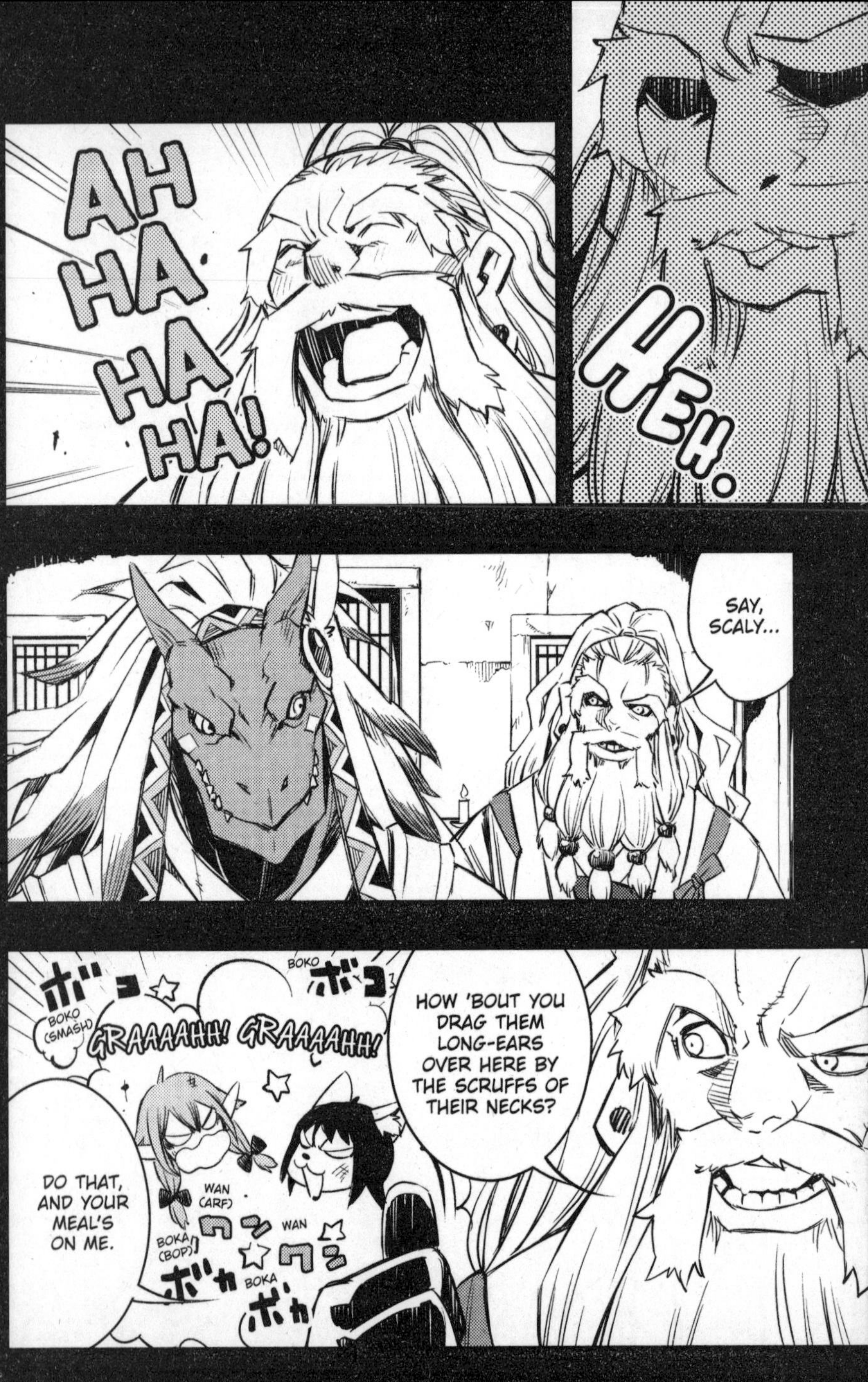
HEH.
AH HA HA HA HA!
SAY, SCALY...
HOW 'BOUT YOU DRAG THEM LONG-EARS OVER HERE BY THE SCRUFFS OF THEIR NECKS?
BOKO ボコ
GRAAAAHH! GRAAAAHH!
ボッ BOKO (SMASH)
DO THAT, AND YOUR MEAL'S ON ME.
WAN (ARF) ワン
WAN ワン
BOKA (BOP) ボカ
BOKA ボカ

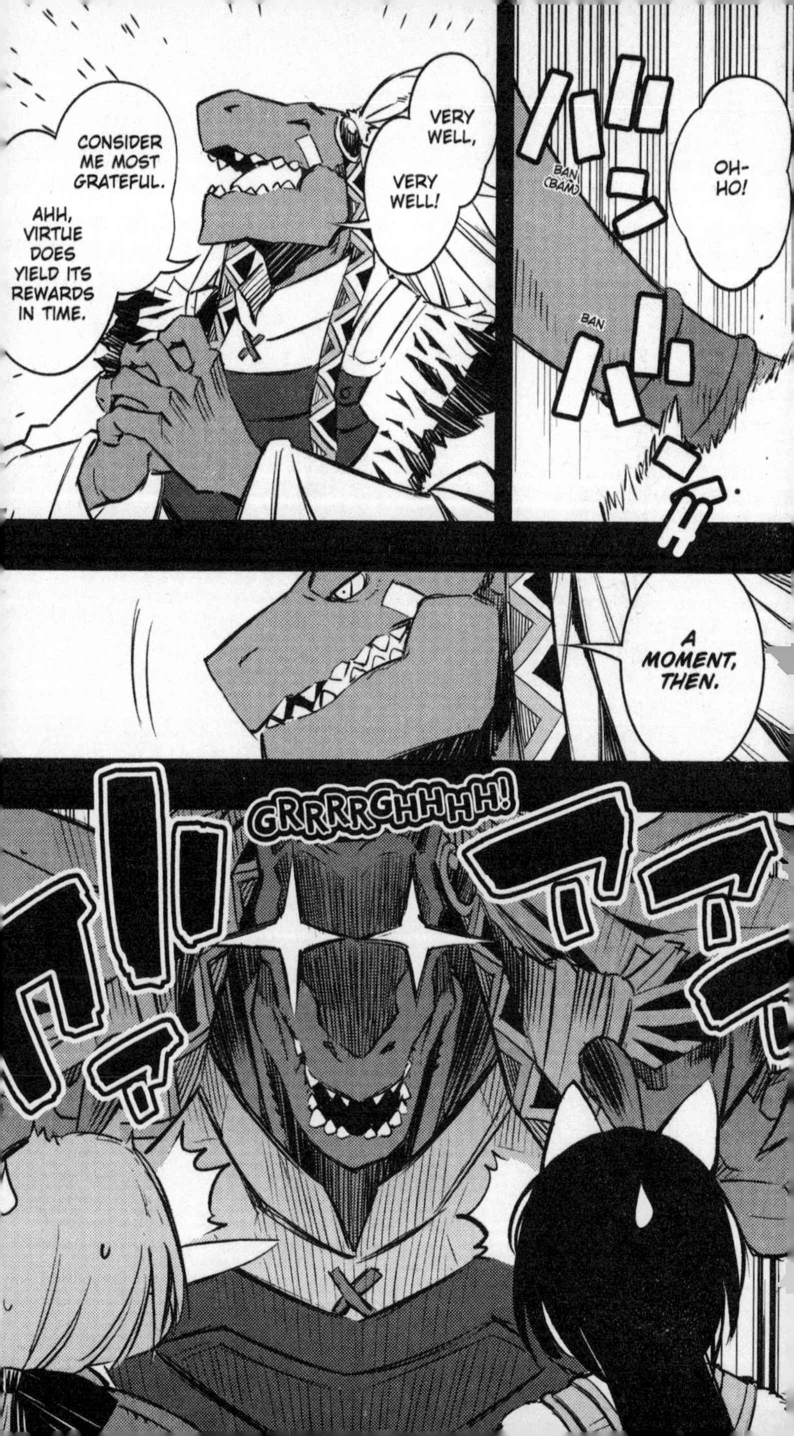
OH-HO!
BAN (BAM)
BAN
VERY WELL,
VERY WELL!
CONSIDER ME MOST GRATEFUL.
AHH, VIRTUE DOES YIELD ITS REWARDS IN TIME.
A MOMENT, THEN.
GRRRRGHHHH!

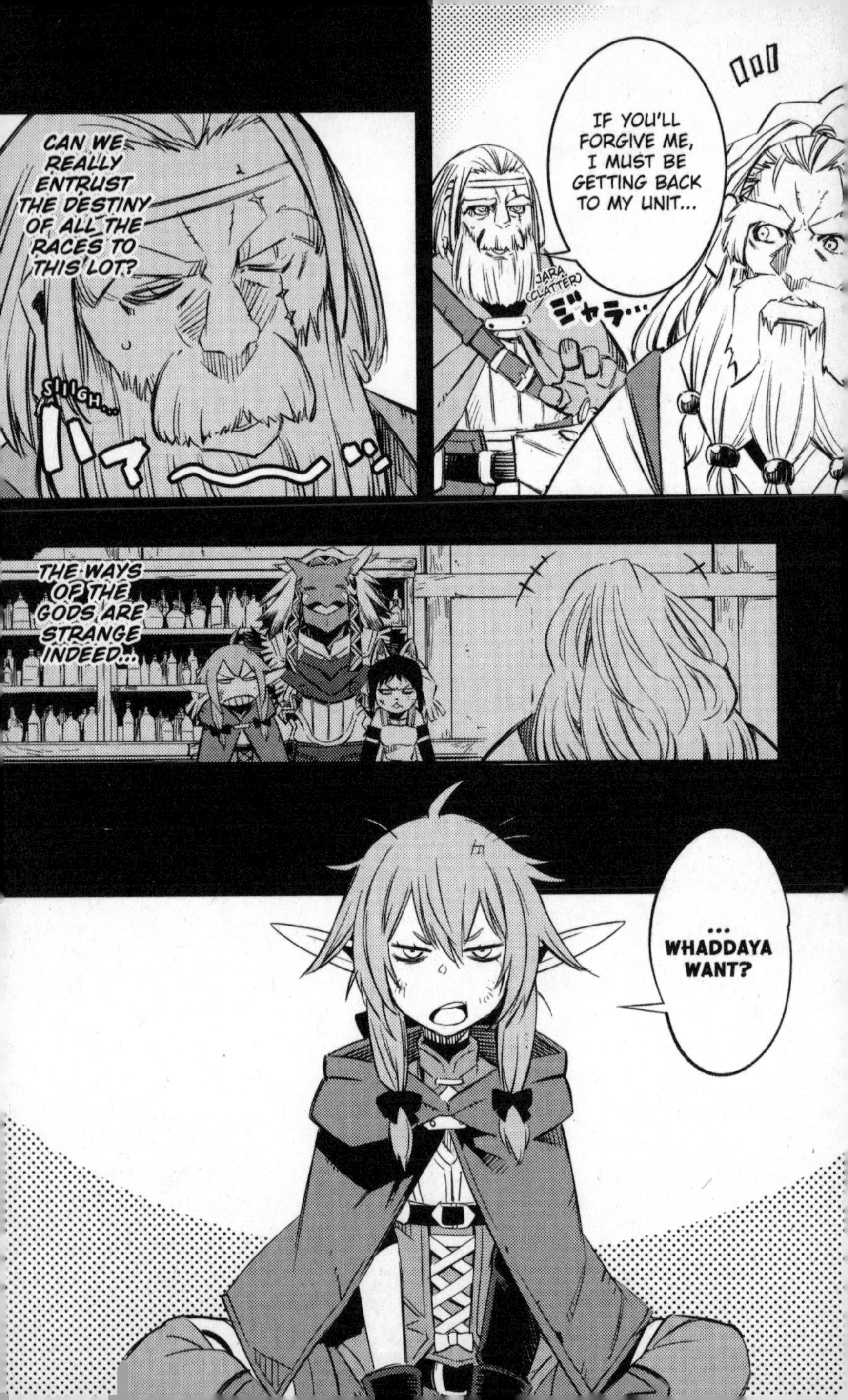
IF YOU'LL FORGIVE ME, I MUST BE GETTING BACK TO MY UNIT...
JARA (CLATTER)
ジャラ…
CAN WE REALLY ENTRUST THE DESTINY OF ALL THE RACES TO THIS LOT?
SIIGH...
ハァ〜〜ッ
THE WAYS OF THE GODS ARE STRANGE INDEED...
...WHADDAYA WANT?

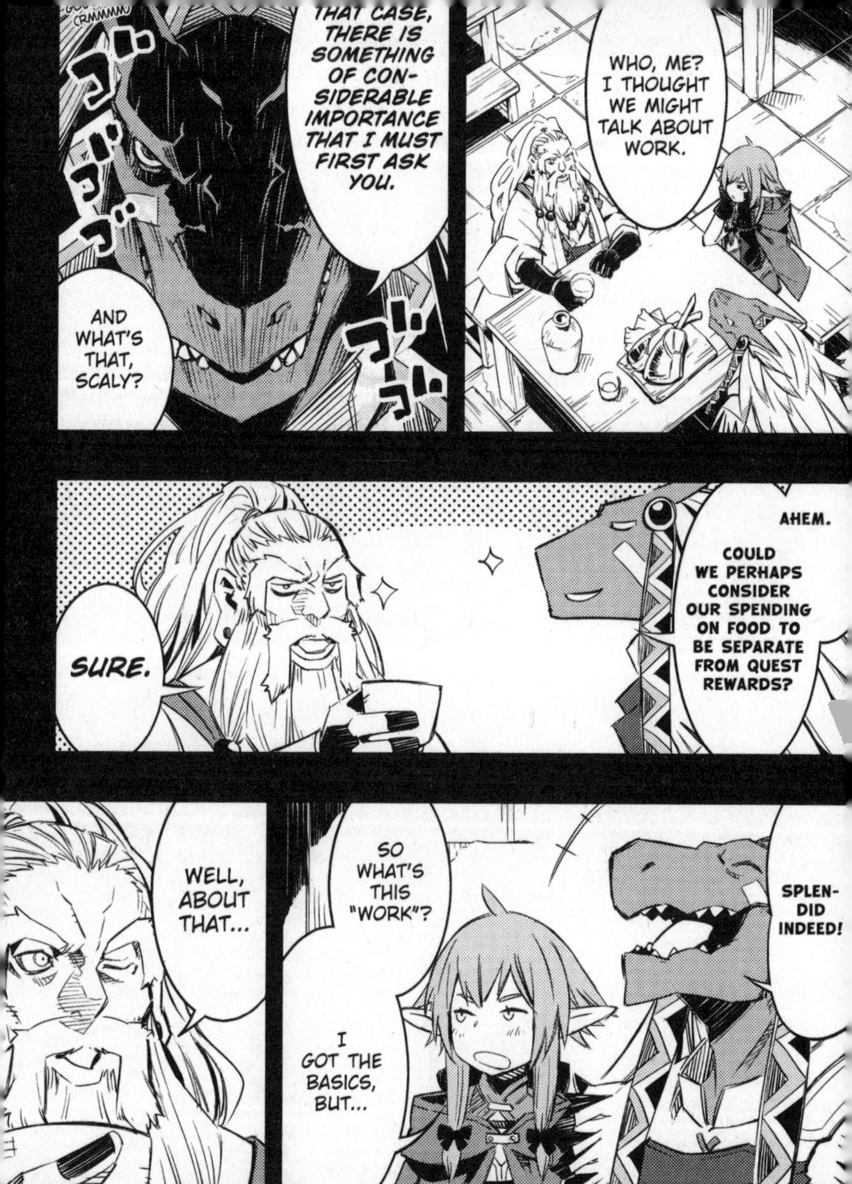
WHO, ME? I THOUGHT WE MIGHT TALK ABOUT WORK.
(RMMMM)
THAT CASE, THERE IS SOMETHING OF CON-SIDERABLE IMPORTANCE THAT I MUST FIRST ASK YOU.
AND WHAT'S THAT, SCALY?
AHEM.
COULD WE PERHAPS CONSIDER OUR SPENDING ON FOOD TO BE SEPARATE FROM QUEST REWARDS?
SURE.
SPLEN-DID INDEED!
SO WHAT'S THIS "WORK"?
I GOT THE BASICS, BUT...
WELL, ABOUT THAT...

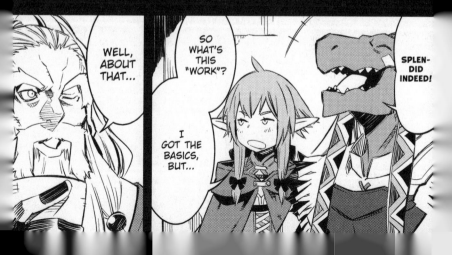

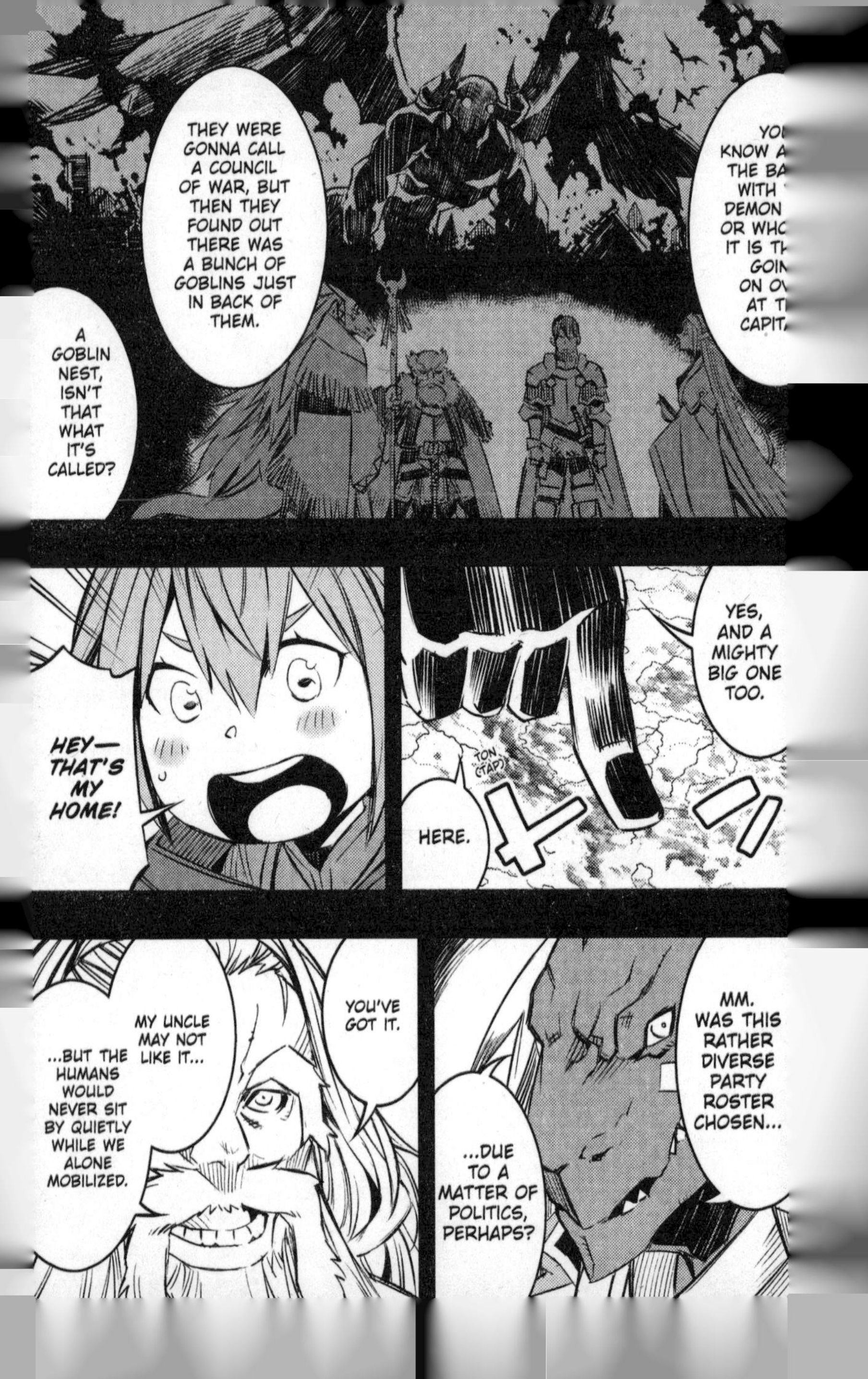
THEY WERE GONNA CALL A COUNCIL OF WAR, BUT THEN THEY FOUND OUT THERE WAS A BUNCH OF GOBLINS JUST IN BACK OF THEM.
A GOBLIN NEST, ISN'T THAT WHAT IT'S CALLED?
YES, AND A MIGHTY BIG ONE TOO.
TON (TAP)
HERE.
HEY—THAT'S MY HOME!
MM. WAS THIS RATHER DIVERSE PARTY ROSTER CHOSEN...
...DUE TO A MATTER OF POLITICS, PERHAPS?
YOU'VE GOT IT.
MY UNCLE MAY NOT LIKE IT...
...BUT THE HUMANS WOULD NEVER SIT BY QUIETLY WHILE WE ALONE MOBILIZED.

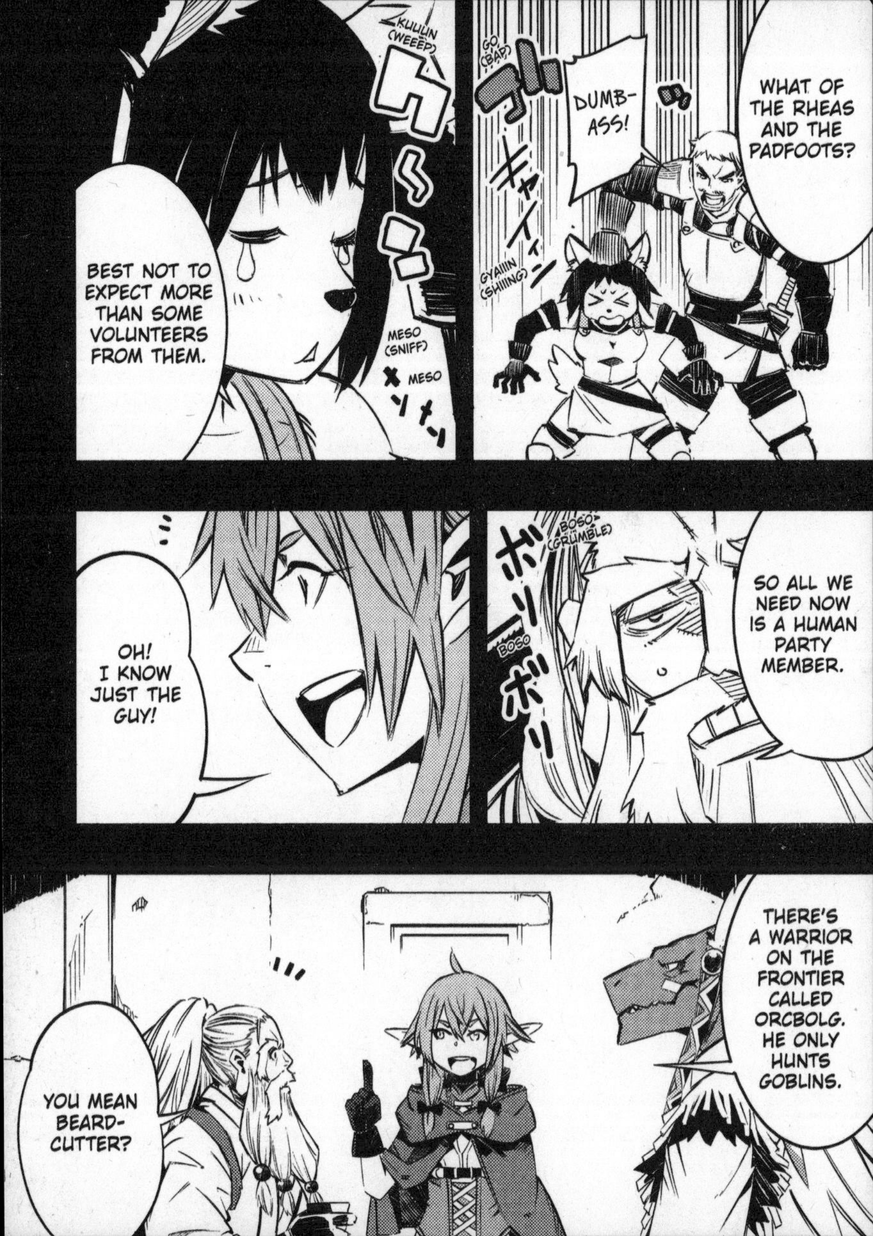
WHAT OF THE RHEAS AND THE PADFOOTS?
GO (BAP)
DUMB-ASS!
GYAIIIN (SHIIING)
KUUUN (WEEEP)
MESO (SNIFF) MESO
BEST NOT TO EXPECT MORE THAN SOME VOLUNTEERS FROM THEM.
BOSO (GRUMBLE)
BOSO
SO ALL WE NEED NOW IS A HUMAN PARTY MEMBER.
...
OH! I KNOW JUST THE GUY!
THERE'S A WARRIOR ON THE FRONTIER CALLED ORCBOLG. HE ONLY HUNTS GOBLINS.
...
YOU MEAN BEARD-CUTTER?

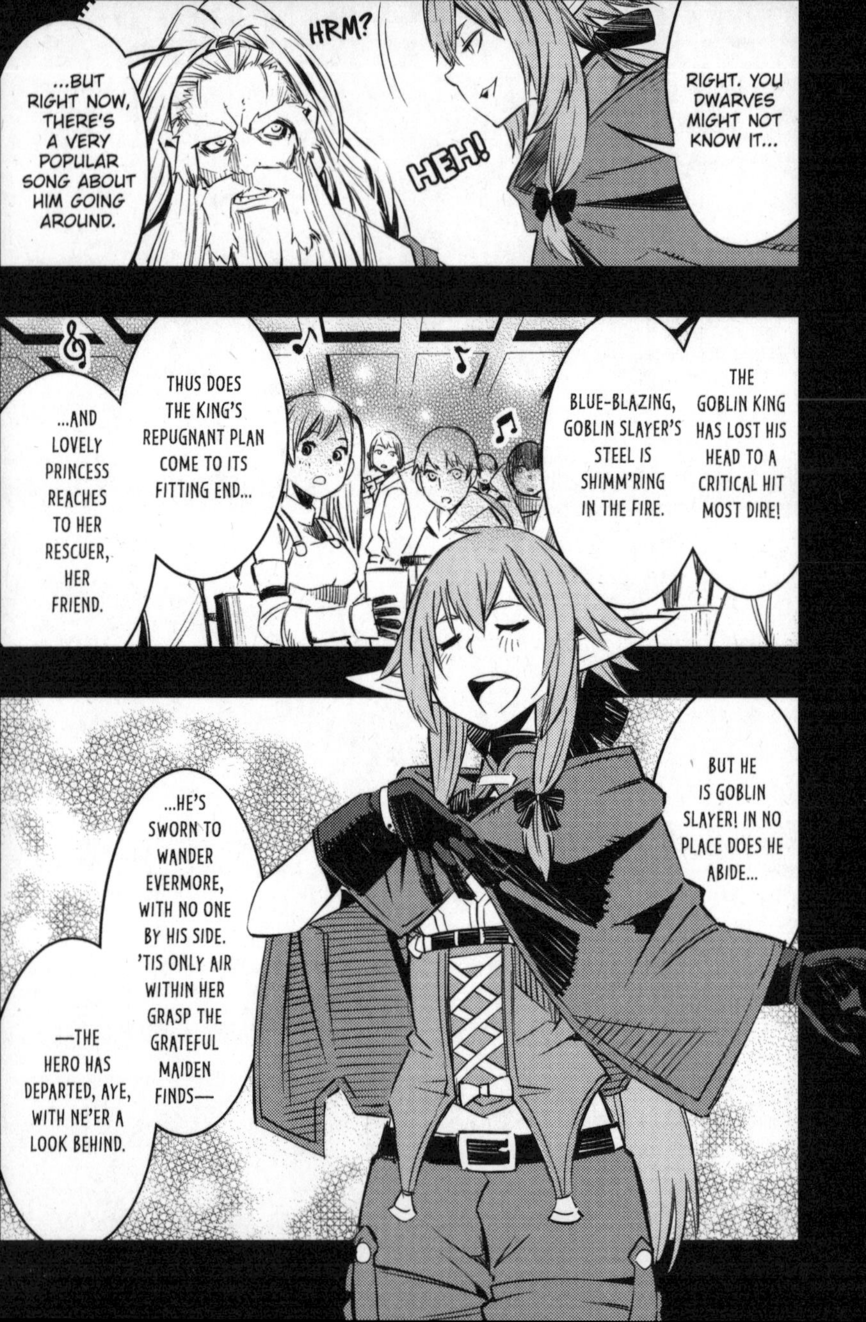
RIGHT. YOU DWARVES MIGHT NOT KNOW IT...
HEH!
HRM?
...BUT RIGHT NOW, THERE'S A VERY POPULAR SONG ABOUT HIM GOING AROUND.
THE GOBLIN KING HAS LOST HIS HEAD TO A CRITICAL HIT MOST DIRE!
BLUE-BLAZING, GOBLIN SLAYER'S STEEL IS SHIMM'RING IN THE FIRE.
THUS DOES THE KING'S REPUGNANT PLAN COME TO ITS FITTING END...
...AND LOVELY PRINCESS REACHES TO HER RESCUER, HER FRIEND.
BUT HE IS GOBLIN SLAYER! IN NO PLACE DOES HE ABIDE...
...HE'S SWORN TO WANDER EVERMORE, WITH NO ONE BY HIS SIDE. 'TIS ONLY AIR WITHIN HER GRASP THE GRATEFUL MAIDEN FINDS—
—THE HERO HAS DEPARTED, AYE, WITH NE'ER A LOOK BEHIND.

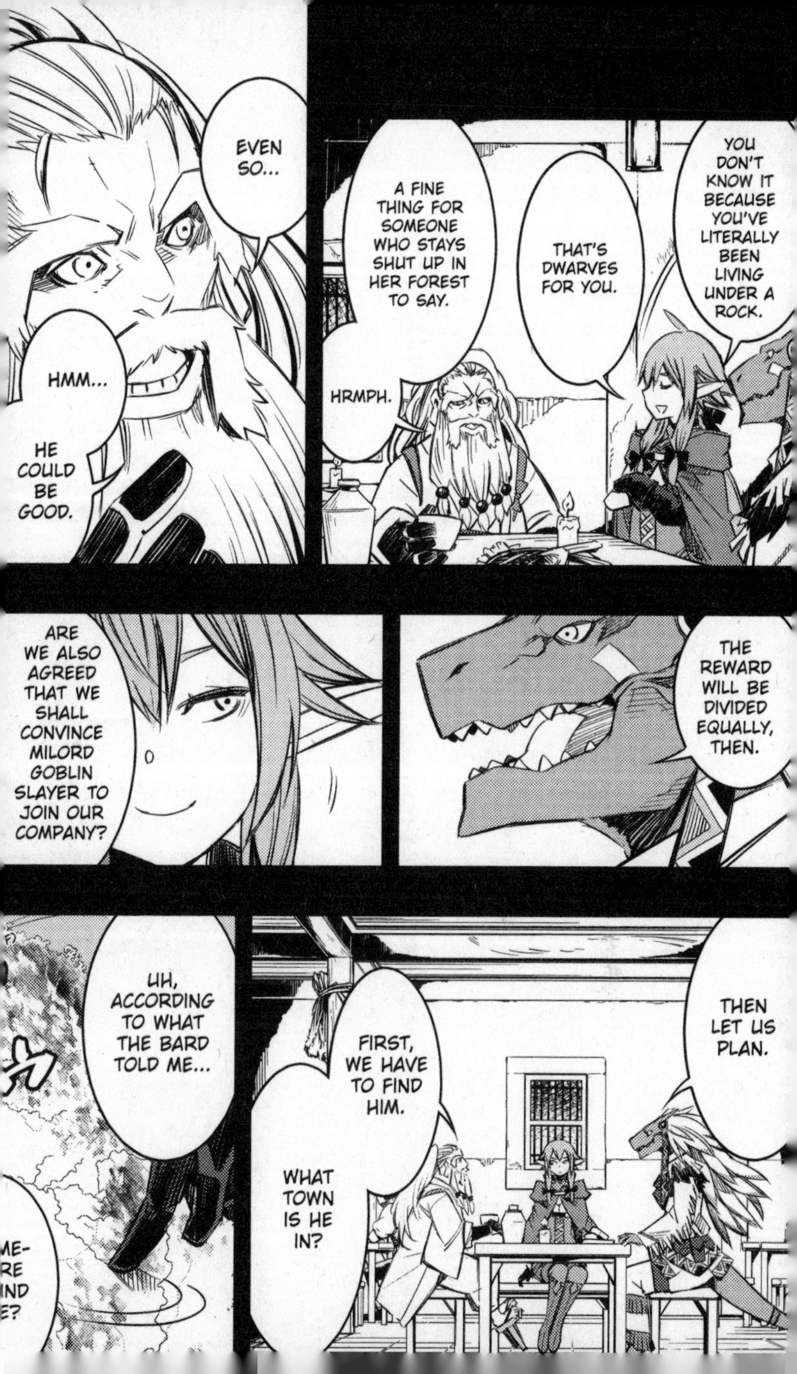
YOU DON'T KNOW IT BECAUSE YOU'VE LITERALLY BEEN LIVING UNDER A ROCK.
THAT'S DWARVES FOR YOU.
A FINE THING FOR SOMEONE WHO STAYS SHUT UP IN HER FOREST TO SAY.
HRMPH.
EVEN SO...
HMM...
HE COULD BE GOOD.
THE REWARD WILL BE DIVIDED EQUALLY, THEN.
ARE WE ALSO AGREED THAT WE SHALL CONVINCE MILORD GOBLIN SLAYER TO JOIN OUR COMPANY?
THEN LET US PLAN.
FIRST, WE HAVE TO FIND HIM.
WHAT TOWN IS HE IN?
UH, ACCORDING TO WHAT THE BARD TOLD ME...

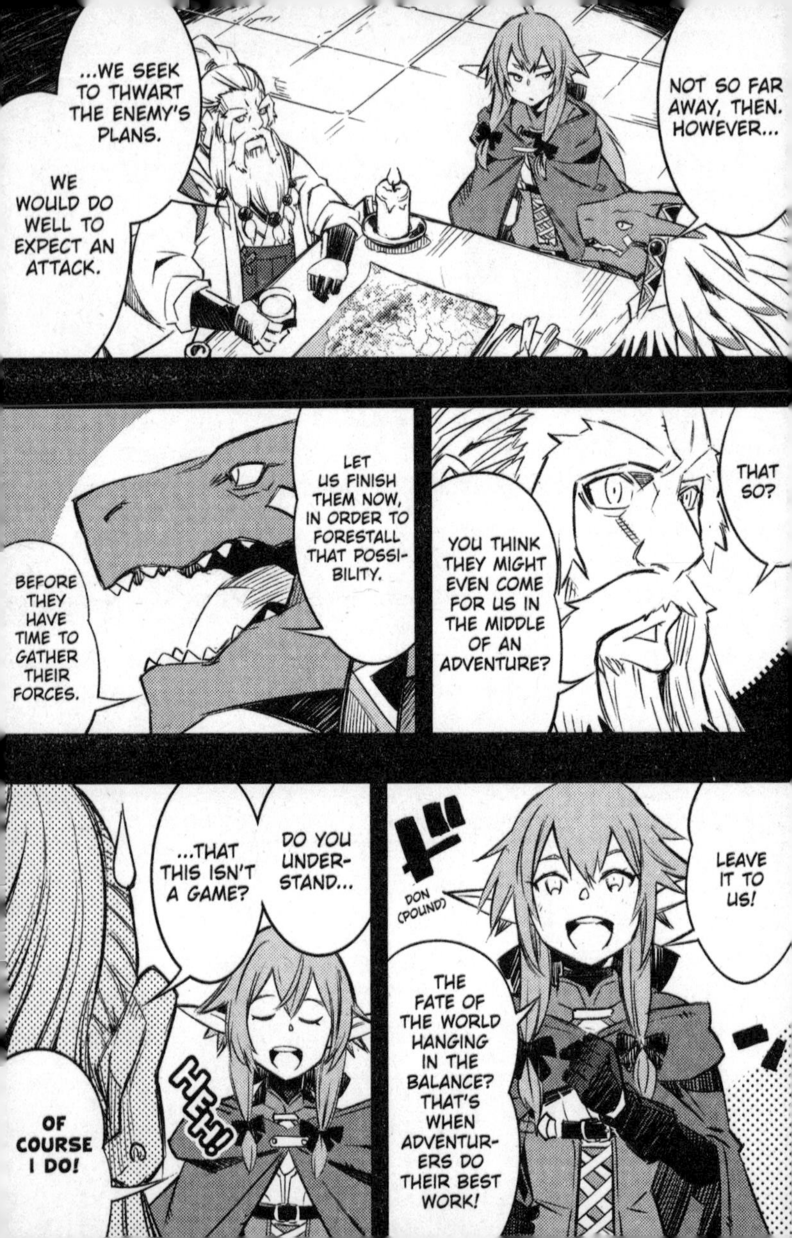
NOT SO FAR AWAY, THEN. HOWEVER...
...WE SEEK TO THWART THE ENEMY'S PLANS.
WE WOULD DO WELL TO EXPECT AN ATTACK.
THAT SO?
YOU THINK THEY MIGHT EVEN COME FOR US IN THE MIDDLE OF AN ADVENTURE?
LET US FINISH THEM NOW, IN ORDER TO FORESTALL THAT POSSIBILITY.
BEFORE THEY HAVE TIME TO GATHER THEIR FORCES.
LEAVE IT TO US!
DON (POUND)
THE FATE OF THE WORLD HANGING IN THE BALANCE? THAT'S WHEN ADVENTURERS DO THEIR BEST WORK!
DO YOU UNDERSTAND...
...THAT THIS ISN'T A GAME?
HEH!
OF COURSE I DO!

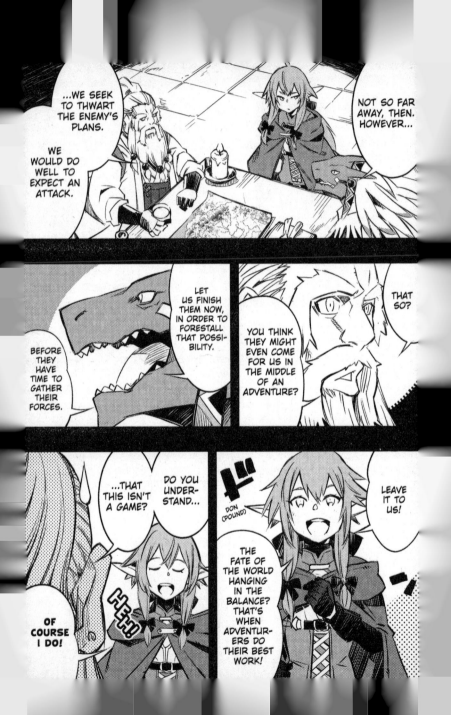

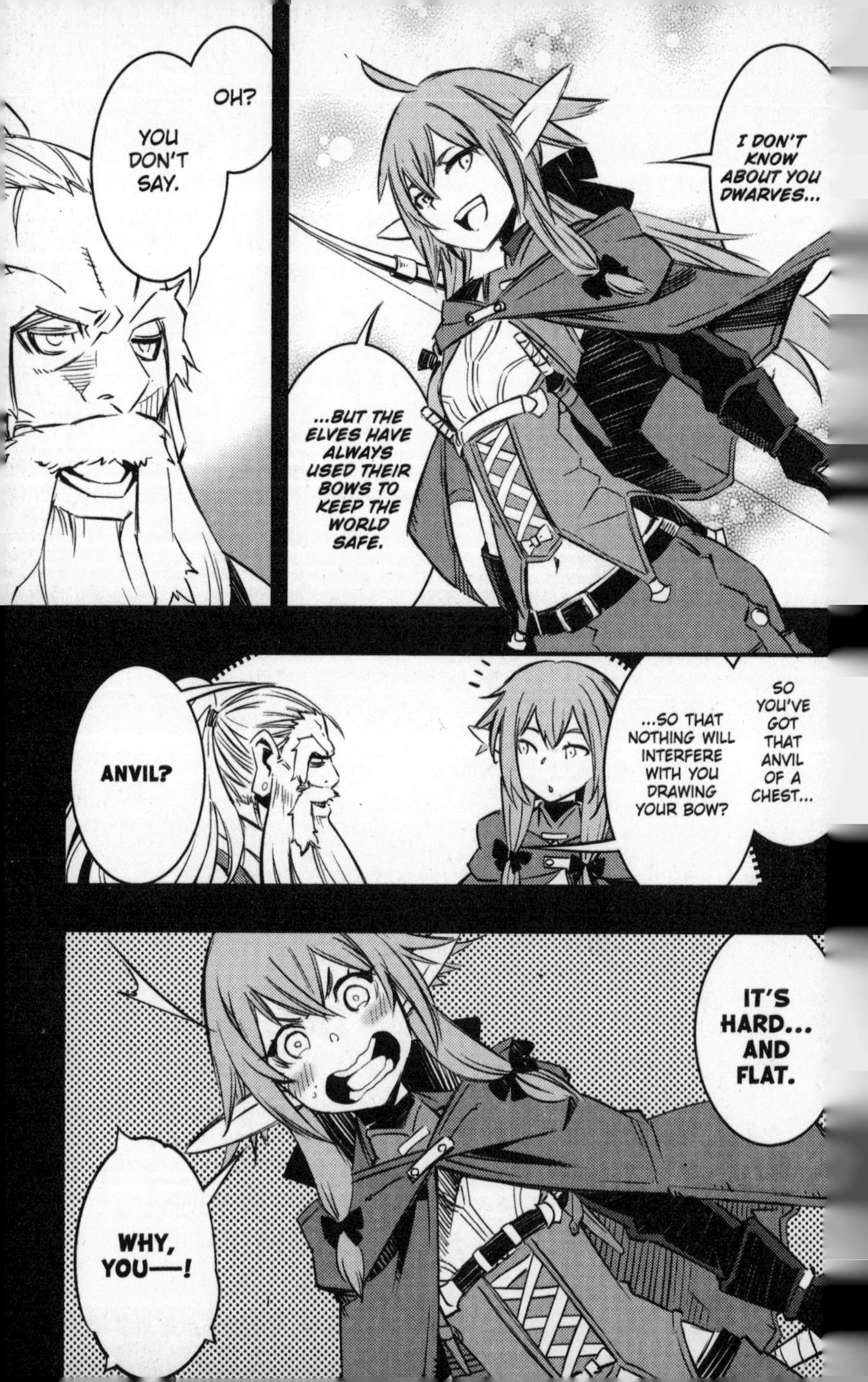
I DON'T KNOW ABOUT YOU DWARVES...
...BUT THE ELVES HAVE ALWAYS USED THEIR BOWS TO KEEP THE WORLD SAFE.
OH?
YOU DON'T SAY.
SO YOU'VE GOT THAT ANVIL OF A CHEST...
...SO THAT NOTHING WILL INTERFERE WITH YOU DRAWING YOUR BOW?
ANVIL?
IT'S HARD... AND FLAT.
WHY, YOU—!

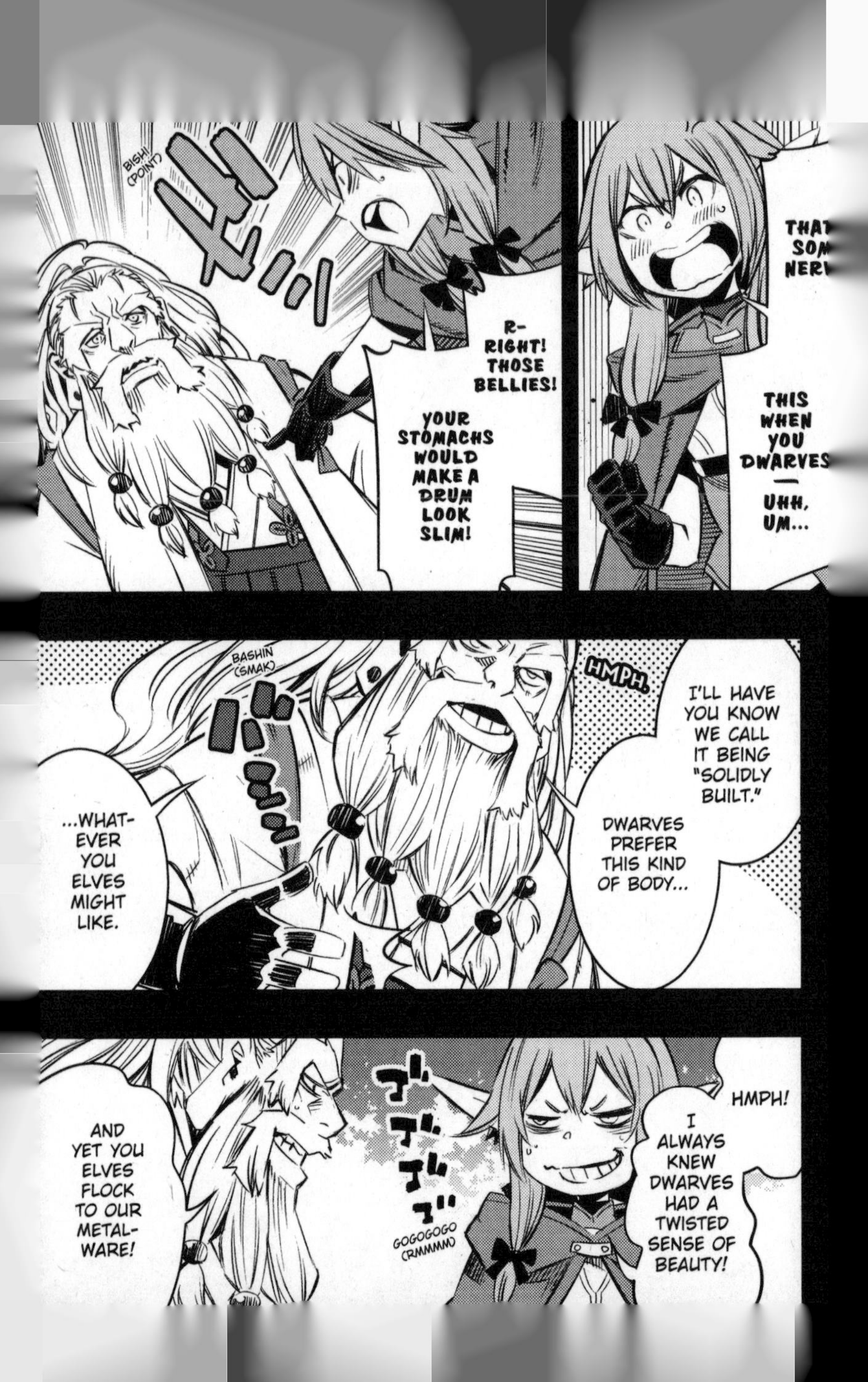
THAT SOM NERV
THIS WHEN YOU DWARVES— UHH, UM...
BISHI (POINT)
R-RIGHT! THOSE BELLIES!
YOUR STOMACHS WOULD MAKE A DRUM LOOK SLIM!
HMPH.
I'LL HAVE YOU KNOW WE CALL IT BEING "SOLIDLY BUILT."
DWARVES PREFER THIS KIND OF BODY...
BASHIN (SMAK)
...WHAT-EVER YOU ELVES MIGHT LIKE.
HMPH!
I ALWAYS KNEW DWARVES HAD A TWISTED SENSE OF BEAUTY!
GOGOGOGO (RMMMM)
AND YET YOU ELVES FLOCK TO OUR METAL-WARE!

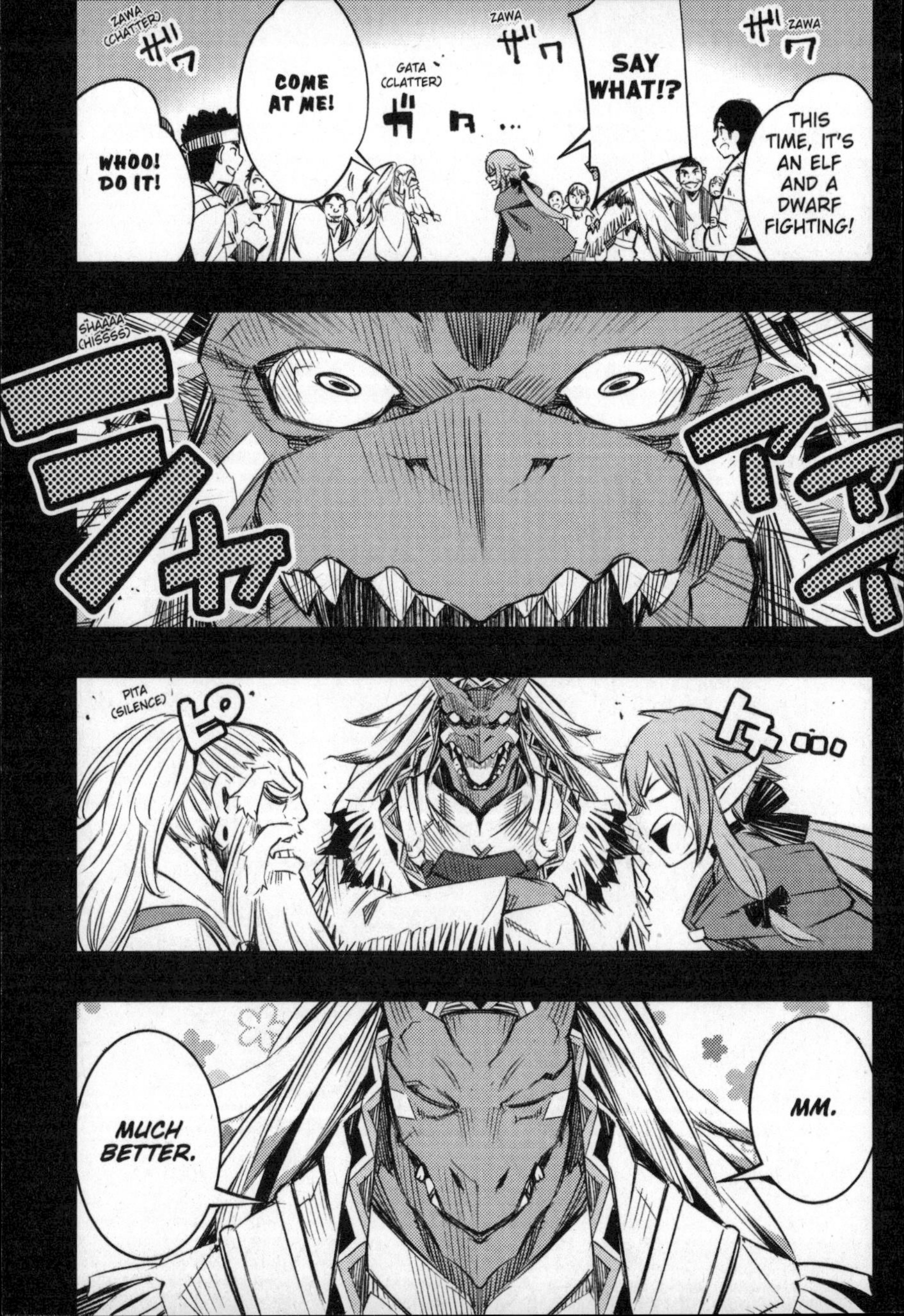
THIS TIME, IT'S AN ELF AND A DWARF FIGHTING!
ZAWA
SAY WHAT!?
ZAWA
GATA (CLATTER)
COME AT ME!
ZAWA (CHATTER)
WHOO! DO IT!
SHAAAA (HISSSS)
PITA (SILENCE)
MM.
MUCH BETTER.

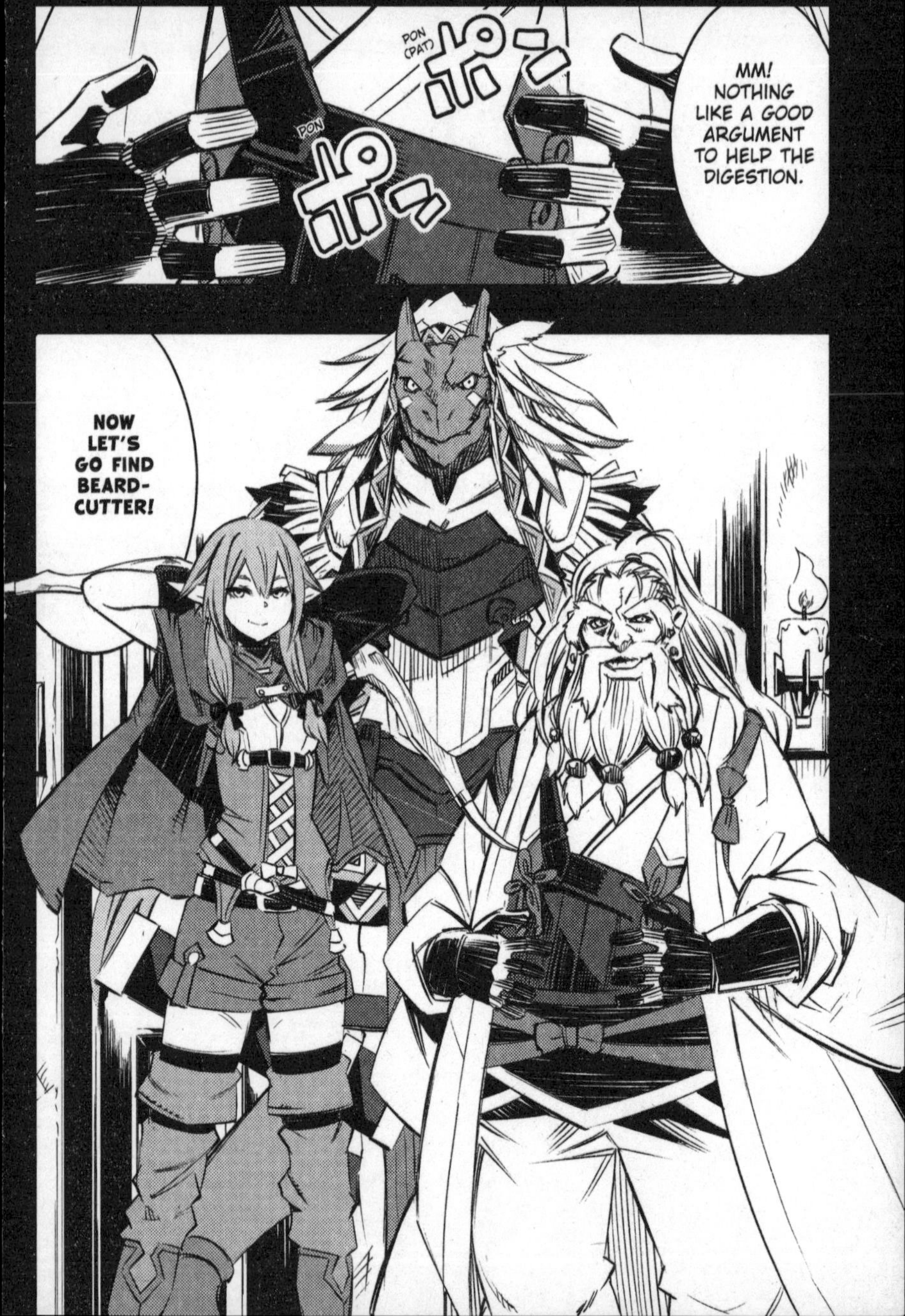

MM! NOTHING LIKE A GOOD ARGUMENT TO HELP THE DIGESTION.
PON (PAT)
PON
NOW LET'S GO FIND BEARD-CUTTER!

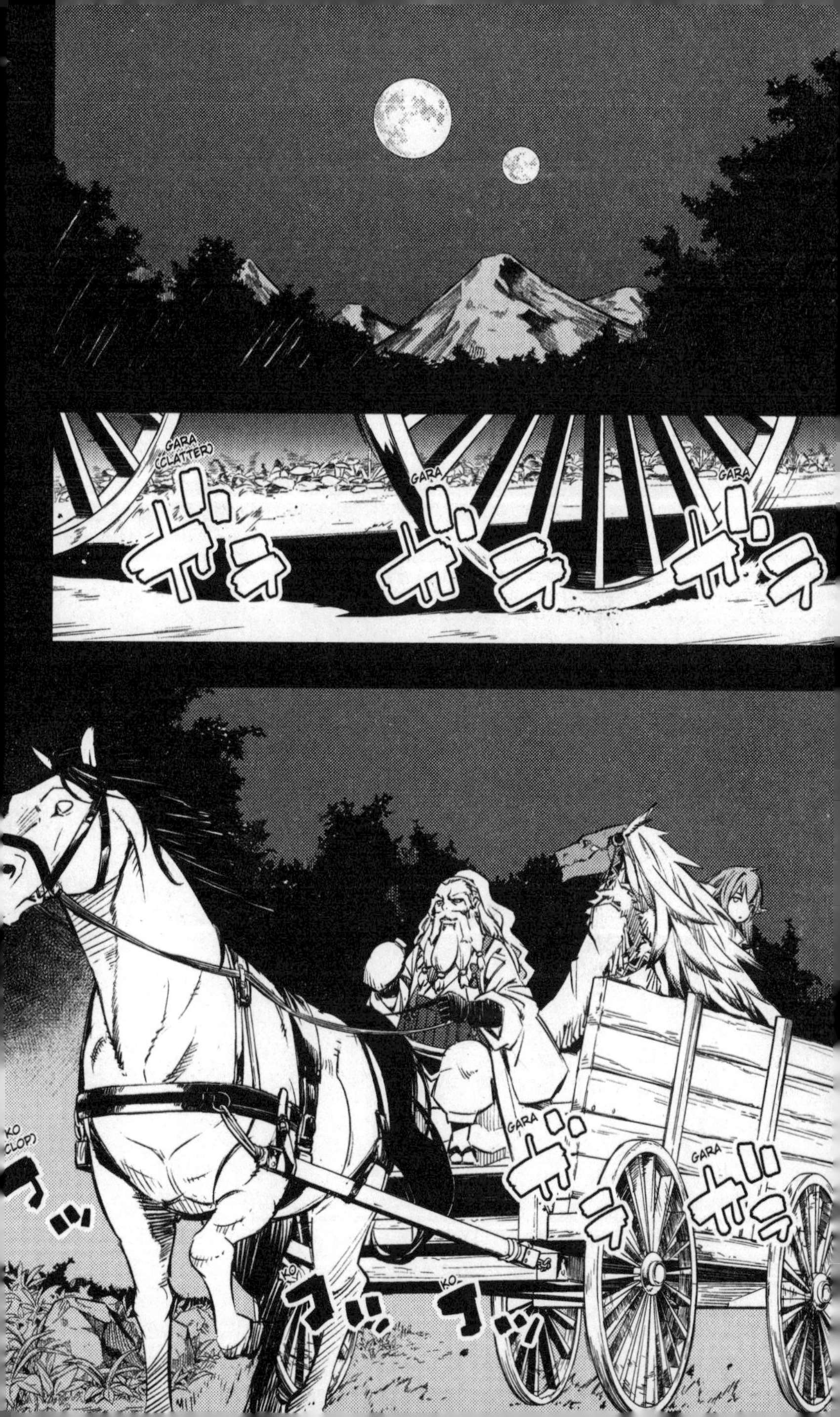
GARA
GARA
GARA (CLATTER)
GARA
GARA
KO
KO

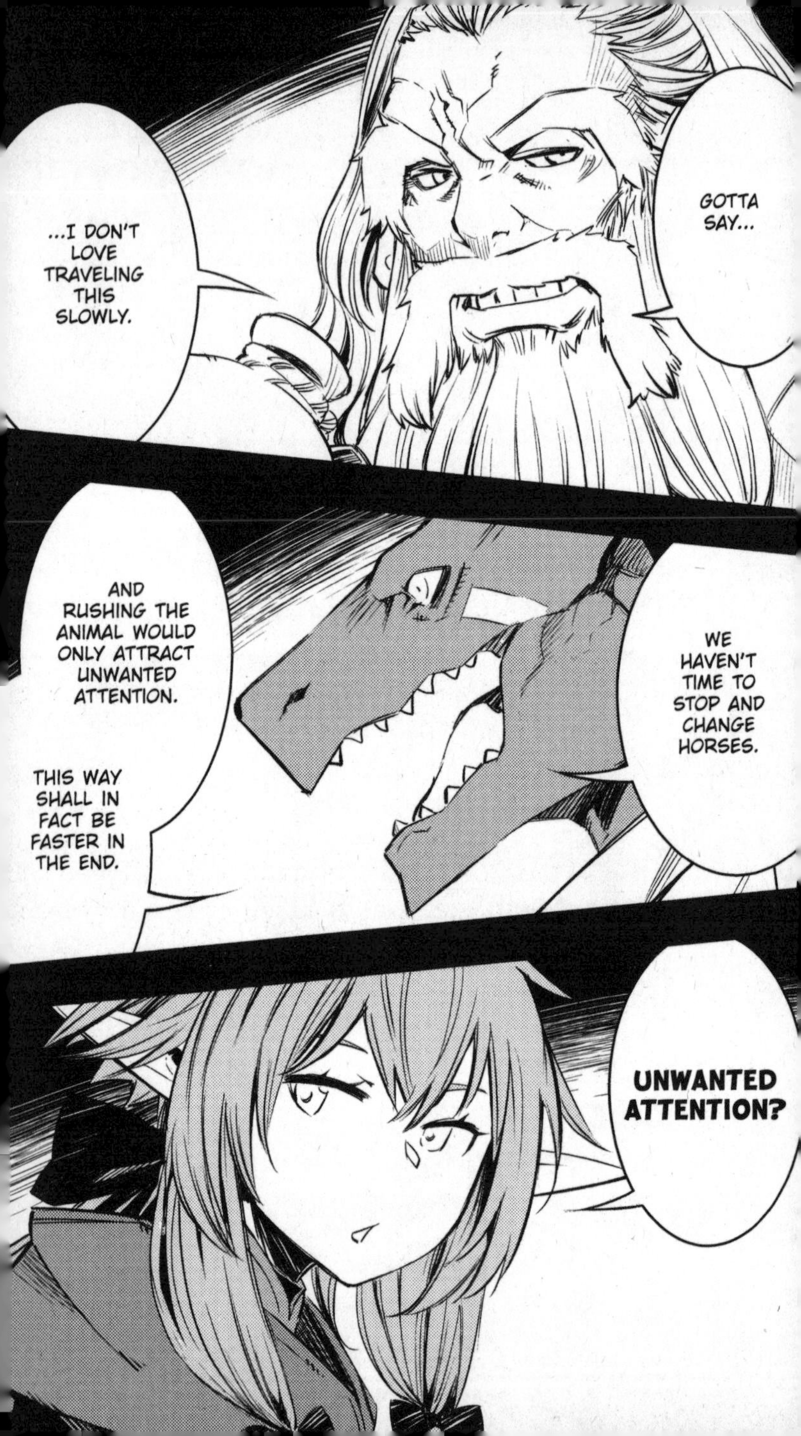
GOTTA SAY...
...I DON'T LOVE TRAVELING THIS SLOWLY.
WE HAVEN'T TIME TO STOP AND CHANGE HORSES.
AND RUSHING THE ANIMAL WOULD ONLY ATTRACT UNWANTED ATTENTION.
THIS WAY SHALL IN FACT BE FASTER IN THE END.
UNWANTED ATTENTION?

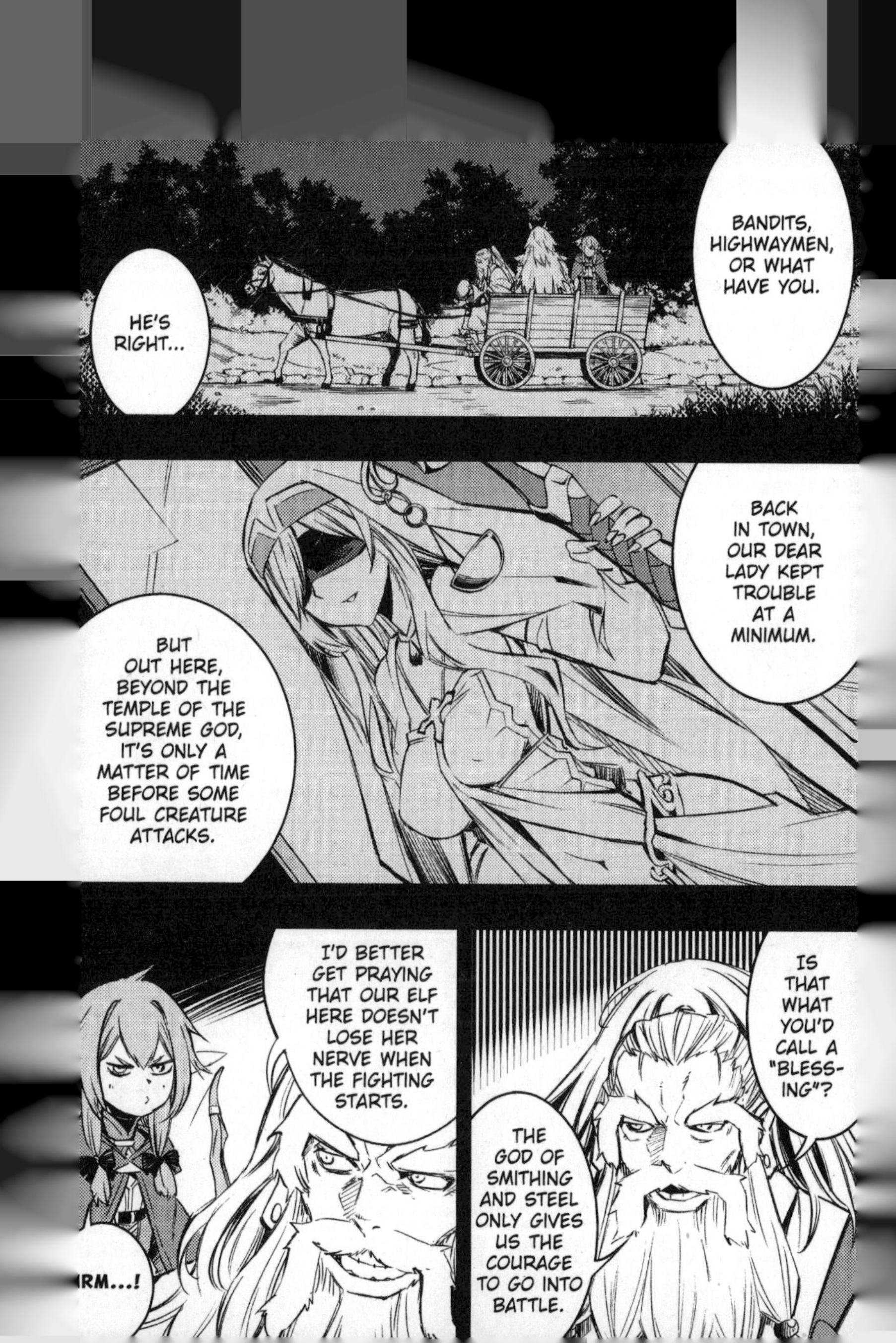
BANDITS, HIGHWAYMEN, OR WHAT HAVE YOU.
HE'S RIGHT...
BACK IN TOWN, OUR DEAR LADY KEPT TROUBLE AT A MINIMUM.
BUT OUT HERE, BEYOND THE TEMPLE OF THE SUPREME GOD, IT'S ONLY A MATTER OF TIME BEFORE SOME FOUL CREATURE ATTACKS.
IS THAT WHAT YOU'D CALL A "BLESSING"?
THE GOD OF SMITHING AND STEEL ONLY GIVES US THE COURAGE TO GO INTO BATTLE.
I'D BETTER GET PRAYING THAT OUR ELF HERE DOESN'T LOSE HER NERVE WHEN THE FIGHTING STARTS.
RM...!

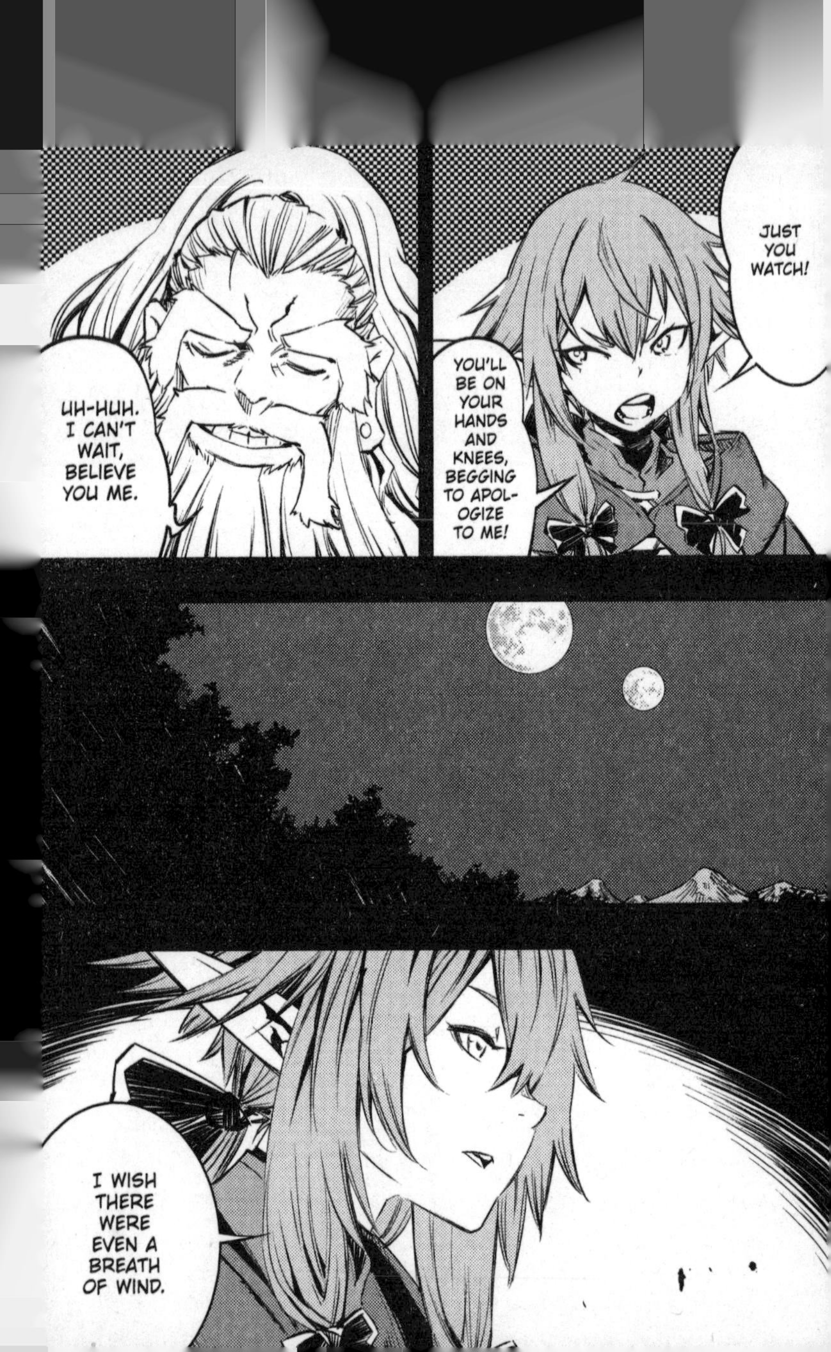
JUST YOU WATCH!
YOU'LL BE ON YOUR HANDS AND KNEES, BEGGING TO APOLOGIZE TO ME!
UH-HUH. I CAN'T WAIT, BELIEVE YOU ME.
I WISH THERE WERE EVEN A BREATH OF WIND.

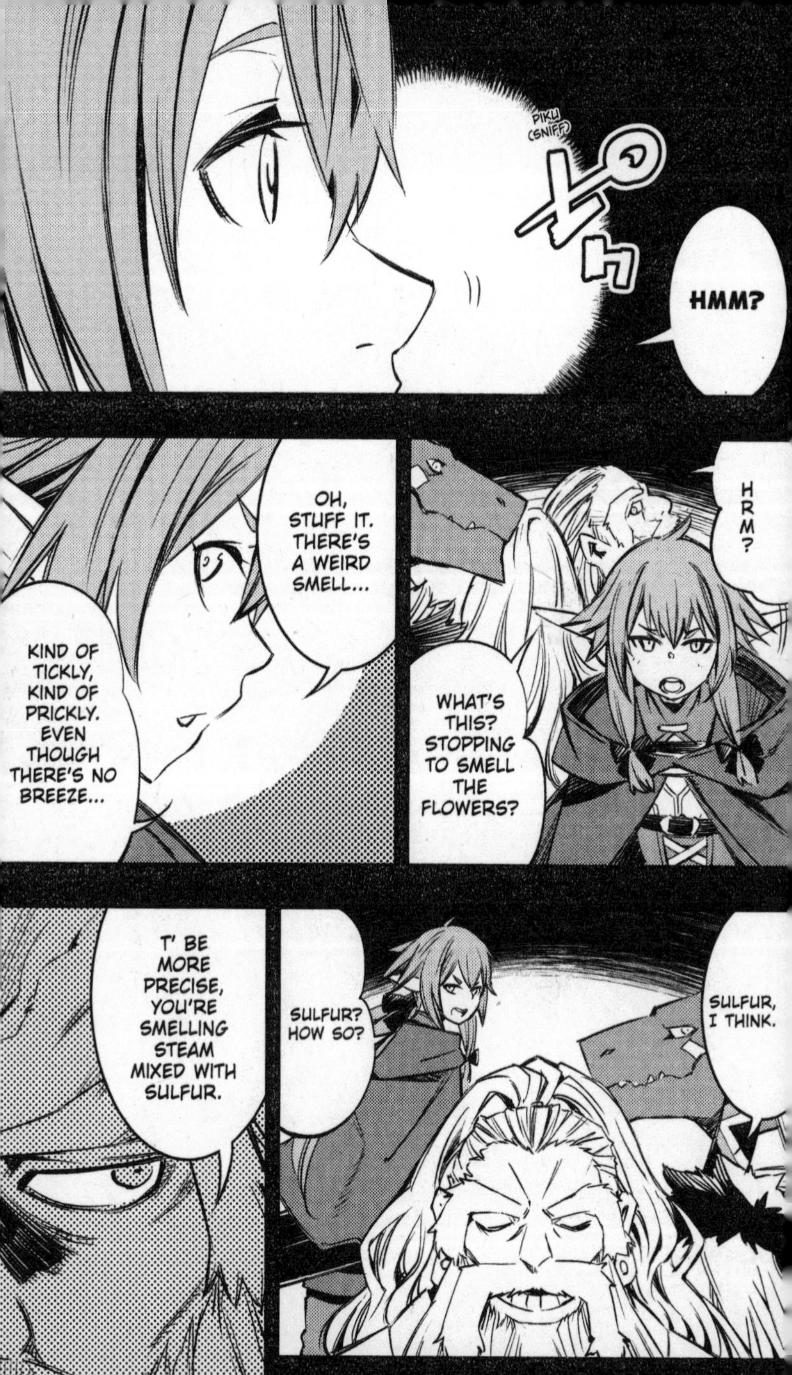
HMM?
PIKU (SNIFF)
HRM?
WHAT'S THIS? STOPPING TO SMELL THE FLOWERS?
OH, STUFF IT. THERE'S A WEIRD SMELL...
KIND OF TICKLY, KIND OF PRICKLY. EVEN THOUGH THERE'S NO BREEZE...
SULFUR, I THINK.
SULFUR? HOW SO?
T' BE MORE PRECISE, YOU'RE SMELLING STEAM MIXED WITH SULFUR.

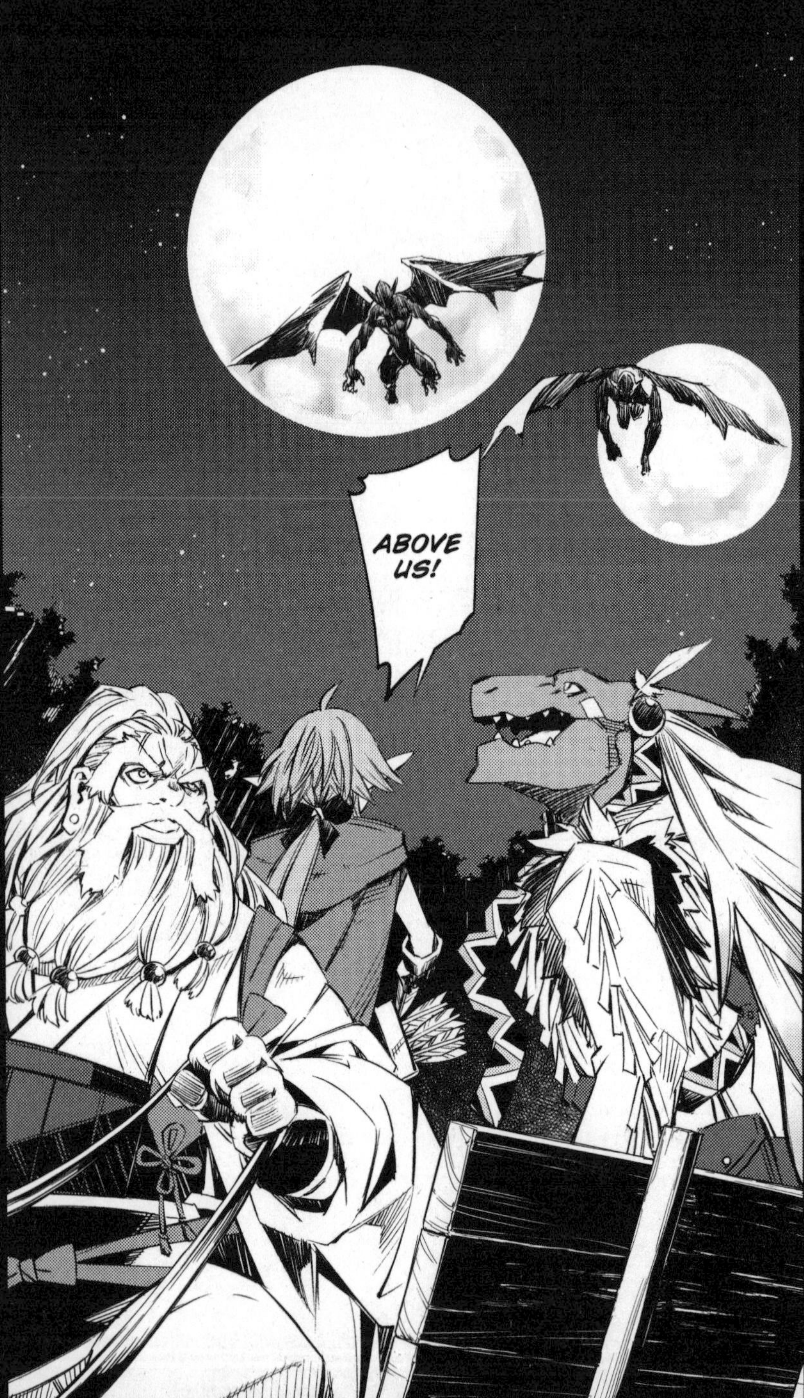
ABOVE US!

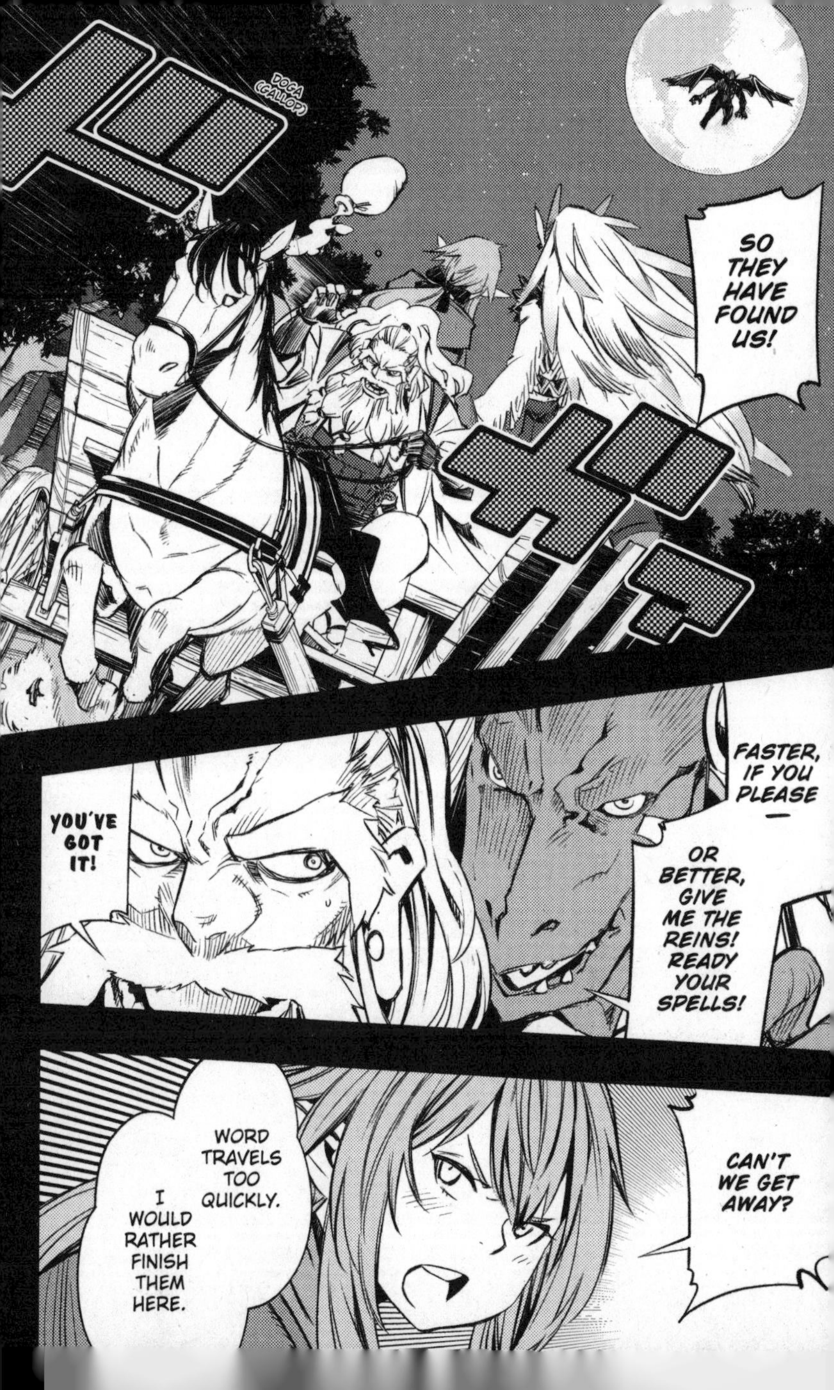
DOGA (GALLOP)
SO THEY HAVE FOUND US!
FASTER, IF YOU PLEASE—
OR BETTER, GIVE ME THE REINS! READY YOUR SPELLS!
YOU'VE GOT IT!
CAN'T WE GET AWAY?
WORD TRAVELS TOO QUICKLY.
I WOULD RATHER FINISH THEM HERE.

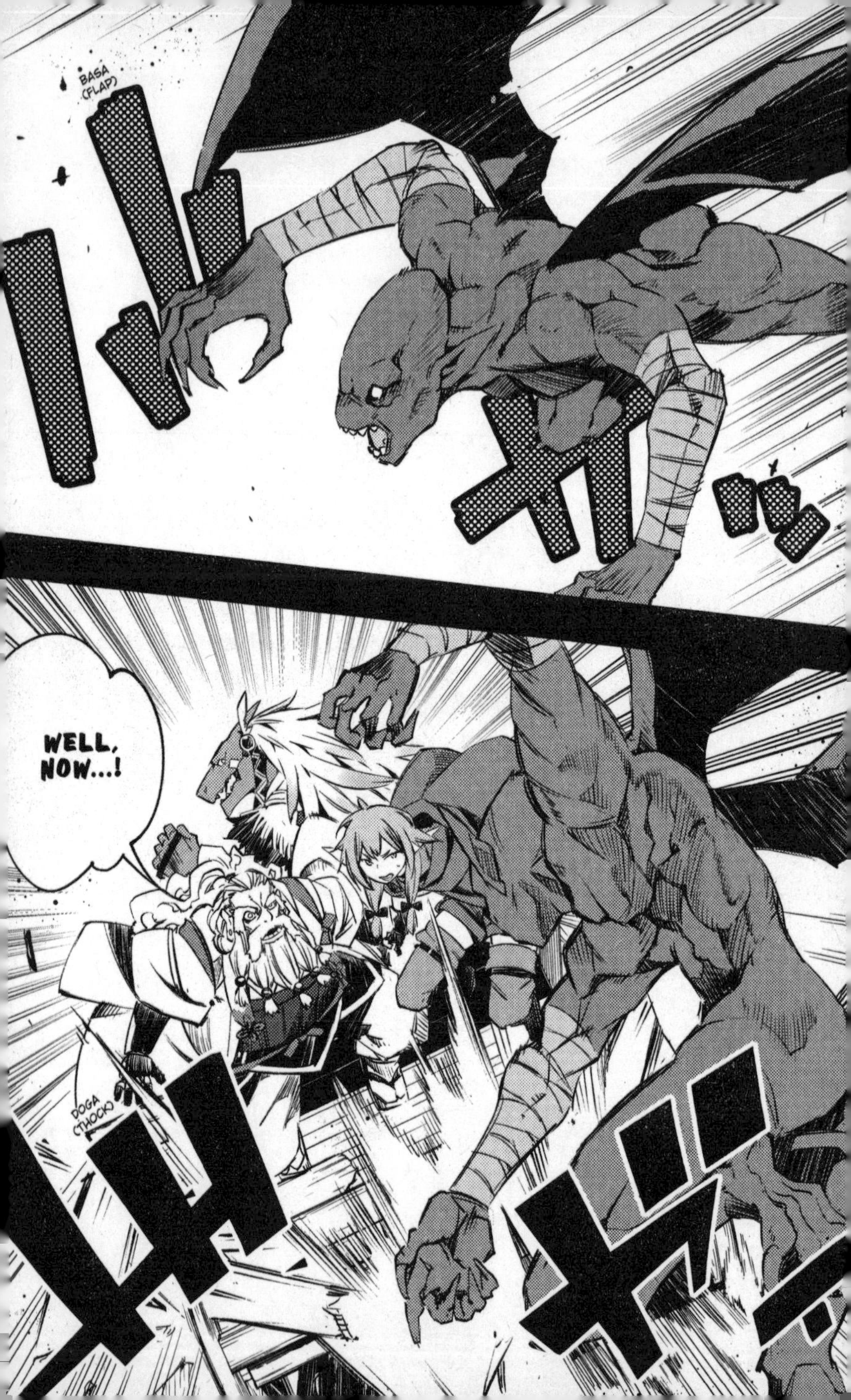
BASA
(FLAP)
WELL,
NOW...!
DOGA
(THOCK)

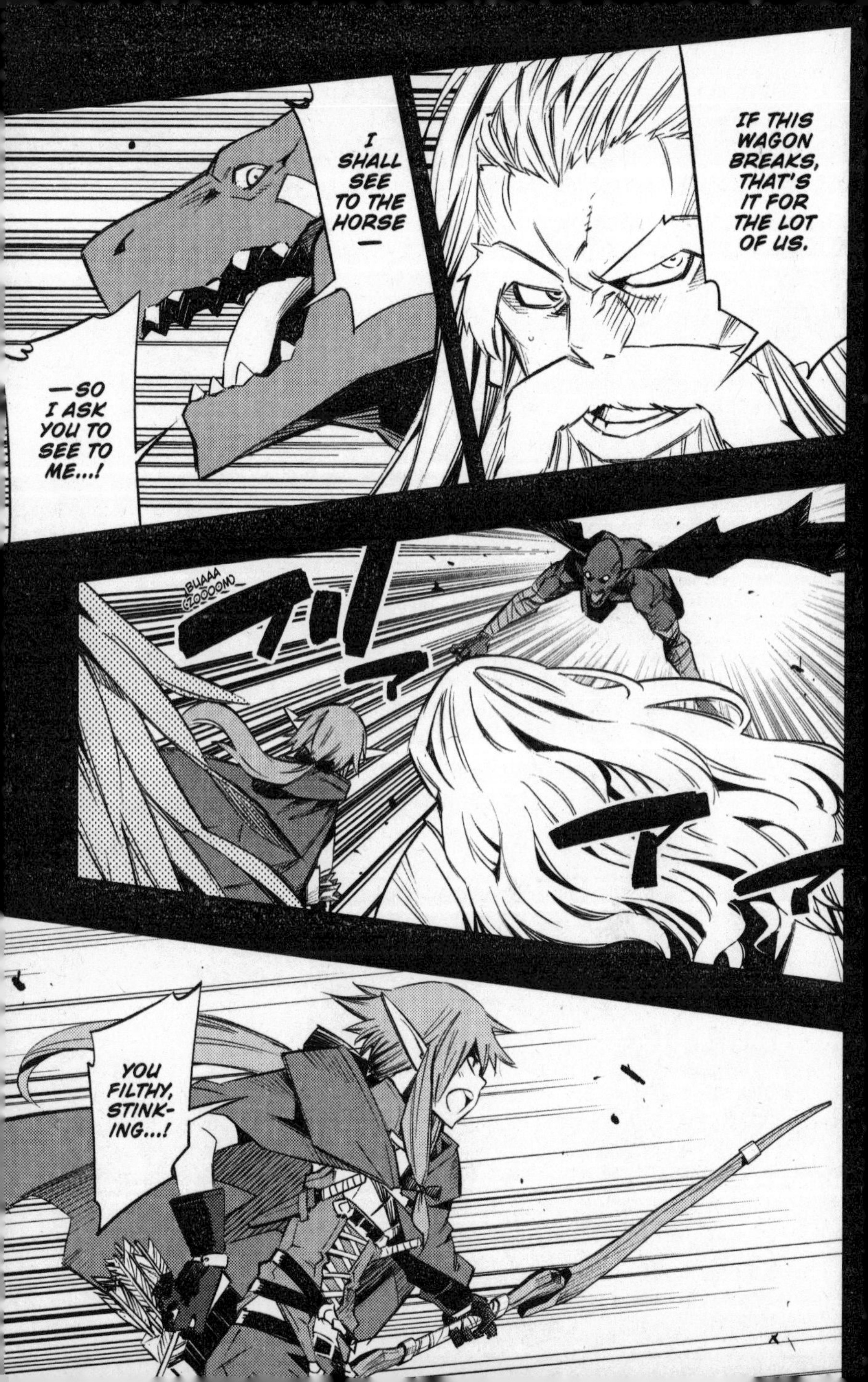
IF THIS WAGON BREAKS, THAT'S IT FOR THE LOT OF US.
I SHALL SEE TO THE HORSE—
—SO I ASK YOU TO SEE TO ME...!
BUAAA (ZOOOOM)
YOU FILTHY, STINK-ING...!

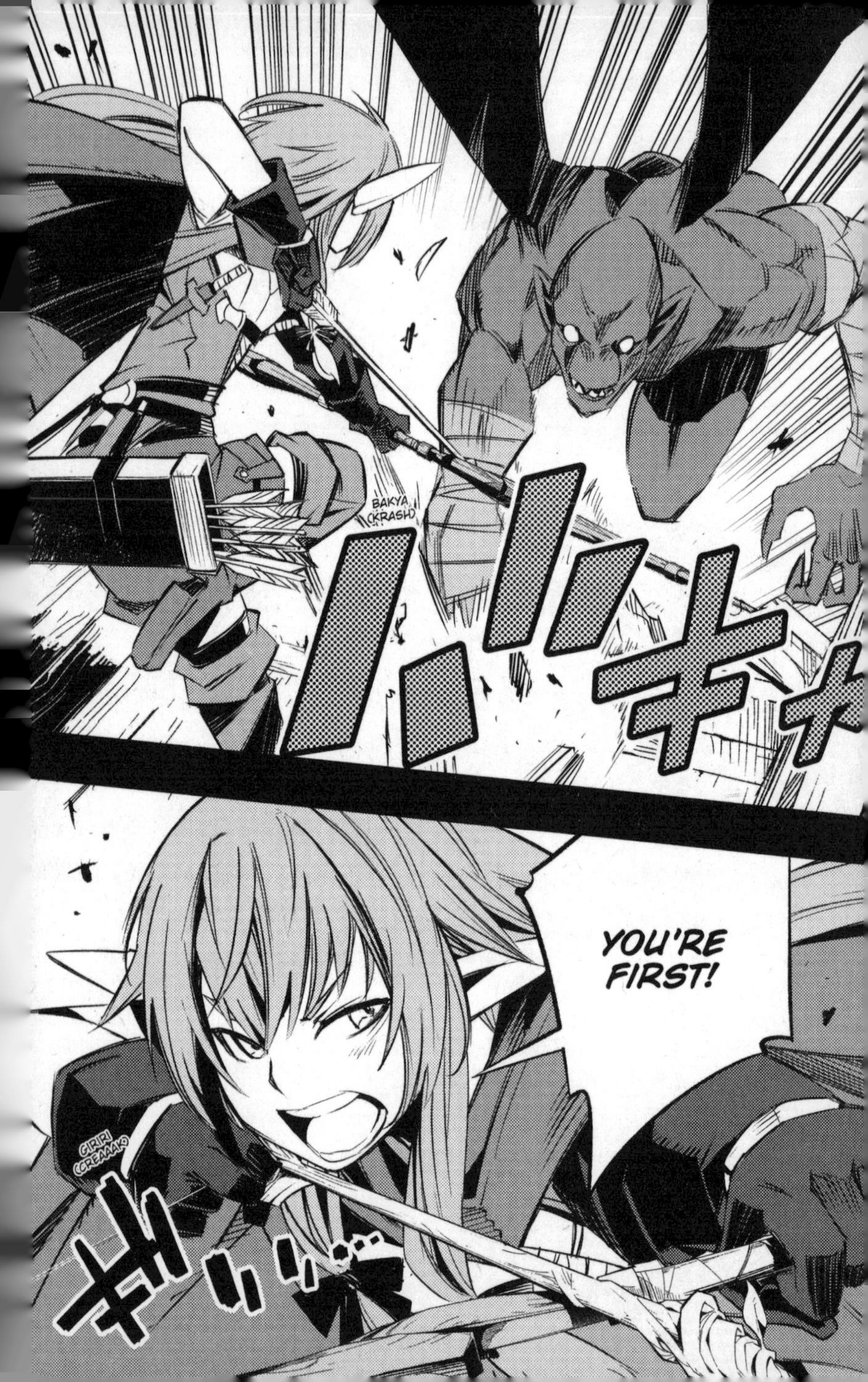
BAKYA
(KRASH)
YOU'RE FIRST!
GIRIRI
(CREAAAK)

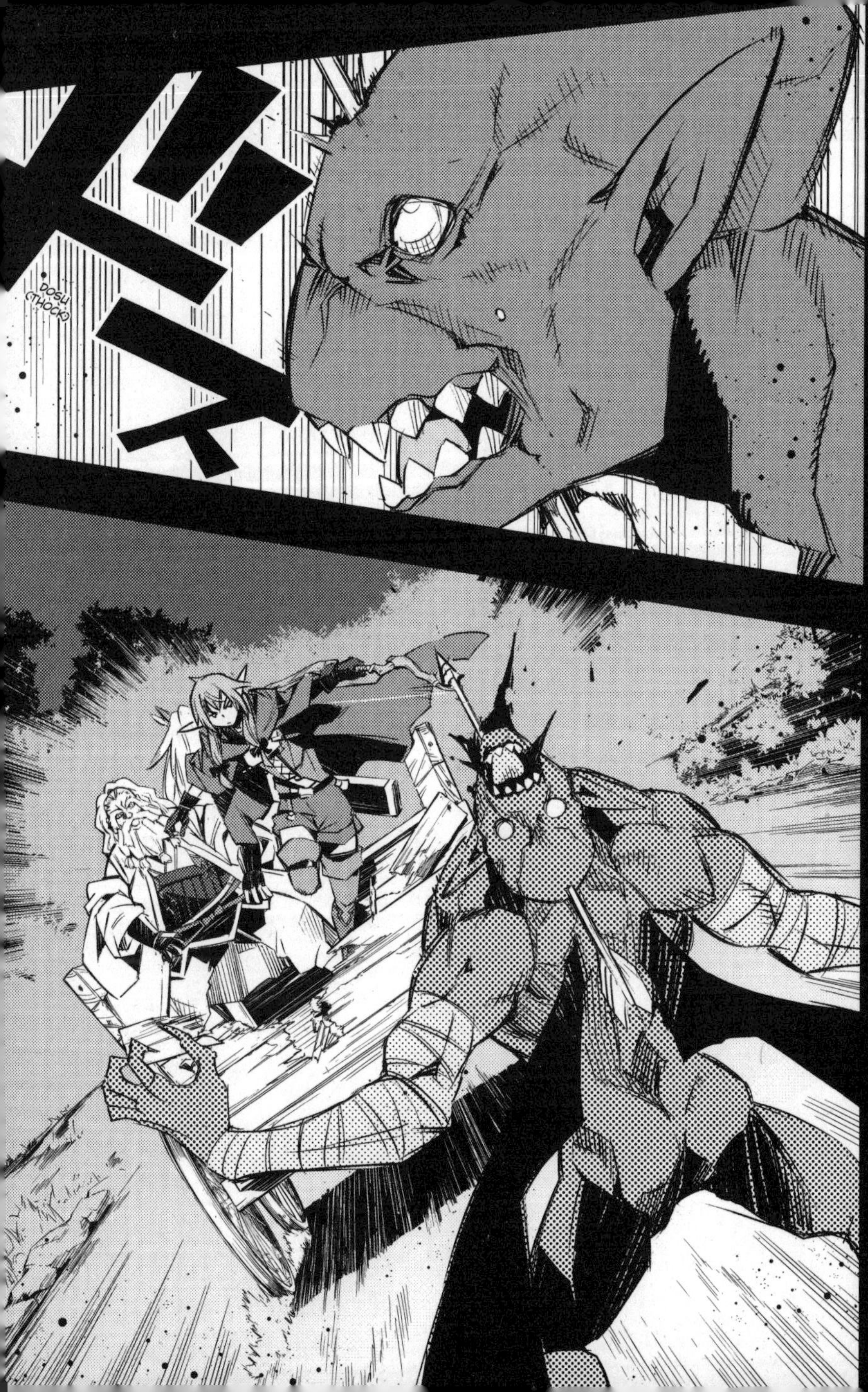
DOSU
(THOCK)

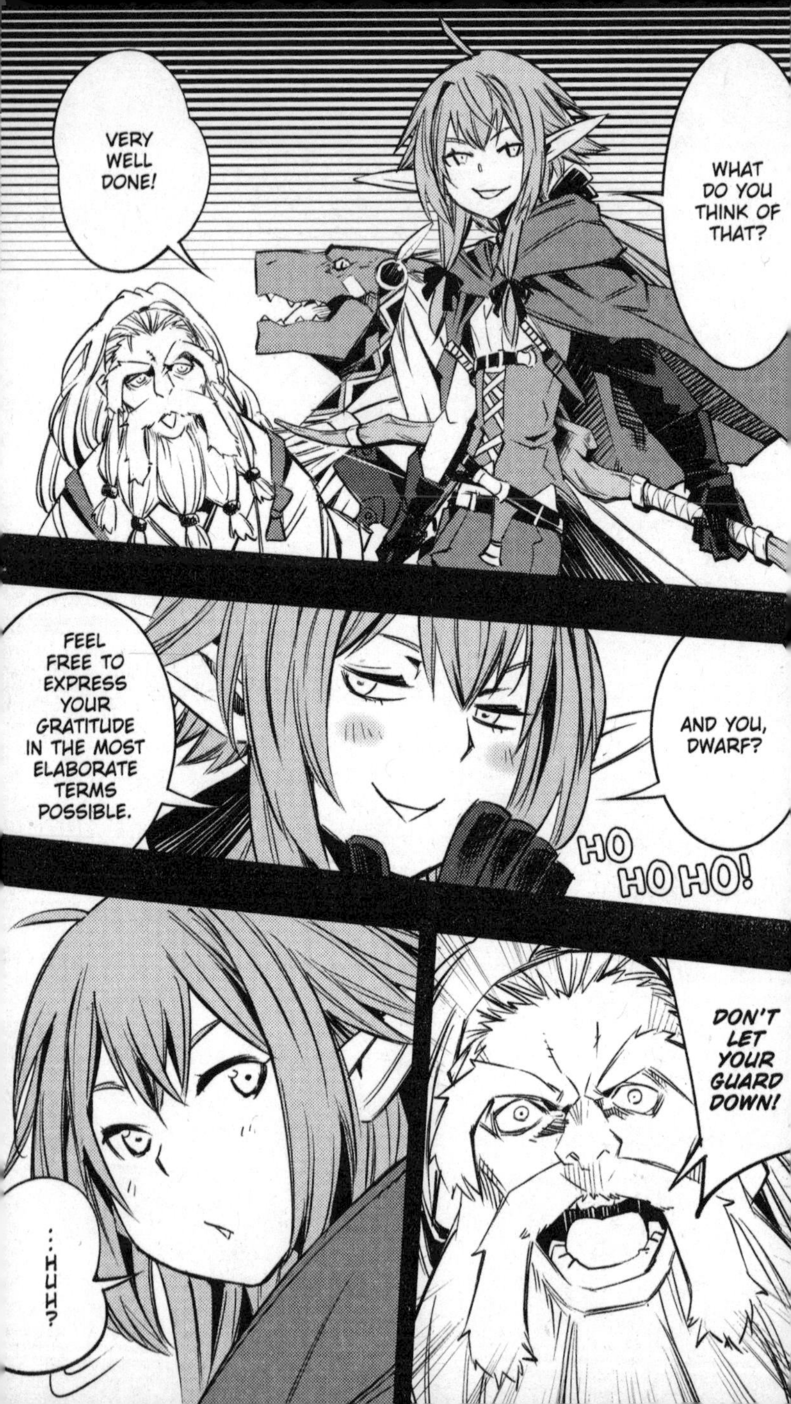
WHAT DO YOU THINK OF THAT?
VERY WELL DONE!
AND YOU, DWARF?
FEEL FREE TO EXPRESS YOUR GRATITUDE IN THE MOST ELABORATE TERMS POSSIBLE.
HO HO HO!
DON'T LET YOUR GUARD DOWN!
...HUH?

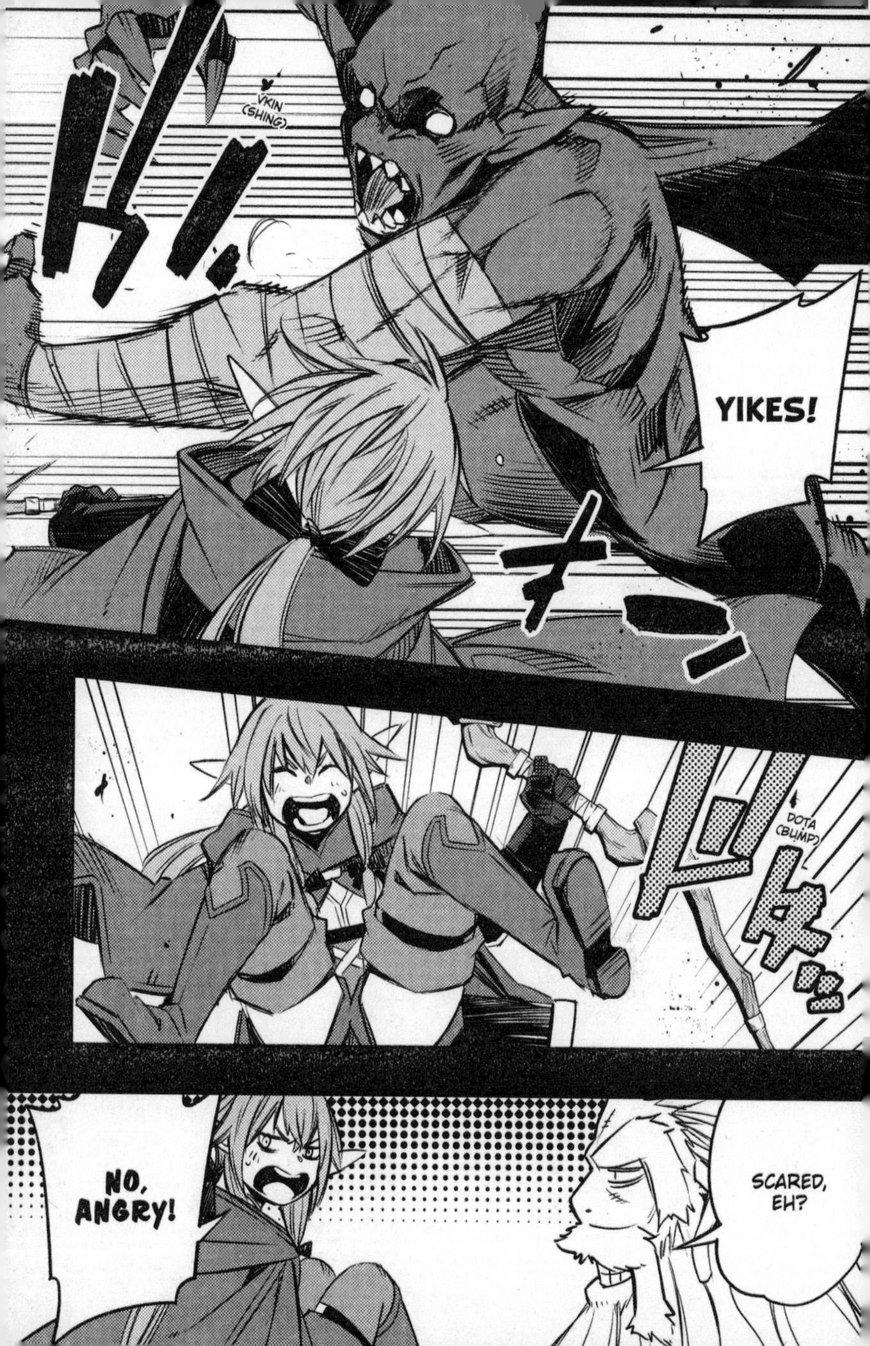
VKIN (SHING)
YIKES!
DOTA (BUMP)
SCARED, EH?
NO, ANGRY!

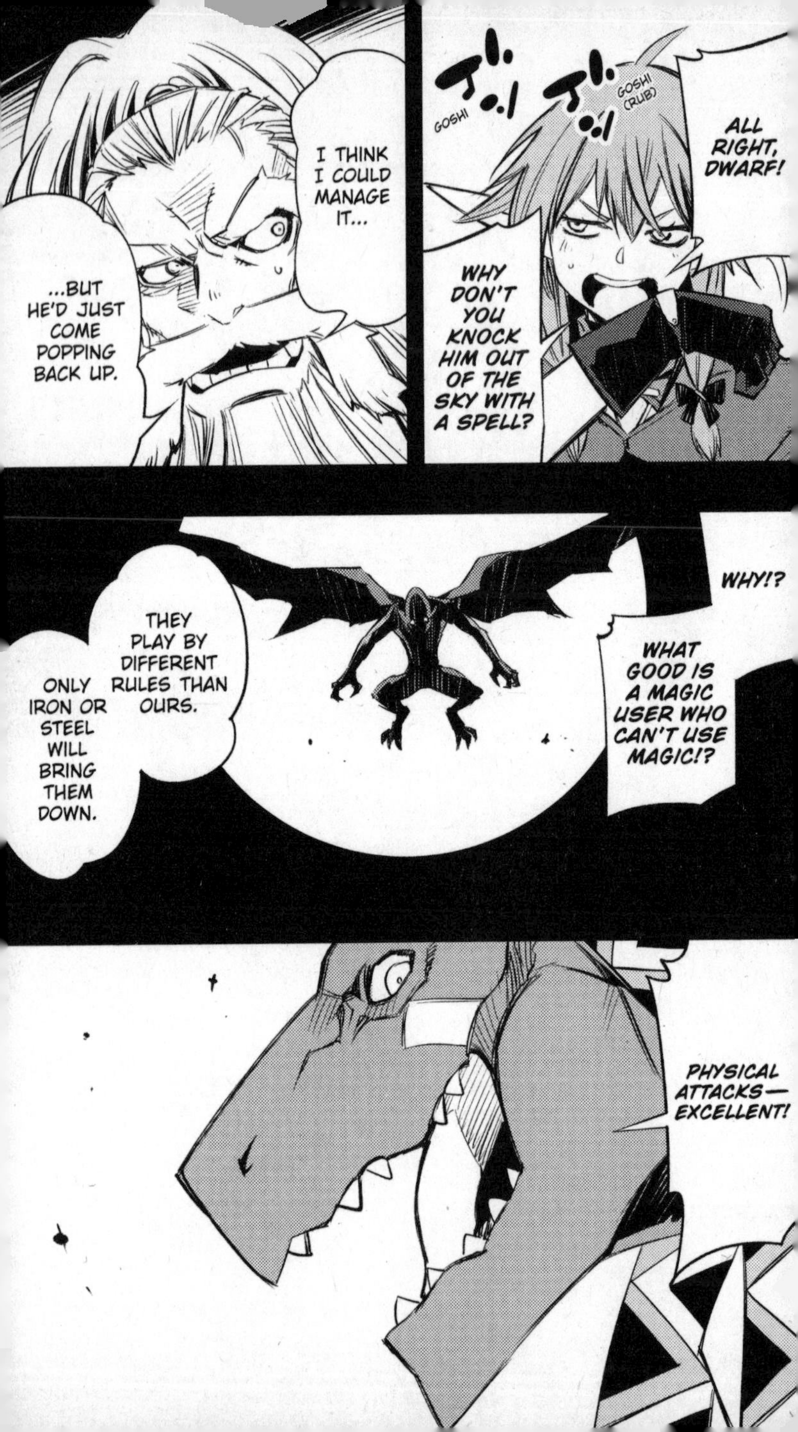
GOSHI
GOSHI (RUB)
ALL RIGHT, DWARF!
WHY DON'T YOU KNOCK HIM OUT OF THE SKY WITH A SPELL?
I THINK I COULD MANAGE IT...
...BUT HE'D JUST COME POPPING BACK UP.
WHY!?
WHAT GOOD IS A MAGIC USER WHO CAN'T USE MAGIC!?
THEY PLAY BY DIFFERENT RULES THAN OURS.
ONLY IRON OR STEEL WILL BRING THEM DOWN.
PHYSICAL ATTACKS—EXCELLENT!

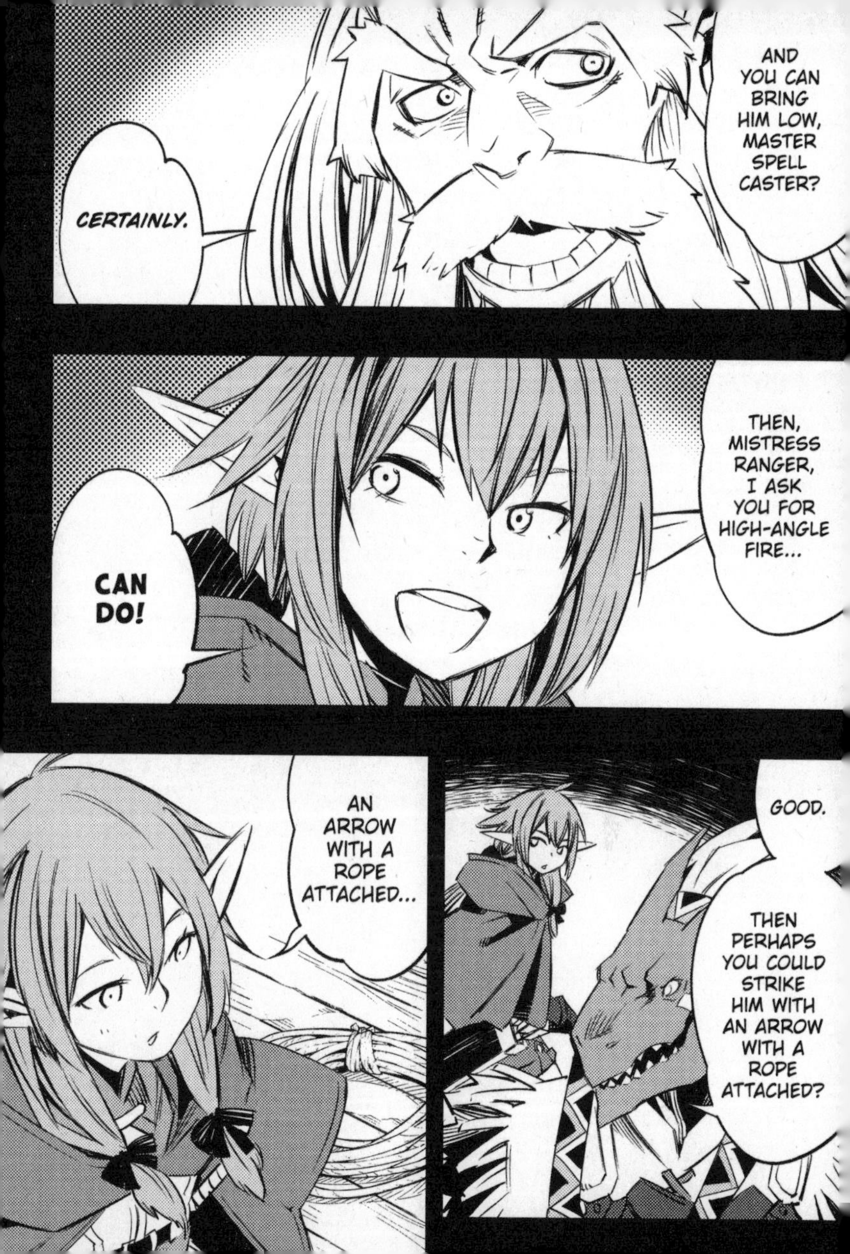
AND YOU CAN BRING HIM LOW, MASTER SPELL CASTER?
CERTAINLY.
THEN, MISTRESS RANGER, I ASK YOU FOR HIGH-ANGLE FIRE...
CAN DO!
GOOD.
THEN PERHAPS YOU COULD STRIKE HIM WITH AN ARROW WITH A ROPE ATTACHED?
AN ARROW WITH A ROPE ATTACHED...

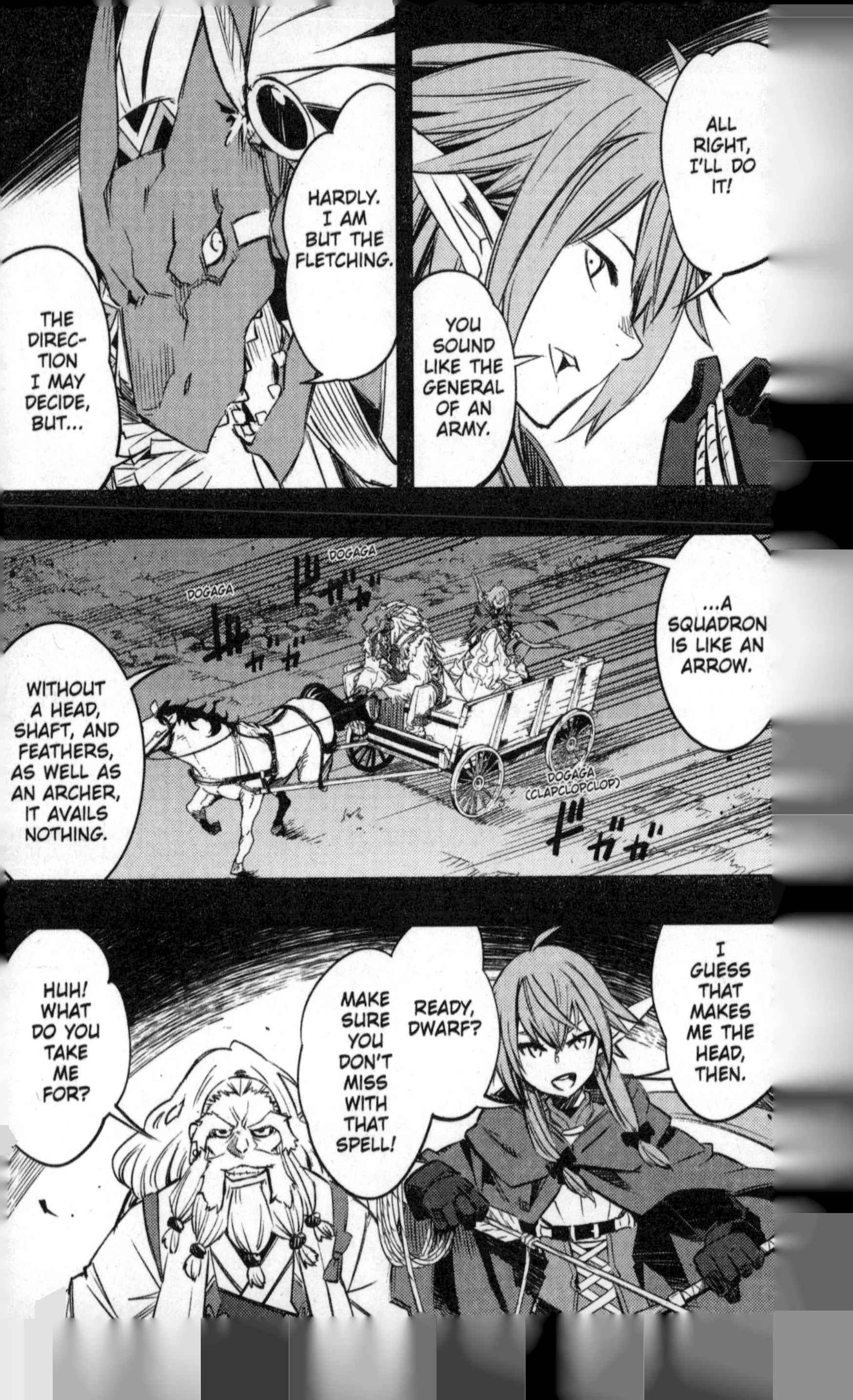
ALL RIGHT, I'LL DO IT!
YOU SOUND LIKE THE GENERAL OF AN ARMY.
HARDLY. I AM BUT THE FLETCHING.
THE DIRECTION I MAY DECIDE, BUT...
...A SQUADRON IS LIKE AN ARROW.
DOGAGA
DOGAGA
DOGAGA (CLAPCLOPCLOP)
WITHOUT A HEAD, SHAFT, AND FEATHERS, AS WELL AS AN ARCHER, IT AVAILS NOTHING.
I GUESS THAT MAKES ME THE HEAD, THEN.
READY, DWARF?
MAKE SURE YOU DON'T MISS WITH THAT SPELL!
HUH! WHAT DO YOU TAKE ME FOR?

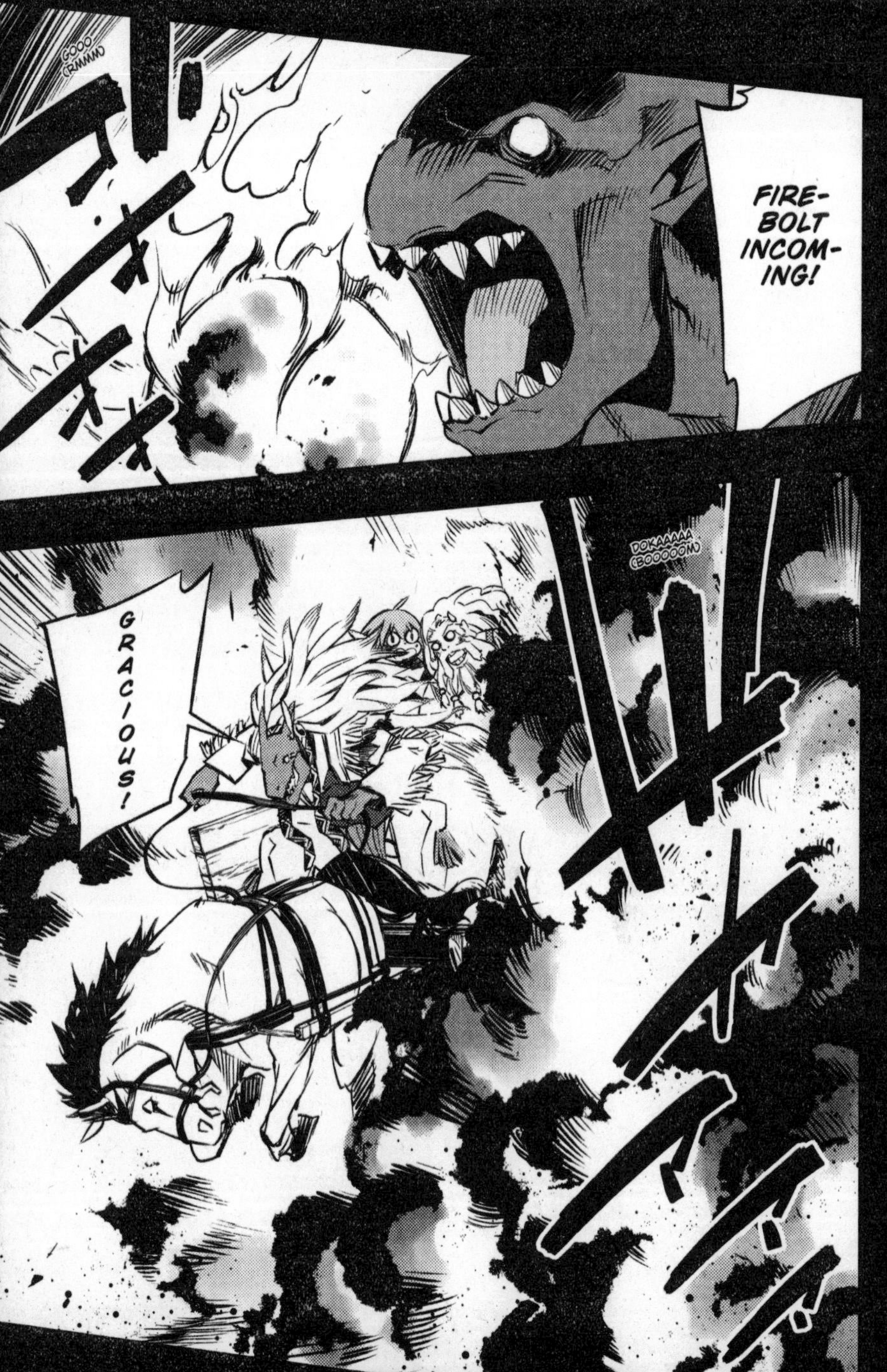
FIRE-BOLT INCOMING!
GOOO (RMMM)
DOKAAAAA (BOOOOOM)
GRACIOUS!

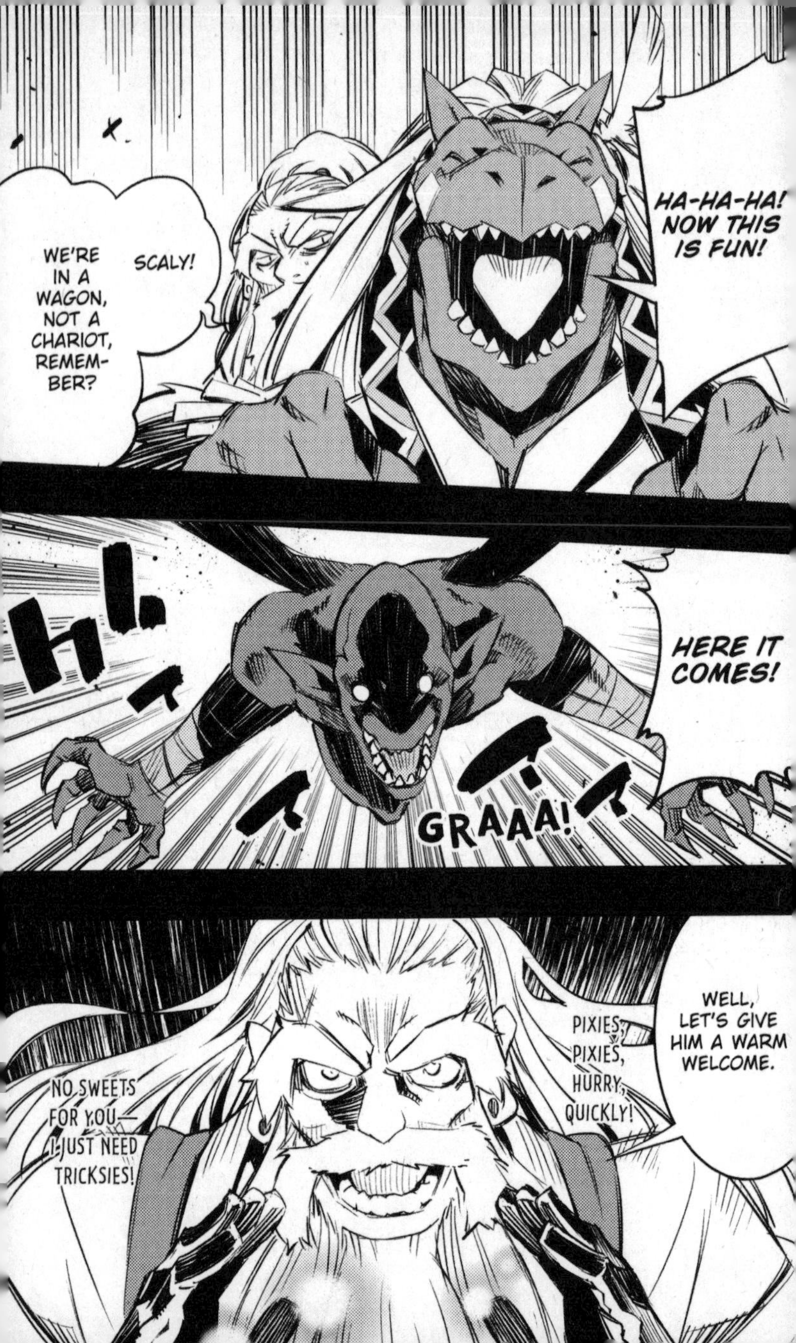
HA-HA-HA! NOW THIS IS FUN!
SCALY!
WE'RE IN A WAGON, NOT A CHARIOT, REMEMBER?
HERE IT COMES!
GRAAA!
WELL, LET'S GIVE HIM A WARM WELCOME.
PIXIES, PIXIES, HURRY, QUICKLY!
NO SWEETS FOR YOU— I JUST NEED TRICKSIES!

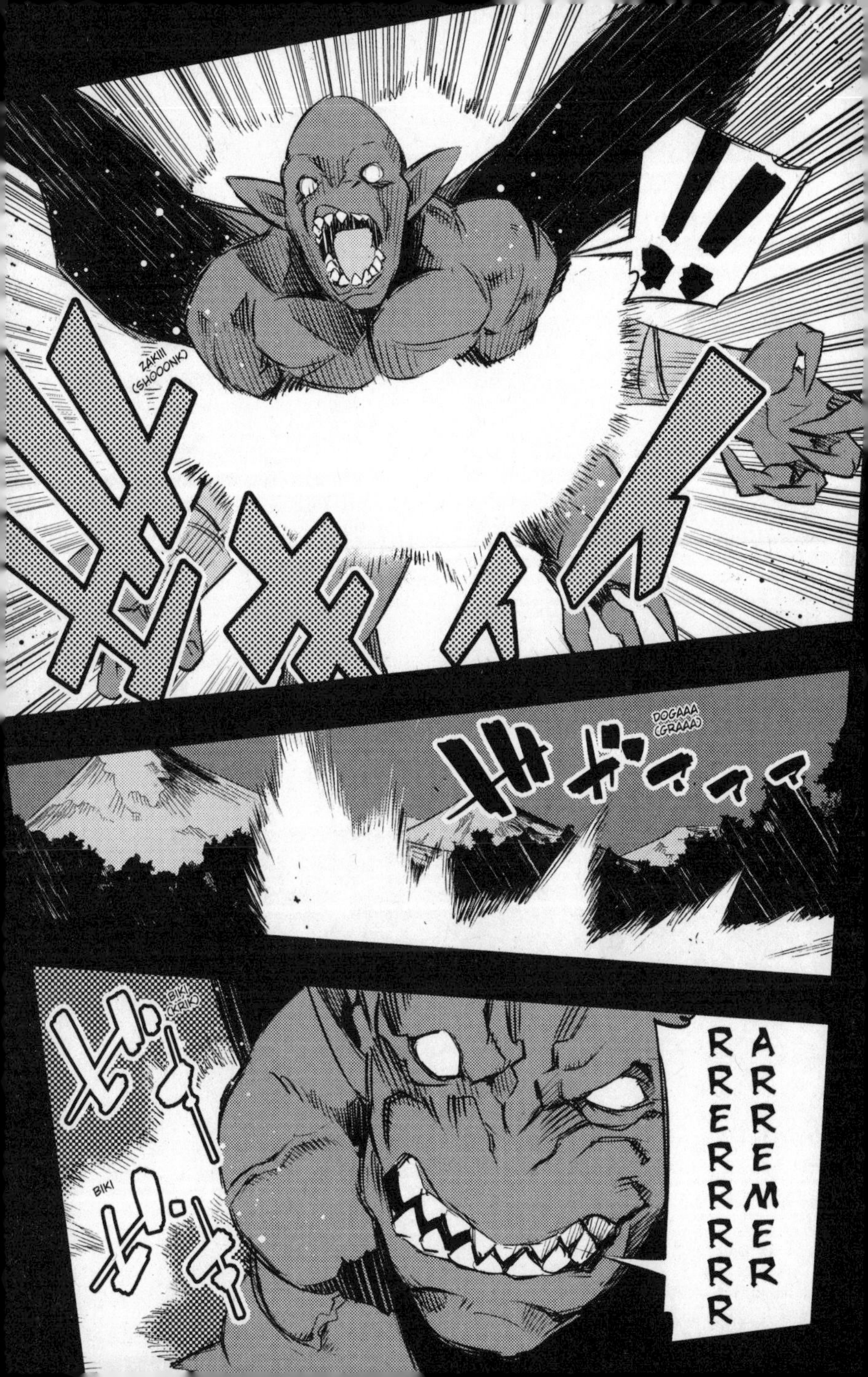
!!
ZAKIII (SHOOONK)
DOGAAA (GRAAA)
ARREMER
RRERRRRR
BIKI (KRIK)
BIKI

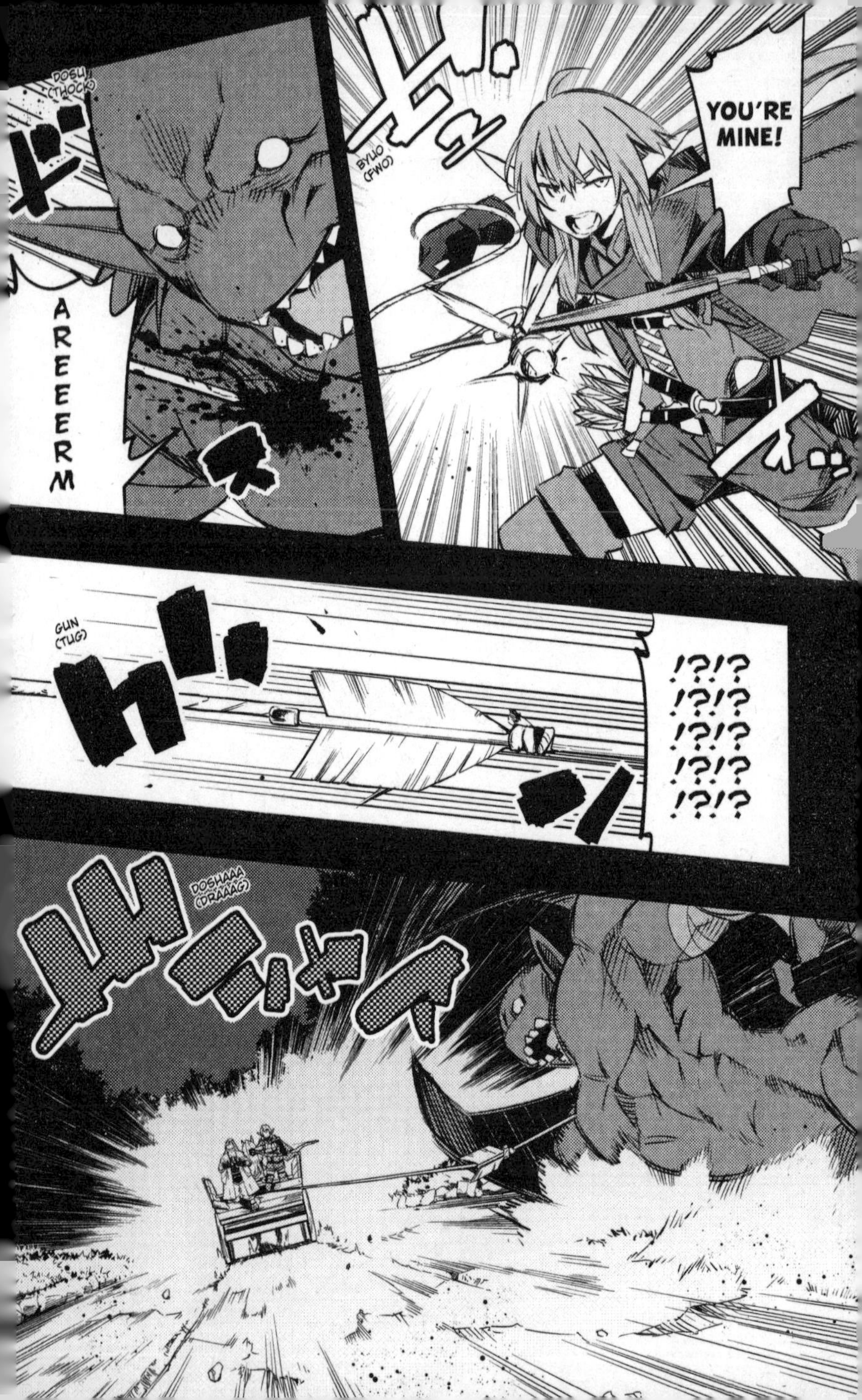
YOU'RE MINE!
BYUO (FWO)
DOSU (THOCK)
AREEEERM
GUN (TUG)
!?!? !?!? !?!? !?!? !?!?
DOSHAAA (DRAAAG)

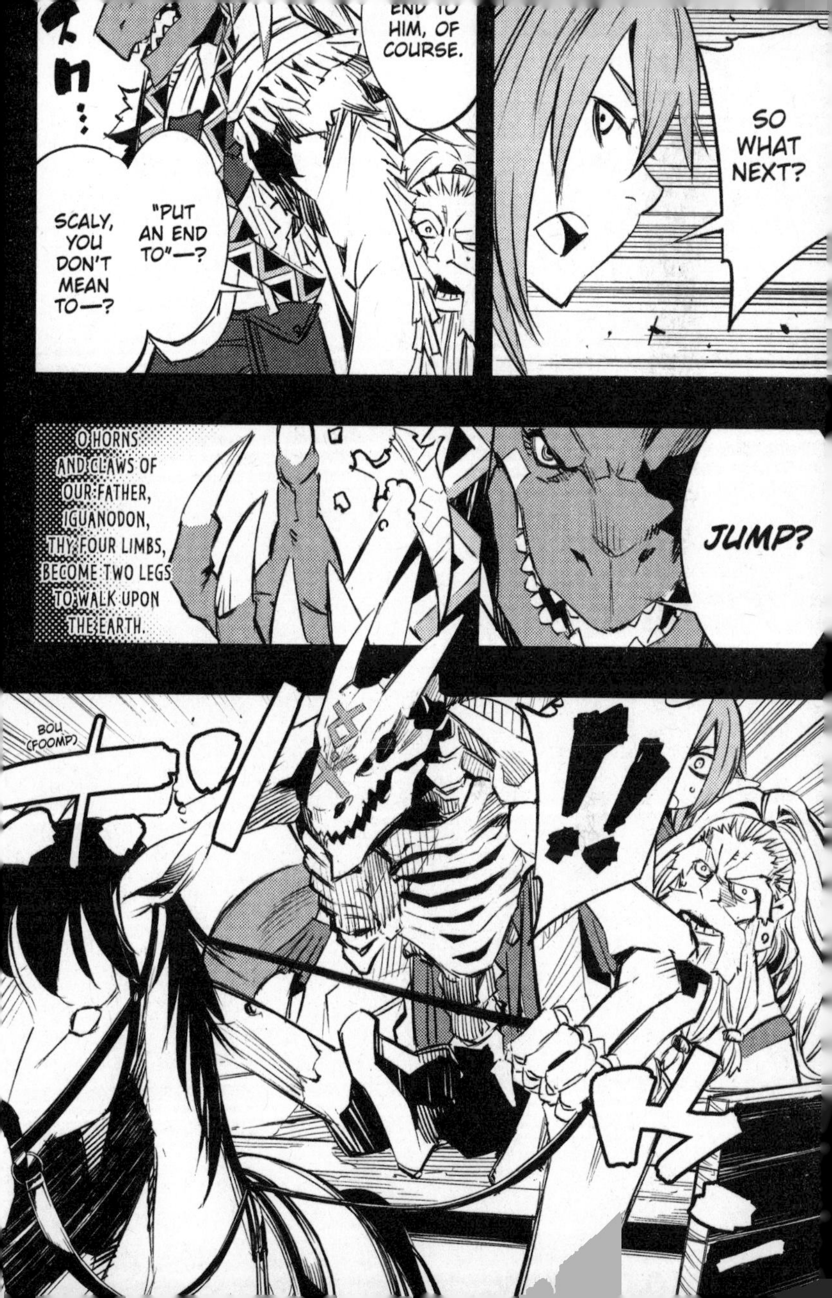
SO WHAT NEXT?
END TO HIM, OF COURSE.
"PUT AN END TO"—?
SCALY, YOU DON'T MEAN TO—?
JUMP?
O HORNS AND CLAWS OF OUR FATHER, IGUANODON, THY FOUR LIMBS, BECOME TWO LEGS TO WALK UPON THE EARTH.
!!
BOU (FOOMP)

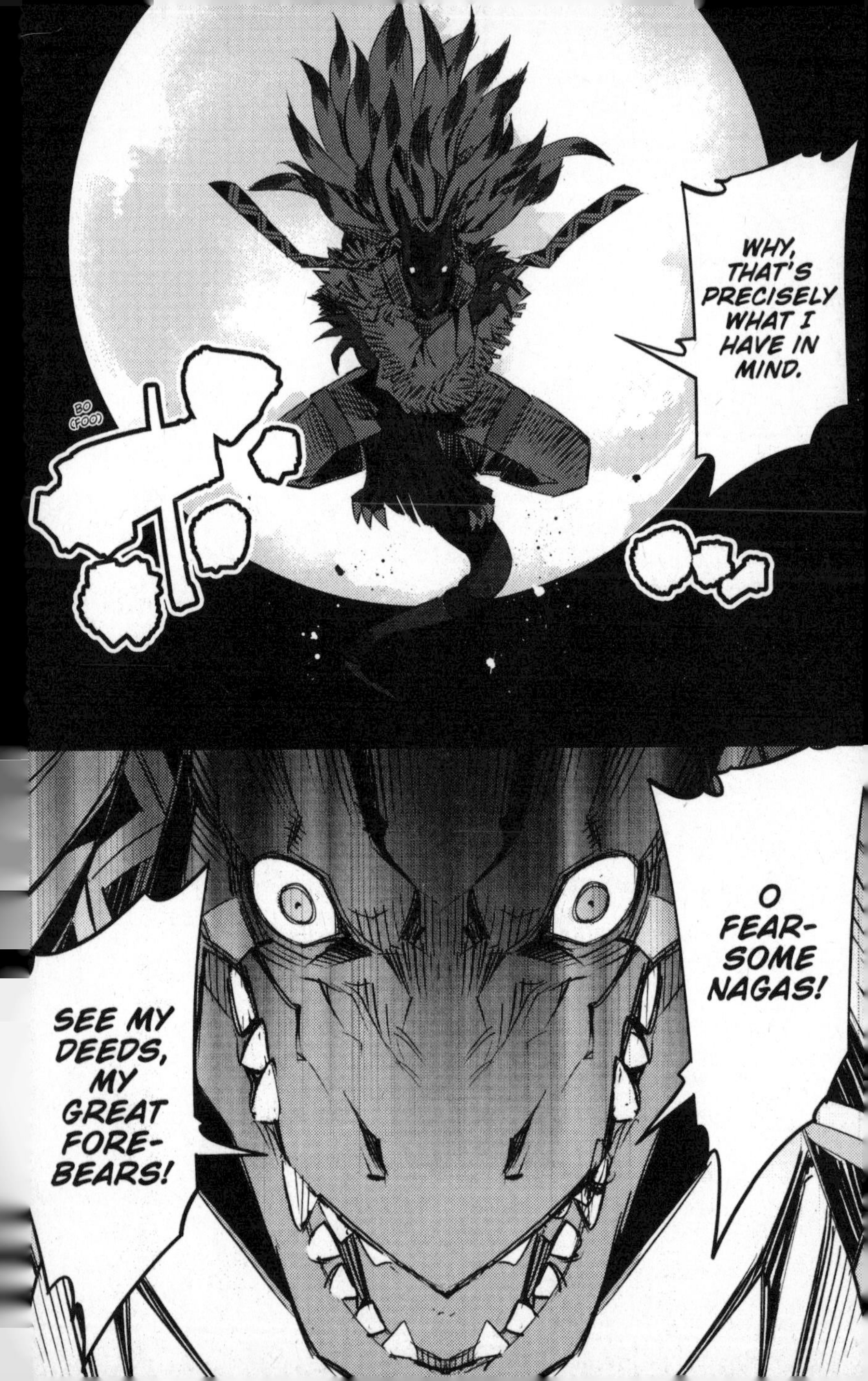
WHY, THAT'S PRECISELY WHAT I HAVE IN MIND.
BO (FOO)
O FEAR-SOME NAGAS!
SEE MY DEEDS, MY GREAT FORE-BEARS!

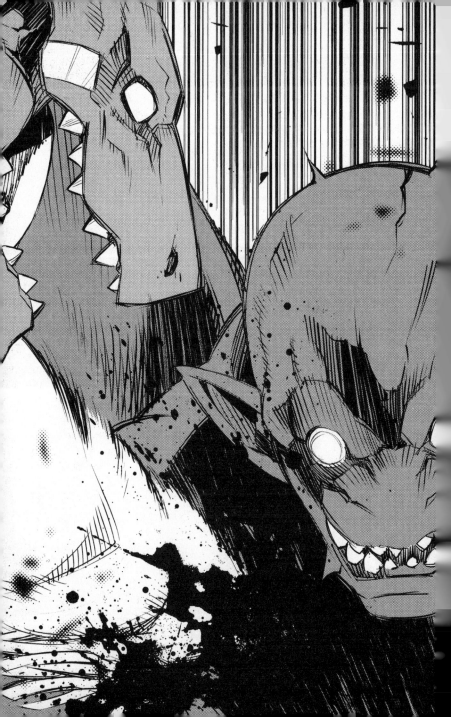

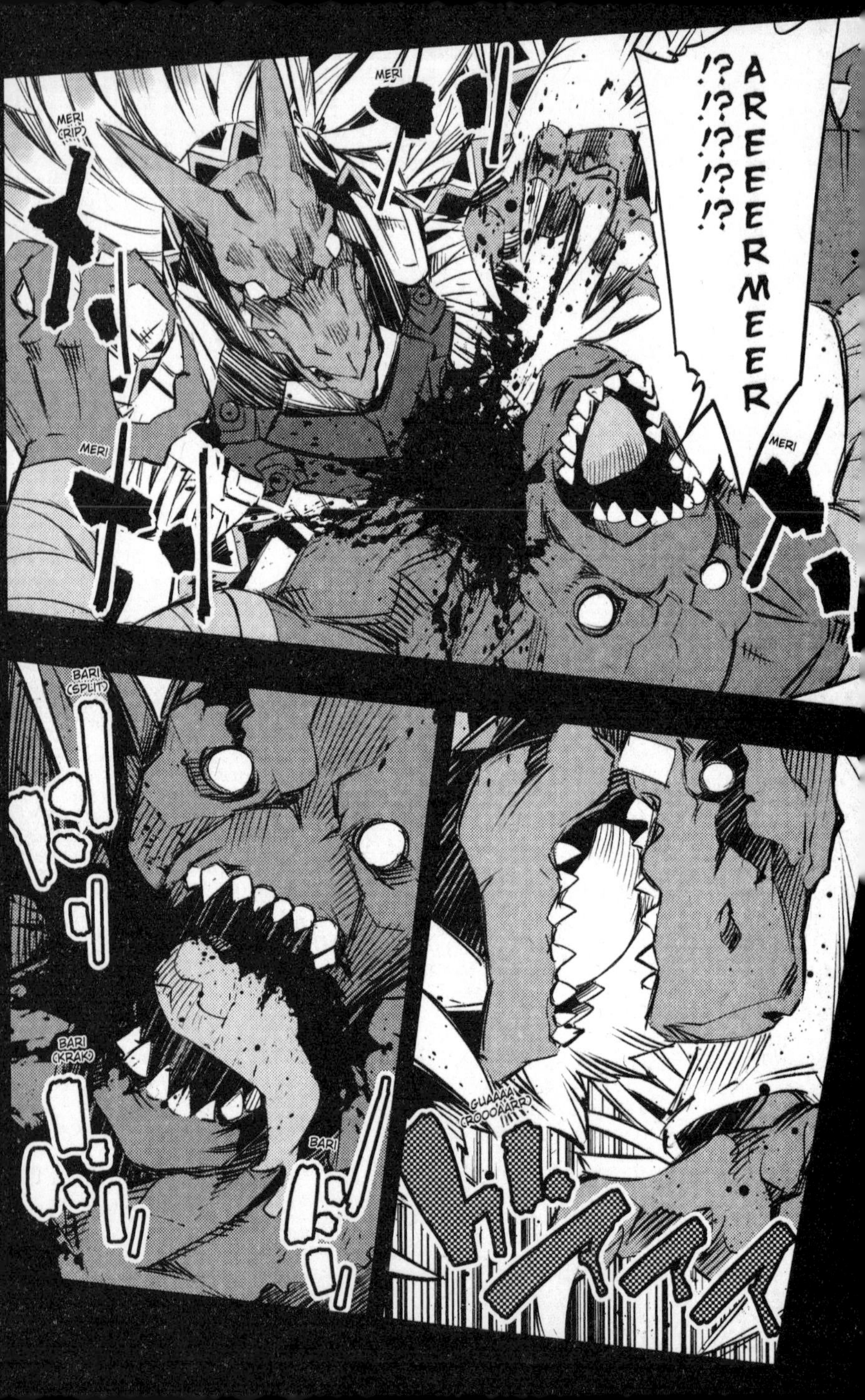
AREEERMEER!?!?!?!?!?
MERI
MERI (RIP)
MERI
MERI
GUAAAA (ROOOAARR)
BARI (SPLIT)
BARI (KRAK)
BARI

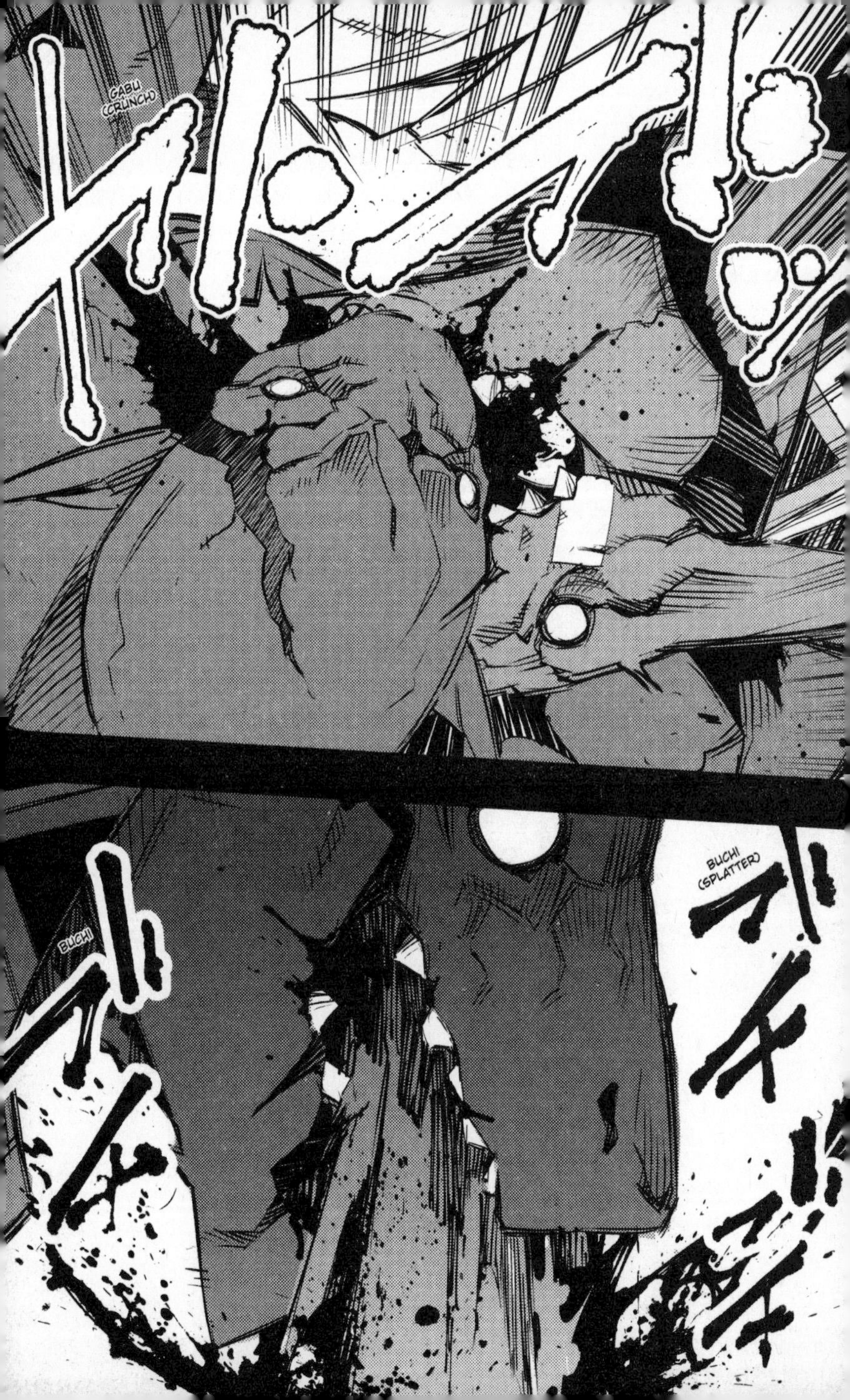
GABU (CRUNCH)
BUCHI (SPLATTER)
BUCHI

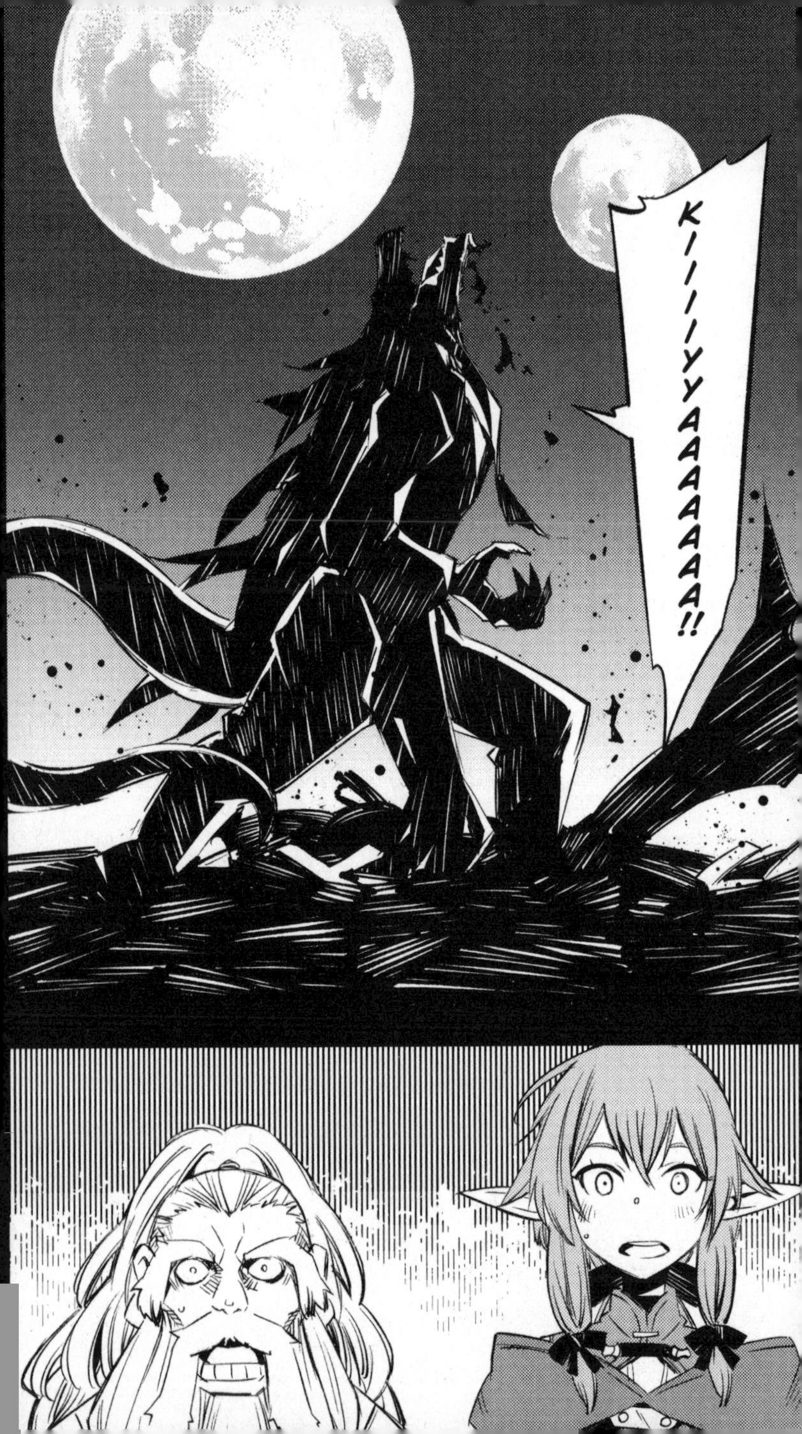
KIIIIYYAAAAAAAAA!!

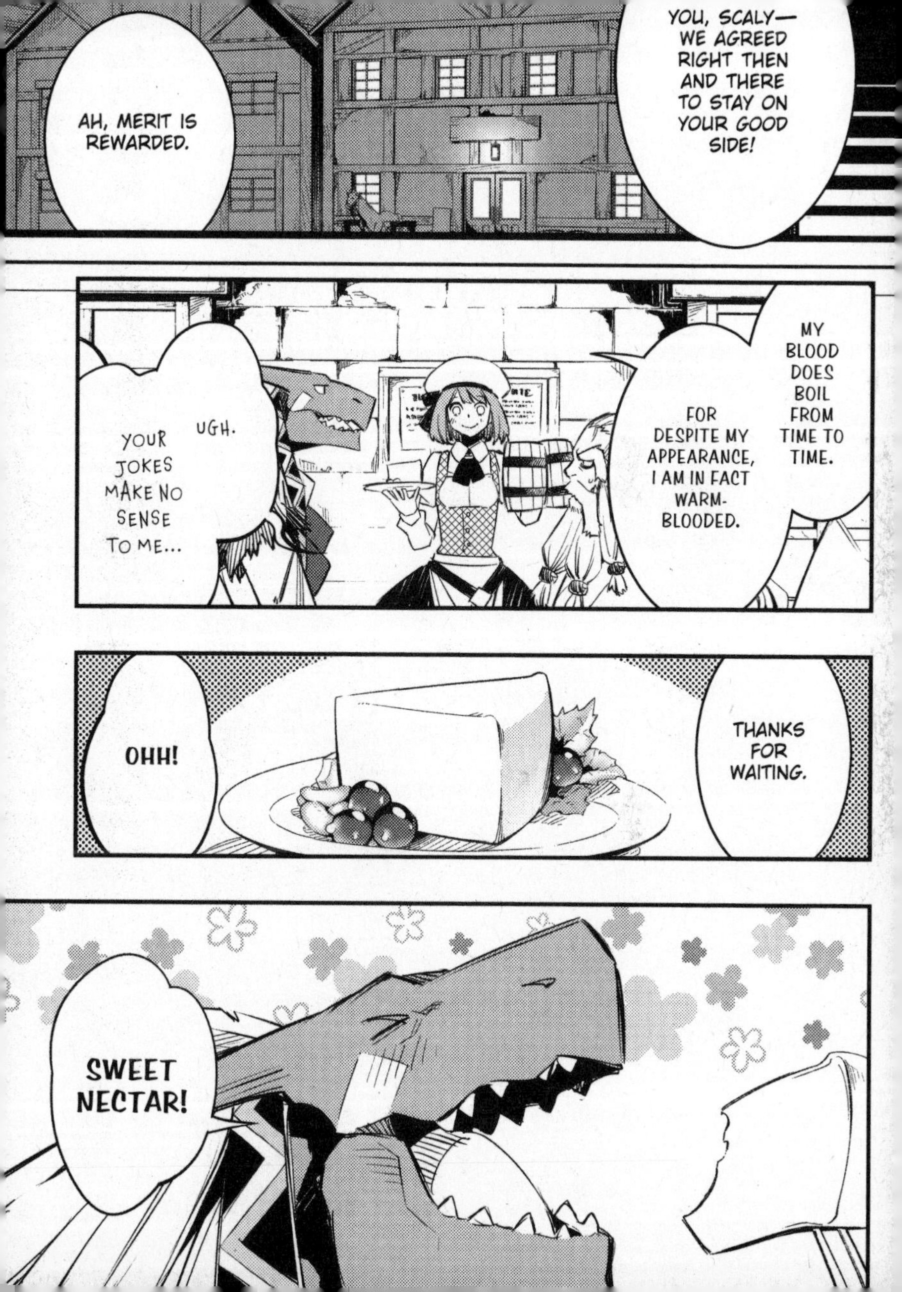
YOU, SCALY—WE AGREED RIGHT THEN AND THERE TO STAY ON YOUR GOOD SIDE!
AH, MERIT IS REWARDED.
MY BLOOD DOES BOIL FROM TIME TO TIME.
FOR DESPITE MY APPEARANCE, I AM IN FACT WARM-BLOODED.
UGH.
YOUR JOKES MAKE NO SENSE TO ME...
THANKS FOR WAITING.
OHH!
SWEET NECTAR!

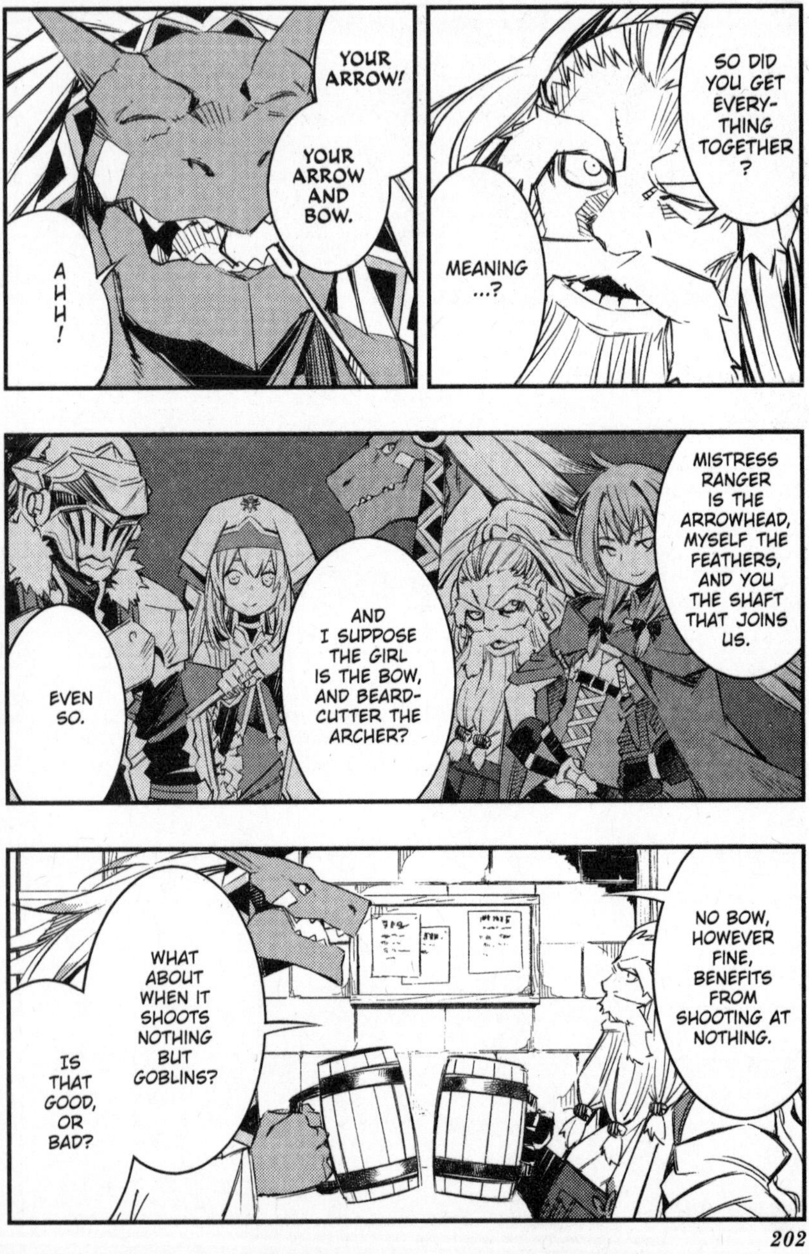
SO DID YOU GET EVERY-THING TOGETHER?
MEANING ...?
YOUR ARROW!
YOUR ARROW AND BOW.
AHH!
MISTRESS RANGER IS THE ARROWHEAD, MYSELF THE FEATHERS, AND YOU THE SHAFT THAT JOINS US.
AND I SUPPOSE THE GIRL IS THE BOW, AND BEARD-CUTTER THE ARCHER?
EVEN SO.
NO BOW, HOWEVER FINE, BENEFITS FROM SHOOTING AT NOTHING.
WHAT ABOUT WHEN IT SHOOTS NOTHING BUT GOBLINS?
IS THAT GOOD, OR BAD?

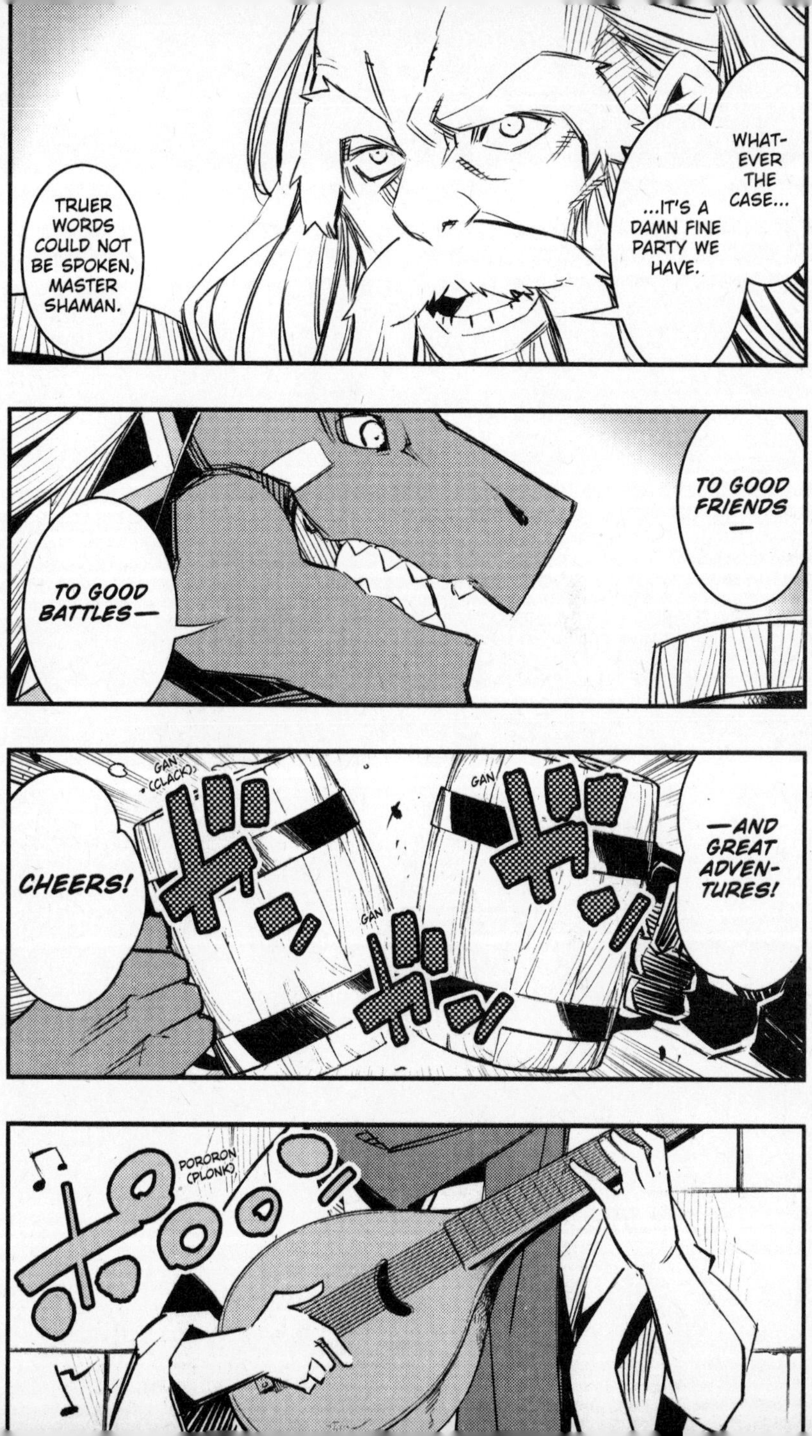
WHAT-EVER THE CASE...
...IT'S A DAMN FINE PARTY WE HAVE.
TRUER WORDS COULD NOT BE SPOKEN, MASTER SHAMAN.
TO GOOD FRIENDS—
TO GOOD BATTLES—
—AND GREAT ADVEN-TURES!
GAN
GAN
GAN (CLACK)
CHEERS!
POROROn (PLONK)

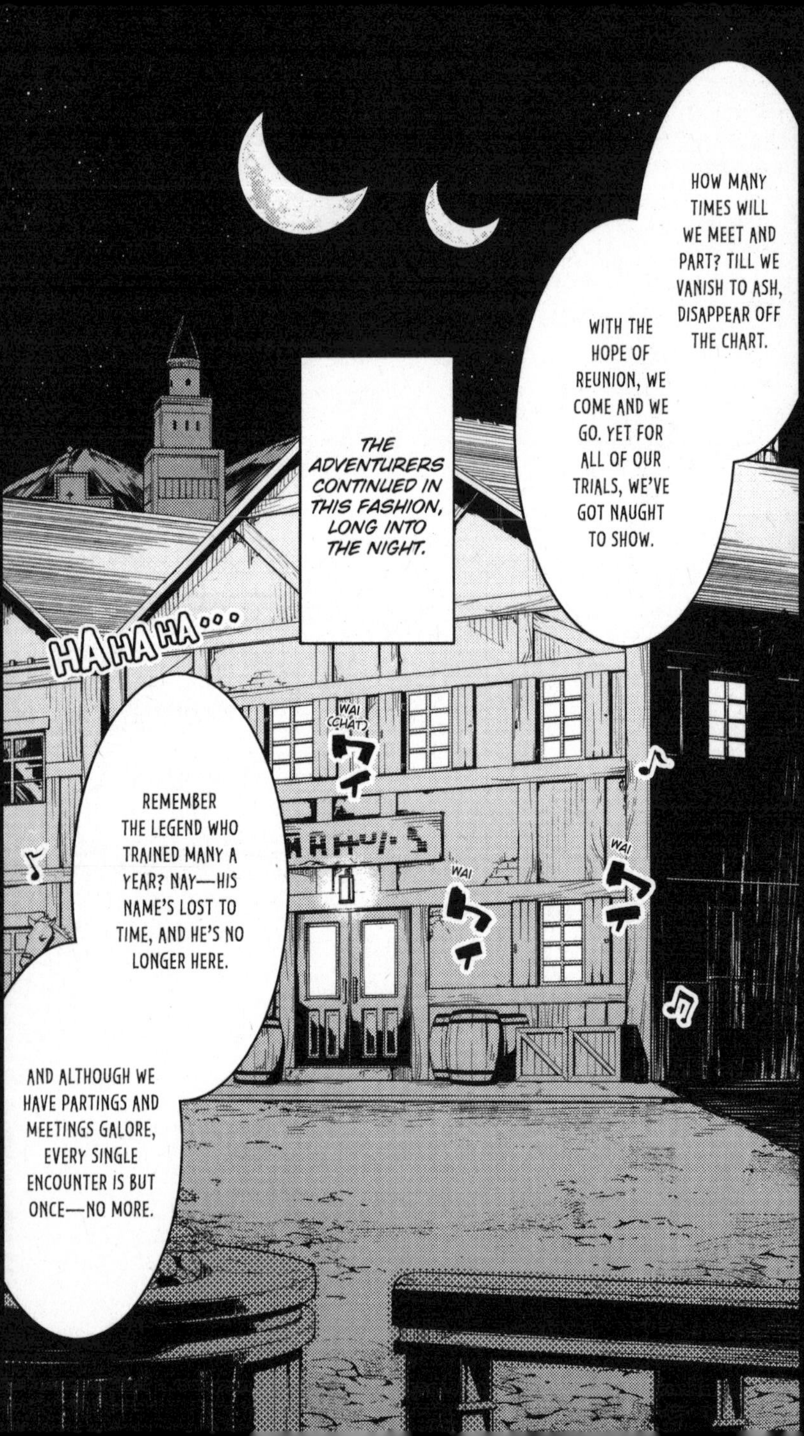

HOW MANY TIMES WILL WE MEET AND PART? TILL WE VANISH TO ASH, DISAPPEAR OFF THE CHART.
WITH THE HOPE OF REUNION, WE COME AND WE GO. YET FOR ALL OF OUR TRIALS, WE'VE GOT NAUGHT TO SHOW.
THE ADVENTURERS CONTINUED IN THIS FASHION, LONG INTO THE NIGHT.
HAHAHA...
WAI (CHAT)
WAI
WAI
REMEMBER THE LEGEND WHO TRAINED MANY A YEAR? NAY—HIS NAME'S LOST TO TIME, AND HE'S NO LONGER HERE.
AND ALTHOUGH WE HAVE PARTINGS AND MEETINGS GALORE, EVERY SINGLE ENCOUNTER IS BUT ONCE—NO MORE.

Chapter 10:
Of Going There and Back Again

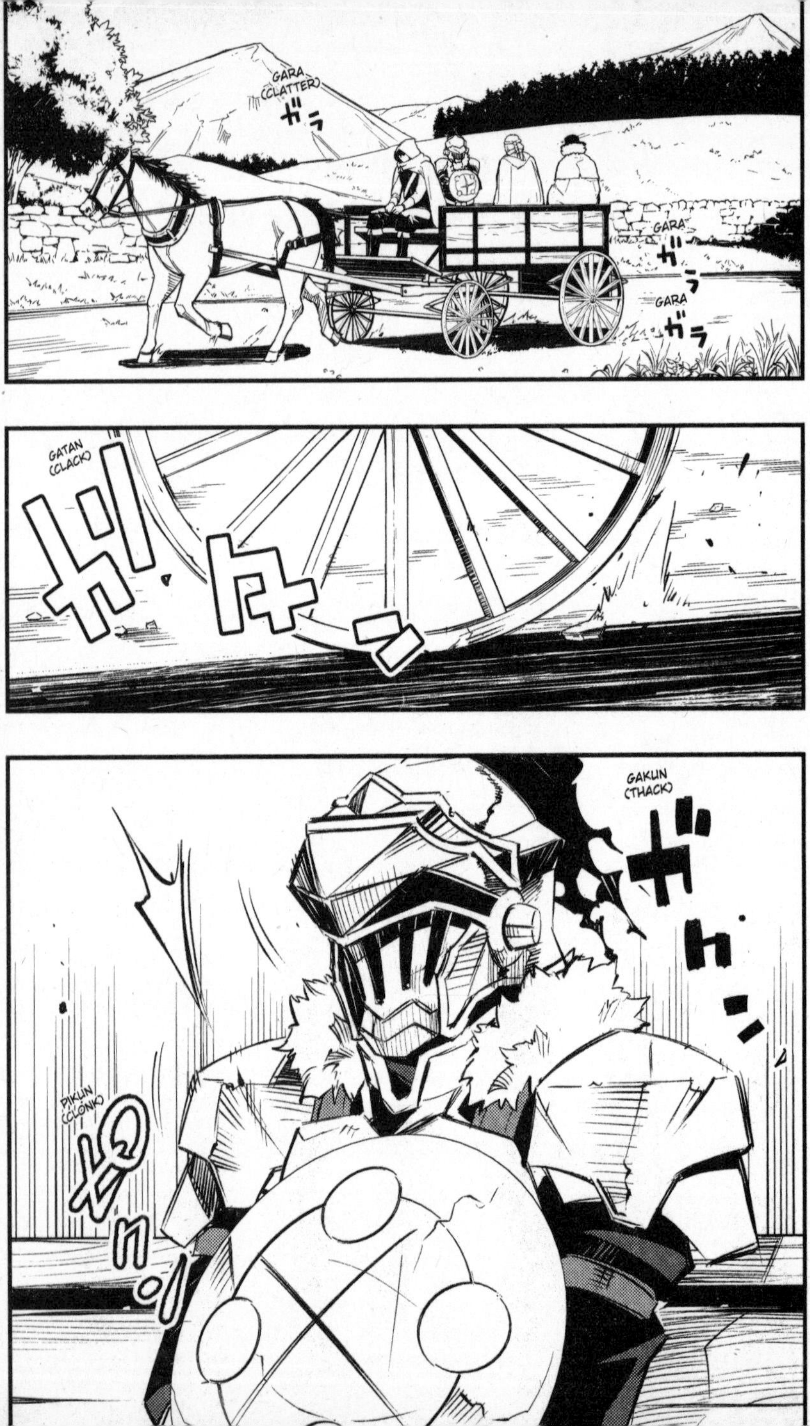
GARA (CLATTER) ガラ
GARA ガラ
GARA ガラ
GATAN (CLACK) ガタン
GAKUN (THACK) ガクン
PIKUN (CLONK) ピクン!

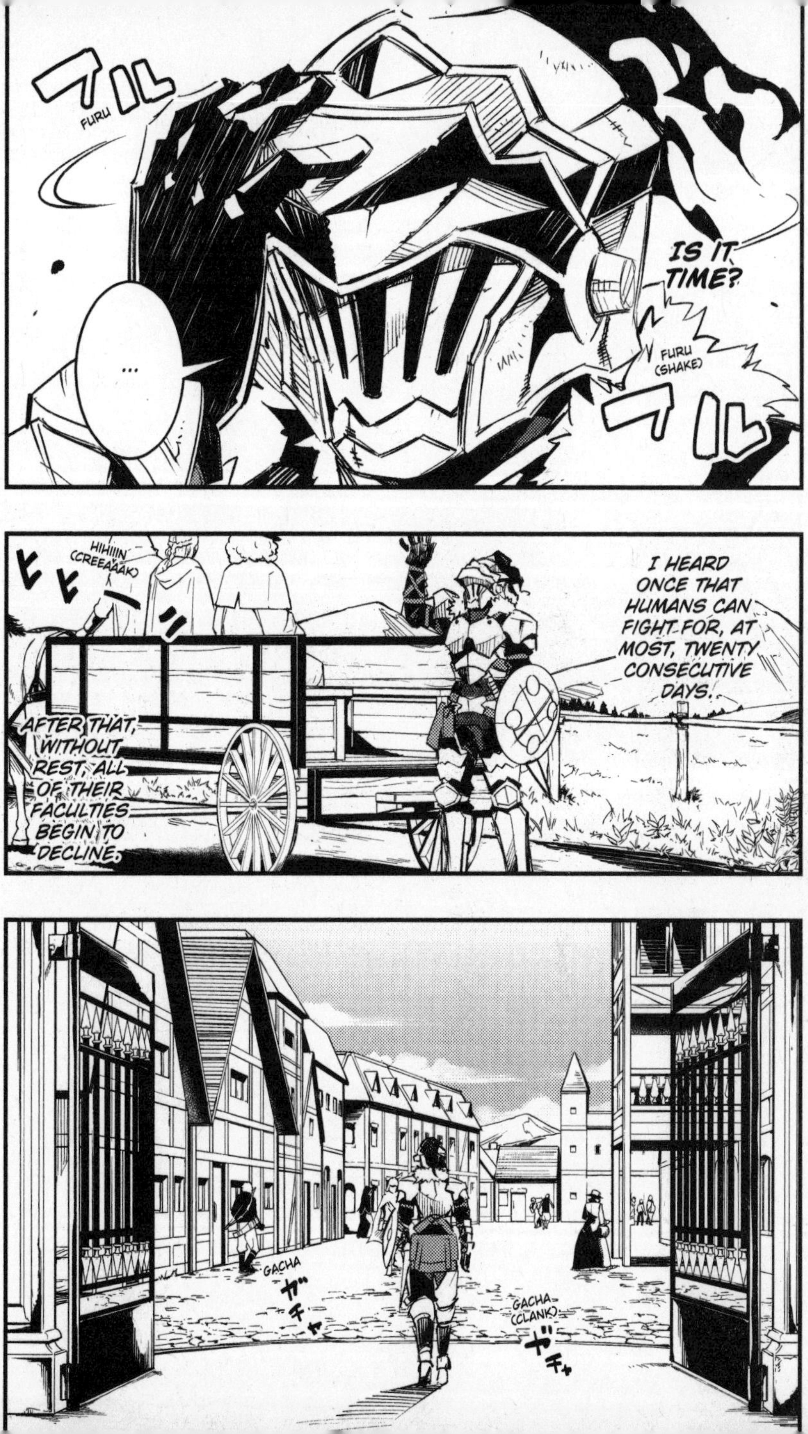

IS IT TIME?
FURU (SHAKE)
フル
FURU
フル
...
I HEARD ONCE THAT HUMANS CAN FIGHT FOR, AT MOST, TWENTY CONSECUTIVE DAYS.
HIHIIIN (CREEAAAK)
ヒヒーン
AFTER THAT, WITHOUT REST, ALL OF THEIR FACULTIES BEGIN TO DECLINE.
GACHA (CLANK)
ガチャ
GACHA
ガチャ

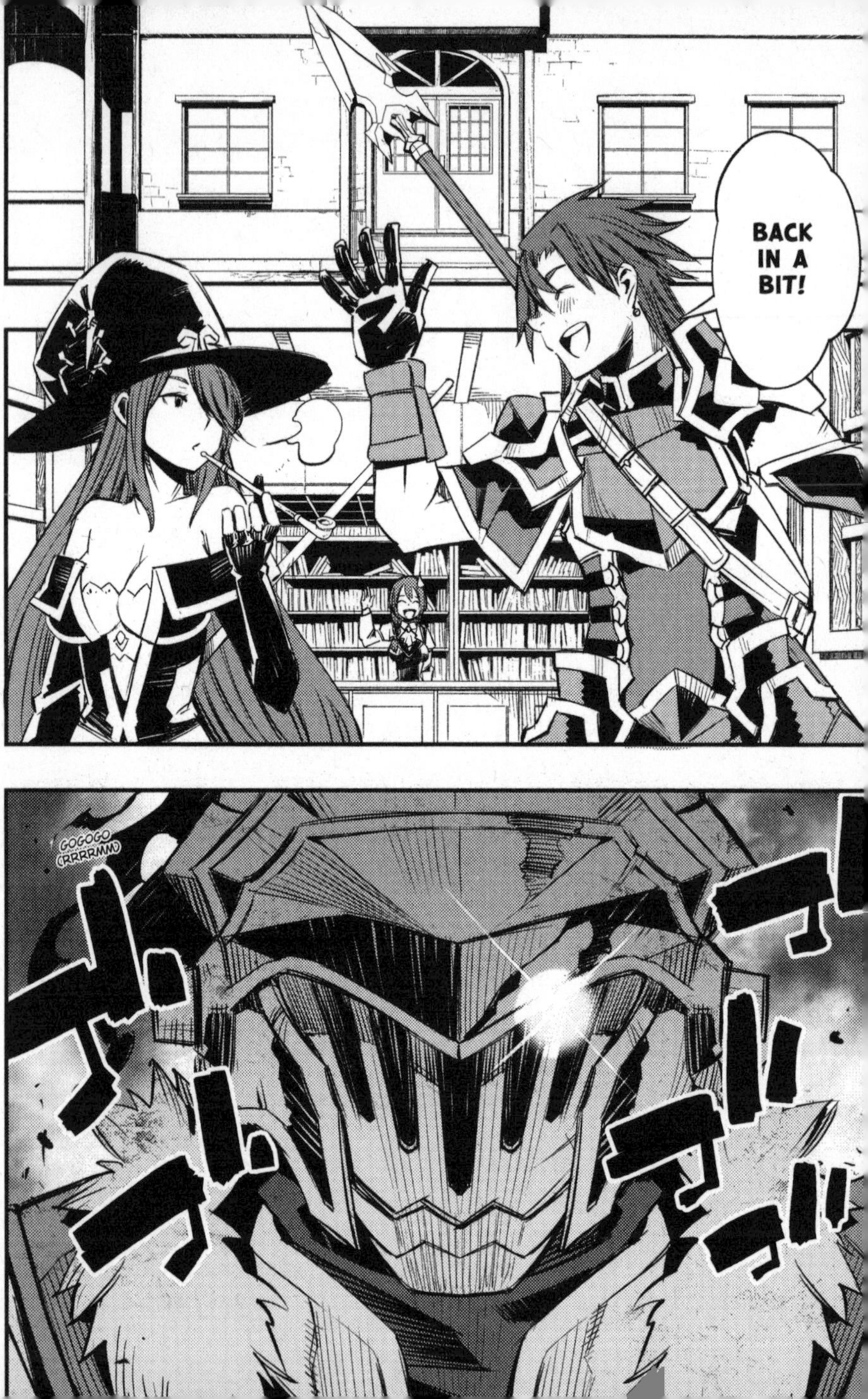
BACK IN A BIT!
GOGOGO (RRRRMM)

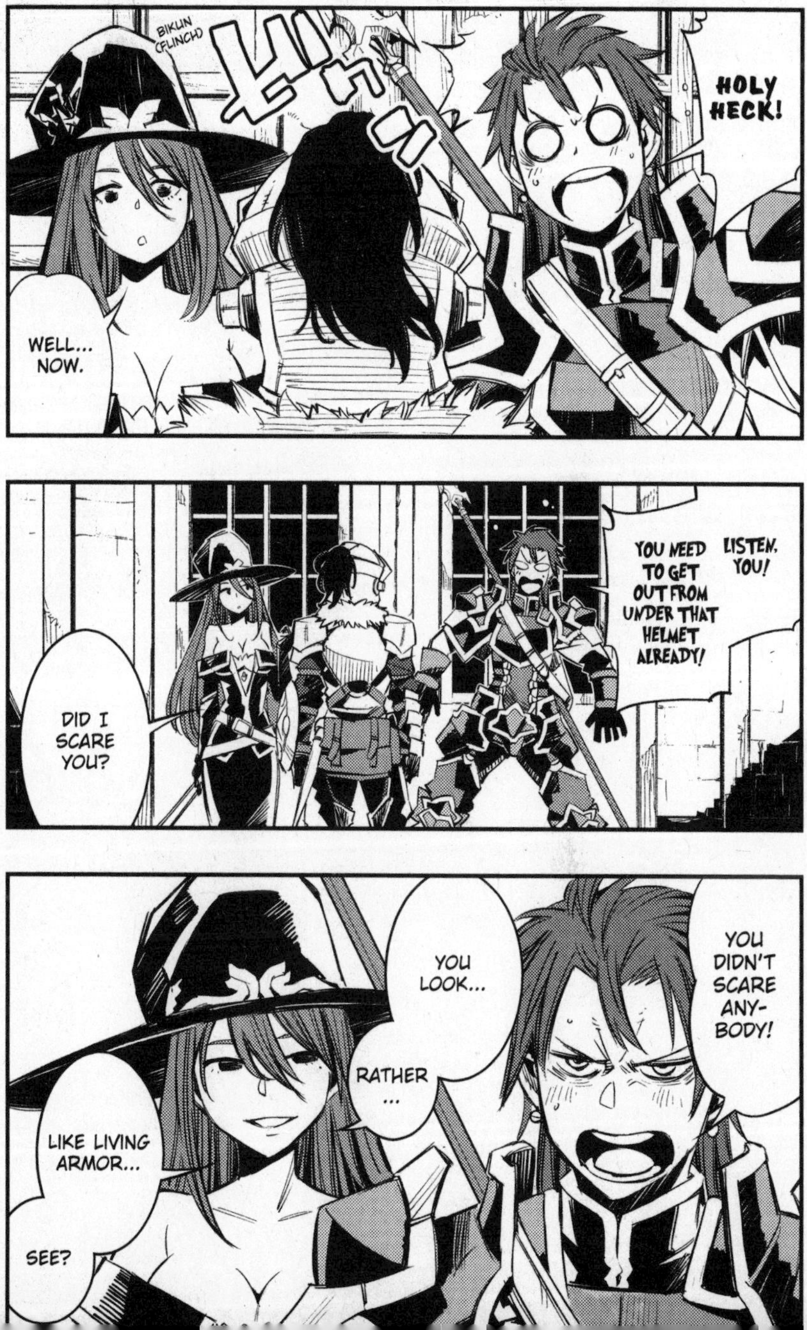
HOLY HECK!
BIKUN (FLINCH)
WELL... NOW.
LISTEN, YOU!
YOU NEED TO GET OUT FROM UNDER THAT HELMET ALREADY!
DID I SCARE YOU?
YOU DIDN'T SCARE ANY-BODY!
YOU LOOK...
RATHER ...
LIKE LIVING ARMOR...
SEE?

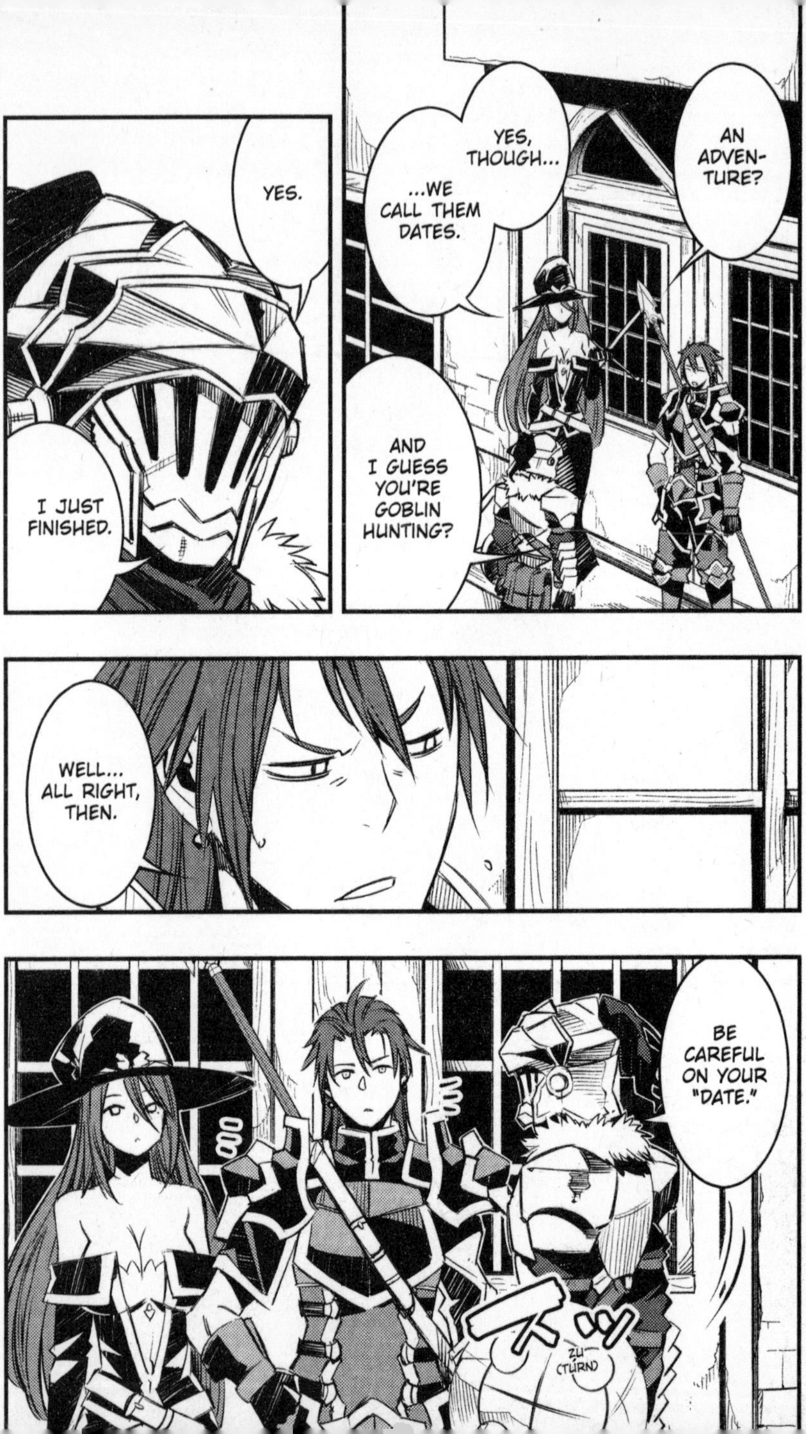
AN ADVENTURE?
YES, THOUGH...
...WE CALL THEM DATES.
AND I GUESS YOU'RE GOBLIN HUNTING?
YES.
I JUST FINISHED.
WELL... ALL RIGHT, THEN.
BE CAREFUL ON YOUR "DATE."
ZU (TURN)

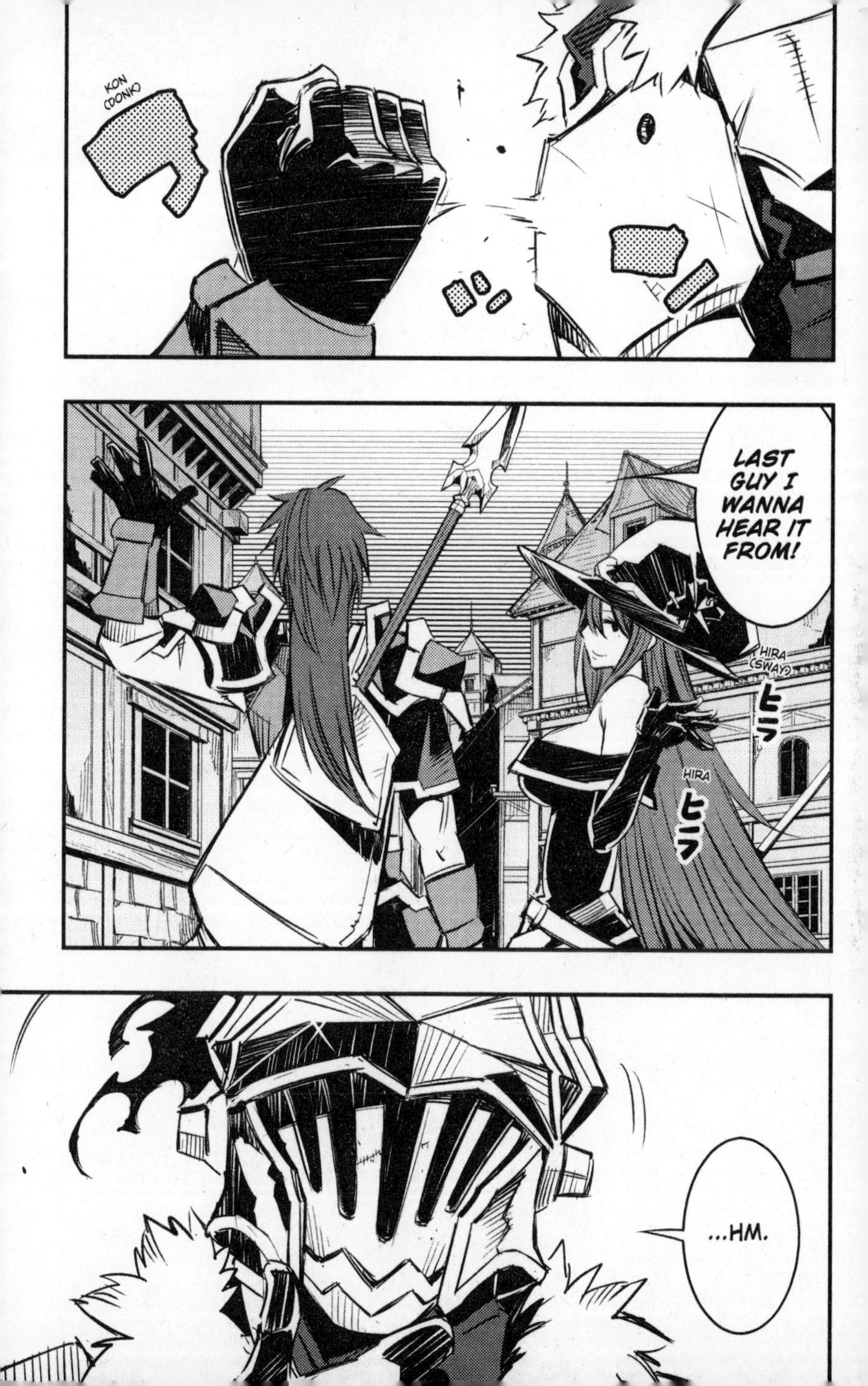
KON
(DONK)
LAST GUY I WANNA HEAR IT FROM!
HIRA
(SWAY)
ヒラ
HIRA
ヒラ
...HM.

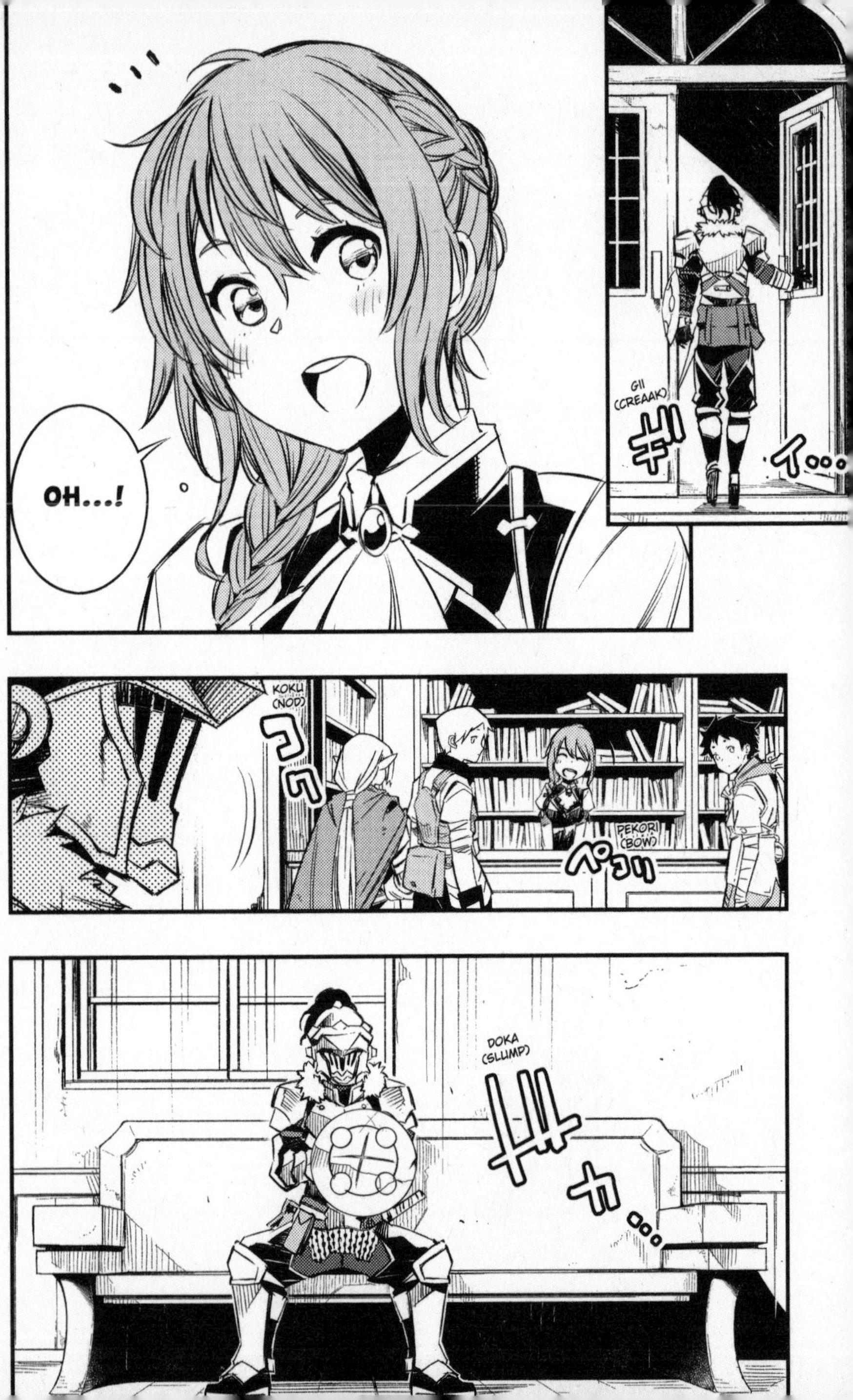
GII (CREAAK)
ギィ…
…!
OH…!
KOKU (NOD)
コク
PEKORI (BOW)
ペコリ
DOKA (SLUMP)
ドカッ…

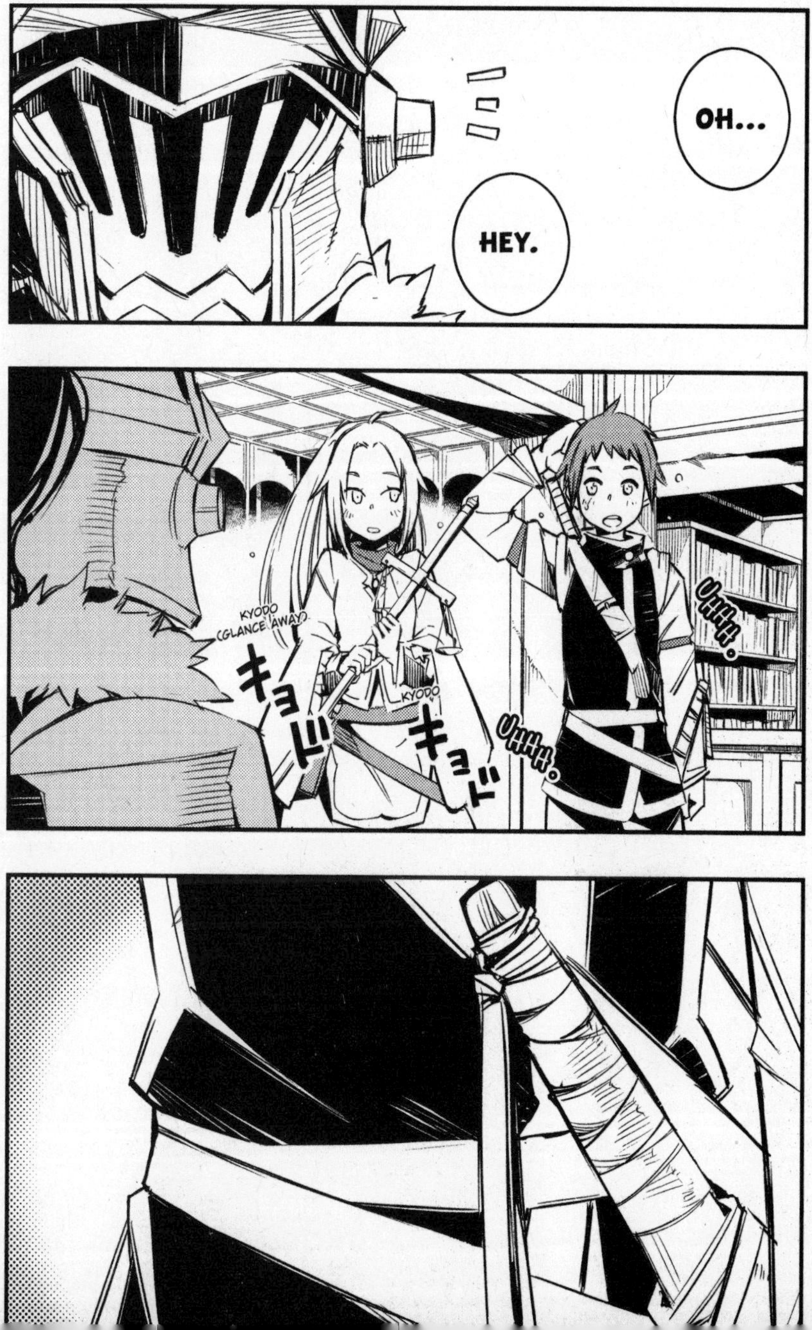
OH...
HEY.
UHHH.
UHHH.
KYODO
キョド
KYODO (GLANCE AWAY)
キョド

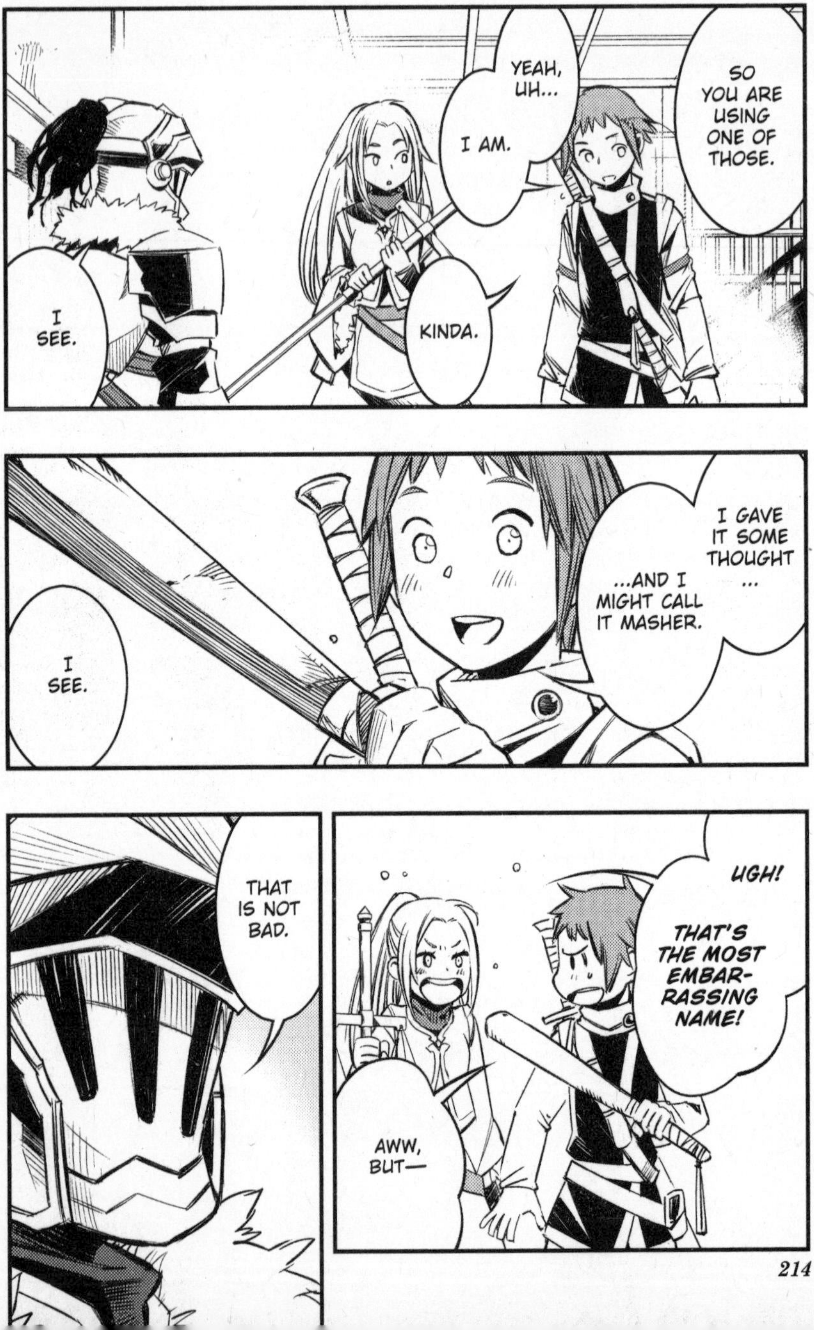
SO YOU ARE USING ONE OF THOSE.
YEAH, UH... I AM.
KINDA.
I SEE.
I GAVE IT SOME THOUGHT...
...AND I MIGHT CALL IT MASHER.
I SEE.
UGH! THAT'S THE MOST EMBAR-RASSING NAME!
AWW, BUT—
THAT IS NOT BAD.

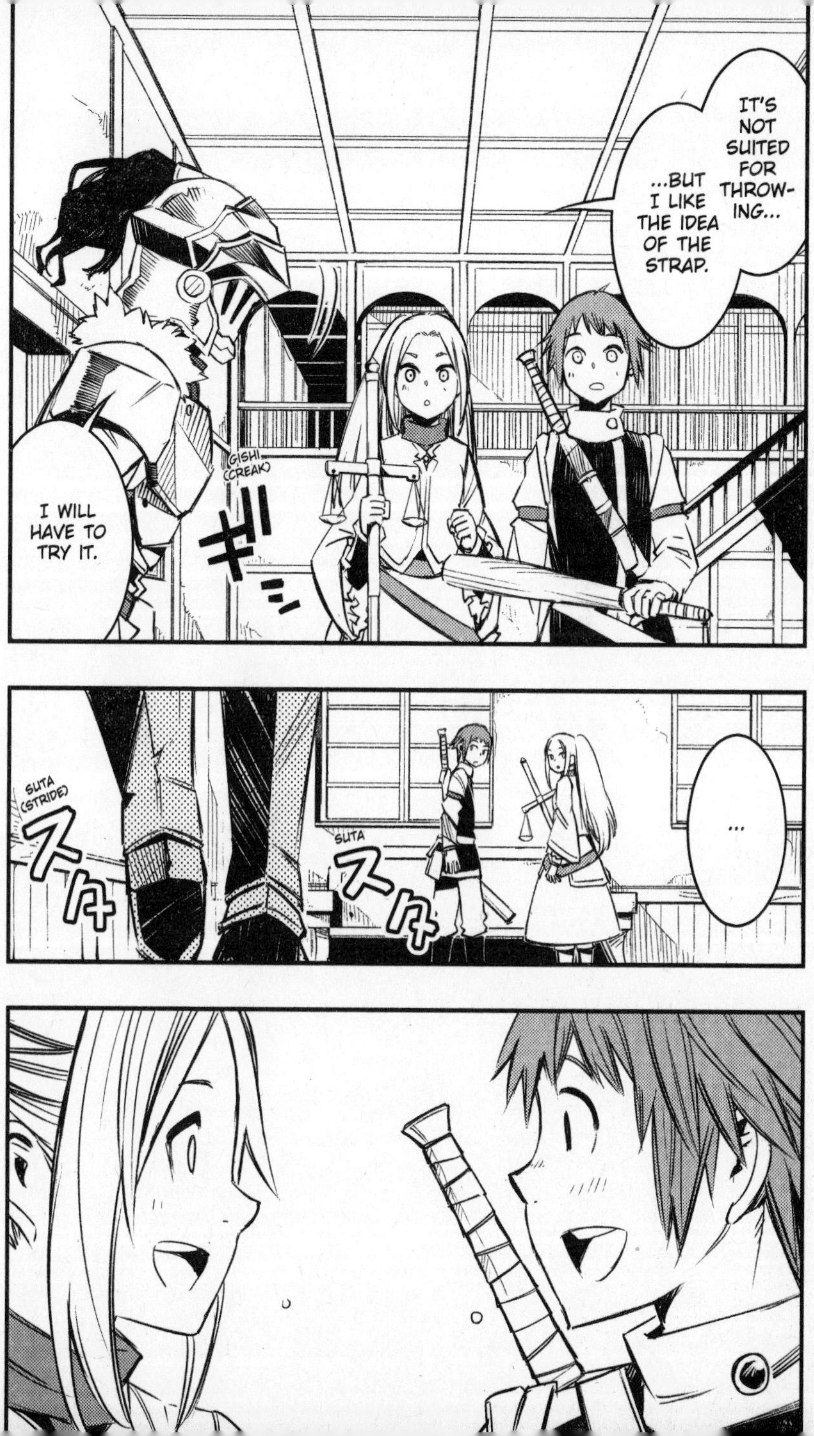
IT'S NOT SUITED FOR THROWING...
...BUT I LIKE THE IDEA OF THE STRAP.
GISHI (CREAK)
ギシ
I WILL HAVE TO TRY IT.
...
SUTA
スッ
SUTA (STRIDE)
スッ

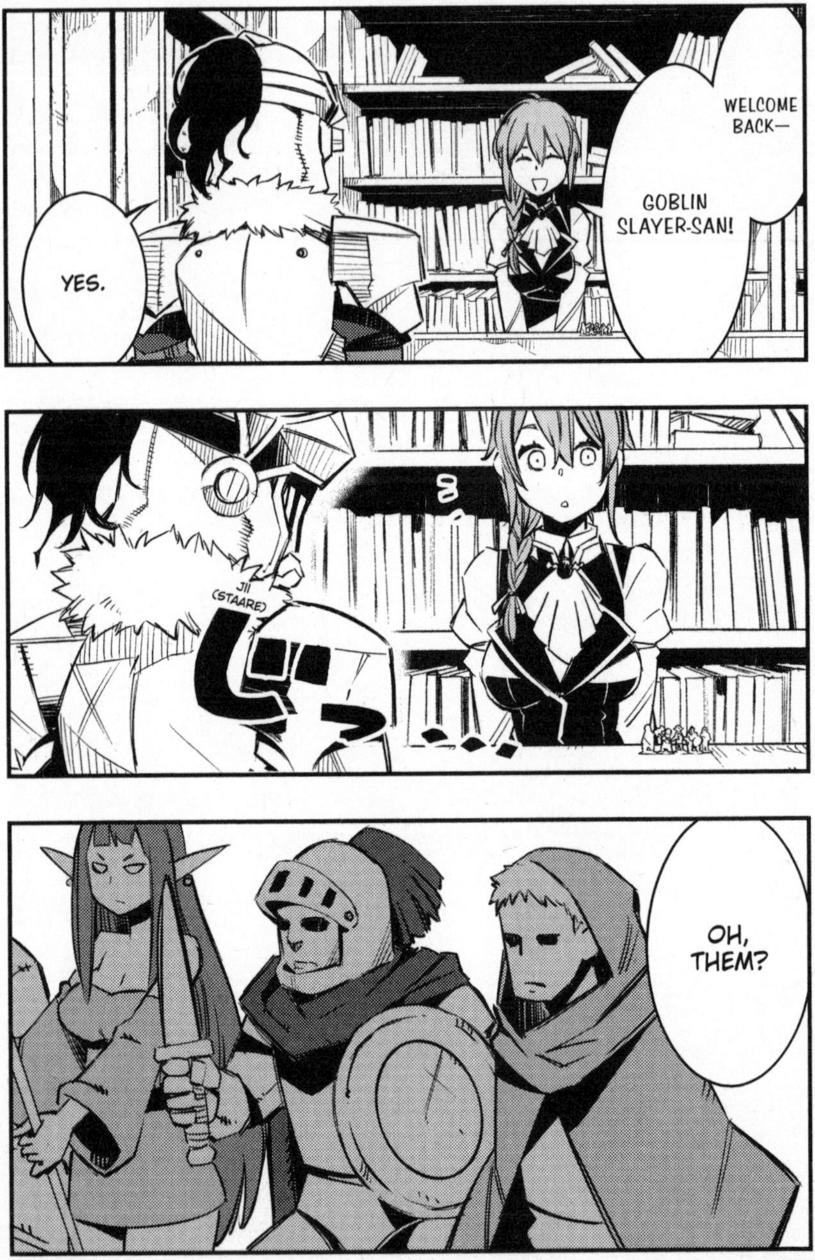
WELCOME BACK—
GOBLIN SLAYER-SAN!
YES.
JII (STAARE)
OH, THEM?

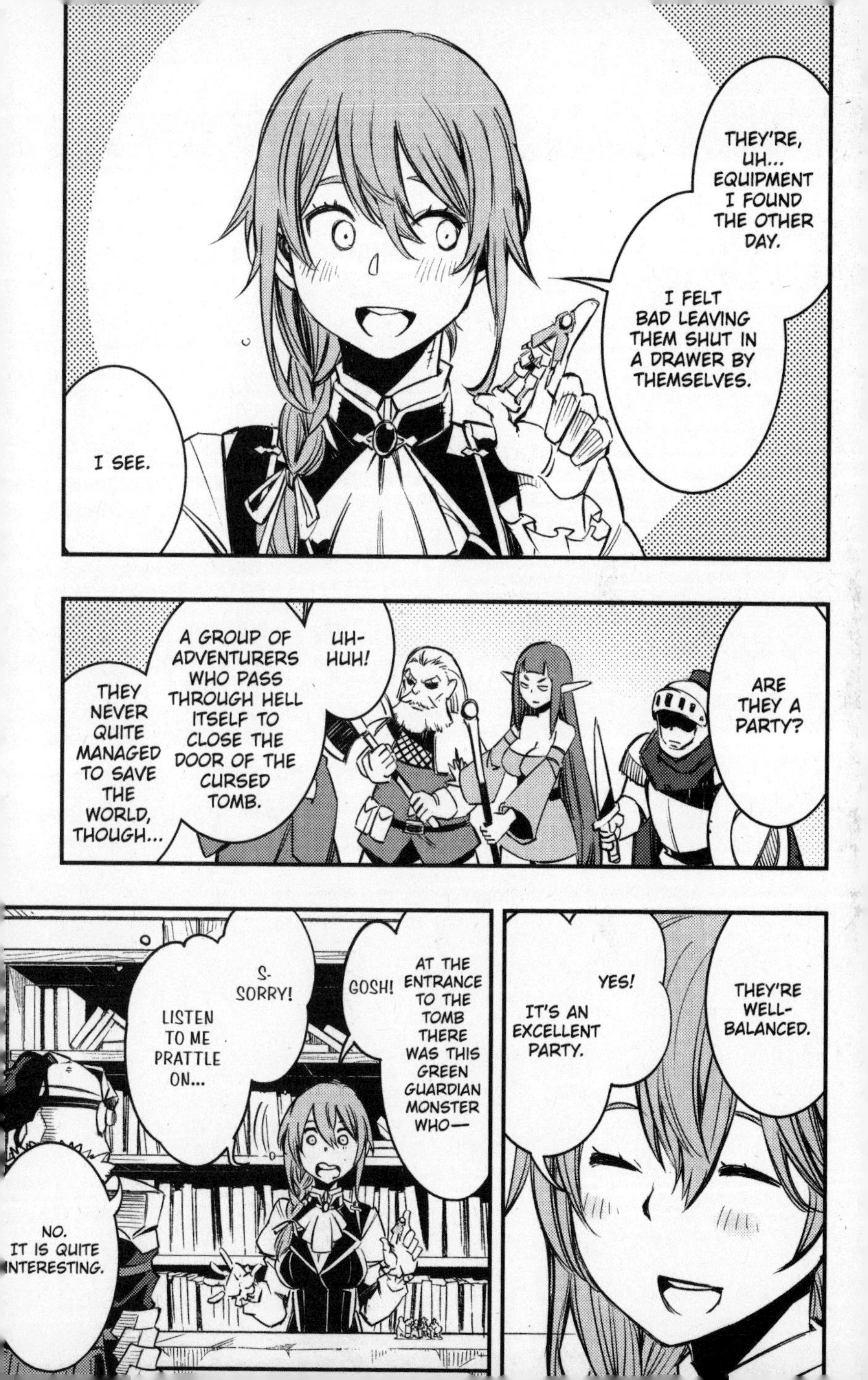
THEY'RE, UH... EQUIPMENT I FOUND THE OTHER DAY.
I FELT BAD LEAVING THEM SHUT IN A DRAWER BY THEMSELVES.
I SEE.
ARE THEY A PARTY?
UH-HUH!
A GROUP OF ADVENTURERS WHO PASS THROUGH HELL ITSELF TO CLOSE THE DOOR OF THE CURSED TOMB.
THEY NEVER QUITE MANAGED TO SAVE THE WORLD, THOUGH...
THEY'RE WELL-BALANCED.
YES!
IT'S AN EXCELLENT PARTY.
AT THE ENTRANCE TO THE TOMB THERE WAS THIS GREEN GUARDIAN MONSTER WHO—
GOSH!
S-SORRY!
LISTEN TO ME PRATTLE ON...
NO. IT IS QUITE INTERESTING.

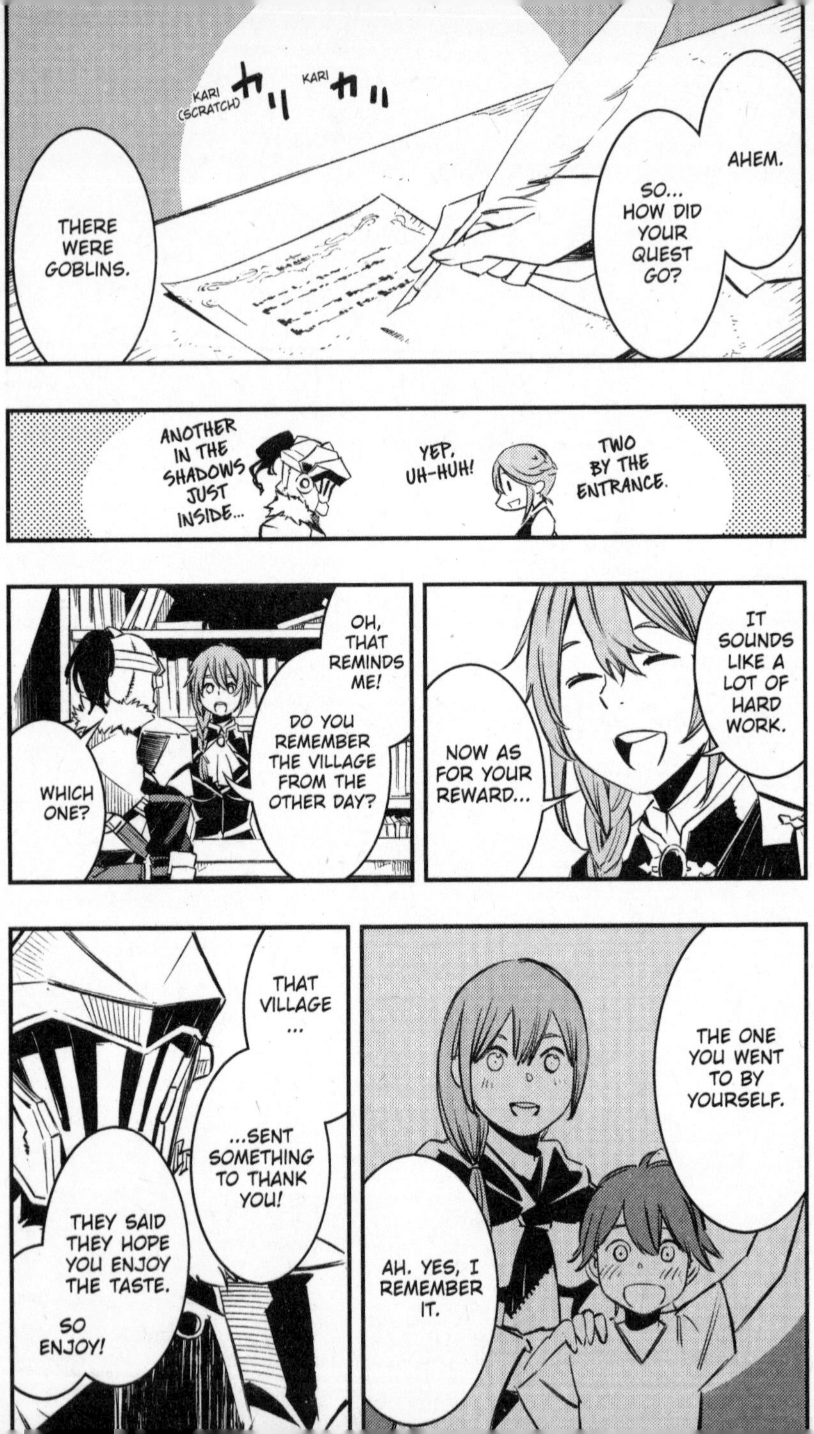
AHEM.
SO... HOW DID YOUR QUEST GO?
KARI KARI (SCRATCH) カリ カリ
THERE WERE GOBLINS.
TWO BY THE ENTRANCE.
YEP, UH-HUH!
ANOTHER IN THE SHADOWS JUST INSIDE...
IT SOUNDS LIKE A LOT OF HARD WORK.
NOW AS FOR YOUR REWARD...
OH, THAT REMINDS ME!
DO YOU REMEMBER THE VILLAGE FROM THE OTHER DAY?
WHICH ONE?
THE ONE YOU WENT TO BY YOURSELF.
AH. YES, I REMEMBER IT.
THAT VILLAGE...
...SENT SOMETHING TO THANK YOU!
THEY SAID THEY HOPE YOU ENJOY THE TASTE.
SO ENJOY!

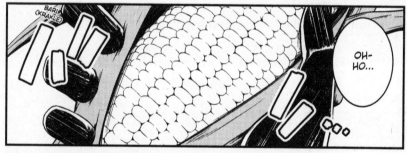

BARI (KRAKLE)

OH-HO...

THIS IS VERY RIPE.

IT SURE IS, HUH?

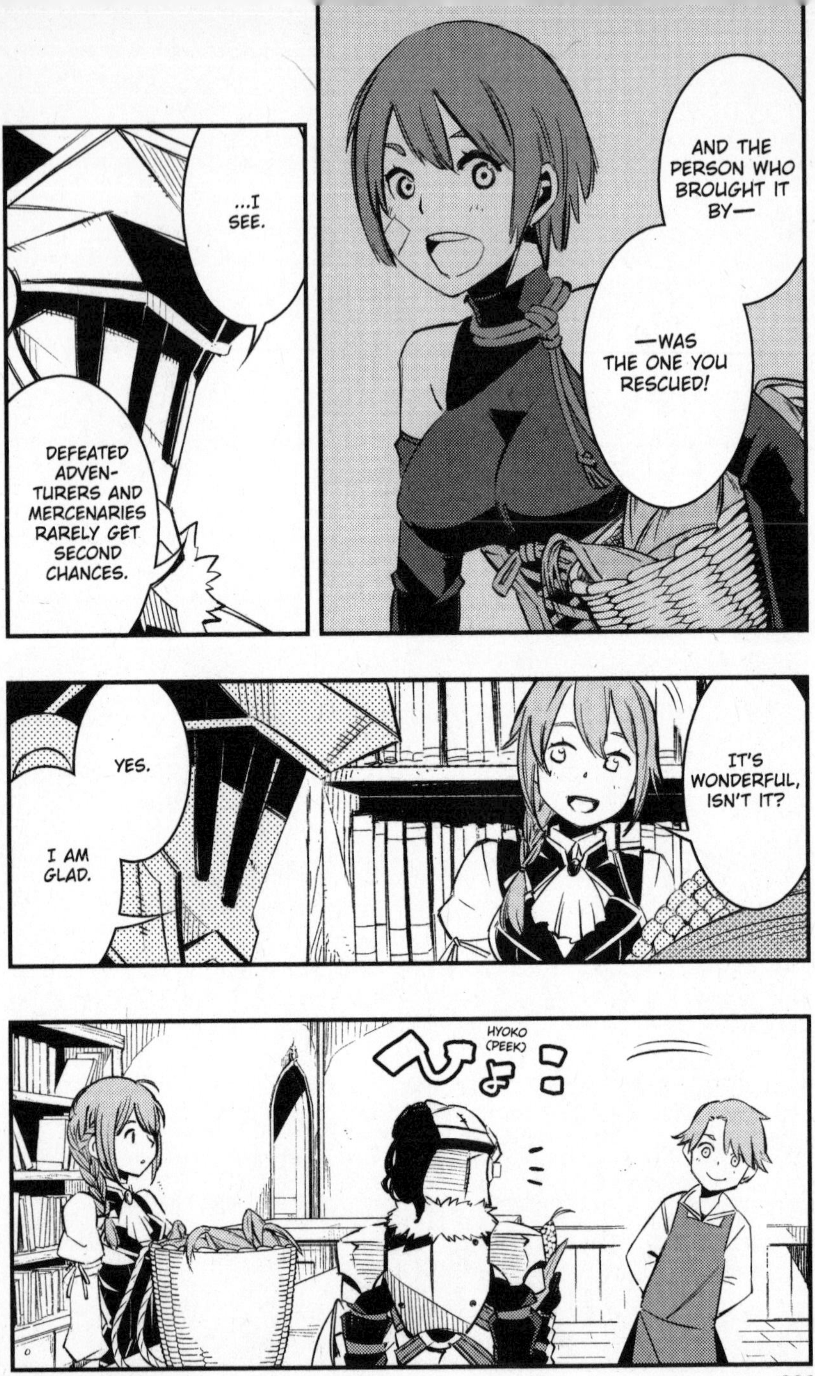
AND THE PERSON WHO BROUGHT IT BY—
—WAS THE ONE YOU RESCUED!
...I SEE.
DEFEATED ADVEN-TURERS AND MERCENARIES RARELY GET SECOND CHANCES.
IT'S WONDERFUL, ISN'T IT?
YES.
I AM GLAD.
HYOKO (PEEK)

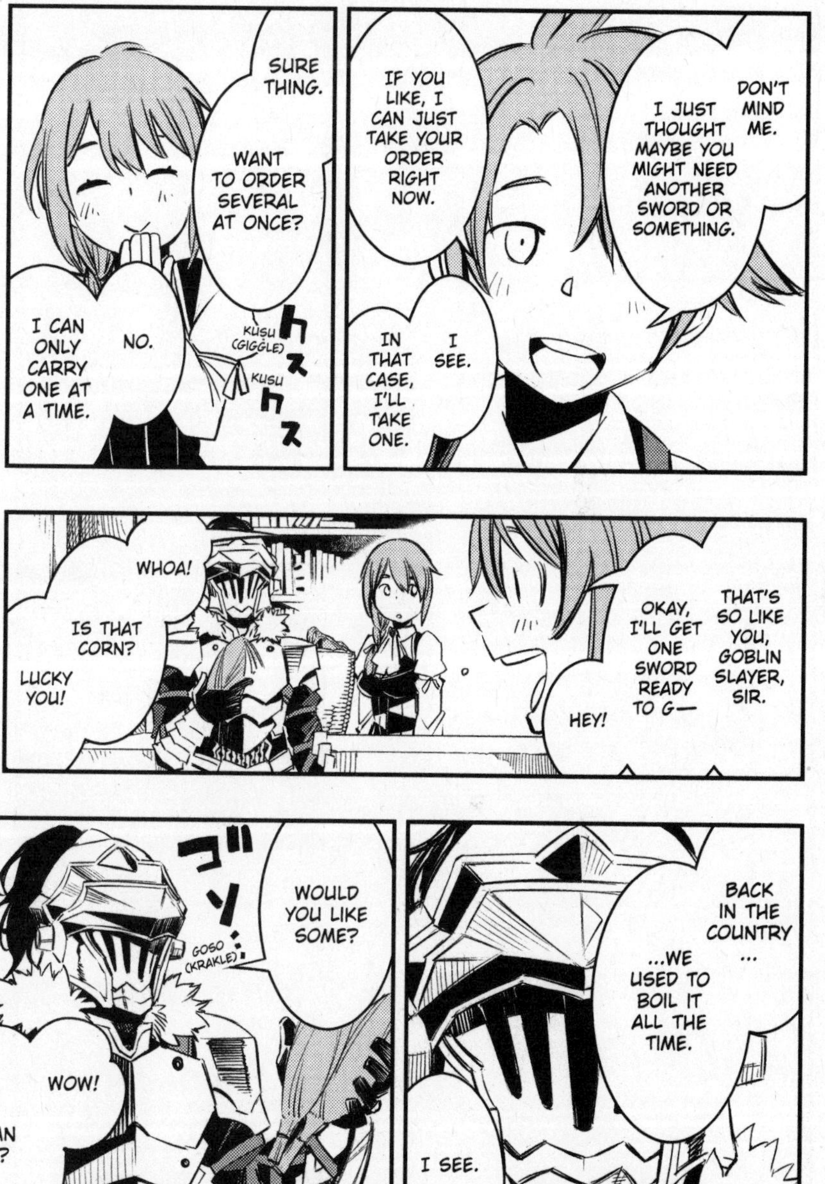
DON'T MIND ME.
I JUST THOUGHT MAYBE YOU MIGHT NEED ANOTHER SWORD OR SOMETHING.
IF YOU LIKE, I CAN JUST TAKE YOUR ORDER RIGHT NOW.
I SEE.
IN THAT CASE, I'LL TAKE ONE.
SURE THING.
WANT TO ORDER SEVERAL AT ONCE?
KUSU (GIGGLE)
KUSU
NO.
I CAN ONLY CARRY ONE AT A TIME.
THAT'S SO LIKE YOU, GOBLIN SLAYER, SIR.
OKAY, I'LL GET ONE SWORD READY TO G—
HEY!
WHOA!
IS THAT CORN?
LUCKY YOU!
BACK IN THE COUNTRY...
...WE USED TO BOIL IT ALL THE TIME.
I SEE.
WOULD YOU LIKE SOME?
GOSO (KRAKLE)
WOW!
CAN I?

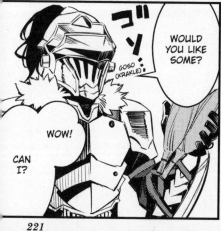

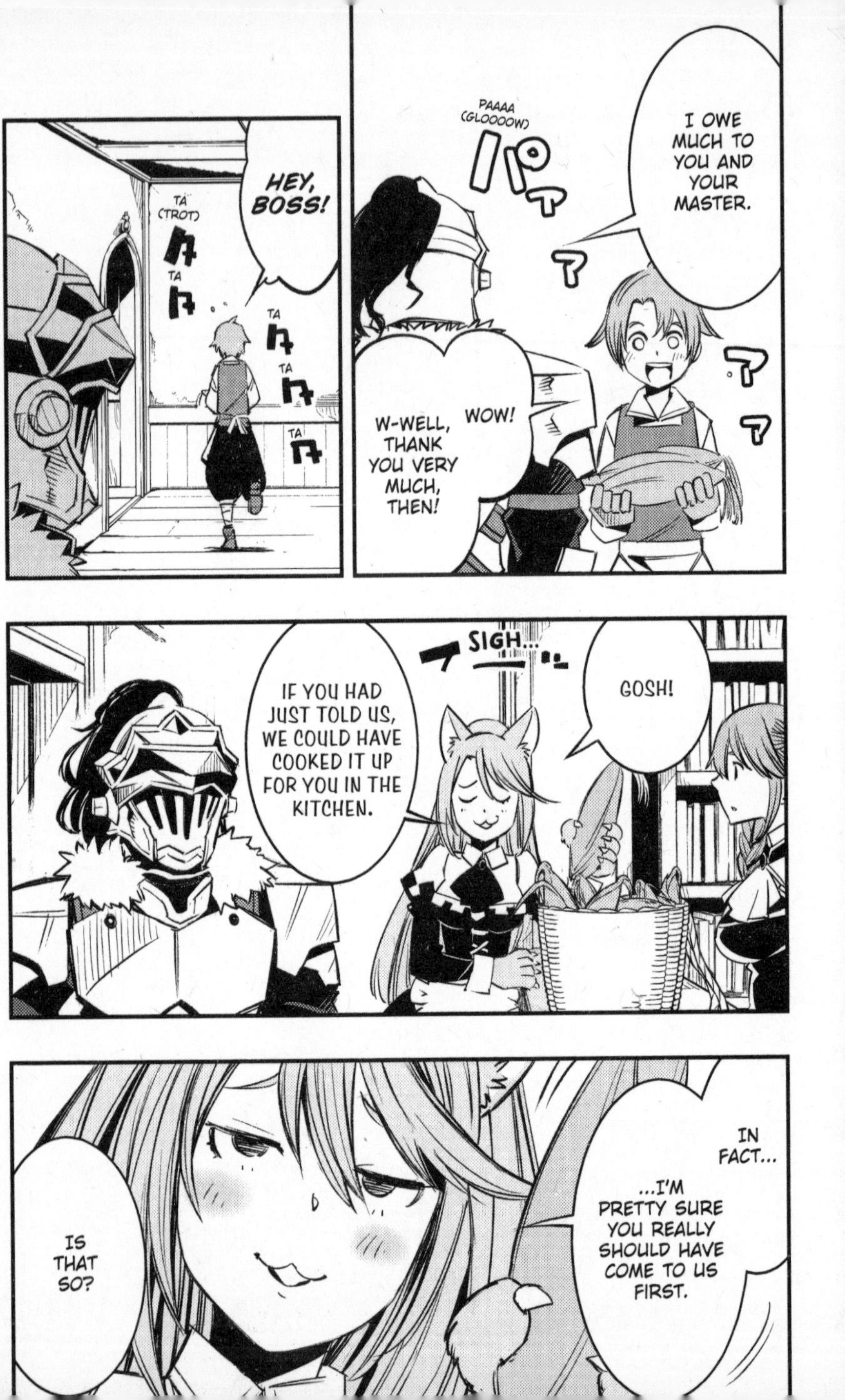
PAAAA (GLOOOOW)
I OWE MUCH TO YOU AND YOUR MASTER.
WOW!
W-WELL, THANK YOU VERY MUCH, THEN!
HEY, BOSS!
TA (TROT)
TA
TA
TA
TA
GOSH!
SIGH...
IF YOU HAD JUST TOLD US, WE COULD HAVE COOKED IT UP FOR YOU IN THE KITCHEN.
IN FACT...
...I'M PRETTY SURE YOU REALLY SHOULD HAVE COME TO US FIRST.
IS THAT SO?

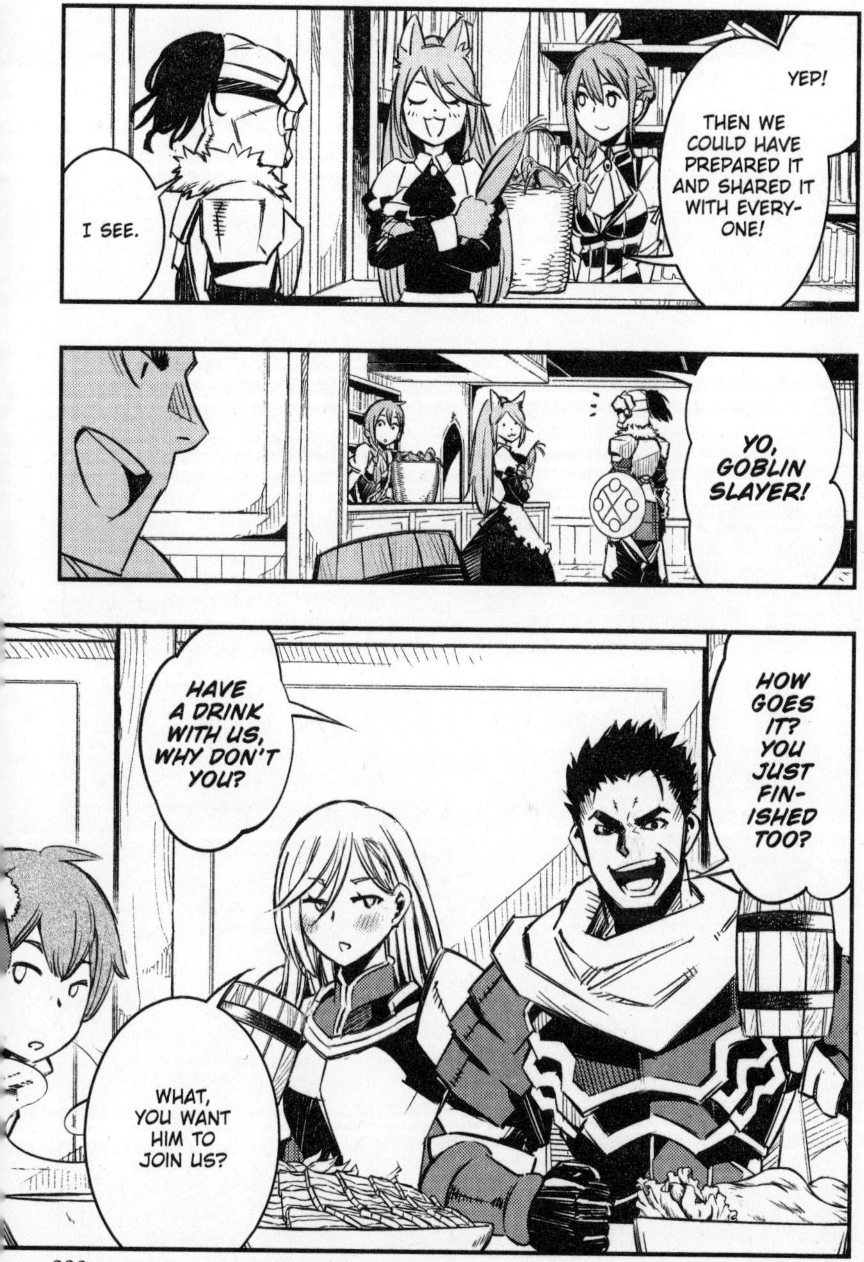
YEP!
THEN WE COULD HAVE PREPARED IT AND SHARED IT WITH EVERY-ONE!
I SEE.
YO, GOBLIN SLAYER!
HOW GOES IT? YOU JUST FIN-ISHED TOO?
HAVE A DRINK WITH US, WHY DON'T YOU?
WHAT, YOU WANT HIM TO JOIN US?

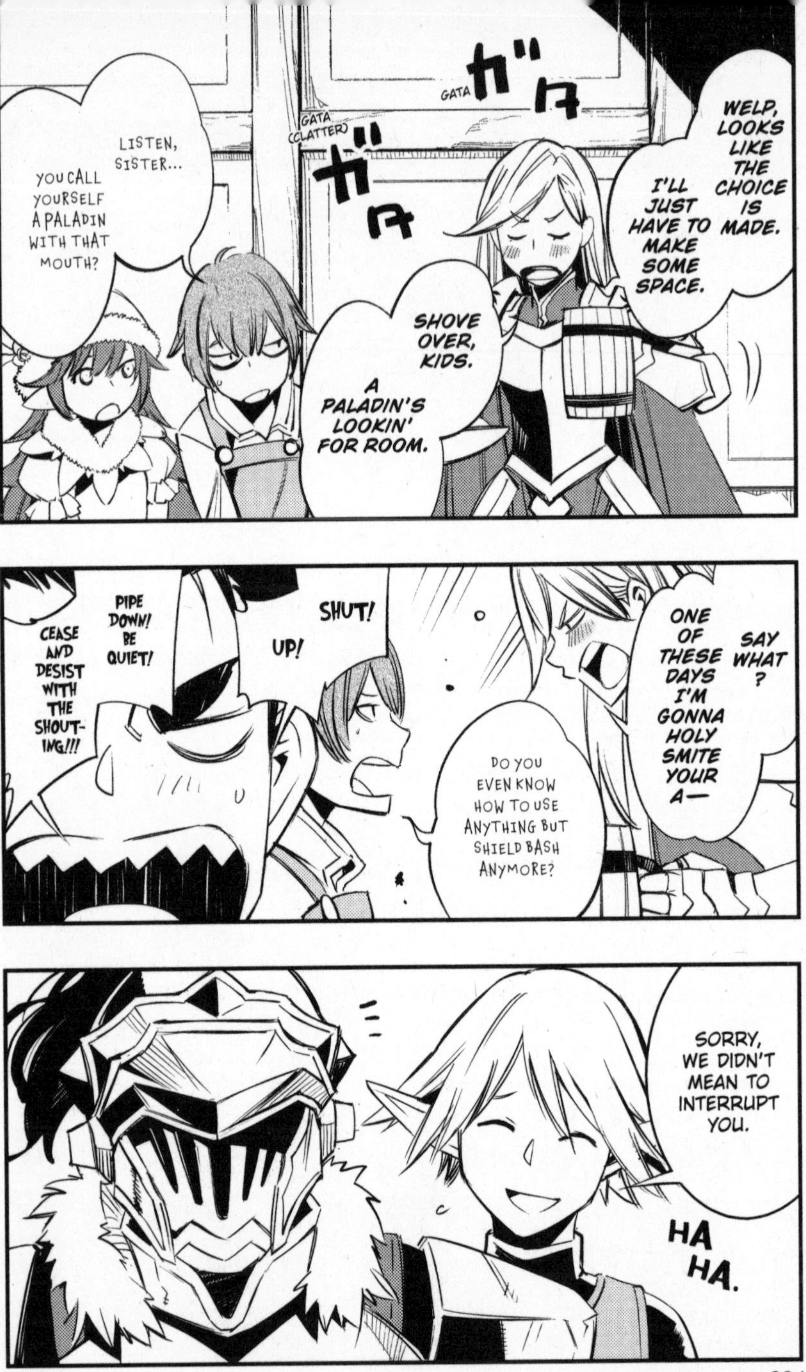
WELP, LOOKS LIKE THE CHOICE IS MADE.
I'LL JUST HAVE TO MAKE SOME SPACE.
ガタ
GATA
ガタ
GATA (CLATTER)
SHOVE OVER, KIDS.
A PALADIN'S LOOKIN' FOR ROOM.
LISTEN, SISTER...
YOU CALL YOURSELF A PALADIN WITH THAT MOUTH?
SAY WHAT?
ONE OF THESE DAYS I'M GONNA HOLY SMITE YOUR A—
DO YOU EVEN KNOW HOW TO USE ANYTHING BUT SHIELD BASH ANYMORE?
SHUT!
UP!
PIPE DOWN! BE QUIET!
CEASE AND DESIST WITH THE SHOUT-ING!!!
SORRY, WE DIDN'T MEAN TO INTERRUPT YOU.
HA HA.

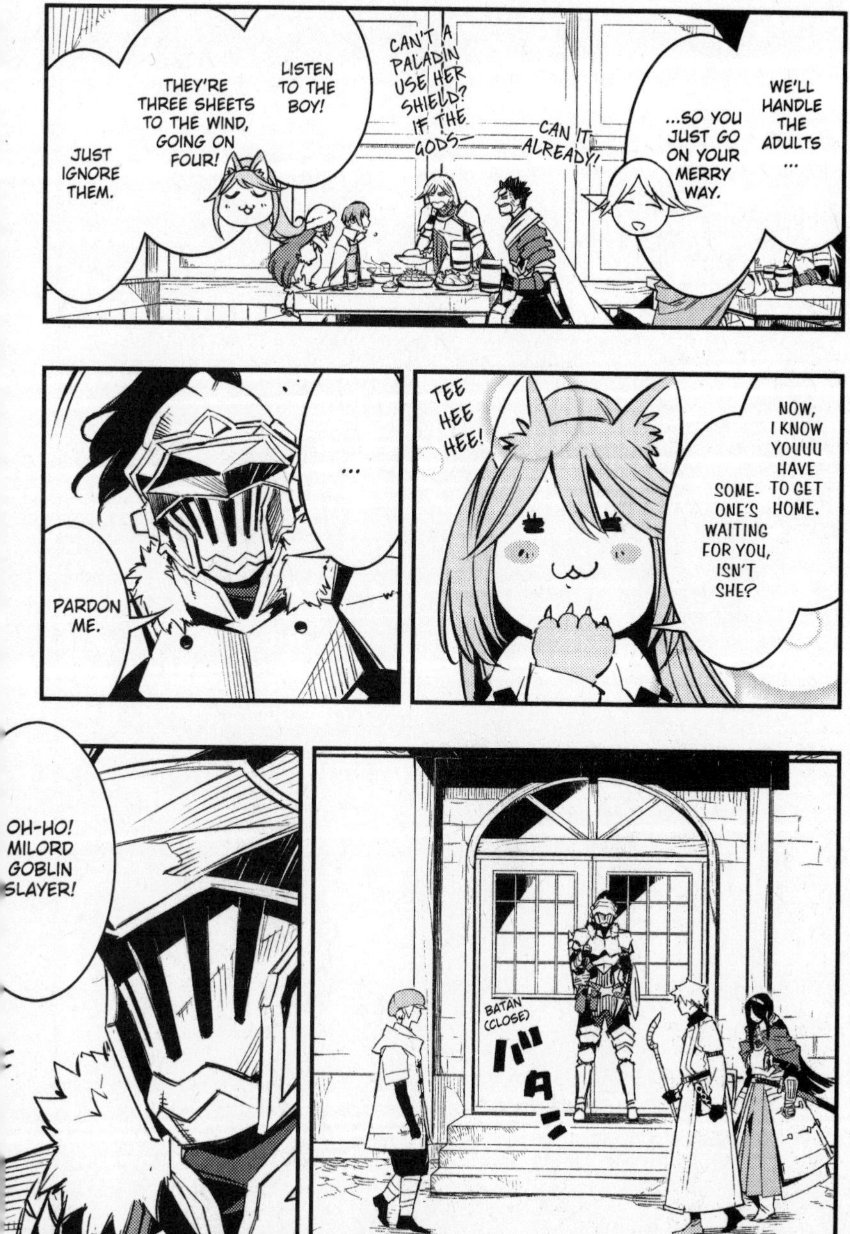
WE'LL HANDLE THE ADULTS...
...SO YOU JUST GO ON YOUR MERRY WAY.
CAN IT ALREADY!
CAN'T A PALADIN USE HER SHIELD? IF THE GODS—
LISTEN TO THE BOY!
THEY'RE THREE SHEETS TO THE WIND, GOING ON FOUR!
JUST IGNORE THEM.
NOW, I KNOW YOUUU HAVE TO GET HOME.
SOME-ONE'S WAITING FOR YOU, ISN'T SHE?
TEE HEE HEE!
...
PARDON ME.
BATAN (CLOSE)
バタン
OH-HO! MILORD GOBLIN SLAYER!

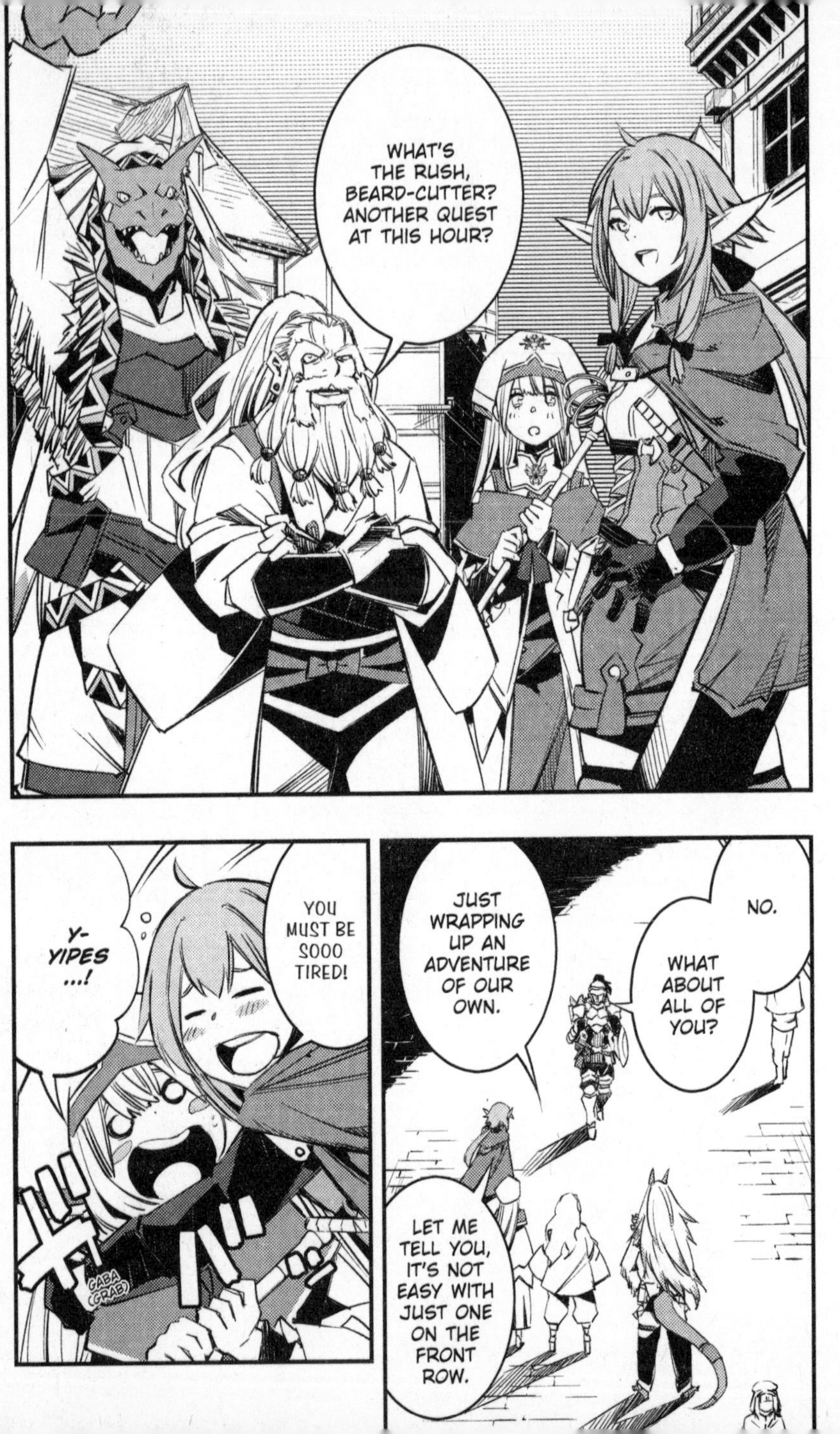
WHAT'S THE RUSH, BEARD-CUTTER? ANOTHER QUEST AT THIS HOUR?
NO.
WHAT ABOUT ALL OF YOU?
JUST WRAPPING UP AN ADVENTURE OF OUR OWN.
LET ME TELL YOU, IT'S NOT EASY WITH JUST ONE ON THE FRONT ROW.
YOU MUST BE SOOO TIRED!
Y-YIPES ...!
GABA (GRAB)

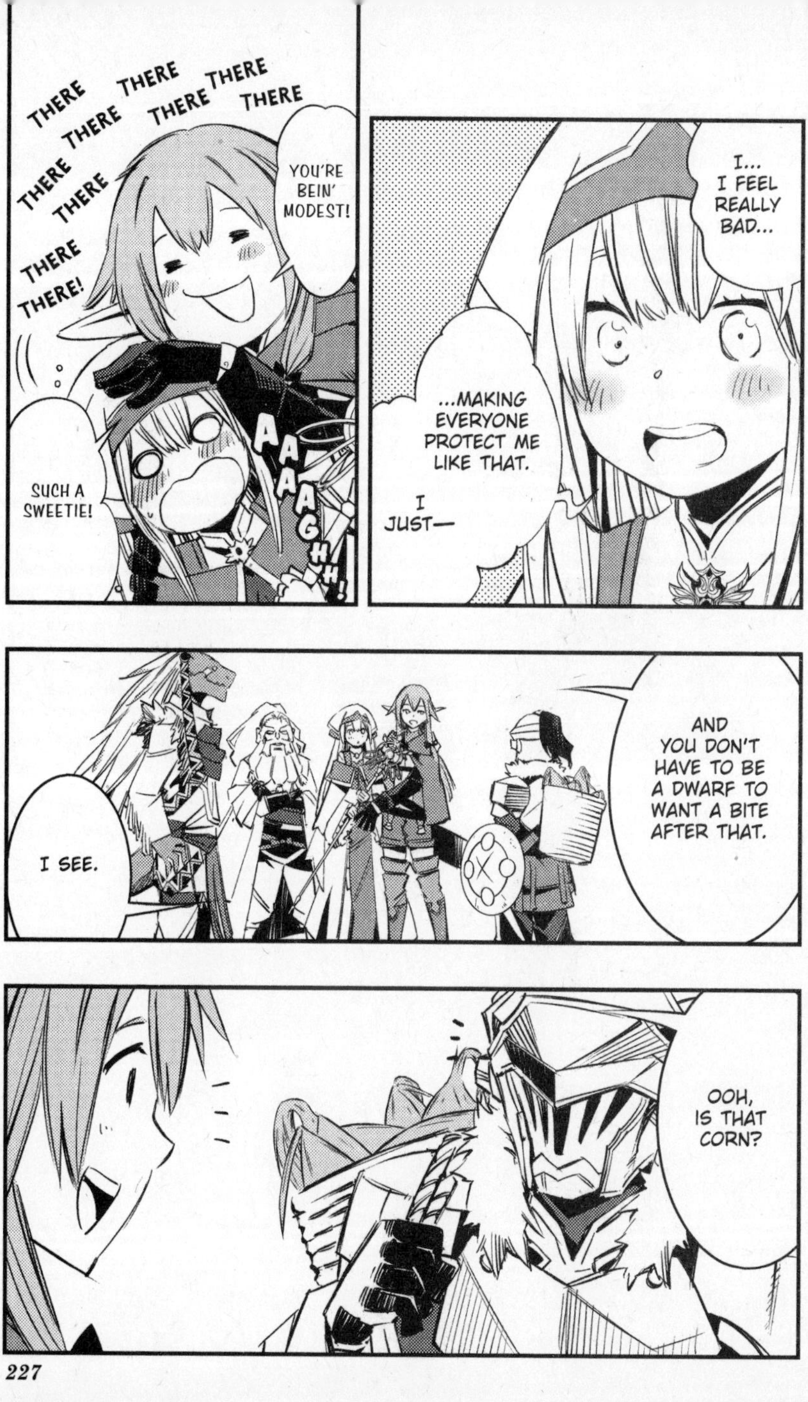
I... I FEEL REALLY BAD...
...MAKING EVERYONE PROTECT ME LIKE THAT.
I JUST—
YOU'RE BEIN' MODEST!
THERE THERE THERE THERE THERE THERE THERE THERE THERE THERE!
AAAAGHH!
SUCH A SWEETIE!
AND YOU DON'T HAVE TO BE A DWARF TO WANT A BITE AFTER THAT.
I SEE.
OOH, IS THAT CORN?

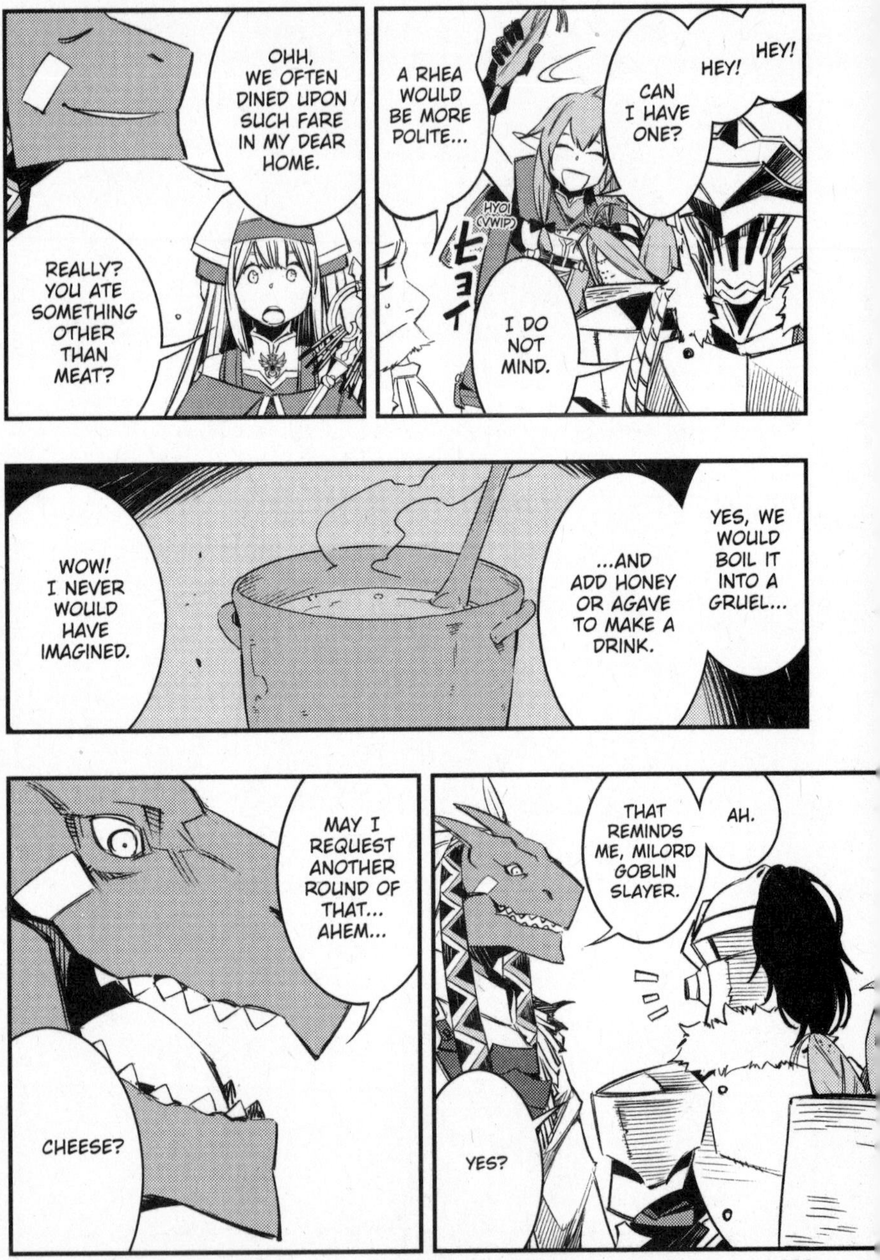
HEY!
HEY!
CAN I HAVE ONE?
A RHEA WOULD BE MORE POLITE...
ヒョイ
HYOI (VWIP)
I DO NOT MIND.
OHH, WE OFTEN DINED UPON SUCH FARE IN MY DEAR HOME.
REALLY? YOU ATE SOMETHING OTHER THAN MEAT?
YES, WE WOULD BOIL IT INTO A GRUEL...
...AND ADD HONEY OR AGAVE TO MAKE A DRINK.
WOW! I NEVER WOULD HAVE IMAGINED.
AH.
THAT REMINDS ME, MILORD GOBLIN SLAYER.
YES?
MAY I REQUEST ANOTHER ROUND OF THAT... AHEM...
CHEESE?

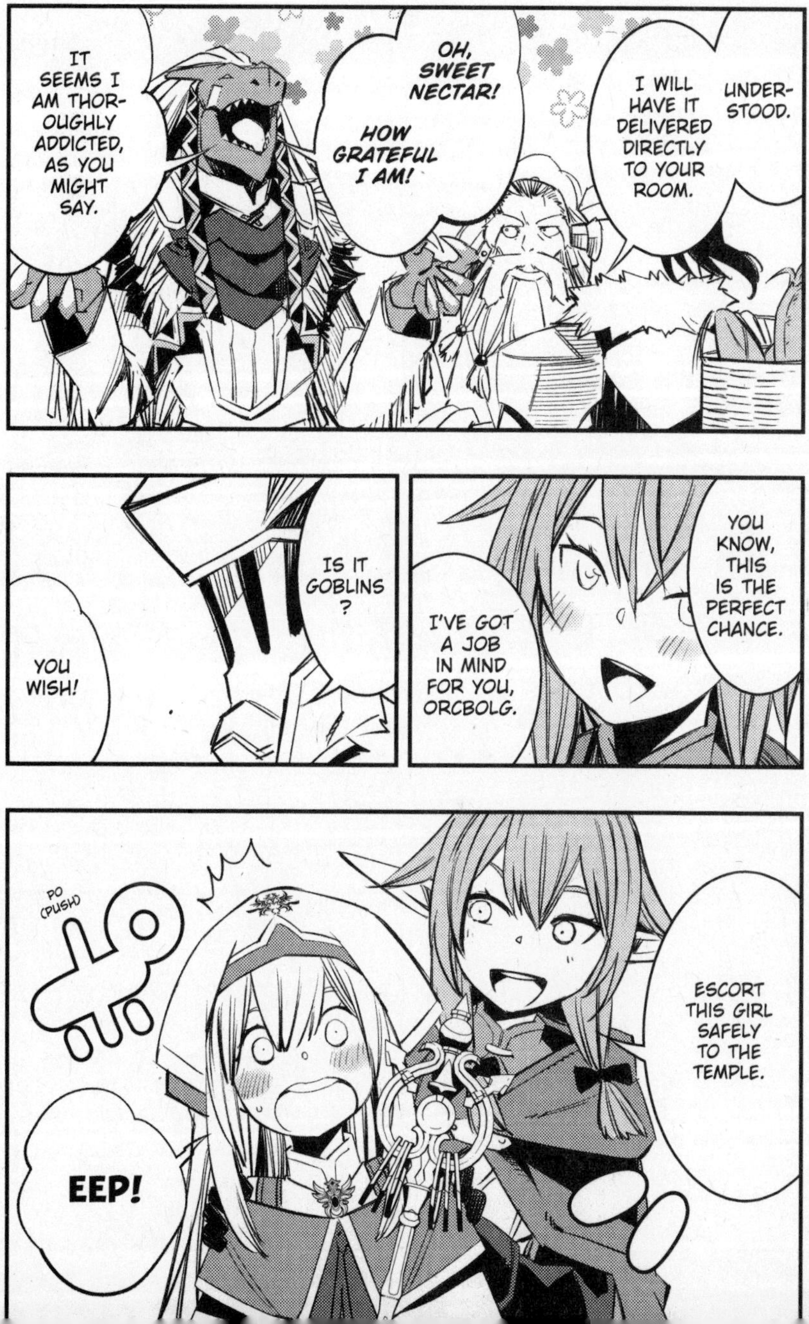
UNDER-STOOD.
I WILL HAVE IT DELIVERED DIRECTLY TO YOUR ROOM.
OH, SWEET NECTAR!
HOW GRATEFUL I AM!
IT SEEMS I AM THOROUGHLY ADDICTED, AS YOU MIGHT SAY.
YOU KNOW, THIS IS THE PERFECT CHANCE.
I'VE GOT A JOB IN MIND FOR YOU, ORCBOLG.
IS IT GOBLINS?
YOU WISH!
ESCORT THIS GIRL SAFELY TO THE TEMPLE.
PO (PUSH)
EEP!

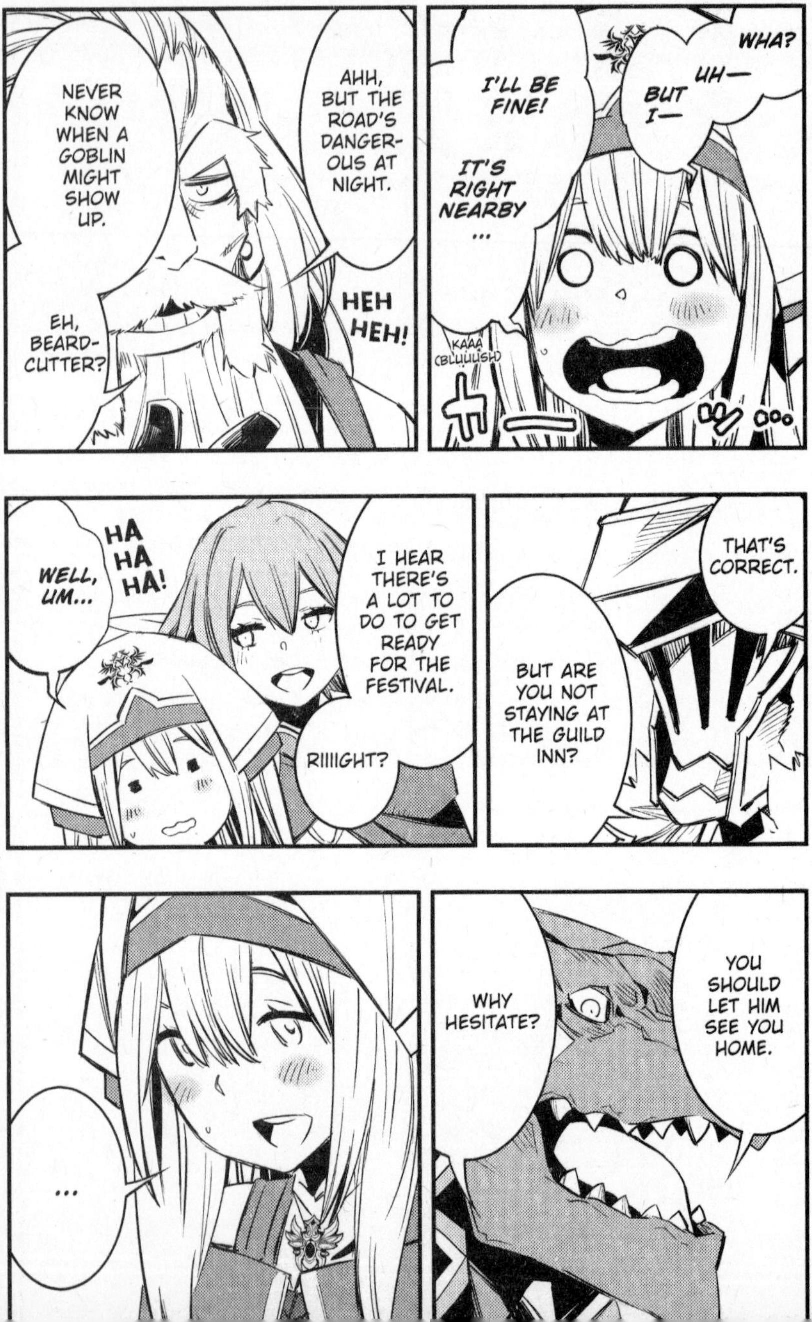
WHA?
UH— BUT I—
I'LL BE FINE!
IT'S RIGHT NEARBY ...
KAAA (BLUUUSH)
AHH, BUT THE ROAD'S DANGER-OUS AT NIGHT.
NEVER KNOW WHEN A GOBLIN MIGHT SHOW UP.
HEH HEH!
EH, BEARD-CUTTER?
THAT'S CORRECT.
BUT ARE YOU NOT STAYING AT THE GUILD INN?
I HEAR THERE'S A LOT TO DO TO GET READY FOR THE FESTIVAL.
RIIIGHT?
HA HA HA!
WELL, UM...
YOU SHOULD LET HIM SEE YOU HOME.
WHY HESITATE?
...

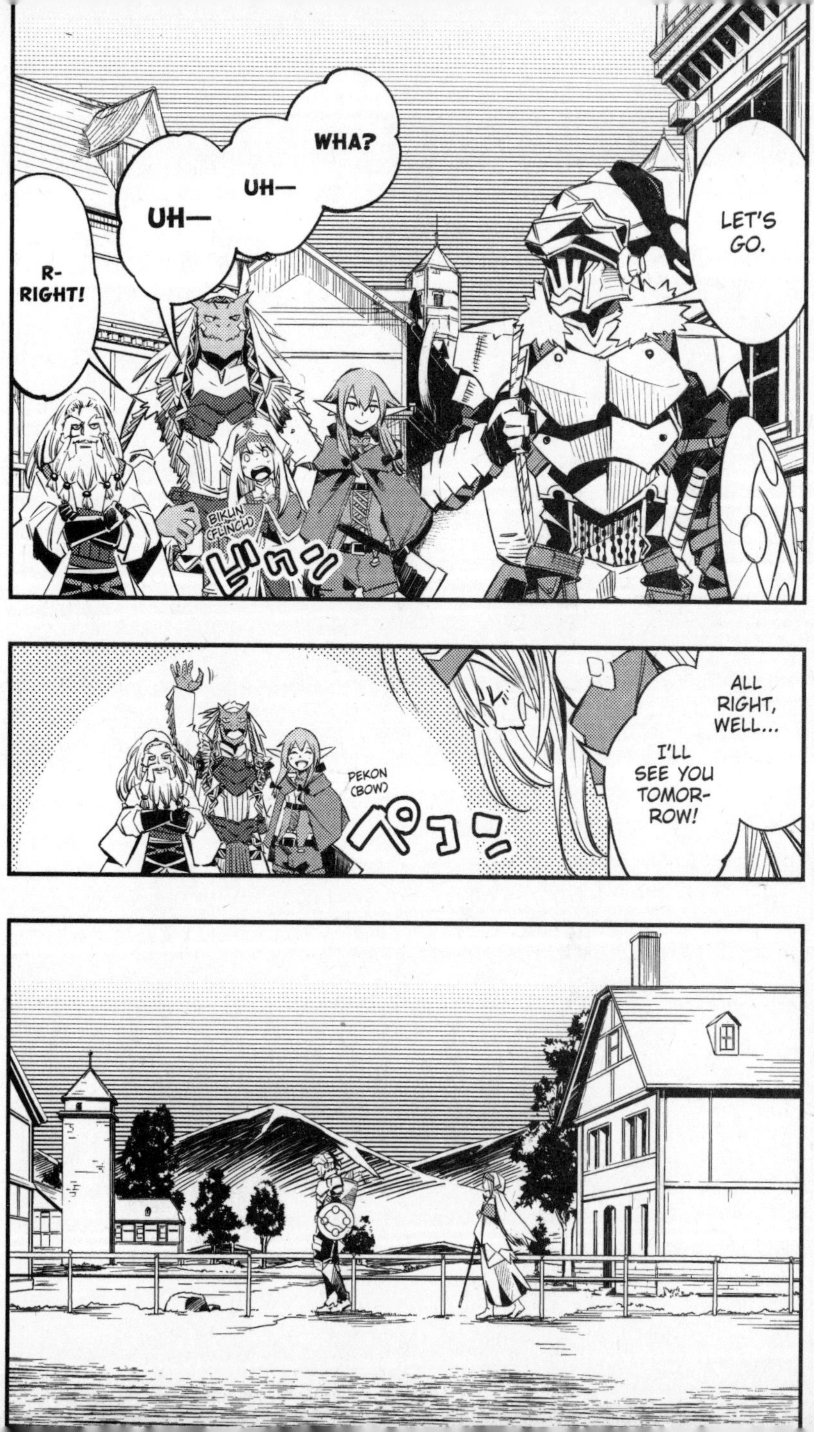
LET'S GO.
WHA?
UH—
UH—
R-RIGHT!
BIKUN (FLINCH)
ALL RIGHT, WELL...
I'LL SEE YOU TOMORROW!
PEKON (BOW)

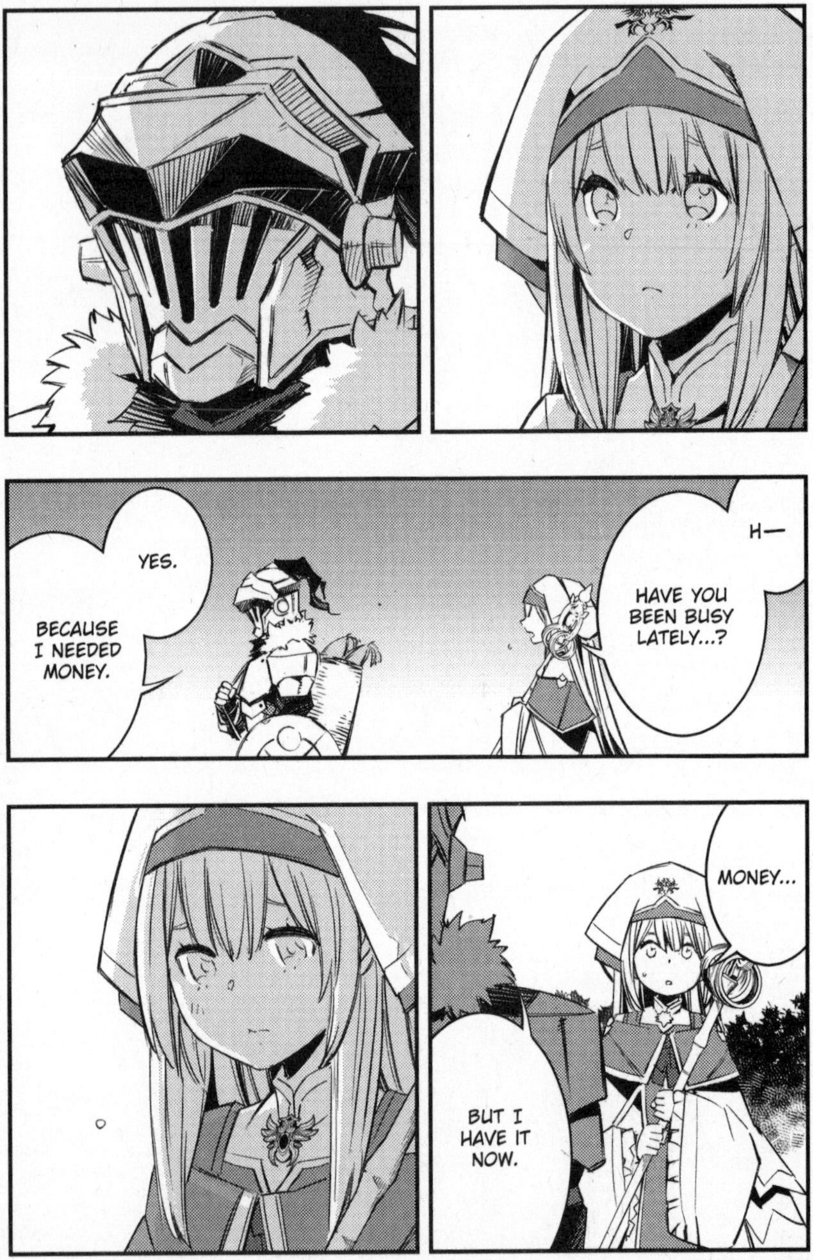
H—
HAVE YOU BEEN BUSY LATELY...?
YES.
BECAUSE I NEEDED MONEY.
MONEY...
BUT I HAVE IT NOW.

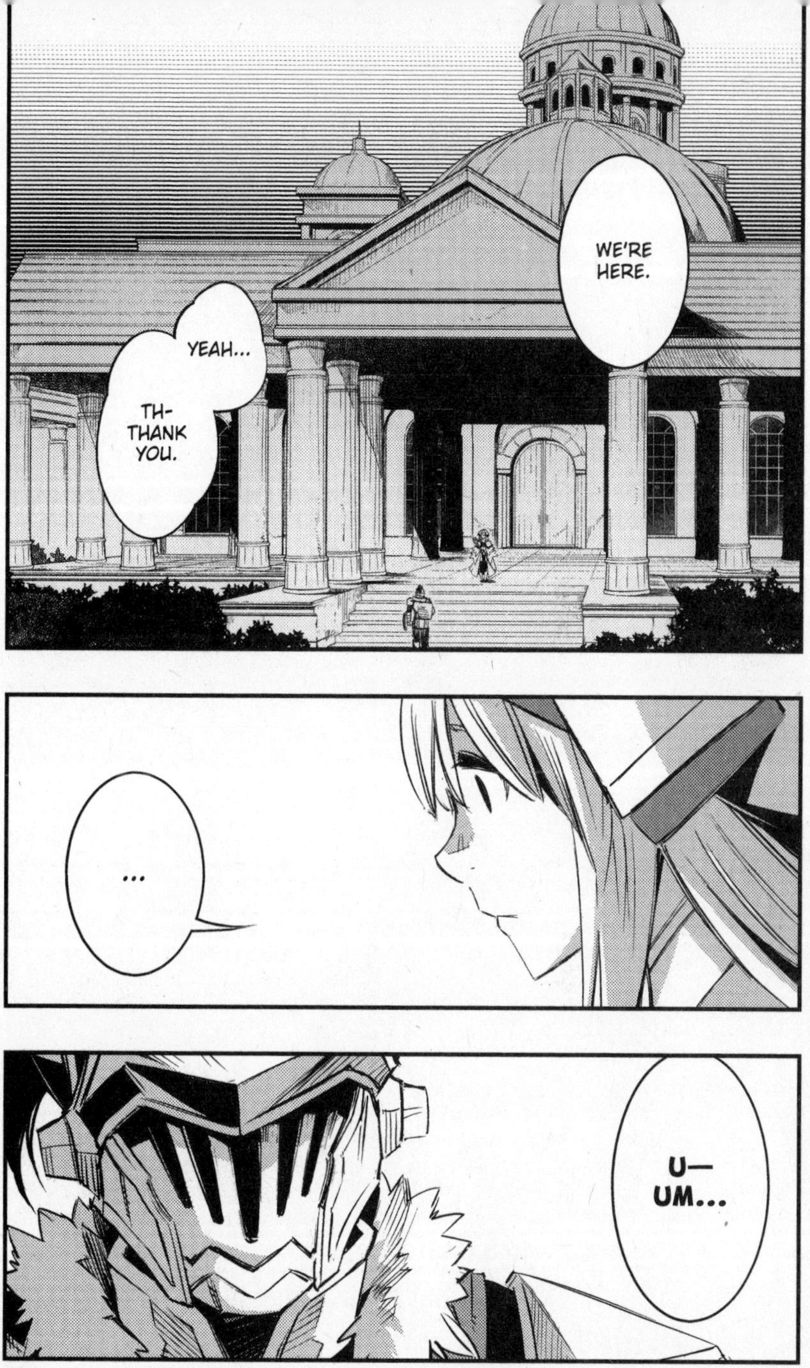
WE'RE HERE.
YEAH...
TH-THANK YOU.
...
U—UM...

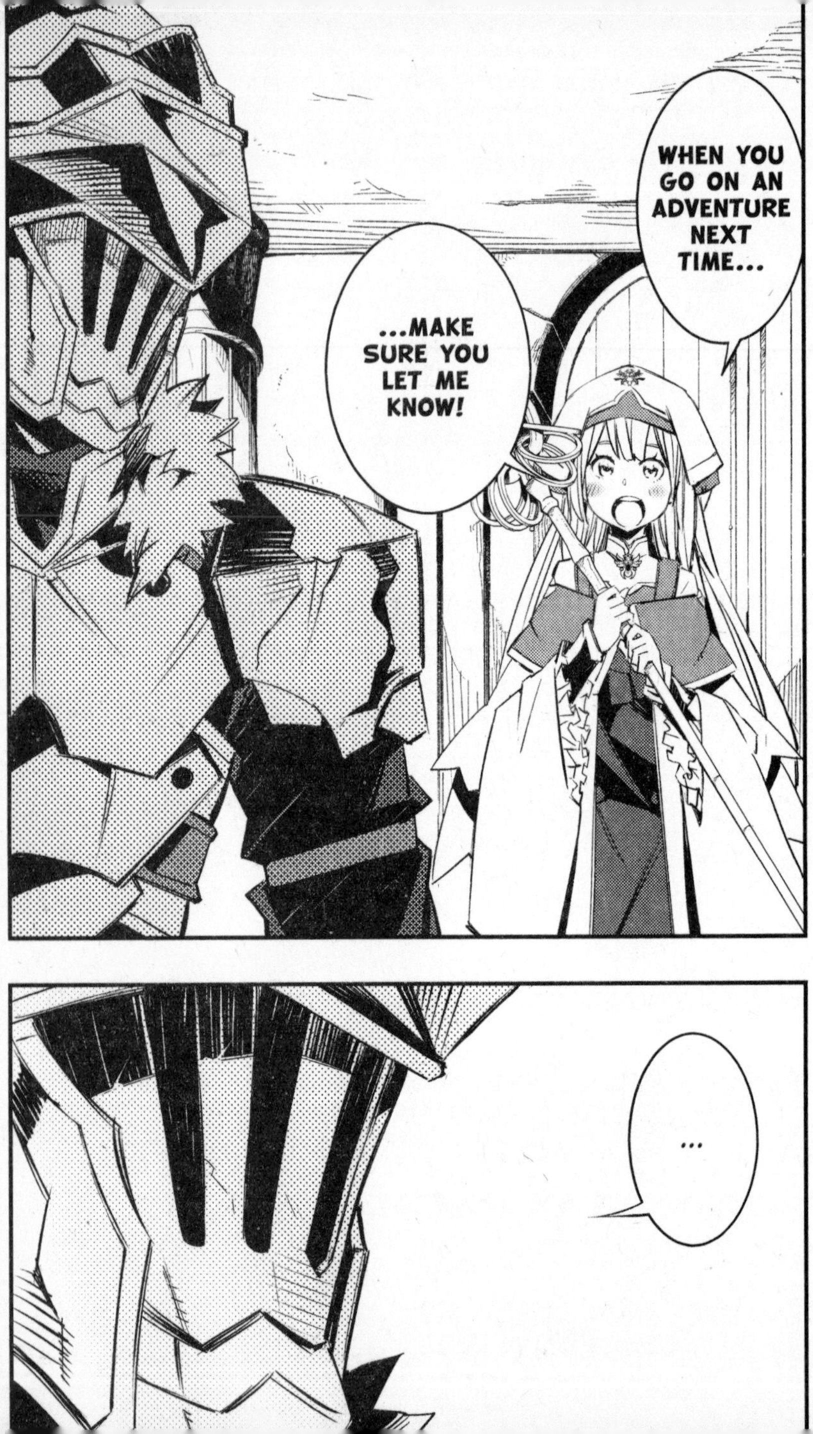
WHEN YOU GO ON AN ADVENTURE NEXT TIME...
...MAKE SURE YOU LET ME KNOW!
...

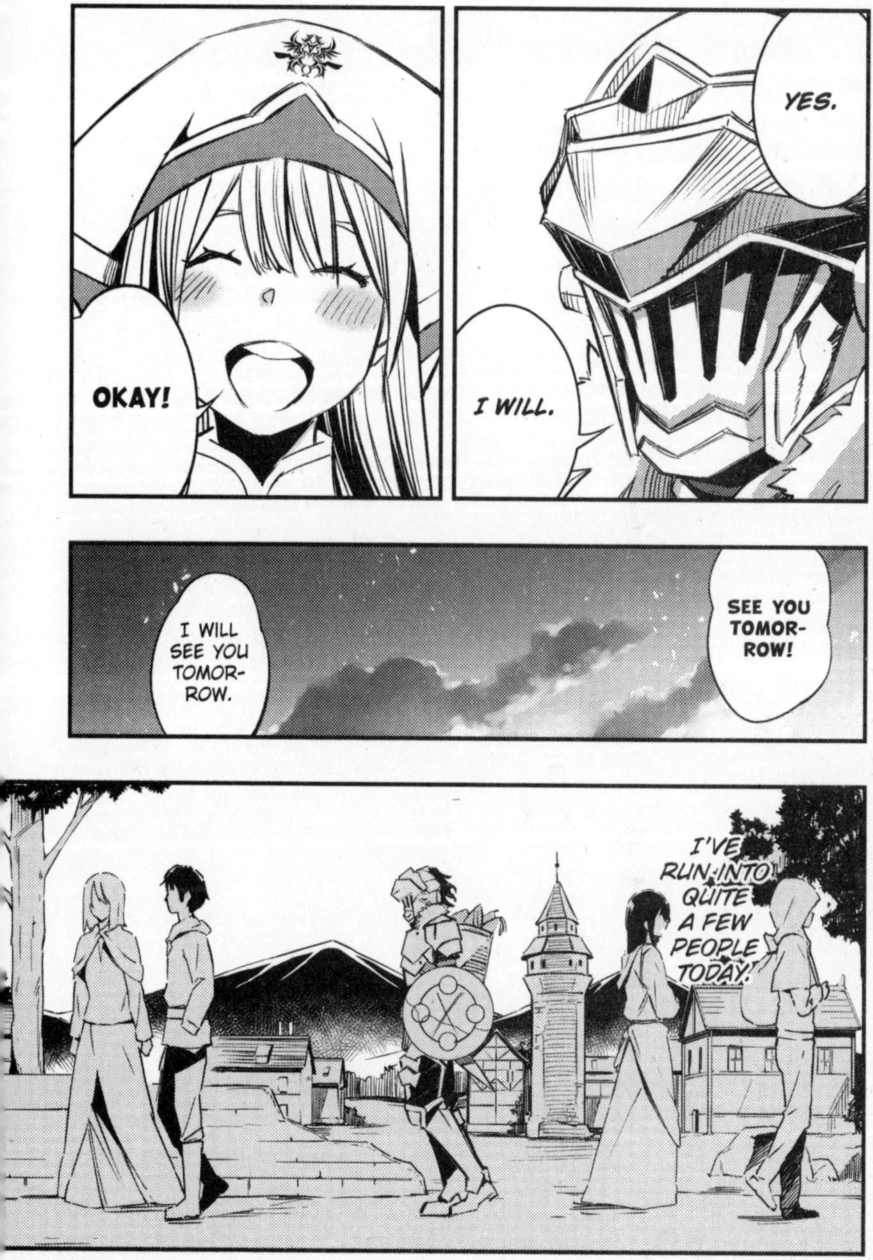
YES.
I WILL.
OKAY!
SEE YOU TOMOR-ROW!
I WILL SEE YOU TOMOR-ROW.
I'VE RUN INTO QUITE A FEW PEOPLE TODAY.

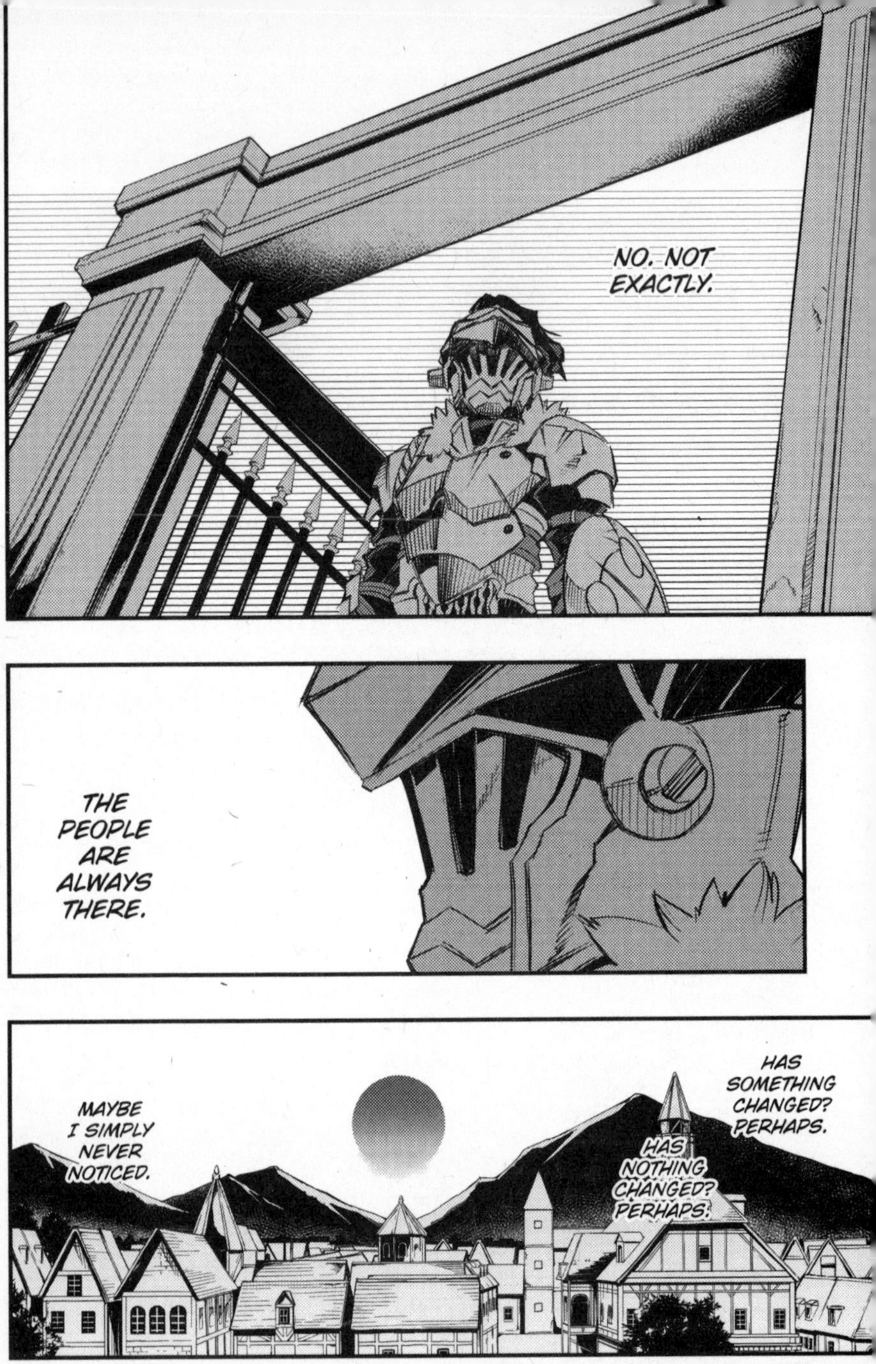
NO. NOT EXACTLY.
THE PEOPLE ARE ALWAYS THERE.
HAS SOMETHING CHANGED? PERHAPS.
HAS NOTHING CHANGED? PERHAPS.
MAYBE I SIMPLY NEVER NOTICED.

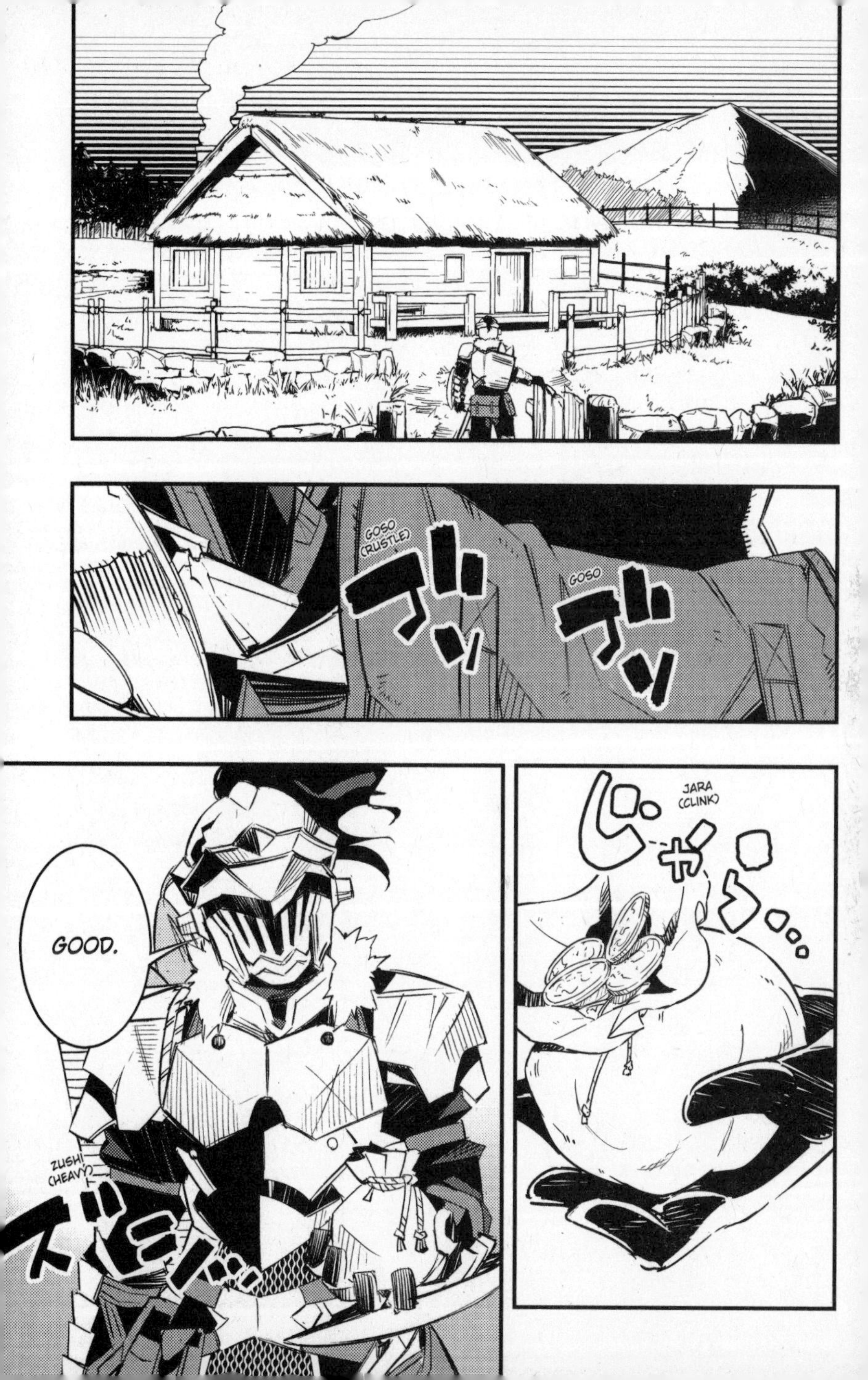
GOSO (RUSTLE)
GOSO
JARA (CLINK)
GOOD.
ZUSHI (HEAVY)

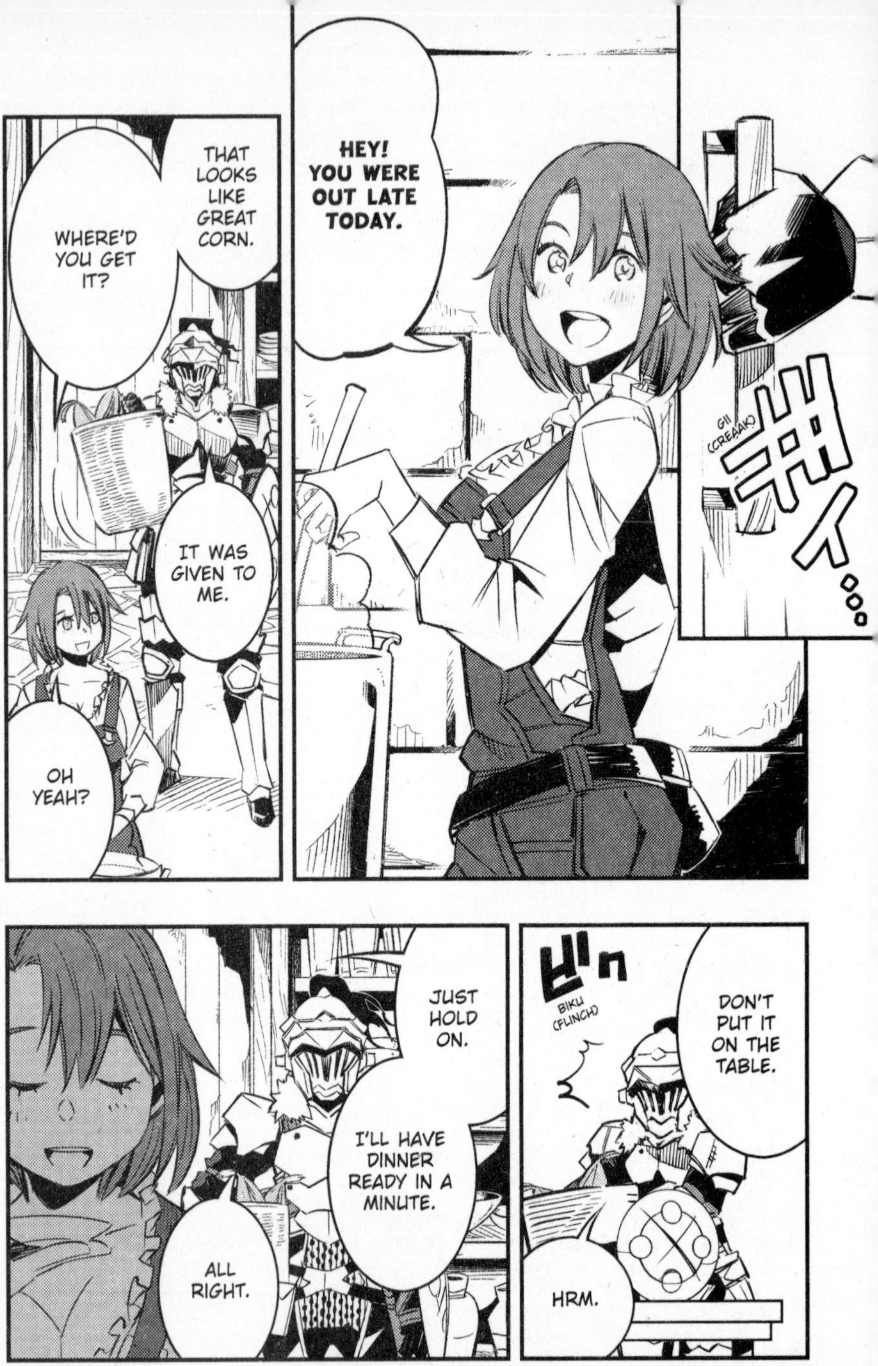
GII (CREAAK)
HEY! YOU WERE OUT LATE TODAY.
THAT LOOKS LIKE GREAT CORN.
WHERE'D YOU GET IT?
IT WAS GIVEN TO ME.
OH YEAH?
BIKU (FLINCH)
DON'T PUT IT ON THE TABLE.
HRM.
JUST HOLD ON.
I'LL HAVE DINNER READY IN A MINUTE.
ALL RIGHT.

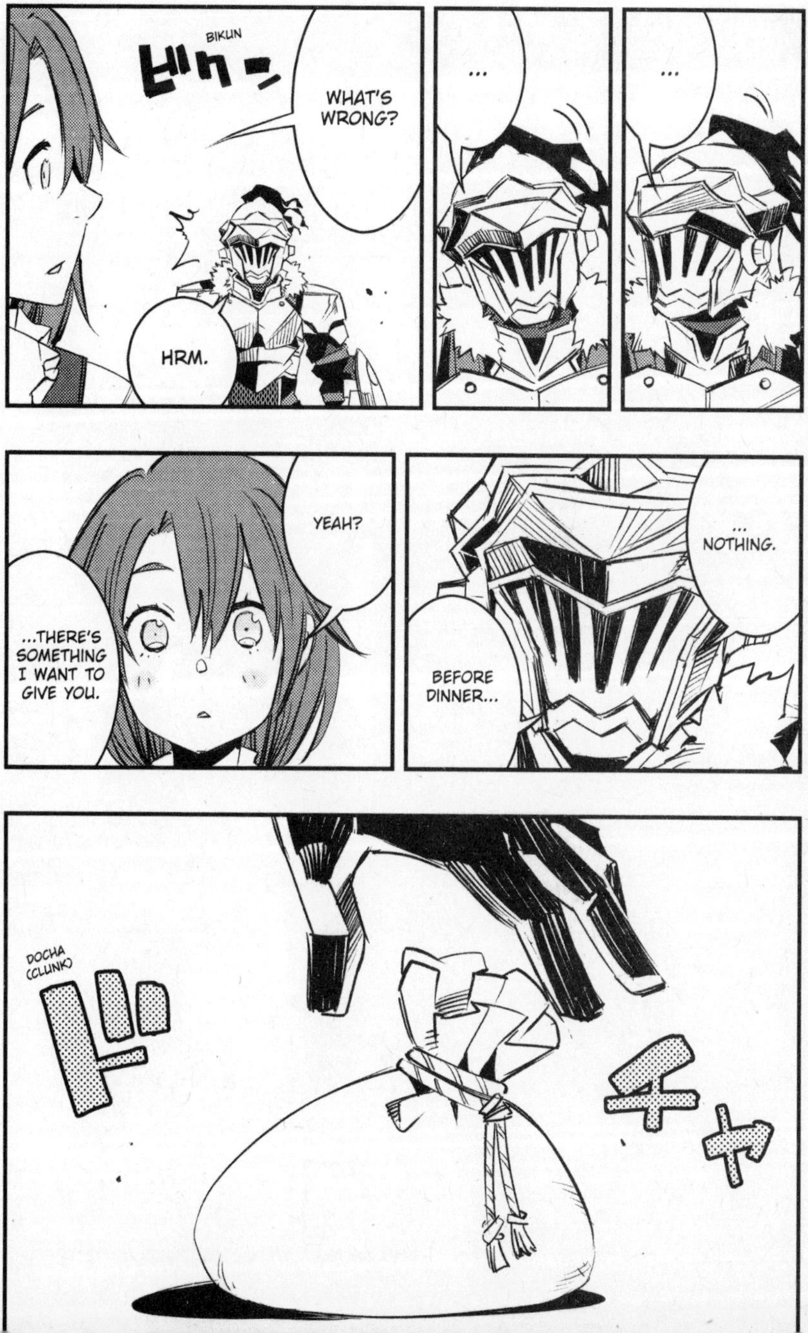
...
...
WHAT'S WRONG?
BIKUN
ビクッ
HRM.
... NOTHING.
BEFORE DINNER...
YEAH?
...THERE'S SOMETHING I WANT TO GIVE YOU.
DOCHA (CLUNK)
ド
チャ

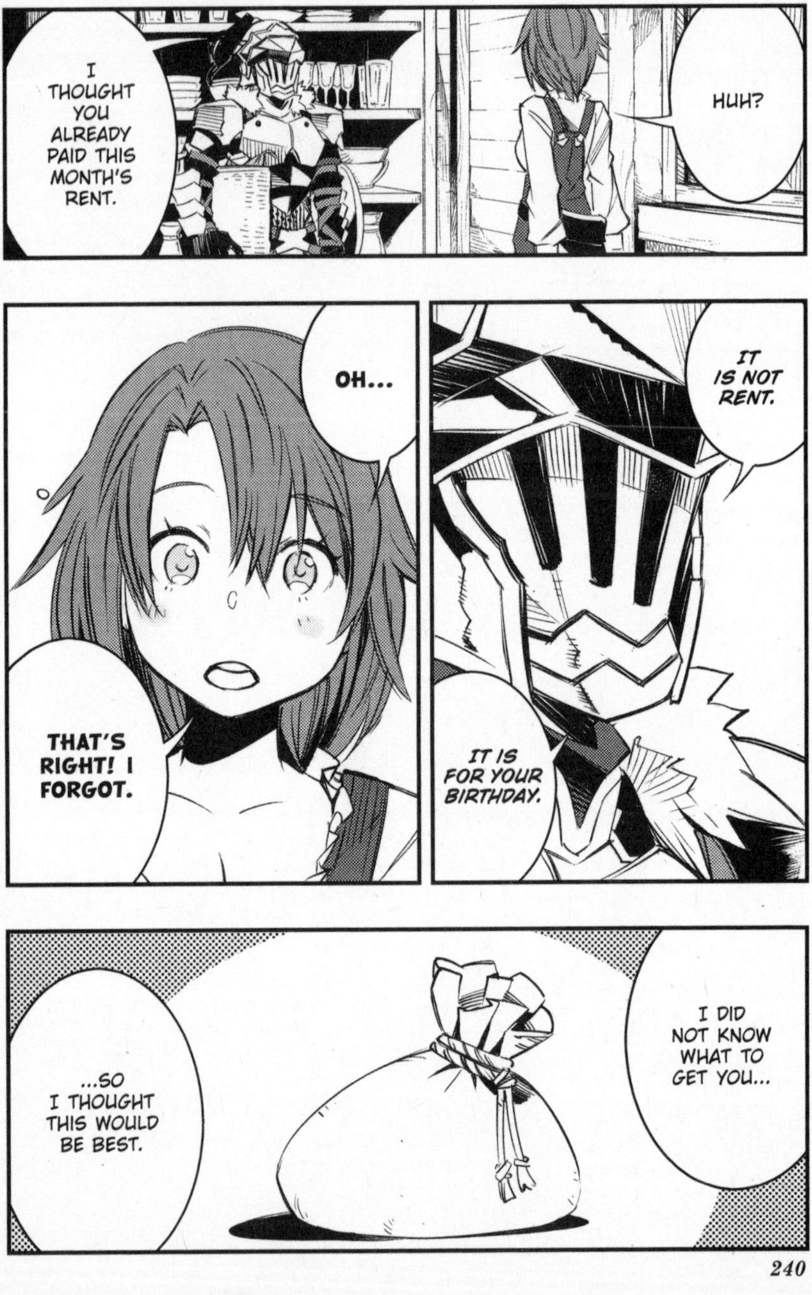
HUH?
I THOUGHT YOU ALREADY PAID THIS MONTH'S RENT.
IT IS NOT RENT.
IT IS FOR YOUR BIRTHDAY.
OH...
THAT'S RIGHT! I FORGOT.
I DID NOT KNOW WHAT TO GET YOU...
...SO I THOUGHT THIS WOULD BE BEST.

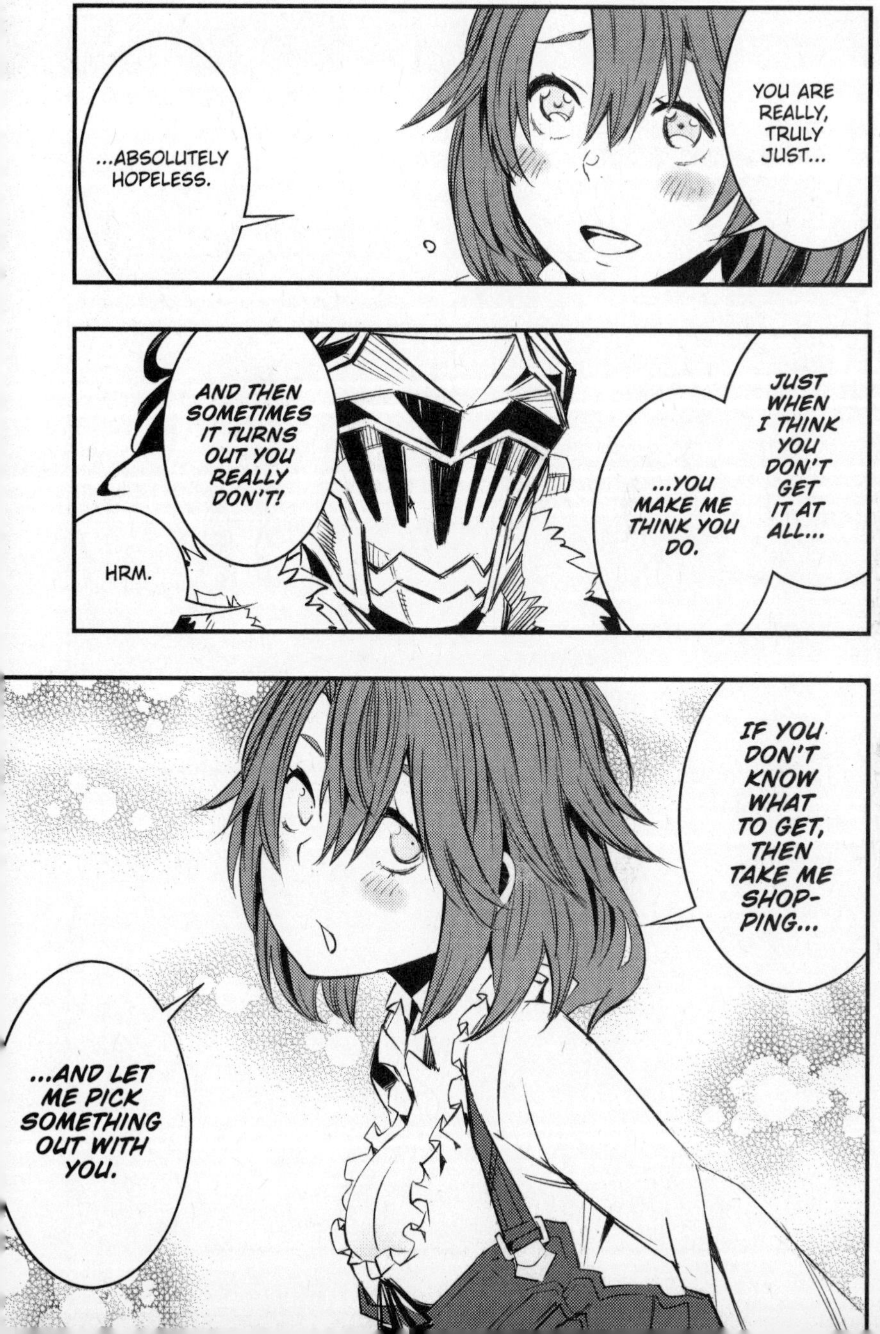
YOU ARE REALLY, TRULY JUST...
...ABSOLUTELY HOPELESS.
JUST WHEN I THINK YOU DON'T GET IT AT ALL...
...YOU MAKE ME THINK YOU DO.
AND THEN SOMETIMES IT TURNS OUT YOU REALLY DON'T!
HRM.
IF YOU DON'T KNOW WHAT TO GET, THEN TAKE ME SHOP-PING...
...AND LET ME PICK SOMETHING OUT WITH YOU.

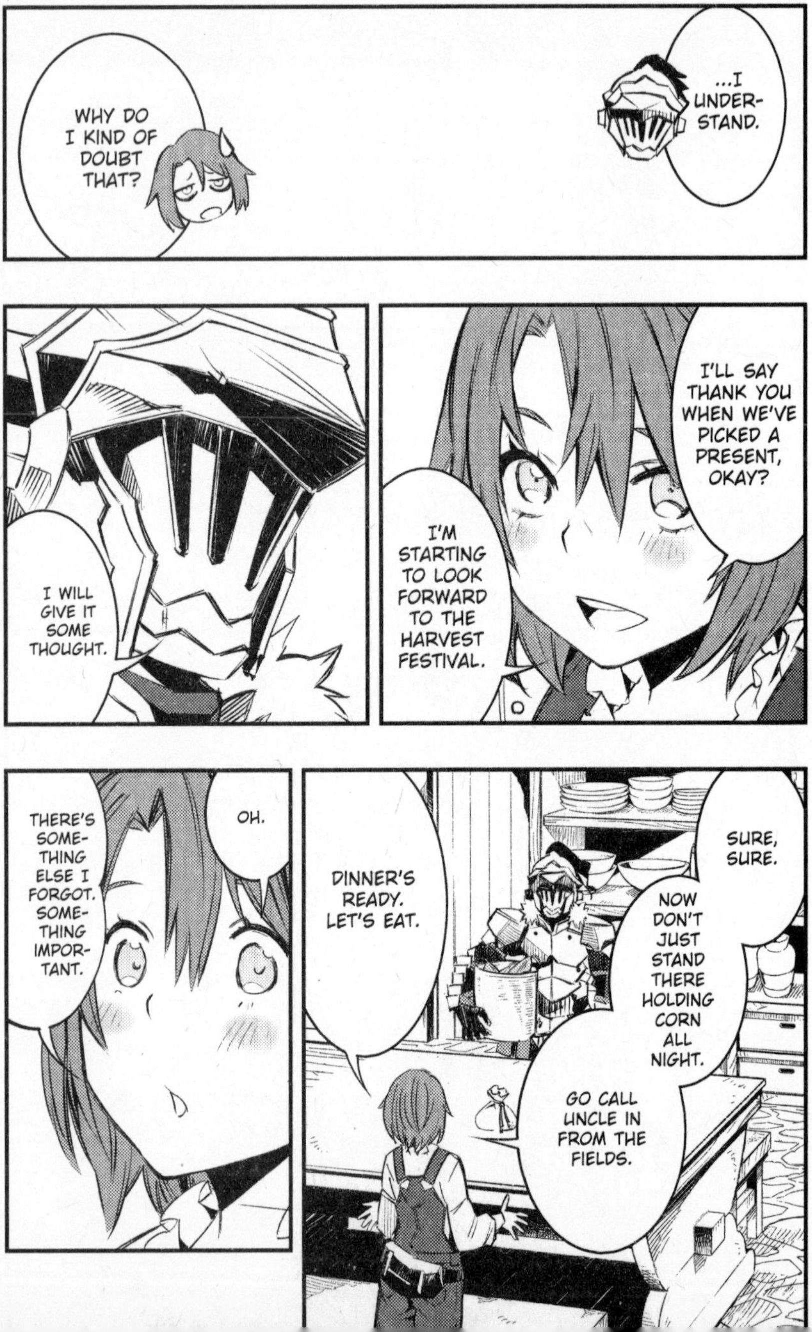
...I UNDERSTAND.
WHY DO I KIND OF DOUBT THAT?
I'LL SAY THANK YOU WHEN WE'VE PICKED A PRESENT, OKAY?
I'M STARTING TO LOOK FORWARD TO THE HARVEST FESTIVAL.
I WILL GIVE IT SOME THOUGHT.
SURE, SURE.
NOW DON'T JUST STAND THERE HOLDING CORN ALL NIGHT.
GO CALL UNCLE IN FROM THE FIELDS.
DINNER'S READY. LET'S EAT.
OH.
THERE'S SOMETHING ELSE I FORGOT. SOMETHING IMPORTANT.

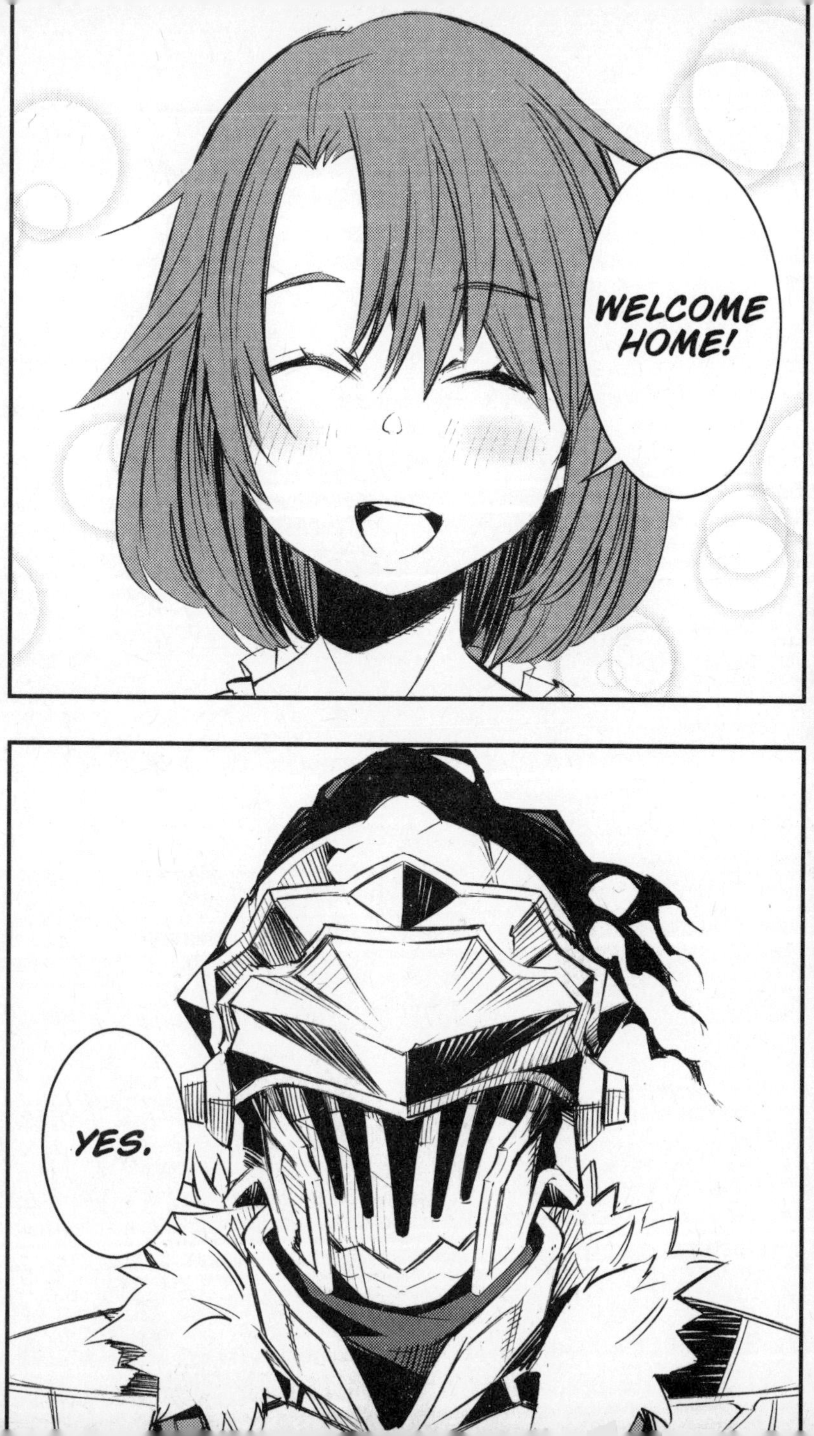
WELCOME HOME!
YES.

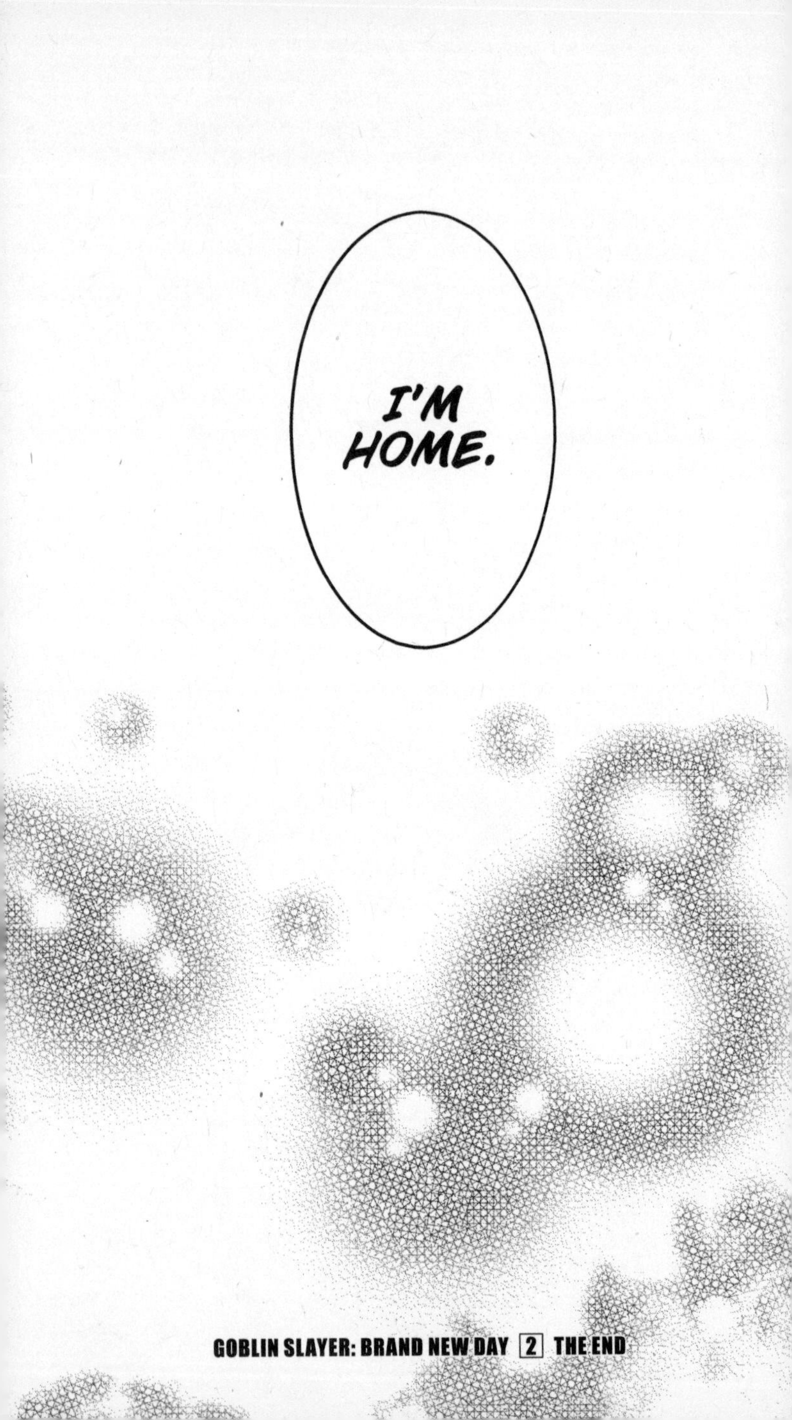
I'M HOME.
GOBLIN SLAYER: BRAND NEW DAY 2 THE END

GOBLIN SLAYER
BRAND NEW DAY

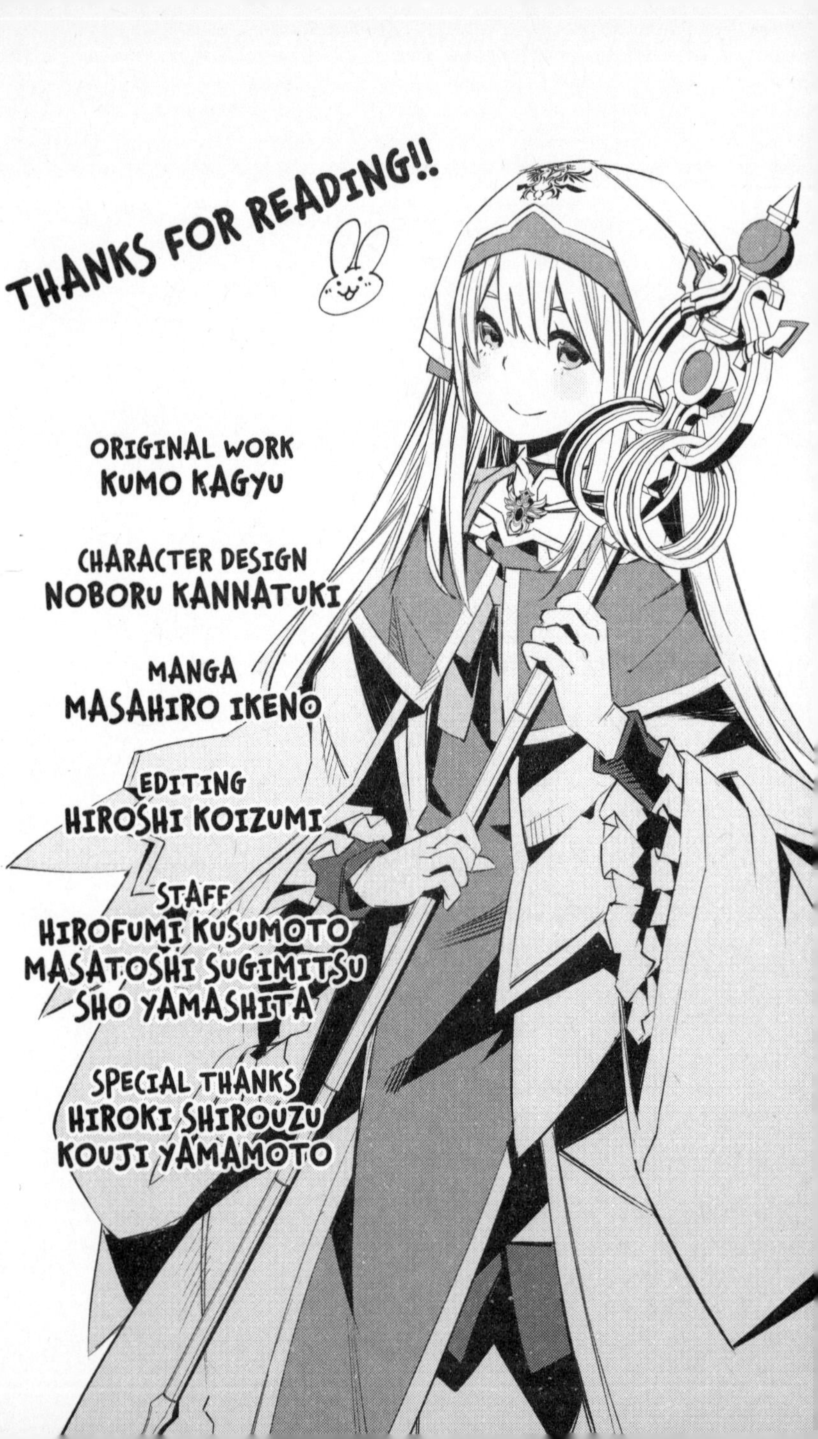
THANKS FOR READING!!
ORIGINAL WORK
KUMO KAGYU
CHARACTER DESIGN
NOBORU KANNATUKI
MANGA
MASAHIRO IKENO
EDITING
HIROSHI KOIZUMI
STAFF
HIROFUMI KUSUMOTO
MASATOSHI SUGIMITSU
SHO YAMASHITA
SPECIAL THANKS
HIROKI SHIROUZU
KOUJI YAMAMOTO

GOBLIN SLAYER

:BRAND NEW DAY:

GOBLIN SLAYER
BRAND NEW DAY 2

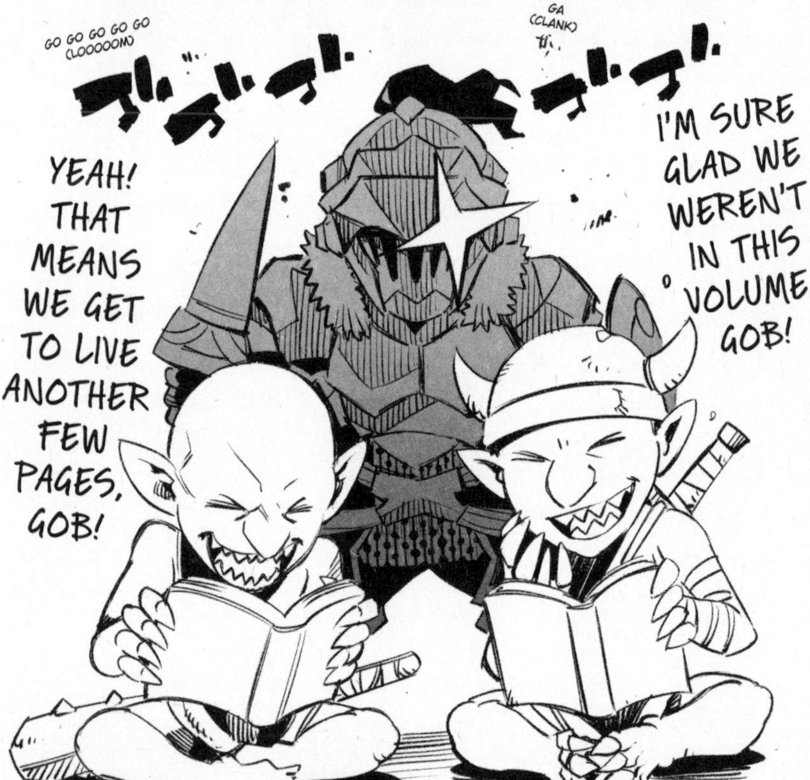
GA
(CLANK)
GO GO GO GO GO
(LOOOOOM)
I'M SURE GLAD WE WEREN'T IN THIS VOLUME, GOB!
YEAH! THAT MEANS WE GET TO LIVE ANOTHER FEW PAGES, GOB!

Turn to the back of the
book for a short story by
Kumo Kagyu!

GOBLIN SLAYER
BRAND NEW DAY

In any event, he removed it when he slept. Tonight, he would accept that risk for a few extra hours. Her birthday present had not been a success. He wished to avoid a second failure the same day.

He unlatched and removed his grimy metal helmet, peeled off the cotton balaclava underneath. He set them on the table, as far from the food as he could.

"How is that?"

"Good," she said, studying him intently, then slowly nodding. "I think it's great."

"I see..."

But how had this changed anything? He didn't know. She was smiling, but that, too, looked the same as it had before. But perhaps, he thought, that was enough. She had said it, hadn't she? Even if he thought nothing had changed, she had said she liked him this way.

With those thoughts in his mind, he took a spoonful of cold stew and sipped it. The flavor hadn't changed, either; it was still, he thought, delicious.

GOBLIN SLAYER
BRAND NEW DAY

glanced around the room. "If there were any troublemakers in this house, I don't think I would have been able to make dinner, see?"

"Hmm..."

That was logical, he thought. But then, what about outside the house? There might be something lurking in the dark just past the window. Consider what had happened just the previous spring. With the festival approaching, the goblins could well be on the move.

"You're always so careful. I think you'll be fine."

"You think so?"

"I do."

He grunted softly. His mind frantically worked to determine what she might want that she was not saying aloud, seeking what might lie behind her words. At the same time, he considered the situation. It was already nighttime. If any were to come, they would probably be only scouts or patrols. What was the likelihood that a horde would suddenly burst into a well-lit room?

It was not zero. So long as the dice of Fate and Chance rolled, there was always a possibility.

But...

"...I will, then."

Today, at least, he would ignore it.

they had met him.

It was just a succession of simple, ordinary days, maybe not even important enough to brag about. His telling wasn't dynamic enough to feel like a proper adventure story—he could only report everything precisely as he had seen it. A third-rate bard would have put on a better performance, but still, it was enough for her.

"Our adventure was really tough. Dragon slaying isn't easy, I can tell you," she offered in return, giggling. She was so busy encouraging his story-telling that her mouth moved more than the hand holding her spoon.

She wondered how long they'd been chatting: it was already dark outside. Maybe it was just because the days were getting shorter. And then she noticed her soup had gone cold. "Oops," she said with a rueful smile.

"Don't worry about it," he said simply, spooning more soup through his visor with a practiced motion. She watched him, resting her chin on her hands, then she murmured:

"Your helmet... Don't you ever take it off?"

"Hrm," he grunted, but not because he was lost for an answer. "It is for safety," he said gravely.

"Are you really that worried?" She frowned, then

her when they were little. Then, word by word, he slowly strung together an entire story.

How two adventurers had come to ask him about the best weapons for roach slaying (two words that brought a frown to her face). How he had shared his experience with them, up to and including the fact that he wasn't sure his experience would be any help to them. How he had gone to a frontier village to slay some goblins and had encountered a little boy who had then saved him at a crucial moment. How, on that quest, he had been able to rescue an adventurer. How the corn had been delivered later on behalf of that adventurer.

Even how, after the quest, the serving girl at the tavern had insisted, for reasons he didn't understand, that he have some food. His surprise at how similar the tavern's stew was to the stew he had on the farm. (That made her smile a little.)

He told her about how Heavy Warrior and Spearman had invited him on an adventure on which they had climbed a tower. How he had been surprised to hear that, during his absence, she had enjoyed some kind of game with High Elf Archer, Guild Girl, Inspector, and Priestess. How he had heard of the adventure Dwarf Shaman, Lizard Priest, and High Elf Archer had shared before

Uh-huh, she added emphatically, puffing out that huge chest. She remarked that the bright yellow kernels almost looked like actual gold and that eating them felt like a waste.

He didn't really understand. He kept his own gratitude constantly in mind, but the gratitude of others toward him made no difference to his own conduct. This was all new to him, and it left him feeling restless—indeed, downright troubled.

"Heh-heh," she said when she saw his look, and her smile only deepened. "You're finding a lot of new people in your life these days."

"Yes." That much he knew. He nodded and spooned some soup through the slats of his visor. Ever since spring—no, even before that, though he hadn't realized it—he had become connected to a great many people. He didn't know if that was really good or bad, but at the least, it didn't feel bad. And that realization alone seemed to him to be a very good thing.

"Some novice adventurers even came to me for advice." The words came to his lips so naturally, he didn't even realize he was speaking.

But when she leaned forward and asked "What kind of advice?" he felt his heart jump for some reason. It felt much like the way he used to brag to

At the Harvest Festival, then.

He didn't know how much he could make up for at the festival, but he had to try. After all, he believed that trying was the only thing he was really any good at.

"By the way, the corn you got—who was it from?"

The question did not, perhaps, indicate that she was unable to endure his silence. She was pointing at the basket of corn now sitting on one of the chairs. He slowly turned his helmeted head to look at it.

"Someone who was involved in one of my quests," he said vaguely. "It was a gesture of thanks, so I brought it back here."

"Really...!"

She nodded, all smiles; as for him, he found it very perplexing. The adventurer he had met whilst slaying those goblins had recovered, and that was a fine thing. But to receive corn was not, in itself, such an unusual event.

"Doesn't it go to show how many people appreciate your work?" she said when he pointed this out. She herself looked rather confused.

"Is that so?"

"Sure is."

"I see."

Interlude:
Of Him and Her, a Little Later —
by Kumo Kagyu

They sat facing each other, spooning stew into their mouths. The only sounds were their breathing and the gentle scraping of utensils. The room was warm. The fresh breeze of late summer blew through, causing the lamplight to waver.

She brought her spoon up as if it were the most blessed thing in the world, then glanced at him and cocked her head. "Hmm?"

Her smile was as small and sweet as a bud waiting to blossom. But as for him, he found himself accosted by an unusual, comfortable discomfort and shifted slightly in his seat. Was it in response to her smile or the gift he'd just given her? He could not tell.

I was trying to be thoughtful in my own way.

Even so, she had not seemed to think his gift was a good birthday present.

That being the case, it really didn't matter how hard he had thought. But failure was no excuse to stop moving—his master had always told him that. Since feeling disheartened was no way to succeed, he should keep pressing forward, so long as he was alive.

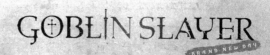

GOBLIN SLAYER 2

Original Story: Kumo Kagyu

Art: Masahiro Ikeno

Character Design: Noboru Kannatuki

Translation: Kevin Steinbach ✣ Lettering: Phil Christie

This book is a work of fiction. Names, characters, places, and incidents are
the product of the author's imagination or are used fictitiously. Any resemblance
to actual events, locales, or persons, living or dead, is coincidental.

GOBLIN SLAYER: BRAND NEW DAY Volume 2
©Kumo Kagyu / SB Creative Corp. Character Design: Noboru Kannatuki
©2019 Masahiro Ikeno / SQUARE ENIX CO., LTD. First published in Japan in 2019 by
SQUARE ENIX CO., LTD. English translation rights arranged with SQUARE ENIX CO.,
LTD. and YEN PRESS, LLC through Tuttle-Mori Agency, Inc.

English translation ©2020 by SQUARE ENIX CO., LTD.

Yen Press
150 West 30th Street, 19th Floor
New York, NY 10001

Visit us at yenpress.com
facebook.com/yenpress
twitter.com/yenpress
yenpress.tumblr.com
instagram.com/yenpress

First Yen Press Edition: February 2020
The chapters in this volume were originally published as ebooks by Yen Press.

Yen Press is an imprint of Yen Press, LLC.
The Yen Press name and logo are trademarks of Yen Press, LLC.

The publisher is not responsible for websites (or their content) that are
not owned by the publisher.

Library of Congress Control Number: 2019938436

ISBNs: 978-1-9753-9921-4 (paperback)
        978-1-9753-0874-2 (ebook)

10 9 8 7 6 5 4 3 2 1

WOR

Printed in the United States of America